RENAISSANCE DRAMA IN ACTION

How did Elizabethan and Jacobean actors stage their plays?

Renaissance Drama in Action is a fascinating exploration of Renaissance theatre practice and staging. Covering questions of contemporary playhouse design, verse and language, staging and rehearsal practices, and acting styles, Martin White relates the characteristics of Renaissance theatre to the issues involved in staging the plays today.

This accessible volume examines the problems posed for modern readers and performers by contemporary verse and language. Looking at both familiar plays such as *The Duchess of Malfi*, *The Changeling* and *'Tis Pity She's a Whore*, as well as less well-known texts, the author offers a fresh look at key issues of staging and interpretation. White examines the evidence for contemporary theatre practice but also draws on the work and experience of modern theatre practitioners such as Stephen Jeffreys, Harriet Walter, Adrian Noble, and Matthew Warchus.

Renaissance Drama in Action offers undergraduates and A-level students an invaluable guide to the main characteristics of Elizabethan and Jacobean drama, and its relationship to contemporary theatre and staging.

Martin White is Professor of Theatre at the University of Bristol, and has taught and directed for 25 years. He is editor of *Arden of Faversham* and author of *Middleton and Tourneur*.

This book is dedicated to Alison, Hannah and Nathaniel

— as is the author

In my own writings I do not always find again the sense of my
first thought; I do not know what I meant to say, and often I get
burned by correcting and putting in a new meaning, because I
have lost the first one, which was better.

Michel de Montaigne

Theory is concerned with reason and the operation of the
intellect, Practice with the operations and movement of the
senses . . . So that the one is the summit and the other the
foundation of the whole fabric of human discourse.

Cesare Ripa, *Iconologia*, 1625

RENAISSANCE DRAMA IN ACTION

An introduction to aspects of theatre
practice and performance

Martin White

London and New York

First published 1998
by Routledge
11 New Fetter Lane, London EC4P 4EE

Simultaneously published in the USA and Canada
by Routledge
29 West 35th Street, New York, NY 10001

Typeset in Garamond by M Rules
Printed and bound in Great Britain by Biddles Ltd, Guildford and King's Lynn

British Library Cataloguing in Publication Data
A catalogue record for this book is available from the British Library

Library of Congress Cataloguing in Publication Data
White, Martin, 1947–
Renaissance drama in action: an introduction to aspects of
theatre practice and performance / Martin White.
p.   cm.
Includes bibliographical references and index.
1. Theater—England—History—16th century.   2. Theater—England—
History—17th century.   3. Theater—England—Production and direction.
4. English drama—Early modern and Elizabethan, 1500–1600—History and
criticism.   5. English drama—17th century—History and criticism.   I. Title.
PN2581.W43   1998
792'.0941'09031—dc21   97–48418
CIP

ISBN 0-415-06738-3 (hbk)
ISBN 0-415-06739-1 (pbk)

CONTENTS

CONTENTS

ILLUSTRATIONS

Paperback cover illustration: the frontispiece to Francis Kirkman's *The Wits* (1673), originally published in the edition of 1662 by Henry Marsh. The use of the depth of the stage may reflect the necessity of playing on diagonals on a thrust stage, or in the round, in order to ensure maximum visibility for spectators.

ABBREVIATIONS

ES   E.K. Chambers, *The Elizabethan Stage*, 4 vols, Oxford 1923; reprinted 1961.

JCS   G.E. Bentley, *The Jacobean and Caroline Stage*, 7 vols, Oxford 1941–68.

ACKNOWLEDGEMENTS

I am but a gatherer and disposer of other men's stuff, at my best value.
Sir Henry Wotton

This book is aimed at students who are interested in approaching plays from the Elizabethan, Jacobean and Caroline periods as performance texts – in the playhouses of those times and in our own. I have tried, therefore, within the texts of the chapters and through the use of a number of case studies, to mix the historical study with examples of later practice. I have also tried, in the course of the book, to address some of the questions that have arisen in discussing and, more especially, working practically on these plays with my students over the past twenty-five years. I am, therefore, deeply indebted to all those students whose enthusiasm, talent and questions have stimulated my own pleasure in these plays. I have relied on their participation in practical projects and full productions to enable me to learn more about Renaissance drama than I could ever have done otherwise. Many of them, I hope, have found pleasure in presenting to an audience plays that many critics have neglected or sold short and in refuting those views by demonstrating their stage-worthiness. There are many other people to whom I owe thanks. Glynne Wickham (who pioneered the study of drama in universities in general and created at Bristol an environment where scholarship and practice go hand in hand) and Peter Thomson read drafts of this book and pointed out many errors in both my facts and wishful fictions. John Marshall and Ted Braun were particularly helpful in clarifying aspects of medieval and twentieth-century practice respectively. The mistakes that remain are, of course, all mine.

While writing this book I became involved at the very edges of the project to construct a replica of the Globe on the South Bank in London. The debates surrounding the various decisions, invariably enlivened by Andrew Gurr's knowledge and imaginative interpretation of information have (like his published work to which I am also indebted) been both a source of new discoveries and, combined with the work of the theatre practitioners at the reconstructed Globe playhouse in London, required me to rethink my own views on the performance of these plays in their own time. Many other scholars have opened up unforeseen routes of enquiry, and I should particularly like to thank Marion O'Connor who has been a constructive source of ideas and advice.

A large number of theatre practitioners from whose performances and productions I have learned a great deal were unconscious collaborators, their work silently observed, noted and then used to provide my examples. Others were more aware of the demands I made on them. At different times over the past fifteen years or so, Peter Copley, Ron Daniels, Peter Gill, Mike Gwilym, Stephen Jeffreys, Helen Mirren, Adrian Noble, Trevor Nunn and Janet Suzman – all of whose ideas I have drawn on, if not directly quoted, in the pages that follow – were not only willing to be interviewed, but were even kind enough to make me feel that they were happy to give up their time and their ideas. Harriet Walter's and Matthew Warchus's major contributions in particular are evident from the Case Studies of their work. And, although it is hard to be precise about their help, mainly because it has been long-standing and pervasive, I also want to express my thanks to my friends Mick Ford, Robert Hickson and Gary Yershon. At Routledge, first Janice Price (who, with Nick Hern originally encouraged this book), then Helena Reckitt and finally Talia Rodgers, Sophie Powell and Miranda Chaytor have all demonstrated more patience and understanding than I could reasonably have expected. I am grateful for a term's research leave that allowed me time to make progress with this book and for financial assistance from the University of Bristol Arts Faculty Research and Conference Funds.

Above all, however, my thanks go to my partner Alison Steele, for reading drafts, asking difficult questions, discussing ideas and being simply the best person I know of with whom to watch, discuss and do plays. And to my children, Hannah and Nathaniel, despite whose gleeful efforts to distract me with often irresistible (and so not always resisted) offers of company, I managed eventually to finish this book.

Martin White
Bristol, August 1997

1

'COMEDIES ARE WRIT TO BE SPOKEN, NOT READ'[1]

Approaching the play

> . . . a Play *read*, hath not half the pleasure of a play *Acted*: for though it have the pleasure of *ingenious Speeches*, yet it wants the pleasure of *Gracefull action*.
>
> Richard Baker, *Theatrum Redivivum*, 1662

Anyone who has read an Elizabethan, Jacobean or Caroline play knows how difficult a task it can be. For anyone preparing the play for performance the challenge is even more taxing since lines over which the eye can move swiftly and easily can present significant and time-consuming difficulties in rehearsal. When lines have to be the spoken expression of an individual character and filled out with action and interaction, each *moment* of the dialogue and the associated action has to be fully explored and understood: approximations and generalisations are, as Stanislavsky said, 'the enemy of art'.[2]

It is precisely this exhaustive analysis that explains why working on a play-text practically (in rehearsal, onstage, or in a class/workshop) invariably teaches one very different things from reading alone, and why the conclusions of critics that are based on textual study alone can often seem wide of the mark, even downright mistaken, to those who have performed the same play. Michael Billington recounts an exchange between the critic John Wain and the actor Alan Howard:

> John Wain remarked that the wooing scene in *Henry V* was simply a joky footnote to the play. Alan Howard, who by then had played the king countless times, picked him up on that and plotted the four or five shifts of movement within the scene. The actor, through practice, has simply spotted things the critic missed.[3]

In this chapter I shall try to outline what I see as some of the problems a student – or performer – might encounter (or possibly overlook) when working on an Elizabethan or Jacobean play, and guided by the experience of theatre artists, my observation of performances and my own practical experience, try to suggest ways in which these hurdles might be approached.

Elizabethan and Jacobean dramatists wrote in what is in many ways to us a foreign language and any attempt to minimise or avoid the difficulties that result from this is misleading. All the actors and directors to whom I spoke or whose views I read during the course of writing this book acknowledged the challenges posed by the language. The director Sam Mendes, for example, describes the first read-through for his production of *The Alchemist* as 'like trying to read a text in Swahili', and David Troughton (preparing to play Fitzdottrel in *The Devil Is an Ass*) likened speaking Jonson's words to 'chewing beef stock cubes'.[4] Jonson may present particular problems, but they are not unique ones, and in my own experience as a director and teacher I know that many students find understanding the words and forms of language a real stumbling-block to their enjoyment of the plays. In fact, the language is often *more* problematic than it might at first sight appear; the bonus is that careful study – rather than being some inward-looking 'academic exercise' with little bearing on performance – can lead to the pleasure of discovering exciting and frequently unforeseen possibilities of interpretation and staging.

Even the audiences at the original playhouses undoubtedly found much of what they heard unusual or complex as the playwrights used old words in new and surprising contexts, invented their own words, recovered some from their classical studies and borrowed others from contemporary languages. The demand for new words was considerable. In his *Art of Reason* (1573) Ralph Lever claimed that 'there are more things than there are words to express things by', and throughout the Elizabethan and early Stuart periods the English language faced the challenge of expressing and describing the flood of technological, geographical and scientific discoveries. The development of a vernacular language became a matter of national pride, and writers strove to demonstrate the superiority of English; as Samuel Daniel wrote in his poem *Musophilus* (1599):

> Or should we careless come behind the rest
> In power of words, that go before in worth,
> Whenas our accents, equal to the best,
> Is able greater wonders to bring forth.
> (II. 951–4)

The playwright Thomas Heywood, in his *Apology for Actors* (1612), made confident claims for the role played by the theatre in refining the language:

> our English tongue, which hath been the most harsh, uneven, and broken language of the world, part Dutch, part Irish, Saxon, Scotch, Welsh, and indeed a gallimaufry of many, but perfect in none, is now

by this secondary means of playing continually refined, every writer striving in himself to add a new flourish unto it; so that in process, from the rude and unpolished tongue it is grown to a most perfect and composed language, and many excellent works and elaborate poems writ in the same, that many nations grow inamoured of our tongue, before despised.

(1841: 52)

Certainly the language of Heywood and his contemporaries was visibly and audibly less rooted in the inflections and conventions of Middle English than that of their grandparents, even of their parents. Indeed, Elizabethan and Jacobean language soon became as different from the English spoken in the early 1500s as it is from the English we speak today.

It may seem unnecessary to make the point, but it is important that any study of the language of these plays is aware of it as *spoken* language. As Hamlet says to Polonius, the court will 'hear a play tomorrow' (2.2.530), and G.K. Hunter's vivid image of the playhouse as a 'rhetorical gymnasium',[5] where language flexed its muscles, is an apt one. Although levels of literacy improved markedly during the period, the transition from an oral culture to one dominated by the written word was still far from complete: despite the fact that London had a substantially higher literacy rate than the rest of the country, only about a third of the capital's adult males – and presumably even fewer of its female population – could read or write. Consequently, although plays were published, some (especially following the issue of Ben Jonson's *Works* in 1616) being prepared and adapted specifically for a reader, plays were generally viewed by their creators as scripts for theatrical production, to be heard and seen rather than read. The author of the *Character* of 'An Excellent Actor' (probably John Webster) underlined the importance of the spoken word:

> Sit in a full Theatre, and you will think you see so many lines drawn from the circumference of so many *ears*, whiles the Actor is the centre [emphasis added].[6]

This strikes me as a perfect image of the Elizabethan and Jacobean playhouse: the actor – the focal point of any performance in any period – at the centre of a circle of listeners. Consequently, playwrights and audiences alike were alert to the skill actors displayed (or did not) in delivering their lines to the best advantage. In the Preface to his tragi-comedy *The Devil's Law Case* (published 1623), Webster wrote of his debt to the actors:

> A great part of the grace of this (I confess) lay in action; yet can no action ever be gracious, where the decency of language, and ingenious structure of the scene, arrive not to make up a perfect harmony.

(14–17)

John Orrell has argued that 'the Globe was an acoustical auditorium, intended to serve the word and the ear more fully than the image and the eye' (Orrell 1983: 140). Although this deliberately and provocatively understates the impact of the playhouse's decoration and the importance of visual stage languages (such as an individual actor's posture and gesture, stage groupings, costume, various elements of the permanent stage structure, portable scenic elements), Professor Orrell is right to stress the centrality of spoken language, and the recreation of the Globe at the International Shakespeare Centre on the South Bank of the Thames (despite flight paths and river traffic), a project in which Orrell has played a significant role, allows us to get at least some sense of the original playhouse's acoustics.[7] The work done so far has produced predominantly favourable responses to this aspect of the reconstruction (though on rainy days, Globe 3's Artistic Director Mark Rylance has observed, the actors need to project with much greater force). But what performances there cannot demonstrate (except, perhaps, at occasional 'authentic' presentations) is the difference in the actual *sound* made by the voices of Elizabethan actors and their modern counterparts. Peter Hall, for example, who describes Elizabethan pronunciation as 'like Belfast crossed with Devon', notes that:

> the resonance and assonance of Shakespeare's text were richer and more complex than the clipped grey sounds of modern English. When I am preparing a Shakespeare play, I still mutter the text to myself in Elizabethan. It reveals the shapes and colours. It *always* makes the words wittier.
>
> (1993: 76)

Barrie Rutter's Northern Broadsides company currently perform Shakespeare's plays in often broad, generally northern, accents, and so strictly speaking do not reproduce 'Elizabethan' English. Nevertheless, they have challenged the notion that there is a particular 'voice' for classic plays (still often characterised, unfairly and quite wrongly, as an 'RSC' voice) and restored much of the original linguistic and vocal energy to performances of the plays, especially as their vocal approach is matched by elements of theatre practice that are in tune with the original expectations and resources of Elizabethan and Jacobean production teams (Holland 1994 and 1995). Writing of Northern Broadsides' production of *Romeo and Juliet*, for example, directed by Tim Supple, and staged in a disused viaduct beneath an old Halifax mill, Robert Butler commented:

> Northern Broadsides have a vigorous aesthetic, a way of doing Shakespeare that is revelatory. Direction and design are kept to a minimum. There are very few lighting cues. The audience sit on two sides facing one another. The actors wear modern dress, but not the sort of stereotypical clothes that prejudge character. Quick and

unsentimental, they never slow up the verse with naturalistic acting, which would duplicate emotions that are self-evident. They trust the text, carry us along with the rhythm of the verse, and, by making the arguments really matter, they transport us effortlessly from the gloom of the viaduct to the heat of Verona . . . this production restores the thrill of narrative: the rapid, jostling succession of events that throws up its own surprises. Shakespeare's promised 'two hours' traffic' here comes in at a miraculous 2 hours 10 minutes.

(*Independent on Sunday*, 13 October 1996, p. 12).

When we speak (and sometimes when we read) a text, a number of obstacles stand in our way. We may initially be floored by syntactical complexity:

> Pray you,
> Since doubting things go ill often hurts more
> Than to be sure they do – for certainties
> Either are past remedies, or, timely knowing,
> The remedy then born – discover to me
> What both you spur and stop.
> (*Cymbeline*, 1.6.95–9)

Changes in pronunciation often make puns (such as 'Do you smell a fault', which would to its original audience have been indistinguishable from 'Do you smell a fart' – and so made more sense of the line (*King Lear*, 1.1.13)) and rhymes (such as in 'Blow, blow, thou winter wind / Thou art not so unkind . . .' (*As You Like It*, 2.7.174–5)) seem laboured (or even, as in the *King Lear* example, disappear). Despite the gradual acceptance in the period of standard grammatical practices, different conventions of word order produce for us easily misunderstood sentences, such as in the following speech from Ford's *The Broken Heart* (1633):

> Orgilus,
> Take heed thou hast not, under our integrity,
> Shrouded unlawful plots; our mortal eyes
> Pierce not the secrets of your heart, the gods
> Are only privy to them.
> (3.1.8–12)

Speaking these lines aloud reveals the particular difficulty of making the word *only* apply to *the gods* rather than sounding as if it is defining *privy*. To many in Ford's audience, the Latinate sentence structure would no doubt have been familiar (and appropriate to the play's classical setting), but the modern actor will not find it so straightforward.

For performers and audiences, however, who unlike readers do not have access to footnotes, the most obvious – and most regularly encountered – problems concern vocabulary. It has been estimated that over 10,000 new words were introduced between 1550 and 1650, of which Shakespeare's share has been reckoned to be anything from 600 to 2,000 (including many words in common use today, such as *gloomy, radiant, leapfrog, frugal, accommodation, admirable, educate, generous* and *tranquil*). John Marston's *Antonio and Mellida*, first performed at Paul's playhouse in 1599, which contains on average a new word every fourteen lines, may be an extreme case of word-coining (and one much pilloried by Jonson) but it derives from a generally shared impulse among contemporary writers. There was no English dictionary until 1604 (Robert Cawdrey's *A Table Alphabeticall*) and so it is not always easy to assess to what extent an audience member actually registered that a word was new, as opposed simply to being unknown to him or her individually. Many of Marston's words – such as *belkt, firking, gerne, houts, loofe, neakes, pantable, peregal, sliftred, spangs, surquedries, tyer, wimble* – must surely have struck the audience as unusual, but just in case they didn't, Marston has a character in the play, Balurdo, draw attention to these inventions:

> my leg is not altogether unpropitiously shaped. There's a word: 'unpropitiously'! I think I shall speak as 'unpropitiously' as any courtier in Italy.
>
> (2.1.106–9)

A cluster of such overtly strange words can be particularly difficult for an actor to deal with, and I suspect that any performer would find the following obscure and obsolete mixture daunting: 'No, no, but careening of an old morphewed lady, to make her disembogue again – there's rough cast phrase to your plastic' (Bosola, *The Duchess of Malfi*, 2.1.31–3). Even if the actor, using footnotes and a dictionary, works out a translation (mine is itself prosaic and none too clear – 'No, no, but scraping clean an old mildewy lady – like cleaning the barnacles from the hull of a ship – so that she can sail forth on new adventures like a boat leaving the river for the open sea: there's coarse plaster to your delicate moulding'), he actually has to *say* Webster's lines and hope to communicate something to an audience. Perhaps unsurprisingly, the line is generally cut.

In such cases, readers and actors at least know they need to look the words up. A more insidious problem is posed by words that still exist in modern usage, and whose modern meaning appears to fit the context, but whose original meaning has become lost or obscure: *honest* (often used to mean 'chaste'), *nice* (coy), *shrewd* (shrewish) and *presently* (immediately) are common examples of such words. *Mere* is another: to the Elizabethans and Jacobeans, although it could carry our modern understanding of 'slight' or 'trivial', it was frequently employed as an enforcing word with the sense of 'total' or 'downright'. The result can be confusing for us when Alice Arden, for instance, claims that her lover, Mosby, seduced her by 'mere sorcery' (*Arden of Faversham*, scene 1, l.200), or when Hamlet, describing the state of Denmark, complains that 'things rank and gross in nature / Possess it merely' (1.2.136–7).

As Harriet Walter points out (see p. 91), although actors often agonise in rehearsal over things which turn out apparently to be of little concern to an audience seeing the finished production, it is precisely because rehearsals *do* explore the text in such detail that actors learn where to place weight, or discover where emphasis may be less important and so are able to give the play its shape and pace. The investigation of possible word meanings – what Ian McKellen calls the exploration of 'every little corner of the text' – is a key part of this rehearsal process, and of direct practical use in preparing to perform these plays beyond the obvious necessity for actors to create meanings from the lines they speak.

In the opening scene of *The Changeling*, for example, Beatrice-Joanna is desperate to avoid her imminent marriage to Alonzo de Piracquo, her father's choice of suitor, now that she has fallen in love with a newcomer, Alsemero. She tries to stall for time:

VERMANDERO: Thou must be a bride within this sevennight.
ALSEMERO: [*Aside*] Ha!
BEATRICE: Nay good sir, be not so violent; with speed
    I cannot render satisfaction
    Unto the dear companion of my soul –
    Virginity – whom I thus long have lived with,
    And part with it so rude and suddenly;
    Can such friends divide, never to meet again
    Without a solemn farewell?
VERMANDERO: Tush, tush! There's a toy.

                        (1.1.190–7)

Two words here will probably be of particular interest to the actor: *speed* and *toy*. To contemporaries, *speed* carried the sense both of 'haste' and 'success'. The first meaning is current with us and fits the context, and although the richness of the word's Jacobean double-meaning will probably be lost to a modern audience there will be no significant loss of understanding. The second word – *toy* – is not glossed at all by the editors of the New Mermaids (1964) or Penguin (1965) editions. The obvious meaning appears to be that Vermandero is referring patronisingly to his daughter's virginity as a 'toy' in the sense we commonly use the word today – a plaything, something childish to be put aside on reaching adulthood. The Jacobeans frequently used it in this sense too; for example, Giovanni in *'Tis Pity She's A Whore* teases his sister after they have made love for the first time:

    I marvel why the chaster of your sex
    Should think this pretty toy called maidenhead

So strange a loss, when, being lost, 'tis nothing,
And you are still the same.

(2.1.9–12)

Alternatively, or in addition, we might perhaps take *toy* to refer to Beatrice-Joanna's professed fears which are, in her father's opinion, trifling, and this meaning, again shared by the Jacobeans and us, is also satisfying in the context of the scene. But there are a number of further meanings which, though now obscure or obsolete, would have been readily understood by the original audience. In the early seventeenth century *toy* could also mean 'an amorous sport' (an obsolete usage now as a noun, but one we retain as a verb in the expression to 'toy with someone's affections'); a 'frivolous or mocking speech' (the gloss given by the more recent Penguin editors); a 'foolish or idle fancy' or 'whim' (the sense in which Middleton uses the word in the opening line of 2.2 of *The Witch* – 'What a mad toy took me to sup with witches?' – and the gloss chosen by the editor of the 1990 New Mermaids edition); a 'foolish or unreasoning dislike or aversion'; and a 'trick'. A number of these meanings fit the context, and although now lost and therefore probably impossible to communicate to an audience directly, they may nevertheless be of practical help in rehearsal. They shed light on the character Vermandero in particular by clarifying and developing both his view that his daughter's duty is to marry when and whom he chooses, and his opinion of the weight of her objections. Moreover, if an audience understands 'trick' as one of the word's meanings, it may suggest to them that Vermandero suspects his daughter's speech is not a valid expression of fear, and reveal his readiness to believe her capable of such a deception. This may in turn help the actress playing Beatrice-Joanna to develop the character and its imaginative past, especially if the line is taken that (as De Flores claims) the qualities that emerge in her as the play progresses are all present at the start and are drawn out by the events that follow. Of course, Vermandero's domineering and insensitive attitude to his daughter and Beatrice-Joanna's wilfulness and deviousness are fully demonstrated in their words and actions throughout the play: for example, following Beatrice's discovery of Alsemero's 'physician's closet' with its potion that will reveal 'whether a woman be with child or no', her immediate response when Diaphanta enters is to exclaim 'Seeing that wench now, / A trick comes in my mind' (4.1.53–4). 'Toy' in this context is therefore what Peter Brook terms a 'vibrating' word – one that cannot and should not be restricted to a single, certain meaning (Berry 1977: 121) – and editorial practice is misleading in generally reducing in the glossary the range of meanings a word might have had for the original audience. For the modern actors playing this scene, though they obviously won't be able to convey that range, just the *knowledge* of the variety of meanings the word may have had for the playwrights might influence vocal tones and physical behaviour and help them establish their attitudes to other characters and events.

8

Emblems and staging

Obscurity is not confined to individual words but may extend to images involving a spoken allusion to a specific visual emblem or imply the physical creation of such an emblem as part of the stage action. Emblem books – collections of illustrations with explanatory verses and mottoes – were extremely popular in England, and the analysis of explicit and implicit emblematic images in the texts and implied performances of plays has become a significant strand of Renaissance drama studies in recent years. The most immediately available examples of emblems in action can be found in contemporary paintings, especially those of Elizabeth I which employ iconography to enforce and establish aspects of the Queen's image and power in what are essentially political portraits. The imagery they employ ranges from the accessible – such as the 'Ditchley' portrait in which the Queen is shown standing on a globe, on a map of England, her toe near to Ditchley House in Oxfordshire whose owner probably commissioned the picture – to the more esoteric. Roy Strong is quick to remind us, however, of the pitfalls that lie in the way of attempts to 'read' the paintings, even when they seem comparatively straightforward:

> It was . . . riddling emblematics that became all the rage in late Elizabethan England and to read these portrait icons correctly requires a mind well versed in late renaissance allegory . . . But we are left wholly baffled by most pictures.[8]

In an exhibition at the Tate Gallery, London, in 1969, an 'Obelisk' designed by Pauline Whitehouse was erected depicting thirteen of the emblems most commonly associated with Elizabeth I. One of these was a sieve, which figures in a number of portraits of the Queen painted between 1579 and 1583. Any bewilderment experienced by the viewer of one of these paintings of the Queen holding what appears to be a kitchen or gardening utensil is dispelled when one learns that the Sieve had been used in Petrarch's *Triumph of Chastity* in which Tuccia, a Roman Vestal Virgin, accused of impurity, seized a sieve and, filling it with water from the River Tiber, ran without spilling a drop to the Temple of Vesta. Once one has the key to the painting's imagery, it can be read as a statement of Elizabeth's renowned role as Virgin Queen, rather than a celebration of her domestic virtues. The Sieve has a further meaning, embodied in the motto inscribed around its rim: *A terra il ben mal dimora insella* (literally: 'The good falls to the ground while the bad remains in the saddle'). This refers to its sieving action in discerning good from bad, the sense in which the emblem is interpreted in Geoffrey Whitney's *Choice of Emblems*, published in 1586, and probably the most popular of all the English emblem books. In other words, the painting's imagery asserts that Elizabeth is not only chaste but wise.

Emblems in books such as Whitney's are composed of three elements: a visual image commented on and explained in a motto (usually in Latin) and a verse epigram (in English). In *The White Devil*, Monticelso and Camillo describe, translate and interpret such an emblem:

MONTICELSO: Here is an emblem, nephew – pray peruse it.
  'Twas thrown in at your window, –
CAMILLO: At my window?
  Here is a stag, my lord, hath shed his horns,
  And for the loss of them the poor beast weeps –
  The word '*Inopem me copia fecit*'.
MONTICELSO: That is,
  Plenty of horns hath made him poor of horns.
CAMILLO: What should this mean?
MONTICELSO: I'll tell you. 'Tis given out
  You are a cuckold.

(2.1.323–31)

The form and function here is essentially no different from that of a literary emblem; it remains verbally expressed. But playtexts frequently imply that a stage image comprising a single figure or a group has been created in the form of a verbal and pictorial tableau that embodies particular relationships or makes abstract themes concrete: in effect a three-dimensional emblem (see Case Studies, pp. 100–8 and pp. 133–43). Some 'emblematic' stage images rely on conventional symbolism and are not dependent on a specific and pre-existing code, nor are they quoted directly from emblem books. For example, when Charlemont describes the water he drinks at his trial as 'thou clear emblem of cool temperance' (*The Atheist's Tragedy*, 5.2.210) the meaning is transparent to us, too, but many links between stage action and images or emblems, like their counterparts in paintings, remain mysterious to a modern audience, or even go unnoticed. As with word meanings, however, awareness of specific emblematic representation may be of direct use in production. Act 2, scene 3 of Middleton's *The Witch* is the shortest scene in the play (55 lines), and is, on the surface, quite straightforward. Francesca, sixteen years old, has given birth to an illegitimate child. The baby's father is Aberzanes, a worthless friend of Francesca's violent brother, Antonio. Fearful of what Antonio might do if he should discover their secret, Aberzanes has taken Francesca to a secret location to give birth. As the scene opens, we see Aberzanes dispose of the baby to an old woman. Once she has gone, Aberzanes explains to the audience that he has paid the woman to leave the child outside the house of Aberzanes's tailor. Aberzanes hopes to get the tailor into trouble with his wife, since she will think it the product of her husband's liaison with their serving-girl, a joke Aberzanes clearly believes the audience will share.[9] Francesca enters, evidently holding a mirror, and studies her face in it:

Alas, sir,
I never marked till now – I hate myself! –
How monstrous thin I look.
. . .
Fie, fie, how pale I am!

(31–35)

This moment may plausibly be read, and played, as the character's misery at losing her baby and her realisation that her lover is a wastrel, mixed with concern that her looks will give the game away as soon as she returns to her brother's house. Later in the play Francesca seeks to destroy the reputation and marriage of her sister-in-law, Isabella, who discovers her secret, but at this stage audience sympathy will probably be wholeheartedly with Francesca, especially given their exposure to the reprehensible Aberzanes. Not Middleton's, however. At least, not entirely. Even if (as seems unlikely) anyone in the original Blackfriars audience was oblivious to his portrayal in Francesca of the notorious Frances Carr (the pun on the names is only one of the clues intended to signal the character's origin to the audience), they would very likely have recognised, in the image of a finely dressed woman holding a mirror, a reference to a contemporary emblem. Marion O'Connor suggests this emblem is that of Vanity and Lust, which certainly fits the context. It seems to me, however, that Middleton may be making a more bleakly ironic allusion to the equally popular emblem of Prudence, who, like Vanity and Lust, was represented as a woman with a mirror. In addition to her mirror, Prudence was also commonly portrayed accompanied by a snake which, in that context, symbolised wisdom.[10] A viewer of the stage image, seeking to complete the image of Prudence, may have found the snake represented (equally ironically) by the remaining presence onstage – Aberzanes, who (fulfilling another symbolic serpentine role) has tempted Francesca into her decidedly imprudent actions. Indeed, perhaps Middleton intended both images – Lust *and* Prudence – to be read simultaneously, so producing a marked tension of response in those in the audience who recognised the emblematic representations and matching the fusion of comic and tragic tones which characterises the play as a whole. Although any of these emblematic associations will undoubtedly be lost to a modern audience, knowledge of them can help keep a modern actress and director clear-sightedly aware of the danger of seeing Francesca wholly as she sees herself, and remind them to keep the balance of understanding and criticism in their presentation of a character who, though young, desperate and vulnerable can nevertheless cold-bloodedly seek to destroy innocent men and women who threaten her own security.

Students often query whether or not 'ordinary' members of the original audience would have been able to interpret these emblematic references in stage action and language, but the sheer profusion of such images, not only in the visual and literary arts but on domestic items surrounding people every day, demonstrates their popularity. In *The Fair Maid of the Exchange* (1607), for example, a play performed at a public playhouse, and which includes considerable detail about embroidery techniques, the character Phyllis describes the images her mistress, Mall, has chosen for the handkerchief she intends to give to her lover:

> In one corner of the same place wanton Love,
> Drawing his bow shooting an amorous dart,
> Opposite him an arrow in a heart,
> In a third corner picture forth disdain
> A cruel fate unto a loving vain.
> In the fourth draw a springtime laurel tree
> Circled about with a ring of poesie: and thus it is:
> 'Love wounds the heart, and conquers fell disdain.'
>
> (Scene 7, ll.869–76)

Something of the effect Moll seeks can be seen in *The Shepherd Buss*, a bedcover (in the Victoria and Albert Museum in London) of white linen embroidered in black silk, which, in addition to images of flowers, fruits and animals, the forlorn lover and a melancholic inscription, reproduces emblems referred to in the speech as well as one taken directly from Whitney: the snake in the grass (Ashelford 1988: 93). However remote we might find certain emblems, therefore, we should not underestimate the ability of the contemporary audience to decode what they saw and heard nor, more importantly, their eagerness to do so: Malvolio's desperate attempt to decipher what he believes to be the code in which Olivia's letter is couched depends largely for its comedy on the audience's (self)recognition of that fact (*Twelfth Night*, 2.5). Ben Jonson, in the Epistle that prefaces *Volpone*, complained that contemporary audiences were obsessed with seeking out hidden meanings even where the writer had intended none:

> nothing can be so innocently writ or carried, but may be made obnoxious to construction . . . Application is now grown a trade with many, and there are that profess to have a key for the deciphering of everything.

Rhetoric

> Use all the *Tropes*
> And *Schemes* that Prince Quintilian can afford you:
> And much good do your Rhetoric's heart.
> *The Devil Is an Ass*, 1.4. 100–2

12

The term 'rhetoric' has gained a somewhat pejorative connotation today, as if the ability to use language well in some way diminishes the truth of feeling that lies behind – too far behind – the actual expression. In *Hamlet*, Polonius's rhetorical posturing leads Gertrude to demand 'more matter with less art' (2.2.95) but Shakespeare's contemporaries generally saw rhetoric (and its cousin, oratory) as arts of persuasion, and instruction in rhetorical skills as the means to learn how spoken and written language might be used to their best and most powerful advantage, employing the basic rhetorical skills of *inventio* (how to conceive the original idea – 'the brightest heaven of *invention*' as the Chorus in *Henry V* calls it), *dispositio* (how to arrange and plan material), *elocutio* (how to employ the various 'ornaments of style', divided between *tropes* such as metaphor, hyperbole, puns, irony and *schemes*, which organised thought rather than individual words and phrases, such as antithesis), *memoria* (how to memorise the material) and *pronunciato* (how best to use gestures, vocal inflections and facial expressions to deliver the material – the sense in which Hamlet uses the word when he tells the Players to 'speak the speech . . . as I pronounced it to you', 3.2.1) (Hussey 1992).

The study of rhetoric was a major part of grammar school education in England. By 1575 there were about 360 such schools, each training its pupils to be fluent in written and spoken Latin, to write and dispute, and to develop the arts of memory. The vast majority of rhetoric manuals used in English schools and universities were in Latin, the standard language of education. Although never produced in the same quantity as those in Latin, there were a number of books in English, such as those by George Puttenham (1589), Henry Peacham (1577, 1593) and, most popular of all, Thomas Wilson's *Art of Rhetoric* (1553), all of which no doubt appealed not only to preachers, lawyers and statesmen eager to brush up their skills (but whose Latin may not have been quite up to the mark), but also to playwrights (Vickers 1994).

Rhetoric, it must be stressed, was a practical pursuit that aimed at equipping a man with the ability to impress others with his command of language and sway them with his persuasiveness. At the age of eleven, a student might study the popular handbook, *Epitome Troporum ac Schematum* (*Examples of Tropes and Schemes*) by Susenbrotus. This comprised a collection of 'tropes', 'schemes' and rhetorical figures that the schoolboy (there was no formal education for girls) would be required to learn by heart, with the result that by the time they left school the vast majority of educated boys would have known a good number of the 132 examples listed in the book. Moreover, they would know how to apply them. In William Kempe's *The Education of Children* (1588), one of the earliest theoretical studies of education, the author suggested that once the pupil had learned the basic tropes and figures he should undertake a series of exercises to put them into practice. One such exercise, intended to develop the ability to 'amplify' language is set out in another widely used textbook, Erasmus's *De Copia* (*Of Copiousness*). Erasmus set students the task of casting a simple sentence in as many different ways as possible. For an example, Erasmus gives the sentence 'Your letter pleased me mightily', which he then proceeds to render in more than 150 different ways, ranging from the mundane – 'I was singularly delighted by your epistle' – to the ornate – 'As I aspire to the love of the Muses, nothing more gladsome than your letter has ever ere this befallen me' (Erasmus 1978: 349, 352).

Much early Elizabethan drama reflects the popularity of this ornate, abundant style, often termed 'copious' after Erasmus or 'euphuistic' after John Lyly's linguistically exuberant prose works, and the comedies he wrote for the Children of Paul's in the 1580s (see Chapter 3). As Jocelyn Powell points out, Lyly's 'artificial' comedies, with their 'fanciful and curious settings', were specifically intended as 'games for the sense, and games for the mind', their effect being 'in the best sense *dilettante*; they exercise the faculties to no other end but their delight'.[11] In later plays this ornate language was superseded as playwrights, in response to the 'form and pressure' of their time, and in particular to the growing interest in human psychology and the spirit of enquiry promoted by Francis Bacon, developed styles in which 'matter' predominated over 'manner'. Indeed, Bacon perceived a contrast between his own writing and the 'delight in their manner of style and phrase' displayed by earlier authors in whom 'the whole inclination and bent . . . was towards *copia* rather than weight'.[12] The closing years of the sixteenth century and early years of the seventeenth saw publication of a number of studies of human psychology, and playwrights sought increasingly to create dramatic language that seemed to be the product of immediate thought, with an inevitable impact on the art of acting (see Chapter 3). There was, of course, no crude evolution by which one fashion replaced its forerunner completely, and later dramatists found themselves with a wide range of styles from which to choose in order to enforce characterisation or theme. Consequently, in later plays, not only do the vocabulary and structure of speeches require analysis, but the possible associations an audience might make with the *kind* of language used have also to be explored: the elaborate, 'copious' style of the early part of the period – the 'amplification' that the Erasmus exercises produced – might be used by dramatists to suggest surface rather than depth (as with Osric in *Hamlet*), or to dramatise expansiveness and scale in a character (as Jonson does with Epicure Mammon in *Volpone*). In similar fashion, the employment of obvious rhetorical devices might be used to hint at possible deviousness or shallowness in a character (the Lawyer and Cardinal in *The White Devil*, Ulysses in *Troilus and Cressida*); formal rhetoric might be used to distinguish public utterances from more 'natural', private speech (*Henry V*) or to distinguish 'real life' from performance (as in *The Roman Actor*: see Case Study, p. 100). The genuineness of a character's attempts at persuasion, where one might expect oratory, might be underlined by the *absence* of rhetoric, such as in *The Devil Is an Ass*, 1.3. (see Chapter 3); deliberate recourse to rhetoric might underline a character's failure to engage with the reality around him, as in *Richard II*; tyrants (like Ferdinand in *The Duchess of Malfi*) might 'double' with their words, and be contrasted with plainer, more direct language (such as Webster writes for Antonio). In other words, *how* things were said could be as meaningful as *what* was said. Actors, necessarily, had to be capable of handing this range of rhetorical strategies, and I discuss this aspect of the actor's art in Chapter 3.

Verse and prose

Elizabethan and Jacobean plays are written in different forms of verse combined in various ways with prose.[13] The verse is predominantly blank (unrhymed) verse, which was first introduced to England by Henry Howard, the Earl of Surrey, in his translation of Book IV of Virgil's *Aeneid*, published in 1554.[14] The title-page referred to it as being written in a 'straunge meter', an attempt to reproduce in English poetry the 'quantative verse' (i.e., dependent on a specific number of syllables in a line) of the Latin original. The first play to employ the meter was *Gorboduc*, written in 1562 by two lawyers, Thomas Sackville (who wrote the first two acts) and Thomas Norton (who composed the other three). This play, like Surrey's translation of Virgil, seems to have been prompted by a Renaissance humanist desire to imitate a classical model – in this case the work of the Roman playwright Seneca. For Sir Philip Sidney the attempt succeeded, and he praised the play for climbing 'to the height of Seneca his style'.[15]

Prior to this time English poetry and plays had commonly been written in end-rhymed lines, often known as 'fourteeners' because of the number of syllables they contained. An example of this form is Thomas Preston's *Cambises* (*c.* 1570). These are the opening lines:

> My counsel grave and sapient with lords of legal train,
> Attentive ears towards me bend and mark what shall be sain.
> So you likewise my valiant knight whose manly acts doth fly
> By bruit of Fame that sounding trump doth pierce the azure sky.

Compare those with the opening lines of *Gorboduc*:

> The silent night that brings the quiet pause,
> From painful travails of the weary day,
> Prolongs my careful thoughts, and makes me blame
> The slow Aurore that for love or shame
> Doth long delay to show her blushing face,
> And now the day renews my grief-ful plaint.

If you read both the above speeches aloud you will need little convincing of the reasons 'fourteeners' did not survive: they easily result in monotonous delivery and gabbling.[16] But blank verse asserted itself as the norm of dramatic verse writing for positive reasons, not because of the limitations of 'fourteeners'. These reasons are not difficult to establish: blank verse closely

approximates the breath and stress patterns of normal speech and was sufficiently flexible to meet the demands made upon it by different dramatists
throughout the period. The turning point that set the seal on blank verse as
the dominant dramatic medium was its almost simultaneous use by Thomas
Kyd and Christopher Marlowe in the late 1580s. In the opening lines of the
Prologue to *Tamburlaine*, Marlowe announced both his intention to be different and the superiority of his chosen medium over its predecessors:

> From jigging veins of rhyming mother wits,
> And such conceits as clownage keeps in pay,
> We'll lead you to the stately tent of war,
> Where you shall hear the Scythian Tamburlaine
> Threat'ning the world with high astounding terms.

Marlowe dramatised the power of Tamburlaine partly by the power of the
language he spoke: 'terms Italianate, Big-sounding sentences, and words of
state', as Joseph Hall described similar writing in *Virgidemiarum* (1597).
Marlowe also explored the dramatic versatility of the verse, a flexibility that in
its most developed form characterises the work of the later Jacobeans. Indeed,
it was this adaptability of blank verse to the changing demands made upon it
that sustained its use and pre-eminence.

This book does not aim to be a manual for performance: there are a number
of studies available that suggest ways actors might develop their skills with
verse and heightened language, most notably John Barton's *Playing Shakespeare*
(1984), and the more technique-oriented books by Cicely Berry (1993) and
Patsy Rodenburg (1993) listed in the bibliography. However, for students of
drama who approach these plays 'practically' (i.e., are alert to their nature as
theatrical rather than literary texts), some awareness of ways in which playwrights controlled the basic verse form for dramatic purposes, and of how
language structures can consequently be as much a guide to our understanding as thematic analysis, is a key part of exploring how these plays work.

Iambic pentameters are lines of ten syllables grouped into five iambic feet in
which the first syllable is unstressed (˘) and the second is stressed (/). Regular
blank (i.e. unrhymed) verse lines go like this:

> In sooth I know not why I am so sad.
> It wearies me; you say it wearies you.
> (*The Merchant of Venice*, 1.1.1–2)

A quick glance at virtually any play, however, even more so a play written
later in the period, will show how frequently the metre varies from this basic
form, and indeed, it is precisely this flexibility that is blank verse's great
strength as a dramatic medium. Apart from the freedom (for writer or actor)

to stress four rather than five beats, variation can be achieved in a number of ways: by letting the stress and sense coincide (as in the *Merchant of Venice* lines) or setting them at variance; by the addition of extra syllables (called 'hyper-metrical' lines and very common in later plays); by reversing the stresses in the first foot or dropping a syllable and beginning on a stressed beat ('headless' lines); by end-stopping lines or running them on (enjambement) to find completion in the midst of a following line; by giving lines stressed or unstressed endings (sometimes termed 'masculine' and 'feminine' respectively); or by having a short line for emphasis or, perhaps, to leave space for implicit stage movement. There is usually a pause in each line – called the *caesura* – which is normally placed after the second or third stressed syllable. This pause may provide a breathing space, indicate a break or change of direction in thought, or mark a 'beat' – a moment in which an idea expressed in the earlier part of the line can be held and focused on before the speaker moves on to the remainder of the line. Further variation can be provided by splitting a complete line between two or more speakers, which may produce added tension and pace, or give a sense of conversation or disputation (see Case Study, p. 161ff.).

Nor is all dramatic verse blank. Rhyme is often used not only to round off a scene (useful in a theatre with no front curtain or blackout), to sum up points in an argument, or to place particular stress and focus on a piece of essential information. It may also be placed in productive contrast with the prose and un-rhymed verse that generally forms the dominant language of the play. For example, in the closing moments of Thomas Middleton's city comedy, *A Trick to Catch the Old One* (*c.* 1604–6), first the Courtesan, and then Witgood, kneel, admit the error of their ways, and pledge themselves to reform their lives. Both speeches are in rhyming couplets and have a formal patterning in their structure. On the face of it, these speeches present a conventional closure, but the use of the rhyme may be employed by Middleton to alert us to the pragmatic artificiality of these speeches and, through this, to the impossibility of rounding off in so neat a fashion the complex issues and social conflicts raised in the play. Such a reading is hinted at, perhaps in Witgood's aside to the audience ('I must confess my follies; I'll down too', 5.2.176) before he begins his rhyming speech, with the physical gesture possibly referring to the action of a performer kneeling to deliver an epilogue to the audience.

A number of plays from the period (such as Shakespeare's *King John* and *Richard II*, Ford's *The Broken Heart* and several of Philip Massinger's) are composed entirely in verse, but – though it is the predominant form in plays such as Middleton's city comedies – no play is written completely in prose. Some verse, however (certainly later in the period), has a form so flexible that it may be difficult for anyone hearing it to distinguish it from prose, while prose frequently has a balance in rhythm and pattern that makes it difficult to distinguish from verse. The commonly expressed view that verse is the medium of the high-status characters and prose of the low is only true in the most general sense, and it is worth remembering, too, that contemporaries did not consider prose as inferior to poetry, merely different. It is more useful, therefore, to think of changes from verse to prose or vice versa within a play as a whole, in individual scenes, or even in single speeches, as indicating a shift of some kind – of mood, of subject matter, from public to personal utterance, sanity to madness, and so on. These shifts mark nodal points to which performers need to be alert in order, in Adrian Noble's words, to 'crack the form'.[17] The reasons for these changes of medium are not always immediately obvious, but I am sure that there is always likely to be a dramatic or theatrical reason. For example, S.S. Hussey comments of the language of the hired assassins Black Will and Shakebag in Sc.3 of *Arden of Faversham* (*c.* 1592), that they 'begin by speaking prose, but at [line] 83, *and for no apparent reason*, move into verse' (1992: 135–6, emphasis added). This early play may not demonstrate the same fluency of medium-shifts as one finds later, and comments on its choice of verse or prose are hampered by the difficulty of establishing the nature of the original text, but one can suggest reasons for the changes that will be of importance in presenting the characters. For example, the moment Black Will shifts from prose to verse is partly to match the 'register' of Greene's preceding lines, but is also, I think, a conscious act of self-aggrandisement on Black Will's part. He is, as we discover in the course of the play, not only violent and bullying, but incompetent, and he is here clearly intent on impressing his prospective employer, Greene. Like some fifth-rate Tamburlaine, Will spends much of the play proclaiming his intentions and abilities in 'high astounding terms' and the playwright is able to comment effectively on the character by this productive disparity between language and action.

Verse and prose may also be intermixed in order to effect stage focus. This is particularly important on an open stage where an audience views from four sides, and which is quite different from the single unified viewpoint of the proscenium stage. Consequently, Renaissance playtexts can to an extent be approached as maps which include – explicitly or implicitly – guides to staging and performance. Simply looking at the *shape* of the dialogue on the page – without any exploration of what is actually said – reveals a chart that tracks the shifts in the scene. Consider the opening scene of *The Changeling*, for example. The play begins with 12 more or less regular iambic verse lines of direct address to the audience, setting up Alsemero's dilemma. This is followed by 43 lines of verse dialogue between Alsemero and Jasperino (the one or two lines of the servants are too short in length to affect the verse rhythm), by the end of which the audience is agog to see the woman who has had such an impact on Alsemero. At line 56, Beatrice enters, accompanied by Diaphanta and servants. Jasperino immediately shifts into prose, and commentates on the stage action for 6 lines, pointing up what is important in the exchange and allowing the audience to get a good look at the new character. That done, Alsemero and Beatrice embark on a conversation, in verse, for 23 lines, during which Beatrice expresses ideas on the relationship between sight, passion and reason that are central to her own character and the play as a whole, and in which she confides to the audience the key, plot-complicating information that she is attracted to Alsemero but already engaged to someone else. At this point, Jasperino again speaks in prose, again for 6 lines, to draw this unit of the scene to a close. It is clear, therefore, that Rowley (whose scene this probably is) has used shifts from verse to prose not for characterisation (Jasperino speaks verse and prose) but to guide the focus of the action, bracketing, as it were, the crucial exchanges between Alsemero and Beatrice, which are expressed in verse, within a frame of prose. A similar point is made by the director, Matthew Warchus, who begins his work on Elizabethan and Jacobean plays by pasting up a photocopy of each act on a large piece of paper:

> Just by looking at the shape of the whole play on paper – at the dense prose sections, the less-packed verse, the long and short scenes – begins to give a hint of the rhythm, the pace of the play and individual scenes.[18]

The important question remains, however, as to the degree to which a 'full and understanding auditory' (as John Webster defined an ideal audience) could then, and can today, distinguish by listening in the theatre between lines in verse and lines in prose: Mike Gwilym, who played Vasques in 'Tis Pity She's A Whore (RSC: 1977), a character who speaks only prose, recalls that he was regularly complimented on his performance by members of the audience who expressed the wish that every actor in the production could speak verse as well as he did.[19] Many in the original audiences presumably had ears so attuned that they were alert to all variations. To an extent, of course, the contrast depends on the particular verse and prose styles involved, which, as I noted earlier, changed over the course of the period. Clearly, though, playwrights must have assumed such changes in medium – or the frequent mix of 'naturalistic' and 'heightened' language – could be signalled to an audience through the actor's delivery, and contemporary actors are invariably praised for the 'tunability', or some such phrase, of their voices (see Chapter 3). Cicely Berry likens the contemporary audience's response to the beat of the verse to that of 'a modern audience listening to Rock or Reggae or Jazz: we know when it is consistent with the message, we very often pick up on the humour in the rhythm, and we know when it is broken' (1993: 53). The significance of shifts in medium or register, added to the fact that our ears are less well attuned than an Elizabethan's, means it is essential that modern actors do not elide the moments of transition or adopt speech tactics that either flatten the verse and prose into one medium or elevate the language generally and indiscriminately, both of which approaches destroy the distinct registers of verse and prose.

Actors and directors generally are aware of the particular skills needed to handle the demands of Renaissance plays, and achieve a balance between technique and individual interpretation.[20] Views differ, however, on how the verse should be approached – often articulated as a choice between 'poetry' and 'meaning'. Peter Hall, for example (acknowledged by many actors as the director most focused on the speaking of verse), writes:

> The rules of Shakespearean verse can be learnt in three hours. But then the actor must make them his, and apply them in his own way. The essence is to speak the lines rather than the individual words. The five-beat iambic line is the unit of communication. By the way he structures his lines, Shakespeare tells the actor when to go fast, when to go slow; where to come in on cue, where to pause. If you observe what he wrote, the scenes orchestrate themselves, their literal and emotional meaning is released and easily communicated to the audience. But, as in music, you must learn the notes correctly before you start to express the emotion.
>
> (1993: 77)

To some, the results of Hall's 'rules' can produce 'a style that can verge on the artificial or even the eccentric', while others find that the more 'naturalistic' or 'conversational' style encouraged by other directors is often achieved at the expense of the rhythmical drive of the language (Wells 1990: 185). There is a range of opinion, too, on the value of, or at least the weight that should be given to, the kind of detailed analysis of form advocated generally (but with different individual emphasis) by those such as Hall, Barton, Noble, Cicely Berry and Rodenburg. John Russell Brown, for example, noting that 'speech is an individual activity as well as a collection of printed signs to be listed, described and decoded' (1989: 50) takes issue with John Barton on where the actor's focus of attention should lie. Barton, he claims:

> pays little attention to syntax and the shape of thought. His actors can sound precious, unreal, and overheated, because they are not taught to seek out the main verb of every sentence, and to organize all its words around this central activity of mind.
>
> (1989: 54)

Charles Marowitz, however, is sweepingly dismissive of the whole approach. In his tendentious book *Recycling Shakespeare* (1991), which according to the Preface 'is directed at two enemies – the academics and the traditionalists' (ix), Marowitz roundly attacks what he understands to be Barton's approach to the texts:

> Language is the end-product of intention and desire. It is because we

want something and try to satisfy our desires in obtaining it that we speak at all . . . It is not to the rules of prosody nor the theories of verse structure that an actor must look in order to find the meaning with which to transfuse Shakespeare's words . . . And to suggest that a speech, a character or an entire play can be 'decoded' by under-standing its prosody or its semiology is grossly to misunderstand the nature of theatrical performance.

(1991: 87)

In fact, it seems to me that Marowitz misrepresents (or perhaps grossly misunderstands) both the detail and general scope of Barton's argument. Throughout *Playing Shakespeare* Barton, and the experienced actors who worked with him, consistently stress the need for the language to be the prod-uct of the character's aims, intentions and attitudes: what we call *motivation* and what Shakespeare, through Hamlet, called 'the motive and the cue for passion' (2.2.554). Only after these motives have been established, Barton argues, should the actor explore the language given to the character to express them:

Playing the *quality* [of the language] leads to bad acting, and going for the intention is more interesting and alive and human. The first is general and the second specific.

(1984: 12)

The text employed for a production is the actor's primary source of hard information about a character's aims and intentions (see Case Study, p. 88ff.), and Renaissance plays require actors to possess particular skills to enable them first to disentangle and then to express the discoveries that arise from their study of that text. The individual words a character uses to confront and manipulate other characters and situations are, as we've seen, frequently alien to us. As part of demystifying the language, Barton tries to help the actor to understand its workings and identify the clues it may contain, knowledge which may clarify an obscure moment and be of direct and practical help in shaping a scene or rela-tionship or in pacing a scene. Such analysis multiplies the options from which an actor or director may choose. The more choices available, the better. If a choice is made that differs from that suggested by the textual structure, know-ing what one is *not* doing will help focus the reasons for doing what one is. Consequently, detailed analysis of the kind Barton and others propose can only be of benefit: for students in developing an awareness of the texts as scripts, and for actors in helping them develop the confidence and skills to deliver to an audience not only the meaning but the 'pleasure of ingenious speeches'.

2

'THE LIFE OF THESE THINGS CONSISTS IN ACTION'[1]

Staging the play

> thou shalt not need to travel with thy pumps full of gravel any more,
> after a blind jade and a hamper; and stalk upon boards and barrel heads
> to an old cracked trumpet.
>
> Ben Jonson, *Poetaster*, 3.4.147–9

During the summer of 1593, Edward Alleyn, the first actor to play Marlowe's Tamburlaine, Dr Faustus and Barabas, was on tour in the provinces while, for the second successive year, London suffered a major outbreak of plague.[2] In the 1590s, as soon as deaths reached around 40–50 a week, the playhouses were closed, forcing companies out on the road, and Henslowe's phrase that a company 'broke and went into the country' is a revealing one. 'T.G.', the author of *The Rich Cabinet Furnished with Variety of Excellent Descriptions* (1616), underlined the threat the plague presented to the actors:

> Player is afraid of the plague, as much as a coward of a musket: for as death is formidable to one, so is poverty and want to the other.

In the middle of summer 1593, when deaths in London were running at more than a thousand each week, Alleyn was in Bristol, from where, at the end of July, he wrote a letter to his wife, Joan (née Woodward), whom he had married the previous October.[3] He expressed the hope that she and the rest of the family would not become ill and gave his advice on how to keep the plague at bay ('every evening throw water before your door and in your backside and have in your windows good store of rue and herb of grace'); he sent back his 'white waistcoat because it is a trouble to me to carry it', thanked her for her letter and asked her to send any further correspondence care of the company at Shrewsbury, West Chester or York – future stops on the tour. Alleyn concluded:

> . . . and thus sweet heart, with my hearty commendations to all our friends I send from Bristol this Wednesday after Saint James his day,

being ready to begin the play of Harry of Cornwall . . . Your loving husband, E Alleyn.

We cannot know for certain, of course, but the phrase 'ready to begin the play' perhaps indicates that Alleyn wrote this letter already made up and in costume and just before going onstage. Moreover, the original manuscript shows that having signed it, Alleyn added to the letter – asking for more news of his wife's 'domestical matters', and making further requests for his 'orange tawny stockings' to be dyed black and for Joan to plant the spinach in September since he would not return from the tour until All Hallows, 1 November (the day when it was customary for Londoners who had left the city for the plague season to return). These afterthoughts – squeezed in at the bottom of the page and vertically in the lefthand margin – were clearly inserted after Alleyn had signed the letter, possibly in his breaks offstage during the performance. Whatever the truth, this letter is as close as we get to the moment at which an Elizabethan actor stepped onstage. Sadly, Alleyn left no thoughts on how he actually acted the part of Harry of Cornwall when he got there. Nor did any other actors set down in writing what they performed in action. Apart from observations within their plays from the large number of writers who were or had themselves been actors or who (like Philip Massinger and Richard Brome) appear regularly to have incorporated firsthand experience of rehearsal and performance directly into their work, the few guides we have to the skills and practices of Elizabethan and Jacobean actors are found in descriptions or reminiscences of performances from the point of view of audiences, playhouse artefacts such as prompt copies and 'plots', the demands and expectations revealed by the texts the actors performed, the possible implications for acting in the relationship between the texts, their performance spaces and audiences, and the various attacks on, and defences of, the theatre that appeared throughout the period (see Chapter 3).

The profession {of acting} has in it a kind of contradiction, for none is more disliked, and yet none more applauded.

John Earle, 1628

Laurence Olivier once identified talent, luck and stamina as the essential elements of a successful career as an actor, and things were much the same in the late sixteenth and early seventeenth centuries. Edward Alleyn retired as an extremely wealthy man, having amassed a fortune from his acting, entrepreneurial activities, investments and land deals, his ownership of the Bear Garden and Fortune playhouse, and his Mastership of the Bears, held jointly with Philip Henslowe. In 1605 Alleyn purchased the manor of Dulwich in south-east London for £5,000 and the neighbouring Rycotes estate, increasing his Dulwich property to 1,100 acres. In 1610 he was made a magistrate and in 1613 he founded the College of God's Gift in Dulwich (now Dulwich College) with an endowment of £10,000. Alleyn's transformation from Elizabethan actor to Jacobean gentleman was, however, exceptional: Joan Alleyn's letter to her husband informing him that a fellow actor, Robert Browne, leader of the company at the Boar's Head, was 'dead, and died very poor' may record a more typical fate.[4] Indeed, very few actors accumulated real wealth. Malevole's advice to Pietro in *The Malcontent* – 'do not turn player. There's more of them than can well live by one another already' (4.4.4–5) – suggests that it was for many actors as competitive, overcrowded and precarious a profession then as it is today. As the quotation at the head of this section reveals, public attitudes to actors were as contradictory then as now, veering between admiration and envy, fascination with their lifestyle (one inn was pointed out to visitors to London as a regular haunt of the actors), criticism of their offstage behaviour (especially their supposed sexual promiscuity), and confusion between the actions and characters they represented onstage and their behaviour off it (see Chapter 3; Skura 1993: 30–46).

Raw talent would have been required, of course, but an actor would also have needed to acquire a range of specific skills: 'T.G.' lists these as 'dancing, activity, music, song, elocution, ability of body, memory, skill of weapon, pregnancy of wit' – very similar to the curriculum of a modern theatre school, in fact – to which should be added the physical and vocal resilience to sustain a punishing schedule. Variety and flexibility were also necessary since, like many supporting actors today (though perhaps more often), the performers had regularly to play more than one part in a play: for example, the Plot of George Peele's *The Battle of Alcazar* (see pp. 41–2) indicates that the majority of actors took more than one role: Samuel Rowley played eight parts – a Moorish Attendant, a Captain, a Messenger, a Moorish Ambassador, a Devil, a Captain of Tangier, Death and a Portuguese Soldier. When considering or proposing original doubling schemes, however, it's worth remembering the difficulty – and hence the time required – of getting in and out of Elizabethan and Jacobean costume. Thomas Tomkis observed in his play, *Lingua*, for example, that a 'ship is sooner rigged than a gentlewoman made ready' (4.6, p. 426) and a courtier in Middleton's *The Old Law* remarks that his doublet needs 'three hours a buttoning' (4.1.160). Both are exaggerations, of course, but exaggerations based on actual experience, and may suggest that conventions of costume change were at times suggestive rather than complete. There are other indications of flexible and imaginative solutions. The 1607 Quarto of the *Fair Maid of the Exchange*, for example, printed a guide to show how 'eleven may easily act' the twenty-two characters in the play, including the two Officers.[5] (I am going to assume for the moment that the printed text represents a performance text.) In this guide, seven of the actors are allocated only one role. Of the other four actors, one plays two parts: Ferdinand (who appears in scenes 3, 7, 9, 12 and 13) and Wood, who also appears in 13 but the actor has a brief – 13-line – time offstage to do the change. Each of the three remaining actors is allocated four parts. The first

(Actor A) plays Berry (scenes 5, 6 and 13); Bobbington (1 and 5); Gardiner (8); and an Officer (12 and 13). The second (Actor B) plays Master Flower (5, 11 and 13); Bennet (8); Scarlet (1); and Ralph (12). The third (Actor C) plays Barnard (2, 6, 10 and 13); Mistress Flower (11 and 13); Ursula (1); and Boy (8). Clearly this doubling scheme presents problems. Two of Actor A's characters (Bobbington and Berry) appear in scene 5: Bobbington enters at l.564 and exits at l.601. Berry enters at l.604, exits at l.612, re-enters at l.729 and exits at l.832. With only three lines separating Bobbington's exit from Berry's entrance a doubling would appear difficult, though not impossible if it involved no more, say, than a change of hat, cloak and accent. Alternatively, it is not inconceivable that another actor stood in for Actor A for those few lines (Berry actually speaks only one line), Actor A resuming the part of Berry at l.729. Actor B's doublings present no obvious problems, but Actor C cannot, evidently, play the parts listed for him given that two of those characters – Barnard and Mistress Flower – both appear in the final scene. Actors A and B already play significant roles in scene 13 and cannot add either role to their allocation. Actor C (who also plays Ursula) obviously specialised in female roles and as the two other female roles in the play (Phyllis and Mall Berry) also appear in scene 13 it seems that Actor C must have played Mistress Flower in the final scene. It appears from this analysis, therefore, that the breakdown is not accurate for the printed text, that the claim for eleven actors is wrong and that twelve is the required number, the extra actor playing at least the role of Barnard. This has the advantage of leaving Actor C to play two female roles and that of a Boy, a typical clutch of parts for a young actor.

The exits and entrances in the final scene, however, in which fourteen characters appear onstage (more than in any other scene) ensure that the maximum number of actors onstage at any one time (from l.2586 to l.2663) is eleven, though it requires some pretty sharp manoeuvring at the very end of the scene to achieve this. Barnard appears at l.2455, but no exit is indicated for him. His plot-line is completed at l.2511, however, after which he has nothing else to say, and there are many other instances in this and other Quartos where essential stage directions are missing. The manuscript prompt-copy of Massinger's *Believe As You List* indicates that the part of Calistus was played by two actors, the role of Demetrius by three.[6] Given this evidence, it seems to me not inconceivable that for this one scene Barnard could be played by another actor, perhaps one of the actors playing Ferdinand, Anthony or Bowdler who enter for the first time in the scene 75 lines after Barnard's final line. This is all possibly too laboured, and David Bradley may be right in thinking that splitting roles in the way indicated in *Believe As You List* was exceptional (1992: 36). But intricate doubling schemes are characteristic of theatre practice throughout the period and it seems reasonable at least to speculate that customs were fluid enough to allow such ingenious solutions when absolutely necessary, such as when touring with a significantly smaller number of actors than were available for London performances. In my experience, when under pressure all kinds of pragmatic solutions may be found to initially seemingly intractable theatre problems. In a touring production of *The Country Wife*, for example, directed by Mike Alfreds for the (then) Cambridge Theatre Company, the single actor who doubled the parts of Old Lady Squeamish and the Quack was required in one scene to be onstage playing both roles simultaneously: the solution found was for the stage-manager to enter and simply hold up the Squeamish costume in front of the actor dressed as the Quack, who spoke Squeamish's lines, after which the stage-manager exited.[7]

Playing multiple parts within one play, some of them only a very few lines in length, some with no lines at all, possibly sharing one part among different actors, presumably meant that performances often focused on some clearly defining characteristic in voice, gesture, make-up or costume: Bottom's list of possible beards in which he might play the part of Pyramus – 'either your straw-colour beard, your orange-tawny beard, your purple-in-grain beard, or your French-crown-colour beard, your perfect yellow' – may reflect the kind of aids the actors sought (*A Midsummer Night's Dream*, 1.2.86–9).

A good memory was certainly needed. A leading actor like Alleyn, for example, would have learned perhaps ten new roles in each season while keeping perhaps twenty old ones fresh in his memory, and a supporting actor, playing a number of parts in each play, 'might need to have as many as a hundred parts committed to memory' (Carson 1988: 37; Beckerman 1962). Bottom's fellow amateur actor, Snug, who admits to being 'slow of study' would not have survived, and even the professionals must have frequently been very shaky on their lines as modern actors who had experience of weekly rep earlier this century recall they were themselves. Peter Copley, a member of the 1995–6 RSC company who began his acting career in 1932, remembers that:

> Lines were learned I don't really know how, but common practice was: the pub after the show, back to digs for supper and a session with the script, down the page with a postcard. And in the usual box set you could during the show, if either very conscientious or very desperate, have your French's acting edition just outside the set door for a quick look at the next scene. How people managed with cue scripts [see pp. 39–40.] which were pretty well abandoned by the Thirties I can't imagine.[8]

An Elizabethan stage offered little opportunity for such concealment however: the Prologue in *Wily Beguiled* (1606) explains to the restless audience that the 'paltry players' are still 'poring in their papers and never perfect', and Burbage was specifically praised for having a voice 'not lower than the prompter', an analogy which seems to hint at how often hard-pressed performers relied on help from offstage (or wherever the prompter was positioned). Lord Letoy, in Richard Brome's play, *The Antipodes* (1638), observes that if an actor was certain at least of the shape of a scene or speech, he might 'fribble' his way through:

>   Well, sir, my actors
> Are all in readiness, and, I think, all perfect
> But one, that never will be perfect in a thing
> He studies: yet he makes such shifts extempore,
> (Knowing the purpose what he is to speak to)
> That he moves mirth in me 'bove all the rest.
> For I am none of those poetic furies,
> That threats the actor's life, in a whole play,
> That adds a syllable or takes away.
> If he can fribble through, and move delight
> In others, I am pleas'd.
>
>   (2.1.14–24)

The quality of 'bad quartos' may reflect the frequency of 'fribbling' caused by memory-lapses, though an actor could clearly also be 'put beside his part' by stage fright (Shakespeare, Sonnet 23) or by the presence in the audience of a professional playwright (less forgiving than the enthusiastic amateur Letoy) who might sit in the gallery, 'and there make vile and bad faces at every line' (Thomas Dekker, *Satiromastix*, 5.2.299–300).

Casting

The popularity of leading actors such as Burbage or Alleyn (whose 'very name . . . was able to make an ill matter good')[9] was matched – perhaps even surpassed – by that of the clowns. Richard Tarlton ('the first English actor to win a national reputation', Leggatt 1975: 100), George Attewell, Robert Wilson, Will Kempe and, later, comic actors such as Robert Armin and Thomas Greene were all star performers in their own right, whom people undoubtedly came to see as much as they did a particular play. When, in 1604, the King's Men adapted *The Malcontent*, a former Children's play, for the adult stage, they introduced a new comic character, Passarello, a major role probably specifically intended to display the talents of Robert Armin.

Although the demands of plays and companies must have required actors to be extremely flexible in their range of parts, it seems that some became associated with a line of roles that suited their personalities or looks, just as popular television actors do today. William Rowley, for example, Middleton's collaborator on a number of plays, was best known for 'fat clown' roles (*JCS*, II: 556) while John Sincler, who was probably a hired man in the King's Men, appears to have made the most of being unusually thin (Nungezer 1968: 326). Stephen Hammerton, when he graduated from female to male roles, thrived on the success his good looks brought him in playing romantic leads, while other actors developed their range as their careers progressed and they got older: Richard Perkins, who worked from 1602 to the closure of the theatres forty years later, was noted for his performances as romantic villain, dignified father, and, towards the end of his career, as honest, plain-spoken old man (*JCS*, II: 526). At times, however, casting was acknowledged to be inappropriate: in Massinger's epilogue to *The Emperor of the East* (1631) he apologised for the fact that the actor 'on whom (forced to it by necessity) The maker did confer his Emperor's part' had been far too young for the role. Only rarely, given the tailor-made nature of most texts, were the demands of a play beyond the cast, but a stage direction printed in the 1640 Quarto of *Messalina* indicates that a song 'was left out of the Play in regard there was none could sing in Parts'.

Rehearsal

We have little idea how, once parts were allotted, individual actors or casts prepared for performances, but rehearsal periods were generally short, which must have required the companies as a rule to work rapidly and in a disciplined way, rather than in the 'chaotic . . . mad hurry' with actors 'drunk, absent, forgetful' envisioned by A.R. Braunmuller (Braunmuller and Hattaway 1990: 57). A contract between Philip Henslowe and an actor, Robert Dawes, dated 7 April 1614 (found among Henslowe's papers but subsequently lost), committed Dawes to 'attend all such rehearsal which shall the night before the rehearsal be given publicly out' and set out the penalties for lateness, being drunk at rehearsal and taking costumes out of the playhouse (Carson 1988: 37–8). The insistence on punctuality and curb on drinking show that such unprofessional behaviour would not be tolerated – there was too little time. Rehearsals have to be called by someone, and that someone has also to decide who is needed to rehearse what. Even though the notion of a director as we have come to understand it in the past hundred years (as the person responsible for 'the interpretation of the play-text and its coherent expression through the full range of the theatre's means of expression')[10] is inappropriate in this context, certain directorial functions are necessary in all productions whatever the period since, as Thomas Heywood wrote, actors' 'imperfections may by instructions be helped and amended' (1841: 43). A number of references throughout the period point to someone involved with productions adopting a function that seems close to directing. Two months before his death in 1566, Richard Edwards was referred to as being in Oxford preparing a lavish production of his (lost) play, *Palamon and Arcite*; Francis Kirkman praised William Beeston (Christopher's son) as 'the happiest interpreter and judge of our English stage-plays' whose 'instruction, judgement and fancy [imagination]' had benefited the 'poets and actors of these times' (Dedication to *The Loves and Adventures of Clerico and Lozia*, 1652); and in Brome's *The Antipodes*, Lord

Letoy's comments to his actors, mixing general and specific points, sound very much like director's notes:

> Let me not see you act now
> In your scholastic way you brought to town wi' ye,
> With see-saw sack-a-down like a sawyer;
> Nor in a comic scene play Hercules Furens,
> Tearing your throat to split the audients' ears.
> And you, sir, you had got a trick of late
> Of holding out your bum in a set speech,
> Your fingers fibulating on your breast
> As if your buttons or your band-strings were
> Helps to your memory. Let me see you in't
> No more, I charge you. No, nor you, sir, in
> That one action of the legs I told you of,
> Your singles and your doubles – look you, thus –
> Like one o' th' dancing masters o' the Bear Garden;
> And when you have spoke, at end of every speech,
> Not minding the reply, you turn you round
> As tumblers do, when betwixt every feat
> They gather wind by firking up their breeches.
> I'll none of these absurdities in my house,
> But words and action married so together
> That shall strike harmony in the ears and eyes
> Of the severest, if judicious, critics.
>
> (2.1)

Although there is frequently no need to block a scene with two, even three, experienced actors in it (though in my experience they invariably work it out for themselves, fix it and then enjoy repeating or varying it), as the numbers onstage rise it becomes correspondingly necessary to organise the moves. Richard Flatter, in *Shakespeare's Producing Hand* (1948) and Patrick Tucker, who has experimented with the use of cue-scripts (see p. 133ff.), argue that in the Folio text of Shakespeare's plays all necessary guides to the performer are implicit in the lines themselves.[11] It is true that Renaissance texts in general contain guides to individual and group actions (see Case Study, p. 133ff.) but that still doesn't seem to me to answer the question of rehearsal entirely. Virtually all extant plays that dramatise the act of staging a performance indicate that one person, rather than the group at large, was charged with the responsibility of 'guiding' the production. Although these representations of play production within plays are frequently of amateur or private performances, they are written by professionals and it seems to me probable that something similar to their descriptions was customary practice in the commercial playhouses.[12]

Companies prepared and staged plays at an astonishing rate compared to general practice in the modern theatre. In the 1630s the theatre companies began to offer the same play on successive days, perhaps for a week or longer, but for most of the period a different play was performed each day and so actors could not use a run of early performances to test and set a role. It seems from Henslowe's *Diary* that the company had on average about three weeks from delivery of the play to its opening performance (Gurr 1992: 209), though a speculative analysis of a single month's work reveals a very pressured timetable. At the Rose in April 1597, for example, the Admiral's Men performed on twenty-five days of the month, during which time they presented thirteen different plays of which certainly three, and possibly four, were new, and another was a revival of a play they had not performed for two years. Henslowe recorded their schedule as follows (figures in brackets indicate the number of known performances to date):[13]

Friday 1	*The Blind Beggar* (22)
Saturday 2	*Vortigern* (12)
Sunday 3	No performance
Monday 4	*Guido* (4)
Tuesday 5	*Alexander and Lodowick* (8)
Wednesday 6	*That Will Be and Shall Be* (9)
Thursday 7	*Five Plays in One* (première)
Friday 8	*A Woman Hard to Please* (8)

Saturday 9 and Sunday 10 – No performances

Monday 11	*Belin Dun* (20)
Tuesday 12	*Alexander and Lodowick* (9)
Wednesday 13	*Times Triumph* (?première)
Thursday 14	*Stukeley* (8)
Friday 15	*Five Plays in One* (2)
Saturday 16	*A Woman Hard to Please* (9)
Sunday 17	No performance
Monday 18	*A French Comedy* (7, but see below)
Tuesday 19	*Belin Dun* (21)
Wednesday 20	*Five Plays in One* (3)
Thursday 21	*Jieronimo* (*The Spanish Tragedy*) (24)
Friday 22	*A French Comedy* (8)
Saturday 23	*Guido* (5)
Sunday 24	No performance
Monday 25	*Five Plays in One* (4)
Tuesday 26	*A French Comedy* (9)

Wednesday 27   *Alexander and Lodowick* (10)
Thursday 28   *Belin Dun* (22)
Friday 29   *Uther Pendragon* (première)
Saturday 30   *That Will Be And Shall Be* (10)

Of the thirteen plays, six were performed once, three twice, three on three occasions, and one was given four performances. Prior to the première of *Five Plays in One* on 7 April, the company had last staged a new play (*Guido*) on 19 March. Easter fell in the last week of March, and Henslowe records no performances from 23 to 28 March (Good Friday was the 25th), which may have allowed the company time to concentrate on preparing its new productions. After the first performance of *Five Plays in One* on 7 April, the next entry marked by Henslowe as 'ne' (presumably an abbreviation for 'new' or 'newly entered') is *A French Comedy*, which was staged on Monday 18 April. In fact, this play had received its first performance more than two years earlier, in February 1595. Whereas all the other plays performed in April 1597 had been staged in the previous month, the last performance (the sixth) of *A French Comedy* recorded by Henslowe had been on 17 June 1595, since when Henslowe had recorded 341 performances on the Rose stage of 49 different plays, of which 21 appear to have been premières. It is likely, therefore, that any actors involved in the previous performance of *A French Comedy* would have needed at least to refresh their memories of the play and production. Indeed, it may well have been completely new to some of those involved and treated as such by the company. Conversely, although not marked 'ne', it appears that the performance of *Time's Triumph* on 13 April may actually have been a première: in any event, no earlier performance is recorded in the *Diary*, so if it was an old play revamped, it, like *A French Comedy*, may also have been treated as new. Between 8 and 18 April, therefore, assuming they rehearsed in the morning of each day on which they performed (though they may well have needed to run bits, or all, of the play scheduled for the afternoon), all day on Saturday 9 (when no performance is recorded) and at least half the day on Sunday 10 and 17, it appears the actors had the equivalent of three and a half days rehearsal before opening *Time's Truth* and two and a half before the revival of *A French Comedy*. During that period they performed five other plays (including the second performance of *Five Plays in One*). Following the première of *A French Comedy* on 18 April they performed on every afternoon (except Sunday 24) and presented their next new play, *Uther Pendragon*, on Friday 29 April, the equivalent of five days rehearsal time (assuming they rehearsed for half the day on Sunday 24). On the nine intervening afternoons they performed six different plays, giving three of them (including *A French Comedy*) two performances each. No play was performed on successive days.

Even allowing for errors in my necessarily speculative analysis (particularly where Sunday rehearsals are concerned) this is a demanding schedule, but one not dissimilar to the experience of actors in weekly rep in the earlier years of this century. Peter Copley recollects:

> The schedule, with small variations, was almost of necessity universal. Tuesday morning 10 a.m.: read play and block Act 1, finish at 2 p.m.; Wednesday morning block Act 2, possibly run Act 1, finish at 2 p.m.; Thursday, block Act 3, finish 12.30 p.m. (matinée 2.30 p.m.); Friday, run play, finish 2 p.m.; Saturday, run play, finish 2 p.m. (matinée 2.30 p.m.): Sunday off for actors but often 24-hour session for stage management and crew (who also might have had to act) striking the previous week's set, fitting up and lighting. Monday, dress rehearsal, finish (well, at Leeds Rep anyway) always in time for extended, relaxing, luxury tea with orchestra plus sometimes a 'mannequin parade' at Debenham & Freebody before first night. Obviously there were variations, like afternoon rehearsals (very unpopular) and sometimes costume parades or even a first dress rehearsal on Sunday followed by a second on Monday (though that was very unusual).[14]

Peter Copley notes that the speed with which productions were prepared resulted in certain conventions of staging (grouping, entrances and exits, etc.) being repeated, but recalls also that:

> in rep performances there was also an element of elasticity, fluidity, invention: nothing had been baked by rehearsal into too firm a shape and surprise was ever round the corner. So alertness, spontaneity, unforced energy were in the air; actors took missed props and missed entrances in their stride, making the most of the unexpected.[15]

Elizabethan actors, working to a similar schedule, undoubtedly developed similar practical solutions. The structure of the plays helped. T.J. King has shown that in Shakespeare's plays, for instance, almost 95 per cent of the lines are spoken by the fourteen principal actors (defined as men and boys who have more than ten lines) which meant that they could work together first, only bringing the supporting actors in at the very end of rehearsal (1992a: 76). Indeed, lines such as these almost seem designed to remind the supporting actors, less familiar with the staging, what to do:

FORTINBRAS: Let four captains
   Bear Hamlet like a soldier to the stage,
   For he was likely, had he been put on,
   To have proved most royal: and for his passage
   The soldiers' music and the rite of war
   Speak loudly for him.
   Take up the bodies. Such a sight as this

Becomes the field, but here shows much amiss.
Go, bid the soldiers shoot.

> *Exeunt marching: after which a peal of ordnance are shot off.*
> (*Hamlet*, 5.2.400–8)

The King's Men in particular demonstrated an enviable continuity in the membership of the company. Between 1616 and 1642, according to Gerald Bentley, seventy-six actors worked for them, of which half were boys and hired men, leading to a familiarity which must have had a beneficial impact on the Company's ensemble playing and ability to work quickly together (*JCS*, I: 70–89). But other companies did not enjoy such continuity, frequently shifting venues and personnel, and even routines with which actors were familiar could go wrong, especially if they involved under-rehearsed extras. In the third act of *Knavery in All Trades* (1664) a group of men in a coffee-house reminisce about the London theatres before the Civil War, especially the actors at the Fortune playhouse (evidently renowned for battle scenes) and, in particular, one Richard Fowler. They recall an incident in a play in which Fowler played 'a great Captain and mighty Warrior', when, in a battle at the end of Act 4:

> he laid so heavily about him, that some Mutes who stood for soldiers, fell down as they were dead e're he had toucht their trembling targets [shields]; so he brandisht his sword and made his Exit; ne'er minding to bring off his dead men; which they perceiving, crawled into the tiring-house, at which Fowler grew angry and told em, 'Dogs, you should have lain there till you had been fetched off', and so they crawled out again, which gave the people such an occasion of Laughter, they cried 'That again, that again, that again.'
>
> (*JCS* II: 440)

Shakespeare may have had something similar in mind when he apologised, via the Chorus in *Henry V*, for the attempt to present the Battle of Agincourt 'With four or five most vile and ragged foils, Right ill-disposed in brawl ridiculous' (4.0.50–1).

Writer-directors

There are sufficient differences between plays to suggest that new problems were constantly faced that cannot always have been solved by conventional staging, by following implicit guides within the text or by committee rehearsals (which never work anyway). It has been proposed that when necessary the dramatist took this 'directorial' role. According to John Downes, Sir William Davenant had seen the part of Hamlet played at the Blackfriars by Joseph Taylor, who had been 'instructed by the author Mr Shakespeare' and Davenant (Downes recalled) subsequently 'taught . . . every particle of it' to Thomas Betterton when he played it in 1662. Downes also claimed that Davenant had himself been instructed how to play Henry VIII by another leading King's man, John Lowin, who when he played the part had 'had his instructions from Mr Shakespeare', advice which Davenant in turn passed to Betterton.[16] Richard Flecknoe, writing in the early 1660s, observed that 'it was the happiness of the actors of those times to have such poets as these to instruct them . . . and no less of those poets to have such docile and excellent actors to act their plays'. The notion of Burbage calmly taking advice on acting from Shakespeare (or anyone else) has been queried, but Flecknoe uses 'docile' specifically in the contemporary sense of 'teachable' (OED) rather than our more common usage of 'placid', and there is other evidence that seems to support his claim. Johannes Rheanus, who in 1613 translated a play, *Lingua*, by Thomas Tomkis, into German, and who had visited England in 1611, wrote in the preface:

> So far as actors are concerned they, as I noticed in England, are daily instructed, as it were in a school, so that even the most eminent actors have to allow themselves to be taught their places by the Dramatists, which arrangement gives life and ornament to a well-written play, so that it is no wonder that the English players (I speak of skilled ones) surpass and have the advantage of others.

Rheanus probably saw Tomkis's play performed by students of King's College, Cambridge, but he stresses that his comments refer to 'even the most eminent actors' and his use of the term 'skilled ones' to distinguish his subject, suggests he is not talking of the amateur actors in the university. The terms 'taught their places' and the 'arrangement [which] gives life and ornament to the play', however, surely refer to the dramatist's role in helping shape the stage picture rather than (or in addition to) teaching the actors the details of their individual physical and vocal performances.[17] Even an absent playwright could provide very clear guides in terms of gesture and positioning, and texts demonstrate the care and originality with which the stage action was imagined and realised. In the opening of the popular Globe play, *The Merry Devil of Edmonton*, for example, the setting and action are contained within the Prologue's lines. Invoking the audience to imagine that it is night-time, and that the place is Edmonton ('Not full seven miles from this great famous city'), Prologue draws the curtains of an onstage bed and describes its occupant and other specific items on the stage:

> Behold him here laid on his restless couch!
> His fatal chime prepared at his head,
> His chamber guarded with these sable slights,
> And by him stands that necromantic chair
> In which he makes his direful invocations,
> And binds the fiends that shall obey his will.

Other texts include very graphic stage directions; for example, the opening of Act 2 of *The Honest Whore* (Part I) specifies:

> Enter Roger with a stool, cushion, looking-glass, and chafing dish. Those being set down, he pulls out of his pocket a vial with white colour in it, and two boxes, one with white another with red painting. He places all things in order and a candle by them, singing with the ends of old ballads as he does it. At last Bellafront (as he rubs his cheeks with the colours) whistles within.

The Bloody Banquet (?1639) contains instructions for some extremely subtle use of action. The final moment of the opening stage direction reads: 'Then enter the old Queen of Lydia, flying from her nephew Lapyrus, with two Babes in her arms, he pursuing her with his drawn sword'. The fleeing is repeated in the action of scene 2 and the movement completed with the appearance of Lapyrus, ready to fight, in scene 3. Whether the dramatist or performers had the original ideas, and, consequently, the extent to which such directions describe what was done rather than specified it, is unknowable. One should always remember the significant differences not only between 'texts' and 'scripts', but between scripts and actual performances that result from the collective activity of those onstage and off. The 'bad' quartos of Shakespeare's plays, for example, frequently contain details of staging not apparent from the later, authorised script. Whereas the stage direction in the Folio text of *3 Henry VI* states merely *Enter Clifford wounded*, the reported Quarto text gives *Enter Clifford wounded, with an arrow in his neck*. This particular detail originates from the source of the play, and the person most likely to have inserted it into the actual performance was, presumably, the playwright himself.[18] Shakespeare and Jonson, like other playwrights, frequently employ theatrical – often specifically acting – images in their plays. *The Tempest*, for example, is often read as a play about the theatre's power to transform and deceive, an interpretation governing a number of recent productions (such as those by the Ninagawa Company, Cheek by Jowl, the RSC and the New York Public Theater). If, developing this idea, Shakespeare can be associated with Prospero, who is dramatist, actor and director, Ariel's promise to follow Prospero's orders 'To th'syllable' (1.2.505) and Prospero's subsequent praise of Ariel's performance of a Harpy, perhaps had their counterparts in rehearsal:

> Bravely the figure of this Harpy hast thou
> Perform'd, my Ariel; a grace it had devouring:
> Of my instruction hast thou nothing bated
> In what thou hadst to say
>
> (3.3.83–6)

Jonson's plays, too, contain many references to theatre practice. Act 3, scene 5 of *Cynthia's Revels* (Blackfriars, Children of the Chapel, 1600), for example, in which Amorphus instructs Asotus in the behaviour of a gallant, takes the form of a rehearsal. The exchanges do not sound very different from those one might hear between an authoritarian director and an (understandably hesitant) actor:

AMORPHUS: 'Tis well entered, sir. Stay, you come on too fast, your pace is too impetuous. Imagine this to be the place of your pleasure, or place where your lady is pleased to be seen. First you present yourself, thus, and spying her, you fall off and walk two turns; in which time, it is to be supposed, your passion hath sufficiently whited your face: then, stifling a sigh or two, and closing your lips, with a trembling boldness and bold terror, you advance yourself forward. Prove thus much, I pray you.

ASOTUS: Yes, sir, pray Jove I can light on it. Here, I come in, you say, and present myself?

AMORPHUS: Good.

ASOTUS: And then I spy her and walk off?

AMORPHUS: Very good.

ASOTUS: Now, sir, I stifle, and advance forward.

AMORPHUS: Trembling.

ASOTUS: Yes, sir, trembling. I shall do it better when I come to it.

(4–19)

Other playwrights were not actors, but may well have been present at rehearsal, adapting the script where staging demands required it and no doubt, as playwrights in rehearsal do now, contributing their thoughts on how a scene might be played and benefiting in turn from the actors' ideas and performances. Before *The Second Maiden's Tragedy* was performed at the Blackfriars in 1611, for instance, a number of substantial changes were made to the prompt-copy, some at the censor's instructions (Clare 1990: 158–65). More than 100 lines were cut, others altered, and five slips of paper, totalling 50 lines, were inserted, containing changes evidently made in rehearsal to introduce topical (though not dangerously satirical) allusions, sharpen characterisation, and clarify certain anomalies in the narrative. One of the slips contains an 11-line speech. Who should speak the lines is not specified on the slip, but the Book Keeper has written 'Enter Mr Gough' on the manuscript immediately preceding the insertion. The primary purpose of the speech is clearly to provide a brief time-lapse between the scene (4.2) in which the Tyrant leaves to visit the tomb of the Lady, and the following scene in which he arrives. The 'journey time' would not have troubled the Jacobeans at all, but the stage direction following the insertion indicates that some scene-setting is required:

Enter the Tyrant again at a farther door, which opened, brings him to the tomb where the Lady lies buried: the Tomb here discovered richly set forth.

(4.3, s.d.0)

It was presumably discovered in the original rehearsals (as I did in my own) that this scene change was complicated enough to cause a hiatus in the action and that a covering speech was required. Middleton (or whoever wrote the lines) may have indicated who should speak them, but as they are clearly a filler he possibly left it to the Book Keeper to assign them. The Book Keeper chose Robert Gough who, playing the minor role of Memphonius, had appeared (and exited) in the previous scene, was not needed in the scene with the tomb, was not changing to play another part and was therefore unoccupied and available.[19]

Actor-directors

Just as the actors who come to Elsinore defer to the First Player, it is possible that rather than (or perhaps in addition to) the dramatist, one of the leading actors took on aspects of the directorial role as well as performing (in the manner of nineteenth-century actor-managers such as Sir Henry Irving, Donald Wolfit earlier this century or Kenneth Branagh today) or perhaps an actor not playing a lead role in a particular production would assume the role. A legal document referring to a dispute between the actors and the theatre manager notes how the Queen's Men organised their affairs at the Red Bull playhouse around 1612. The actors explained that the presentation of plays 'required Divers officers and that every one of the said Actors should take upon them some place and charge'. Only one of these tasks is identified – responsibility for the 'provision of the furniture and apparel': perhaps the planning and staging of the play was another, and evidence points to the fact that one or two of the sharers in a company were not cast in each production, leaving them free to play an offstage role in the staging.[20]

In 4.3 of *The Second Part of The Return from Parnassus* (one of a trilogy written for performance by members of St John's College, Cambridge), two college actors, playing Burbage and Kempe, criticise the standard of acting at the university, claiming the student performers 'never speak in their walk but at the end of the stage, just as though in walking with a fellow we should never speak but at a stile, a gate, or a ditch, where a man can go no further'. They then audition some students. 'Observe how I act it and then imitate me', 'Burbage' tells one student, and proceeds to deliver one of the most celebrated speeches from Hieronimo in *The Spanish Tragedy* – one of the real Burbage's roles. In *Hamlet* the situation is reversed as a student (played by the real Burbage) instructs a professional actor to 'Speak the speech, I pray you, as I pronounced it to you' (3.2.1), where 'pronounced' (as in the rhetorical exercise of 'pronunciato') means 'delivered', and would have included such aspects of performance as modulation of the voice, gesture, posture and facial expression. Commenting on this scene, David Mann observes that it would 'be of great interest to know whether this was common practice . . . and indeed whether it was used as a training technique' (1991: 142).

Documenting the production

The prompt-copy

Although performances in any period are fluid, and subject to the vagaries of actors and audiences, the agreed scheme of a production, arrived at through rehearsal, has to be recorded in the form of a prompt-copy. This includes the text that the actors will speak (the 'allowed book' passed by the censor in the case of the Elizabethans) as well as information about the physical conduct of the performance.

Believe As You List, written by Philip Massinger and performed by the King's Men in 1631, survives in the author's manuscript, and includes additions made by Edward Knight, the company's Book Keeper, in preparing it for his own use during performance.[21] Although an experienced stage-manager can mark up a text to a degree before rehearsal, the majority of detailed decisions about who does what and when emerge from working on the play before its first performance or perhaps during the play's run. It seems likely that Massinger's play was performed at the King's Men's indoor Blackfriars play-house, but the stage practice in these respects was presumably very similar in outdoor playhouses.

Knight did everything that a modern stage-manager does to make up a prompt-copy, except put in details of onstage moves. He added music cues, including a note of the moment for singers to take up positions ready to sing at the arras; he inserted stage-management notes on furniture and props – 'Table ready: & 6 chairs' (2.1.66), 'the great book of Accompte ready' (2.2.203), '2 chairs set out' (in the gap between the third and fourth acts), 'all the swords ready' (5.1.8 – they are brought on at l.103 of the following scene). He added stand-by cues for actors well in advance of their entrances, and in one instance – 'Mr Hobbs: called up' – indicated that an actor was perhaps to be summoned from front-of-house duties for a single short appearance. When inserting stand-by cues Knight used the actors' own names in line with theatre practice (still followed today) of giving actors their calls to the stage in their own names rather than their characters' to avoid confusion ('which Antonio?') among actors with a rapid turnover of plays that frequently repeat the same character names; he put in further detail on precisely where certain lines were to be spoken (adding 'within' to an Officer's line, 2.2.119, for example); he wrote down who was to be ready to open the stage trap ('Gascoine & Hubert', musicians or hired men) in the fourth act (4.1.26), and when they were to be in position; inserted an instruction that the actor who is to ascend through it should be in place (4.1.67, about 50 lines and a scene break – probably unmarked in performance – before he appears); and put in cues for those who were to enter on the upper level. Stage directions and marginal notes indicate the small number of properties that the actors would be expected to collect from the props table: a poinard, a halter, brown bread and a wooden dish of water. Knight also drew up a list of personal properties that the actors would collect (presumably directly from him) before the beginning of the performance and keep with them during it:

Act I: A writing out of the book with a small piece of
       silver for Mr Swansson
          .3. notes for Mr Pollard:
Act 2: A writing for Mr Taylor:
Act 3: A letter for Mr Robinson
          .2. letters for Mr Lowin
Act 5: A letter for Mr Benfeild

The Book Keeper would have been responsible for ensuring that performances ran smoothly – a role similar to that of a stage-management team today. According to John Higgens's definition in his *Nomenclator* (1585), it was also the Book Keeper who 'telleth the players their part when they are out and have forgotten' (King 1992: 10) and he may perhaps have been responsible, too, for helping to shape the action overall in rehearsal. Actors always enjoy sending up themselves (or, at least, other actors) and relish even more the chance to mock 'ham' acting. The mechanicals' rehearsal in *A Midsummer Night's Dream* is littered with theatre jargon – 'bill of properties', doing the piece 'in action' and 'according to his cue' – and the problems Peter Quince (on the book) encounters trying to run a rehearsal while coping with the doomed attempts of his leading actor, Bottom, to achieve a 'condoling' tone in one moment, before vocally 'tearing a cat' the next, may well reflect directly Edward Knight's experience in the playhouse.

The production of any performance is a collaborative activity, and it's almost impossible, even when one is directly involved in a production, to disentangle exactly what each person has contributed. In general terms, however, the playwright perhaps advised on the general arrangement of the stage, leading actors gave advice to the hired men as well as to the apprentice boys on details of their performances, and the Book Keeper ensured that rehearsals (and performances) ran smoothly, organised scene changes and supervised revivals.

The actor's part

Actors did not receive a copy of the whole play as they do today, but only their own 'parts' (also called cue-scripts), a practice that originated in the medieval theatre and survived into the early years of the twentieth century. Written out by a scribe (possibly before the play as a whole had been completed and before the prompt-copy had been copied out) the parts gave only the character's own lines and his cues – though no more than the two or three final words of the preceding speech – with no indication of exactly where in the play the lines were located. Although a few medieval examples have survived, there is only one extant part for an Elizabethan or Jacobean professional actor – that of the lead role of Orlando in Robert Greene's *Orlando Furioso*, almost certainly played by Edward Alleyn for the first time at the Rose in February 1592. The part (which differs in a number of respects from the printed Quarto text) is made up of pieces of paper between 10–16 in. in length pasted together to make a long roll about 17 ft long and 6 in. wide, and comprising about two-thirds of the leading role. It is unknown whether actors went to the first rehearsal with their lines more or less known, or used their scripts in rehearsal. Although the part includes several textual alterations and annotations made by Alleyn, the absence of positional and other notes often characteristic of modern actors' scripts might suggest the former practice. The opening stage direction in Marston's *Antonio and Mellida* ('Enter with parts in their hands'), however, may imply otherwise, though in this instance the scrolls may have been carried by the actors to help create the impression of pre-performance behaviour rather than being a replica of actual rehearsal practice, the contrived sense of chaos contrasting with the order of the performance that followed.

Alleyn would undoubtedly have had access to the precious complete man-uscript of *Orlando Furioso*: indeed, he filled in a line that the scribe who wrote out the part had been unable to read. Other actors, especially those with a number of parts, or infrequent appearances, must have found getting a sense of the total shape of a play they had heard, possibly piecemeal, but not read, much more difficult, particularly given the sporadic performance schedule. (Hence the importance of the Plot; see below.) Peter Quince's rebuke to Flute for speaking all his part at once, 'cues and all', and to Bottom for missing his two-word cue, presumably reflect these problems (*Midsummer Night's Dream*, 3.1.93–5). During rehearsals for his production of *Henry V* at the RSC in 1994, Matthew Warchus experimented with a set of cue-scripts:

> It's very exciting, with all the actors waiting to hear their cue in the scene, and simply not knowing when it's going to come. Or for the actor who is speaking, not knowing exactly who is going to intervene, or when. It raises the whole level and energy of listening, which in turn makes the spoken language more active, more persuasive.

The Plot

When we mean to build,
We first survey the plot, then draw the model.
Lord Bardolph, *2 Henry IV*, 1.3.41–2

Whatever the organisation of rehearsal was (and I suspect it will remain con-jectural) the agreed production plan would have had to be written down (as it is in the modern theatre) in order to run a particular performance or allow a production to be revived, especially if there were changes in the venue or cast.

As we have seen, some of this information was recorded in the prompt-copy, but someone (again possibly the Book Keeper) also prepared a 'Plot' (or 'platt' or 'platform'). Seven Plots survive; three are more or less complete (*The Dead Man's Fortune*, the second part of *The Seven Deadly Sins* and *Frederick and Basilea*), two are only partial fragments (*2 Fortune's Tennis* and *Troilus and Cressida*),[22] one (*1 Tamar Cam*) is a printed transcript of a manuscript that no longer survives, and the last – a fairly complete fragment for *The Battle of Alcazar* – is the only Plot for which the playtext also survives. All these Plots belonged at one time to Edward Alleyn and though they therefore provide definite evidence of production practice only at playhouses with which he was directly associated, I think it safe to assume they are typical of production practice generally.

Assuming Burbage's cue-script for *Orlando Furioso* is also typical, the parts given to the actors contained no indication of the time-lapse between speeches, the shape of the sections of the play in which they were to be spoken, or even where in the total span of the play the lines appeared. It was necessary therefore to prepare a unit-by-unit outline – the Plot. The form of each surviving Plot is the same. Each contains the staging outlines of a play, divided into sections, and providing details of entrances and exits, some sound and music cues and stage-management notes of properties, furniture and other requirements such as a chariot (*Alcazar*) and specific locations such as 'behind the curtain' (*Alcazar*), 'in prison' (*Dead Man's Fortune*), or 'Enter Nemesis above' (*Alcazar*).

The Plot of *The Seven Deadly Sins* has a label (written in the same hand as the Plot) with the title – 'The Booke and Platt of the second part of The 7 deadly sins' – pasted on the outside of one of its halves. The fold in the centre of the Plot possibly indicates that it acted as a cover for the Book, ensuring that both documents remained together. The word 'plot' in Elizabethan usage meant 'ground-plan', and the Plot and the prompt-copy, if put together, would provide material very similar to that in a stage-manager's marked-up book used in a modern theatre.

Unlike the surviving prompt-copies which contain very little and sometimes nothing of the agreed blocking, the Plots provide some evidence of actual staging not transferred to the printed text. Evidence such as this reminds us that however careful we are in using texts as guides to performance there remain (as in theatre performances of all periods) elements of visual presentation central to an audience's understanding, experience and enjoyment of a production that are unrecoverable: the text and performance can never be considered synonymous. For example, the opening of the third act of *The Battle of Alcazar* is printed as follows in the Quarto of 1594:

Enter the presenter and speaks.

Lo thus into a lake of blood and gore,
The brave contentious king of Portugal
Hath drenched himself, and now prepares amain

With sails and oars to cross the swelling seas,
With men and ships, courage and canon shot,   5
To plant this cursed Moor in fatal hour,
And in this Catholic case the king of Spain
Is called upon by sweet Sebastian.
Who surfeiting in prime time of his youth,
Upon ambitious poison dies thereon.   10
By this time is the Moor to Tangar come,
A city 'longing to the Portugal,
And now doth Spain promise with holy face,
As favouring the honour of the cause,
His aid of arms, and levies men apace,   15
But nothing less than king Sebastian's good
He means, yet at Sucor de Tupea,
He met some say in person with the Portugal,
And treateth of a marriage with the king.
But ware ambitious wiles and poisoned eyes,   20
There was nor aid of arms or marriage,
For on his way without those Spaniards king Sebastian went.

Exit.

The Plot, however, reveals that (at least in the specific performance for which it was made) the following dumb-show took place after line 10:

Enter Nemesis above. Enter to her three Furies bringing in the scales. To them enter three devils. Then enter to them three ghosts. The Furies first fetch in Sebastian and carry him out again, which done they fetch in Stukley and carry him out, then bring in the Moor and carry him out. Exeunt.

The specified props help to establish still more precisely the nature of the action: the scales are an emblematic property that suggest a judgement scene, while other props noted by the side of the description of the dumb show – '3 vials of blood and a sheep's gather' (i.e., liver, lungs and heart) – imply that the action included a gory and realistic presentation of the murder of the three men. (This general level of violence in the stage action is further indicated by the later calls for 'Dead men's heads & bones banquet blood', 'brand and chopping knife' and 'raw flesh'.) As I have noted, movement and gesture are frequently guided to some extent by the spoken lines, and it is therefore unsurprising that records of dumb-shows contain the most detailed information on staging in the Plots. In *The Seven Deadly Sins*, for instance, we find:

A sennet. Dumb Show. Enter King Gorboduc with 2 Counsellors . . .
The Queen with Ferrex and Porrex and some attendants follow . . .

After Gorboduc hath consulted with his Lords he brings his sons to several seats. They envying on one another Ferrex offers to take Porrex his crown. He draws his weapon. The King, Queen and Lords step between them. They thrust them away and menacing each other exit. The Queen and Lords depart heavily.

With this amount of information (I assume the attendants bring the seats with them) it is perfectly straightforward to reconstruct the framework of the staging. In a number of instances exits are not indicated in the Plot (but were presumably obvious from the lines spoken onstage); in others (such as the direction that 'Sloth passeth over'), while it is not certain exactly what is intended, entering from one door and, possibly after other moves, exiting by another, seems the most likely interpretation (though see Sprinchorn 1992 for other – in my view unworkable – ideas).

The exact purpose of the Plot, the point at which it was drawn up and the use to which it was put have been matters of some disagreement. The Plot of *The Seven Deadly Sins* has a hole about one-third of the way from the top and it is usually assumed that this enabled the plot to be hung up backstage for the actors to use as a guide to the action as they had no scripts, and possibly to assist the Book Keeper in running the show (though why the hole is not nearer the top, which would seem the more natural place to make it, is unclear to me). The Plot of *The Seven Deadly Sins*, for example, is about 18×12 in. (45 cm $\times$ 30 cm) and written in a large neat hand to make it easy for a group of actors under pressure of performance to consult it in a hurry. David Bradley, in a lengthy and detailed analysis, concludes that although a Plot may have been helpful to a limited extent during run-throughs or rehearsals, the form of the Plot, the nature of the information it contains and the manner in which that information is presented make it unlikely that it provided a primary guide to the actors and crew during performance. Bradley concludes that it was put together during rehearsal, mainly in order to allocate the roles and tasks to the cast and crew available, and then in performance possibly used as a cue-sheet by the musicians. The Plotter (as Bradley calls him) set down the agreed stage action, added action and moves not clear from the text or varied the text, and worked out exactly who was to play which of the parts that needed to be doubled or who should appear in dumb shows where the dramatist has not been specific. He also wrote down details of how the dumb shows were to be handled, presumably once the actors had worked them out. In other words, he used the Plot to fit the play to the available actors and resources, and to fit the actors to the play. Some, but not all, of this information was then transferred to the prompt-copy. The actors' lines (either in their heads or written on the scrolls) and the Plot were then all that was required to restage the production, or to reshape a production to different performance conditions, for example when reviving it or when the company was on tour, perhaps enabling the valuable prompt-copy to remain in London.[23]

CASE STUDY: MATTHEW WARCHUS[24] – *HENRY V*: TEXT, REHEARSAL, PERFORMANCE

The story of the warrior king was evidently popular with Elizabethan theatregoers, and Shakespeare's play (written in 1599) was one of four plays about Henry V staged in the closing years of the sixteenth century. The Quarto title-page claimed it was performed publicly 'sundry times' by the Lord Chamberlain's Men, and it was staged at court in 1605. The extent to which it survived as a commercial box-office hit is questioned by Gary Taylor, however, who observes that the play was reprinted far less often than other plays by Shakespeare and was referred to only rarely. Aaron Hill's 1723 adaptation (he removed the comic scenes and enhanced the romantic aspects) restored the play to the stage, and in 1738 a version closer to the source text was staged at Covent Garden. It continued to be performed, often as a vehicle for star actors such as John Philip Kemble and William Macready, and it offered opportunities for the spectacular stagings that were popular in the mid to late nineteenth century. In Charles Kean's 1859 production at the Princes' Theatre, London, Ellen Tree played the Chorus as Clio, the Muse of History, and Kean, as Henry, in an interpolated scene following Henry's victory at Agincourt, crossed the stage on a real horse, cheered on by 500 extras. *Henry V* has been one of the most popular plays with twentieth-century audiences, and it is significant that it has often been staged at times of national conflict: productions starring Frank Benson and Lewis Waller coincided with the Boer War, and a production of the play was presented each year of the First World War. It was performed at the Old Vic in 1937, Drury Lane in 1938 and broadcast on BBC Radio in 1939. Laurence Olivier (who had played the lead in Tyrone Guthrie's 1937 production) delivered speeches from it in the film *Words for Battle* and in patriotic rallies at the Albert Hall. Olivier's celebrated film version, made in 1944, in which he also starred, was produced as part of the war propaganda effort and dedicated to 'the airborne troops of Great Britain and Canada'. The text was shaped accordingly: Henry's decision to kill the prisoners, for example, was omitted, while the killing of the boys by the French was emphasised and contrasted with the English sense of chivalry. Kenneth Branagh's post-Falklands film, released in 1989, comments directly on Olivier's: the famous Globe playhouse opening sequence is replaced by a film studio setting, the glitteringly colourful battle scenes are replaced by an emphasis on the mud and blood of infantry warfare and a greater concentration on the acts of violence portrayed by Shakespeare. The English Shakespeare Company toured a production directed by Michael Bogdanov (1986) but the size of cast demanded by the play has meant that in recent years it has been seen most often in productions by the RSC (or by earlier incarnations of that company) who staged the play in 1951 (Richard Burton as Henry), 1964 (Ian Holm), 1975 (Alan Howard), 1984 (Kenneth Branagh), in 1994–5 with Iain Glen and, most recently, with Michael Sheen in the title role. In 1997, the play was included in the first full season at the reconstructed Globe in London, with Mark Rylance as Henry.

The director of the 1994 RSC production was Matthew Warchus. It opened at Stratford on 2 May 1994, with set designs by Neil Warmington, costumes by Kandis Cook, lighting by Alan Burrett, sound by Paul Slocombe and music by Mark Vibrans. The setting was a disused theatre, brought alive by the Chorus, who began the play by throwing a lever to light the stage. The production explored 'the overlays of history, the historicising of Henry and the Agincourt campaign into a peculiarly national myth'.[25] The upstage area often held tableau images of a heroicised version of what the audience witnessed and, as the play progressed, a front section of the stage floor lifted and opened and a tomb, engraved with the dates of Henry's life, pushed its way to the surface. In the following informal discussion, Matthew Warchus enlarges on some of the problems he encountered in staging *Henry V* and the solutions he, the actors and the production team found.

Pre-rehearsal preparation

Can you remember your reactions the first time you read the play, knowing you were about to direct it?

I found the play quite difficult to understand. I couldn't discover on first reading what was exciting about it as a play, but I remember finding the choruses beautiful and resonant and familiar – because they're so often quoted, I guess – but I just didn't engage with the play or with the character of Henry. I found Henry's lengthy, rhetorical speeches daunting, the comedy not funny and difficult to read, and I thought there were some very bizarre twists – even thinking, on a first reading, 'Why is this whole scene in French?', for example. In the middle of the Battle of Agincourt, there's an extended, almost Benny Hill-type glove sequence that all seems very weird, and the last scene has got a lot of convoluted Elizabethan language, coded language that's difficult to understand. It actually read like a patchy, long, cumbersome play. And so I read it again, but I didn't really come to a different conclusion until I'd rehearsed it.

So you didn't go into rehearsal having worked all those things through?

No, I didn't. But before going into rehearsal I did a lot of background reading, looked at the Folio and Quartos, watched Olivier's and Branagh's films and chose a specific text [Gary Taylor's Oxford edition]. That, and a lot more detailed reading of the text made me feel that there was something to be found in the play that was against how it's often perceived, even though I had no idea how to capture that, or even if it was at all possible to do so. The play presents different versions and viewpoints of the story. Instead of just acting one perspective – the English establishment perspective – the play also gives you Pistol's, Bardolph's and Nym's perspectives on the battle, and then even gives you the French perspective on it as well by immersing you in the French language and making you feel as an audience that you actually speak French for part of the play. And it also gives you a woman's perspective on it by spending that time with Alice and Catherine: immediately after all that Harfleur aggression, men, animal stuff, suddenly there's two women. Not only have you shifted into a feminine tone, but you've also shifted into a different language. And so it is very much a multi-perspective exploration of a historically famous event. But I think that Shakespeare is also talking about history – our relationship with history. The value and importance of Memory. Our potential to learn and change – to reach a higher level of understanding, contrasted with our tendency to waste experience, to forget, and so repeat mistakes.

So, by the time you went into rehearsal, although you hadn't solved all the problems you've been talking about, you'd clarified them more for yourself, looked at the play in its wider literary and cultural context, established the text you were going to perform, and got a sense of how you wanted to approach the play?
Yes. I think I'd identified various big ideas that I thought the play confronted. I hadn't discovered whether or not Shakespeare found a pattern to link those ideas, or even if the play had a clear message at all. All I'd found out about it was the possibility that Shakespeare had juxtaposed various ideas, and that by having so many of them, clearly and purposefully put, strongly delivered, almost with disregard to each other, he maybe builds up not so much a message as a complex experience for the audience.

It seems to me that in the midst of all the things a director does in preparation – background research, textual study, looking at past productions, and so on – there is often a key image that fires his or her imagination for the production and, in a sense, draws all that disparate thinking together. Was there such an image for you?
Yes. The main stimulus for me was the beginning of *Henry VI* Part I. I became very interested in the order that the history plays had been written in because I was trying to understand why a writer would write his final statement of history in the way that Shakespeare had written *Henry V*. I looked at the first part of *Henry VI* and I started to think about the order in which the history plays had been written: in other words going *Henry VI* Parts I, II and III, *Richard III*, and then *Richard II*, *Henry IV* Part I, *Henry IV* Part II, and *Henry V*, means that you begin with Henry V's funeral and end with his marriage. In other words, you begin with a dark time of English history and finish with the golden moment. There's maybe sense in the order of that curve which is more politically and poetically eloquent than just doing everything chronologically. In particular, if you imagine that the original audience had seen *Henry VI*, then I think that must have affected hugely their view of *Henry V*: if you have experienced very dark and turbulent views of history, very negative and cursed, you arrive at a golden moment with a sense of relief. But because you know exactly what follows – i.e., Henry VI follows Henry V – then the structure operates more like Pinter's play *Betrayal*, or Sondheim's musical *Merrily We Roll Along*,

in that you head towards something climactic and glorious but always with the knowledge that it's going to be followed by disaster. And that's the only way that I could ever show this glory onstage as a final event. Then I could commit to the idea of optimism – a new tomorrow with the prospect of Anglo-French union in peace – without feeling cheap.

So on the assumption that most of your audiences won't have seen or read Henry VI *{even though Katie Mitchell's production of* Henry VI *ran concurrently at The Other Place in Stratford} what was your solution to mediate the play's climax of triumph?*
It lay partly in the way we played the Chorus and partly through the ever-present image of Henry's tombstone. The reason we came up with the idea of the tombstone is that *Henry VI* Part I starts off with a fantastic opening scene. Black everywhere, and you get the impression that there's thunder.

Of course the original theatre might have very well been draped . . .
. . . with black, I'm sure. And in the middle of the stage Henry V's coffin onstage, the most famous warrior king, a hero, and somebody runs on, interrupting the scene and says, France is being lost, it's slipping through our fingers. And someone says don't speak this in front of Henry's body, in front of Henry's coffin, since 'the loss of those great towns Will make him burst his lead and rise from death' [1.1.63–4]. And this gave me the idea of people breaking out from the past; and from there to the idea of the play being in a derelict theatre which comes alive by an act of imagination. These things don't completely follow through but this is the general idea: that the ghosts, the spirits that the Chorus talks about are there, that the theatre is haunted by history, and this is why the stage was excavated during the course of the production. Starting at Harfleur, the stage is lifted away, and under it you find Henry's tomb which eventually rises up and comes out. And that's taken directly from the images in *Henry VI* Part I.

And the derelict theatre setting also enables you to pick up the images of theatres, acting and roles that are so central to the play?
Yes. The Chorus in particular won't let us forget that. It's as though our imaginations were lengths of elastic tied to him in the theatre at one end and stretching towards Southampton, Harfleur, Agincourt and elsewhere. We keep springing back, but the tension is energising and exciting.

Can you say more about the theatrical references in the staging?
When the Chorus came on originally and said, 'I want you to imagine', what he's really saying is, 'Imagine that you're there' or, 'imagine that these events are in the theatre, that the armies are here, the horses and everything is here', and I got this feeling that that was a completely new twist. It seemed like a television documentary, through which we're used to being put into history, into the event as it's happening. I wanted to get this idea of something from the past suddenly coming alive in the theatre. I thought of ghosts summoning up, and then immersing you in, a story, so you took everybody as being real,

and then finishing it with a freeze round a treaty table, almost as if they were in a glass cabinet in a museum, so that the characters and events have suddenly retreated back into history again. I wanted to honour Shakespeare's idea of a theatre coming alive by an act of imagination on the part of the audience. So we knew that anything that appeared in that space would have to be the sort of thing you would see in a theatre. A lighting bar could come down and form trenches and a landscape for a battlefield; in the back wall of the stage is supposedly a big shutter through to the scenic workshop, but when it opens up it turns out that Southampton or France is the other side of it; the French court is really just an old blue curtain that comes in on a flying bar. Everything had to look just like simple theatre things, except the floor opening and moving, which was to be a 'supernatural' thing, as if by reliving certain aspects of the story one had actually conjured them up.

The rehearsal period

I'd like to move on to the work in rehearsal. The opening scenes of the play can be difficult can't they – for actors and audience?
The opening court sequence (scenes 1 and 2) *is* difficult, because it's the beginning of the play, it's very history-orientated, and your instinct as a director is that the audience won't be ready for this, they won't tune into it. But I thought we should try to get the audience to appreciate how exciting the pre-decision debate of war is in these first two scenes. The problems are often dealt with by cutting the text.

Or by playing it comically, as in the Olivier film.
Yes. I think that these scenes are crucial: Henry says he's delaying seeing the French ambassador because 'never two such kingdoms did contend Without much fall of blood . . .' [1.2.24–5] and so he sets the stakes for this early part of the play. I think it's fantastic that there's so much talk before the decision to invade is taken. This young prince is being buffeted in this sea of words, trying to come to a decision, because he knows what's at stake. What he's saying is that on this decision hangs the fate of thousands of people, and I had this image of a sword hanging over the scene, like the Sword of Damocles. And I also had this idea of this court scene being rather like a self-contained historical event in a museum, so we put museum-type cordons around the stage, and other people, the rest of England, come and look at it, almost like an exhibit that they can't get to, but can see being acted out. And during that scene all those mothers and husbands and children, like those that Henry says will be 'mocked' out of their lives by the Dauphin's tennis-ball joke, were there onstage watching this happen. And that idea of the rest of England being there waiting and watching started very early, about the third time I read the play. I imagined a huge plinth, a sort of very high platform, the court taking place on it, very high up, and the citizens and peasants with farming implements and old clothes [1940s period], just standing looking up, waiting, standing

round the base while this event that was going to affect their destiny was played out above. In terms of design that just became too extravagant to do in practice, but we tried to keep that feeling. So this opening section of the play is to do with words and history, the past, taking decisions, the meaning of leadership and the practical logistics of protecting a country when the King's away.

So how did you address the problems in rehearsal?
We tried the scene in different ways: we did it as a board meeting, for example, with a long table with glasses of water and everyone armed with files or clip-boards, things like that. The actors played Shakespeare's text but it sounded very naturalistic in that context. Henry made Canterbury come and sit down next to him, and everyone had to move round the table, and Canterbury had to stand up in the board meeting and make a speech about why the battle would be honourable, and everyone who spoke had to stand up to make their point. And things like that helped to involve everyone in the scene, its arguments and issues. So when Canterbury – having spent hours in the library and discovered this amazing fact about the succession – revealed it, it was a cause for great laughter and celebration around the table. The scene is nothing to do with Canterbury waffling on – his speech is as concise as it can possibly be to try and give all that important information.

But while the information is very important, there is a difference, isn't there, between the amount which is said to Henry and the fact that the actual decision is really yes or no? Canterbury's line after so much factual detail – 'so that as clear as is the summer's sun' – seems designed to raise a laugh, and it usually gets one, doesn't it?
If people laugh that's fine, but it would be good if the laughter was in a context of exhilaration rather than tedium. What Canterbury says is a fantastic shedding of light on something, and a revolutionary discovery, and it really does mean that it would be a just war, because the French have been lying all this time, and the English are in the right. The list of names in his Salic law speech *is* extensive, but the fact is that there are so many examples of the lies that the French have told – not only did this happen but also this person only inherited because of his grandmother, and then this person because of his wife, and so on. But what I really wanted to put over is all the references to women in that speech, so I asked the actor to stress daughter, grandmother, mother, rather than King Pepin, Louis IX, and so on.

And that ties in closely with the end of the play, when the focus is again on family re-lationships – son, daughter, father and so on?
Yes, that was a pattern we noticed. But at that earlier point Henry asks a very concise question, 'May I with right and conscience make this claim?' [1.2.96], which may seem simple, but *right* and *conscience* are two different things that need separate answers. And then the practical questions of security at home have to be answered. It's Canterbury's 'honeybee' speech [1.2.183–220] that seems finally to sway Henry so we tried to make that particular conversation

into almost a separate scene by bringing Canterbury and Henry to a bench near the front of the stage so that the sequence could change rhythm and focus. It required a lot of rehearsal to find ways to show all those things happening and so make it not just a scene in which you have a man who uses too many words blustering around, a corrupt churchman trying to get something achieved for an ulterior motive, but a scene full of complex exchanges of ideas. It never seemed difficult, however, because we felt we were working hand in hand with the scene by taking that attitude to it, and so things moved quite quickly.

At the point of decision at the end of the second scene, after the departure of the Ambassadors, you created a thrilling image of swords lowered down to the stage on the ends of chains. Was that derived from your Sword of Damocles idea?
Yes. The arrival of the swords was meant to mark a decision point – a shift from talk to action. I wanted to make the first part of the play feel like we're on a cliff, and that we stay on the edge of the cliff for a long time, for more than half an hour, before we step over, so that by the time we get to the second Chorus – 'Now all the youth of England are on fire' – the play has changed gear.

Did you cut these opening scenes at all?
No, not at first. In fact we rehearsed the whole play without any cuts whatever for six or seven weeks, out of a total rehearsal period of nine weeks.

How extensive were the cuts you eventually made in the play as a whole?
By the time we opened for previews we had made a few cuts and the production lasted just over four hours. By the opening night we had taken off another twenty minutes, including cutting the Chorus speech that opens Act 5.

That decision to cut the Chorus is a pretty substantial one, isn't it, given the points you made earlier? The Chorus is one of the means by which our responses are challenged or guided: we often find ourselves saying in response to the Chorus, 'But that's not true, we haven't seen that', which keeps us very aware that what we hear and what we see are not always the same thing.
Sometimes that's so, and absolutely vital. I used to say in rehearsals that the Chorus's voice is like a chronicle voice, but that the scenes that surround the Chorus are like documentary scenes, underlining the gulf between chronicled history and documentary history. But the fifth Chorus didn't seem like that. We kept cutting lines from it and eventually decided we could lose it all. However, we realised that the Chorus couldn't be absent from the play for so long and spent a lot of time looking for a way he could return without that speech being there. At the last minute I decided he should appear on the battlefield at Agincourt – it was one of my favourite moments in the production, and a fruitful cut, I think.

It seems to me that in addition to cuts to aid understanding or to shape particular interpretations some cuts are made simply to meet other, often pragmatic, constraints. Terry Hands, for example, observed that the cuts in the last scene in his 1975 RSC production were forced upon him by the audience who are keen to get home (Beauman 1976: 228).

I sympathise with Terry Hands's dilemma because when I reworked the production a few months into its run it was in the last scene that I eventually made most cuts. The last scene is an incredibly difficult scene to understand, and the area I found most difficult – and eventually cut – is the section that begins 'God save your majesty . . .' [5.2.272].

Terry Hands cut precisely this section, which he described as 'courtly circumlocutions' (Beauman 1976: 228) *that held up the important remainder of the scene.*

I think there's more going on here than that description suggests. The King and Queen of France, Burgundy and the French and English lords re-enter [5.2.271], presumably having resolved those things in the treaty that were a stumbling-block before. The French King says nothing, but this strange thing happens between Burgundy and Henry. In the earlier part of the scene when Burgundy has his very long speech about the destruction of France [23–67; given to Chorus in Hands's production] there's nothing to suggest the manner he adopts on re-entering. We used to joke in rehearsal that when they go off-stage he drinks a bottle of Burgundy to celebrate the treaty, then comes back on and can't stop laughing and cracking rude jokes. But Burgundy's manner *is* very different from earlier in the scene, and the frame of mind Henry is in is also very unclear. After the by-play with Burgundy, which is all very obscure now, Henry says that he 'cannot see many a fair French city for one fair French maid that stands in my way' (306–7), and the French King says but you do see them 'perspectively', which I think is a very good word for this play. He means 'you're looking at it in a very different way from the way you used to understand things, you're now looking at our French cities the way we look at them. You've only ever seen them as property and something to gain, but now you see them with a change of perspective, cities changed into a maid, equal to Catherine', to which Henry replies, in effect, 'You should be grateful for that, for my love, otherwise I'd be raping more cities.'

But the actors still have to say Shakespeare's lines.

Exactly. So you start to try and translate it and work out what's happening. Possibly Burgundy is laughing at this twenty-seven-year-old man, who has no way of relating to women, no experience of it, and who is, in a rather adolescent way, being frustrated – Henry has kissed Catherine and that's confused him; he says there's 'witchcraft in your lips' [267], and he's thrown by it. And suddenly these people come back in.

Iain Glen pulled back from her at that moment, and played the line 'Here comes your father' like one of a couple caught kissing on the sofa. It very much emphasised his nervousness and inexperience, I thought.

The whole purpose of the scene for Henry is to get Catherine to say either 'I do love you' or at least 'I could love you'. Burgundy is laughing, maybe all the rest of the court are laughing, maybe the audience is laughing as well. Maybe

51

the only person who isn't laughing is Henry, who's saying 'You should be thankful that I love her, otherwise . . .'; in other words maybe what is happening is that Henry is about to throw in the treaty and that all the efforts, all the fantastic heroic efforts of war, all his achievements and all of Burgundy's and the French king's attempts to formulate this treaty, maybe everything in the end is going to be completely blown apart because Henry can't get Catherine to say 'I love you'. This section of the scene demonstrates the fragility of any political situation that can be changed by someone's private personal feelings being misunderstood or frustrated. If that's the case this is a really exciting, tense moment, like the point of decision that Henry comes to at the opening of the play, and maybe Uncle Exeter intervenes (like he does earlier in 1.2.174), saying it's all right, it's all right, the treaty's done, we've got the treaty, everything's OK. The French King's agreed to everything, the only thing he hasn't agreed to is the clause about calling you his son. And the French King says 'Nor this I have not brother so denied, But your *request* shall make me let it pass.' The French King is prepared to look beyond the complexities of political division and treaty towards a more significant *personal reconciliation* – can Henry do the same? Then, for the first time, Henry seems to get something; he says 'I pray you then, in love and dear alliance . . .' – completely new sorts of words from him. Maybe he's kneeling to the French King, he's certainly a son-in-law going to a prospective father-in-law, saying please can I marry your daughter. Purely domestic, not political at all, a family moment. And the King replies, 'take her fair *son*.' It's another stage in Henry's development, in his rites of passage. He stops simply having an emotional, reflex reaction – they've done that so I've got to do this. It's gone beyond his personal fears and insecurities to a higher level of understanding, and maybe all these things are happening in this dense section of the scene, over about 50 lines. We tried repeatedly to stage it to draw these out, but it wouldn't click. I thought it worked in rehearsal a couple of times, because I was very much seeing it through my understanding, but in the theatre it just wouldn't click. The last scene is often interpreted as one of resolution, rather than as a scene of a new crisis, the last in a series of battles Henry has to fight – and win. [See John Wain, quoted on p. 1.] So it would have been satisfying to be able to deliver this reading of the scene, but in the end we had to cut it. The version we finally arrived at tried to recreate that moment where Henry might throw the whole treaty away, and to catch his insecurity and isolation, but with about half the lines. [In the section from 5.2.272 to the end of the scene, 39 lines were cut from a total of 86.] The most painful losses from cutting any text are those that you reckon you understand, or you are excited about because the scene, or that part of it, is revealed to be much more exciting than you first thought. But when you have to lose those because you can't make it read without doing a small lecture on it first it's really disappointing, because you feel that you're having to deliver a more simple version of a scene and therefore of the play.

You were talking earlier about what you called bizarre twists that seemed problematical on first reading, such as the glove sequence in the middle of the battle of Agincourt.

I had trouble making sense of the Battle of Agincourt part of the play. We'd followed where the text says excursions and alarums, and we'd arranged stage fights for those bits, but then comes this string of short scenes – Pistol and Monsieur Le Fer [4.4], the French lords saying 'O diable', all is lost, everything is lost [4.5], and killing the prisoners [4.6] – and it's actually quite difficult through these to give the audience the impression that the Battle of Agincourt is still going on. In other words there's a long shot of the battle and then there's these close-ups, which is a fantastic idea, particularly with this Boy wandering through it all. This reminded me of the scene in *Schindler's List* when everyone's being thrown out of the ghetto and although the film's shot in black and white there's one little girl in a red coat going through. In the same way, Shakespeare's taking a huge broad canvas and then focusing on this tiny moment and individual, saying that really a battle is actually only hundreds of thousands of tiny moments, happening simultaneously; it feels like a vast event but in fact it's one person trying to kill another person, one person running away, one of them hiding, somebody stealing from someone else. It isn't one huge concerted effort, it's lots of tiny things happening. But to keep the overall arc of the battle going in the theatre is a difficult thing to do. I also had a problem with the fact that just as the battle sequence is coming to an end, immediately before the reading of the numbers of dead, Shakespeare returns to the glove episode. Henry names the battle Agincourt, sends his heralds to accompany Montjoy to count the dead, and then he says 'there's the man with the glove' and the focus moves to that business. I was finding it difficult because I didn't find the glove business particularly funny during rehearsals. I found it awkward because I wanted to stay in 'Agincourt mode'. And then I said OK, let's go wholeheartedly, let's forget the war, and I started to rehearse that section as though it was not at the end of a battle. We found lots of jokes, we turned the fights into comedy fights, like slapstick, and I gave the actor playing Fluellen licence to go all out for comedy in that section. And then we ran it. We went in one direction completely during the battle scenes, and then just started going completely in the other direction with the glove section, and at that point the herald walks on with the names of the dead, and you go whack, back, and I realised that the shift of tone is there because once you've had all that battle, if you go straight into the names of the dead, as an audience you're emotionally drained and tired. You're in a serious frame of mind and the names of the dead are just another thing in the same melody, the same tune is being played. But if you've actually gone through all that battle and all those terrible and disturbing things that you've seen – boys being killed, prisoners being killed, terrible atrocities – and *then* you get the whole theatre going whoosh with laughter at this joke. You've released an awful lot, and you share a celebratory energy in the same way as the soldiers who've just found out that they've won. And then the names of the dead come. All your defences are down, and it's a huge emotional shock. And it's at times like that that you really get the sense of mastery in the writing, of an author knowing that the scene's got to go somewhere else before it goes to the names of the dead, otherwise it's not going to go straight to people's hearts because too many defences will be up. By first igniting the whole theatre with laughter, everyone's defences are down.

4.6, a really short scene (40 lines) which comprises mainly the description of the deaths of the Earls of Suffolk and York, is often heavily cut, leaving just the killing of the prisoners. Did you consider doing so?

No. Exeter's speech, too, is part of the radical, almost subversive view of war the play encompasses. In the middle of the battle a man stands crying, saying that he saw his two close friends embrace as they were dying. Even now, I'm sure, that kind of information would be censored during a war, and I'm certain that would have been a shocking thing then, too: not their embrace or their kiss, but the fact that in the midst of the battle, and in tears, a soldier could describe so personal a moment. And a few moments later the prisoners are cold-bloodedly murdered. I find that juxtaposition astonishing too.

The other event in 4.6 is the killing of the French prisoners. In the text the prisoners are brought onstage at the start of the scene and so one assumes that they're there for a reason, and that reason seems to be that they're to be killed. But the action is often played offstage.

Yes, we brought the prisoners onstage, and as part of that we brought Pistol with M. Le Fer, so we had anonymous prisoners and we also had these people we know – we've seen Pistol and M. Le Fer earlier in that almost comic grotesque scene (4.4) being played between them in two languages. Pistol hopes he's going to make an absolute fortune by ransoming his prisoner, its going to change his life. So we brought them all together, and Henry, thinking the French army has regrouped, orders the prisoners to be killed, and we had Henry (who's just been saying he's close to tears at Exeter's speech) go to the front of the stage and, to set an example, kill one, two, three prisoners. Pistol is standing there with his prisoner and he's not going to kill Le Fer because that's his fortune, and so Henry drags Pistol's sword across Le Fer's throat and disinherits Pistol of everything. The idea was really just to try and get this shock and show how the command for every soldier to kill his prisoners is not only horrific for the French soldiers but also a terrible affront for their English captors, many of whom are relying on ransoms – that's what they've come for.

And the killing of the boys was juxtaposed with that?

Yes. As the audience watched Pistol staggering away from the corpse of Le Fer, having lost everything, the stage blacked out. The audience heard screams of other people's throats being cut and in the blackout the boys entered unseen and lay down on the top of the prisoners' bodies. Then spotlights came on at the start of 4.7 illuminating the boys' bodies with the prisoners' bodies underneath them. It's fascinating the way Shakespeare puts the two events adjacent to each other in the text. The most important thing for me was not which act was right or wrong but rather that both events caused an accumulation of dead people.

You began by saying that Henry has a lot of lengthy, rather daunting, rhetorical speeches. I suppose the most famous is the Crispin Day speech before the Battle of Agincourt. I remember in Terry Hands's production how Alan Howard showed consciously that Henry was having to remember all his rhetorical training lessons in order to come out with a speech of sufficient persuasive power, whereas Iain Glen played the Crispin Day speech as very much a personal and direct speech to the onstage characters. He played it quite quietly, too, certainly compared with the great rhetorical flourish that Olivier gives it in his film.

For the last four days of rehearsals we had a mock-up of the ramps so we could do the fighting, and I suddenly realised that by having the ramp Henry could speak to people in front of him downstage and still be seen by the audience – he could even sit down for the Crispin's Day speech and the sightlines would still be OK. After one rehearsal we were all sitting on the ramp while I was giving the company notes. Everybody was listening, and I thought, hang on, so I said to Iain, 'just come here, sit here', and I went and sat with the other actors, and I said to him 'just talk to us about Crispin's Day'. At first he was still quite 'big', because we'd been doing it that way, but gradually he changed it, made it more intimate, and everybody was listening intently, and he finished, and I remember a wonderful silence. I was very moved – almost tearful; I think we all were.

I think there's also something in that whole notion in the play of 'we happy few, we band of brothers'. I imagine the theatre company, this little group of men, taking on these enormous artistic and social challenges, and economic ones too, especially if they were in a period of transition between the Theatre and the Globe, and uncertain of their survival.

That phrase is so important, I think. To have a king saying to a whole section of society, and by implication to everybody who's watching the play as well, that we can actually be brothers on the same level. If it's said very honestly, it shakes the whole hierarchy.

The cynical view of course would be that it's a highly constructed, political speech . . .

But sometimes a naive view can be more exciting. If he means it at that moment, then the whole hierarchy goes into spin. Henry, the man on the battlefield, says, 'We would not die in that man's company, That fears his fellowship to die with us' [4.3.38–9] and there's a tone in that speech that I find a contrast to 'once more unto the breach'. Harfleur sounds like 'we'll still fight, we're going to win', but there's a sense in the Crispin's Day speech of a recognition that they may well die but they'll be remembered, and that's a very different thing. I was driving to rehearsals one day down Clapham High Street where there's a war memorial, and it had some poppies round it even though it was spring, it wasn't even November, and I thought that memory really is kept alive for the First and Second World War. And then I thought, what do we do on St Crispin's Day, because Henry says, and Shakespeare says through Henry, that St Crispin's Day, 'will ne'er go by, From this day to the ending of the world, But we in it shall be remembered'. It's 25 October, and we don't do anything on Crispin's Day, this day goes by repeatedly and we don't actually remember it. And so that fervent hope, that belief, has evaporated. And when I got into rehearsals, I immediately contacted people who I thought might know whether or not, when the play was written, 25 October was a public holiday to mark the battle. And it wasn't. It seems they weren't 'remembering' Agincourt even then. So both Shakespeare's audience, and ours, hear Henry in all honesty and faith saying that this day 'shall ne'er go by From this day to the ending of the world, But we in it shall be remembered' and know that he's wrong. And perhaps the expression is so extreme – 'From this day to the ending of the world' – because Shakespeare is deliberately drawing attention to the fact that it's actually not true. And that idea, if that is deliberate, very subtly and secretly sprinkled in there, is very much like the Chorus at the end of the play reminding the audience at the very moment of Henry's triumph that he would reign only for a 'small time' and that in his son's reign France would be lost and 'England bleed' – that all these achievements that seem fantastic while we've been abroad, that we've been celebrating now, soon evaporated.

You staged the scene before the walls of Harfleur (3.3) by having Henry speak out to the audience, imagining the Governor to be downstage, and then turn upstage as the Governor actually enters on the raised level. This strikes me as being in line with how it would probably have been staged originally.
We didn't stage it like that at first, and in fact it wasn't changed until during the previews. We rehearsed the scene in a very realistic way, with everyone facing upstage, and Henry actually spoke a lot of that with his back to the audience, facing upstage.

The Folio stage direction quite specifically doesn't have the Governor appear until the line before he replies to Henry, which seems to indicate that what you did is very much what Shakespeare had in mind in terms of shifting focus with great freedom: the theatre itself first becomes the town of Harfleur he's going to threaten, and then we move back and the stage's upper level becomes the actual city walls.
It certainly seems to work best like that. It's another discovery that comes from trusting the text, as with the shifts in tone between scenes we discussed earlier.

Elizabethan actors had very short rehearsal periods. There obviously wasn't a director in the sense that you're a director, but when we were talking about the first scenes you were saying that it took a great deal of rehearsing to get clear the various levels and shifts in direction implicit in the text. Obviously notions of acting and staging vary from one period to another, but having directed a number of Elizabethan and Jacobean plays, how does that notion of working square with your experience?
Shakespeare not only had a very profound and complex view of the world, but also of how the theatre can reflect that view. If the majority of people watching the play and performing it didn't engage with that at all then the writing

surely wouldn't be nearly as complex as it is. If there were stock scenes there could be stock characters. From working on the plays I get the sense that Elizabethan actors must have been really fast thinkers and creators and experimentalists.

What I've found working with actors is that if you don't really do any directing, don't really comment, then they develop very interesting things, but what often can arise from that is a kind of very mumbled meaning to a scene in terms of its relationship to the play. A scene with two people arguing might actually be supposed to be telling you something else rather than simply that those two people are arguing. And when you apply it to a whole play, certainly Shakespeare, you get the feeling that occasionally the scenes are actually speaking a slightly different message from the experience of the characters within them, and that Shakespeare wants to communicate or express ideas by juxtaposing things, by showing things in a different light and that it's the way scenes go against other scenes that's most important. It's the importance of perspective again. Actors can't really take that on board, their priorities are rightly elsewhere, and my job as a director is to make sure that the audience can hear not only the characters but also the playwright, can hear – in the broadest sense of the word – something the playwright is saying. What a playwright may be revealing can only be understood through the complete experience of a play, not through individual moments of it. It's only by those moments being structured and put into other contexts that some kind of meaning or comment comes about, and that's what theatre is. It doesn't always find solutions or conclusions, but comments by structuring and making a pattern – perhaps an erratic pattern or simple pattern, but some kind of a pattern. And that's really something that the individual characters can't help with at all. They can't be interested in that – it's like asking a radish in a salad to do something cucumberish as well, in order that the salad has got all these other elements in it; but in a play, as in a salad, you want the radish to be a radish, a cucumber's got to be a cucumber, the lettuce a lettuce – but we're still having a mixed salad. You can't ask actors – I'm sure that you *never* could ask actors – to take that on. And it's either the author acting as a director, or the author and someone else being a director, to make sure that the play is a play, not a series of biographies.

3

'SPEECHES WELL PRONOUNCED, WITH ACTION LIVELY FRAMED'[1]

Performing the play

> Does he not act it rarely?
> Observe with what a feeling he delivers
> His orisons to Cupid; I am rap'd with it.
> Philip Massinger, *The Roman Actor*,
> 3.2.175–7

> Actors, you rogues, come away; clear your throats, blow your noses and
> wipe your mouths ere you enter, that you may take no occasion to spit
> or cough when you are non plus. And this I bar, over and besides, that
> none of you stroke your beards to make action, play with your codpiece
> points, or stand fumbling on your buttons, when you know not how to
> bestow your fingers. Serve God, and act cleanly.
> Thomas Nashe, *Summer's Last Will and Testament*

The contrasting tone of these two quotations – one verse, one prose; one from
the point of view of the audience, the other from backstage – identifies problems of discussing the art (and artifice) of acting, and the difficulty of
distinguishing what may be the sublime, affecting impact of a performance
from the conscious process and technical means by which it is achieved and, as
important, repeated. These problems are rendered even more acute by the
distance between us and Elizabethan and Jacobean performances and by the
almost total absence of sustained, detailed observations of identifiable actors in
action. Richard Flecknoe's description of Richard Burbage is particularly valuable, therefore, especially if it is read in the light of John Webster's *Character*
of 'An Excellent Actor', apparently based on Burbage, roles known to have
been played by Burbage (especially Hamlet) and other references to his skill as
an actor:[2]

> It was the happiness of the actors of those times to have such poets
> as these to instruct them and write for them; and no less of those
> poets to have such docile and excellent actors to act their plays, as a
> Field and Burbage; of whom we may say he was a delightful Proteus,

58

so wholly transforming himself into his part and putting himself off with his clothes, as he never (not so much as in the tyring house) assumed himself again until the play was done, there being as much difference betwixt him and one of our common actors as between a ballad singer who only mouths it and an excellent singer, who knows all his graces and can artfully vary and modulate his voice, even to know how much breath he is to give to every syllable. He had all the parts of an excellent orator (animating his words with speaking, and speech with action) his auditors being never more delighted than when he spake, nor more sorry than when he held his peace. Yet even then, he was an excellent actor still, never falling in his part when he had done speaking, but with his looks and gesture, maintaining it still unto the heighth, he imagining 'Age quod agis' only spoke to him, so as those who call him a player do him wrong, no man being less idle than he, whose life is nothing else but action; with only this difference from other men's, that as what is but a play to them is his business, so their business is but a play to him.

Flecknoe made his observations in *A Short Discourse of the English Stage*, a brief essay appended to his play *Love's Kingdom* (1664). It has been argued that not only was this published more than forty years after Burbage's death, but also that Flecknoe (who died around 1678 but whose birth date is unknown) may possibly never have seen Burbage act, so rendering his comments derivative or based on hearsay. But Flecknoe's opinions, even if retrospective, are substantiated by other evidence, and nothing he says contradicts contemporary aesthetic judgements of acting in general or Burbage in particular. Nevertheless, we should note, as Flecknoe and other commentators do, that Burbage was exceptional (there being, in Flecknoe's words, 'as much difference between him and one of our common actors as between a ballad singer . . . and an excellent singer'), and that judgements of him refer only to the highest standards of contemporary acting.

> *It was the happiness of the actors of those times to have such poets as these to instruct them and write for them; and no less of those poets to have such docile and excellent actors to act their plays, as a Field and Burbage; of whom we may say he was a delightful Proteus . . .*

I considered the implications of the opening references to instruction in Chapter 2. Let us look in more detail at the remainder of Flecknoe's report. Comparisons of characters in Elizabethan and Jacobean plays to Proteus – the water spirit who could change his shape at will – are common, though the analogy is not always employed in a positive sense. The ability to shift shape, to dissimulate, is also frequently used in plays to signify untrustworthiness and hypocrisy in a character, such as Shakespeare's Proteus in *The Two Gentlemen of Verona* or Richard III in *3 Henry VI*, who boasts that he can 'wet [his] cheeks with artificial tears' and 'Change shapes with Proteus for advantages / And set the murderous Machiavel to school' (3.2.184, 192–3), or Jonson's deceitful courtier whose ability to 'change and vary with all forms he sees', makes him a 'subtle Proteus . . . anything but honest' (*Cynthia's Revels*, 3.4.42–4). Similar criticism was extended from the characters they played to the actors themselves, whose evident capacity to substitute feigned personalities for their essential selves was regularly the focus of anti-theatrical tracts.

Jonas A. Barish points out, however, that 'the polyvalence of Renaissance symbology meant that most emblems could be assigned different, even contradictory meanings', and he observes that in *L'Aminta* (1573), a pastoral by the contemporary Italian playwright, Torquato Tasso, Proteus is characterised as 'the benign presiding genius over the entire realm of theatrical illusion' (1981: 106–7). It is undoubtedly in this positive theatrical sense that we should understand Thomas Heywood's description of Edward Alleyn as a 'Proteus for shapes', Thomas Randolph's praise of Thomas Riley as 'a Proteus, that can take / What shape he please, and in an instant make / Himself to anything' (Preface to *The Jealous Lovers*, 1622) and Flecknoe's reference to Burbage. The term also suggests the actor's ability to perform a series of different roles (several in one week given the repertory system employed) and his considerable dexterity and flexibility within a single role – within the play overall, within individual speeches, even within the length of a single line; what Trevor Nunn terms the need for actors in these plays to be able to 'turn on a sixpence'.[3] Flaminius, in Philip Massinger's *Believe As You List* (though himself a shifty character) sums up the task confronting the actor:

> I am on the stage
> And if now, in the scene imposed upon me,
> So full of change . . .
> . . . I show not myself
> A protean actor varying every shape
> With the occasion, it will hardly poise
> The expectation.
>
> (3.1.12–18)

A speech from another Massinger play, *The Roman Actor*, illustrates these points in action, particularly the speed with which thoughts and their resulting actions must be radically switched. The Emperor, Domitian, has caught his mistress, Domitia, trying to seduce Paris, the actor. Although indicative of his confused state of mind, the speed of shifts required of the actor playing Domitian is also partly necessitated by the fact that the Guard accompanying Domitia will, of course, carry out one instruction until it is rescinded by another. I have marked with an asterisk the points at which these shifts of attitude and focus occur:

> O impudence! take her hence,
> And let her make her entrance into hell,
> By leaving life with all the tortures that
> Flesh can be sensible of. * Yet stay. * What power
> Her beauty still holds o'er my soul! What wrongs
> Of this unpardonable nature cannot teach me
> To right my self and hate her! * Kill her. * Hold.*
> O that my dotage should increase from that
> Which should breed detestation. * By Minerva
> If I look on her longer I shall melt
> And sue to her, my injuries forgot,
> Again to be receiv'd into her favour
> Could honour yield to it! * Carry her to her chamber,
> Be that her prison till in cooler blood
> I shall determine of her.
>
> (4.2.138–152)

In response to Macbeth's question 'Who can be wise, amaz'd, temp'rate and furious, loyal and neutral, in a moment' (2.3.108–9) one might answer 'The actor playing that speech or any like it'. Actors today, often more used to the seemingly logical connections of naturalistic characterisation, and trained to conceal their art rather than display it, can find such demands daunting: once accepted, though, they can find the opportunities exhilarating.

. . . so wholly transforming himself into his part . . .

It is common in Elizabethan and Jacobean plays for the actors to interact in some way with the audience to acknowledge its presence as an audience and the play as a play (see Case Study, p. 100ff.). As part of this strategy actors are required to shift (often with considerable speed) between different combinations of focused onstage scenes, 'secret' exchanges with other onstage characters within those scenes, and direct engagement with the audience through asides or soliloquies. A few lines from *The Atheist's Tragedy* (2.1.105–122) are sufficiently typical to use as an example. Borachio, at D'Amville's instigation, comes onstage disguised as a wounded soldier, claiming to have returned from the wars with news of Charlemont's death. Following a lengthy and very detailed description of Charlemont's death in battle, Borachio produces a scarf belonging to Charlemont as the final proof with which to convince both Charlemont's lover, Castabella, and his father, Montferrers, of his death. D'Amville's lines to the audience are in italics; those to the onstage characters in normal type; D'Amville's asides to Borachio are underlined; and Borachio's asides to D'Amville are in bold. It's worth trying this in action.

BORACHIO: And here's the sad remembrance of his life,
         (Shows the scarf.)
 Which for his sake I will for ever wear.
MONTFERRERS: Torment me not with witnesses of that
 Which I desire not to believe, yet must.
D'AMVILLE: Thou art a screech-owl and dost come i' night
 To be the cursed messenger of death.
 Away. Depart my house, or, by my soul,
 You'll find me a more fatal enemy
 Than ever was Ostend. Be gone. Despatch.
BORACHIO: Sir, 'twas my love –
D'AMVILLE: Your love to vex my heart
 With that I hate? Hark, do you hear, you knave?
 <u>O th'art a most delicate sweet eloquent villain.</u>
BORACHIO: **Was't not well counterfeited?**
D'AMVILLE: <u>Rarely</u>. Be gone; <u>I will not here reply</u>.
BORACHIO: **Why then, farewell. I will not trouble you. (Exit.)**
D'AMVILLE: *So. The foundation's laid. Now by degrees*
 The work will rise and soon be perfected.
 O this uncertain state of mortal man!

Partly as a consequence of such strategies, Brecht's notions of staging and performance have for some time been promoted as a particularly useful model for the modern actor of Jacobean plays (Heinemann 1985). It is a view undoubtedly strengthened not only by Brecht's dominance as a theorist-practitioner in the late twentieth century, but also by his own acknowledgement of Shakespeare's influence and importance and the obviously closer correlation between the supposed theatre practice of the Elizabethan stage and that of the Epic – as opposed to the Naturalistic – theatre. Although Brecht recognised the need for actors 'to feel their way into their character's skins' in rehearsal,[4] his aim (with certain key exceptions) was substantially to reduce the audience's empathetic engagement and by employing a range of 'distancing' devices in individual performances and overall staging keep them alert to the constructed nature of the events portrayed before them – the process usually termed 'alienation'. Flecknoe's phrase 'wholly transforming himself', however, suggests a close identification of actor and role on the part of the spectator observing Burbage. Indeed, the evidence provided by audience members from the opening of the professional playhouses until their closure, and self-referential remarks within plays themselves, suggest that 'good' acting was expected to present a convincing portrayal of a character's behaviour so 'to the life' (in Thomas Heywood's words) that the spectators, 'as being wrapt in contemplation', apparently felt 'as if the Personator were the man Personated' (1841: 21). Moreover, in both children's playhouses (though less extensively; see below) and those occupied by adult performers, audiences were at times clearly intended to respond emotionally to the action onstage. The Prologue to Thomas Dekker's *If This Be Not a Good Play, the Devil Is in It* (Red Bull, 1612) sets out the route by which emotions were transferred from playwright to audience via the actor:

> That man give me, whose breast fill'd by the Muses
> With Raptures, into a second them infuses:
> Can give an actor sorrow, rage, joy, passion,
> Whilst he again (by self-same agitation)
> Commands the hearers, sometimes drawing out tears,
> Then smiles, and fills them both with hopes and fears.

Reports of performances throughout the period testify to actors' successes in achieving these aims. In the early 1590s Thomas Nashe observed of Alleyn or, possibly, the youthful Burbage's acting, that:

> How would it have joy'd brave Talbot (the terror of the French) to think that after he had lain two hundred years in his tomb, he should triumph again on the stage and have his bones new embalmed with the tears of ten thousand spectators at least (at several times), who, in the tragedian that represents his person, imagine they behold him fresh bleeding? . . . there is no immortality can be given a man on earth like unto plays.
>
> (1972: 113)

Thomas Middleton recalled that spectators at *The Duchess of Malfi* (1613) cried ('For who e're saw this Duchess live and die, / That could get off under a bleeding eye'), while in a Commendatory Poem attached to the Beaumont and Fletcher First Folio (1647) Francis Palmer described an audience fully caught up in the action portrayed onstage:

> But when thy tragic Muse would please to rise
> In majesty, and call tribute from our eyes,
> Like scenes we shifted passions, and that so,
> Who only came to see turned actors too.
> How didst thou sway the theatre! make us feel
> The players' wounds were true, and their swords steel!
> Nay stranger yet, how often did I know
> When the spectators ran to save the blow!
> Frozen with grief, we could not stir away
> Until the epilogue told us 'twas a play.[5]

Not all were so admiring, but it was, presumably, precisely the players' success in generating powerful reactions to 'lifelike' representations that fuelled charges against stage performances for arousing dangerous desires in their audiences. Detractors of the theatre (often, as in the case of Gosson and Munday, practitioners themselves) concentrated on precisely its ability to 'enchant' and 'ensnare' spectators, a much more likely image of the playhouse's impact on its audience than the worthy defences offered by the theatre's supporters that seem undermined by virtually every play that survives (Kastan 1986; see also Cartelli 1991 and Case Study, p. 100ff.).

To identify such audience responses is not, however, to assert that the actors who produced them were similarly ensnared – at least, not intentionally – during the act of performance itself. As Harriet Walter points out, actors are paid to imitate, not to feel, and need at all times 'a super-sensitivity to the here and now'. Nevertheless, as she also notes, an actor may need, in rehearsing a role, to recover some personal experience (however remote) comparable to that of the character (see Case Study, p. 88ff.) and, crucially, discover some means to 'trigger' what she calls 'the learned pathway' during repeated performances. It was to address this specific issue, and avoid clichéd repetition, that the Russian director, Konstantin Stanislavsky devised a system of exercises designed to enable the actor to reproduce a character's emotions 'truthfully' – and on demand in performance – and so give the performer conscious control over these invariably capricious responses. Among the exercises Stanislavsky devised is one based on emotional recall, in which the actor first remembers an actual event from his or her own life in which the emotion required by the play (or something very close to it) was actually generated, and then methodically creates in his or her mind, in detail, the full *physical* circumstances which produced and accompanied it. The actor then refines that construct until the recollection of a single element is able, within the performance, to spark off the emotional response: for Marcel Proust, for instance, though in another context, the sensation of childhood was encapsulated by savouring a cup of tea.[6] Interestingly enough, the Roman writer Quintilian dealt in considerable detail with the means by which an orator should 'assimilate [himself] to the emotions of those who are genuinely affected', by the use of *visiones*, by which he meant 'fantastic . . . daydreams . . . whereby things absent are presented to our imagination with such vividness that they seem actually to be before our very eyes', commenting that 'on the stage I have often observed the eyes of the actor through his mask inflamed with fury'.[7] Thomas Dekker, in the Prologue to *If This Be Not a Good Play* quoted above, refers to the actor's 'self-same agitation' in generating a response in his audience, and Francisco, Duke of Florence, perhaps the most successful of the many performer / characters in Webster's *The White Devil*, appears to demonstrate how actors might have employed similar means to create realities from their, and their audience's, imaginations:

To fashion my revenge more seriously,
Let me remember my dead sister's face:
Call for her picture: no, I'll close mine eyes
And in a melancholic thought I'll frame
Her figure 'fore me. Now I ha't – how strong
Imagination works. How can she frame
Things which are not.

(4.1.98–104)

Absorption (or apparent absorption) of the self within another personality was a key charge against actors and was frequently aligned with magic – as Heywood himself notes, 'so bewitching a thing is lively and spirited action' (1841: 21). But trying to ascertain rules for how all actors operate is futile, and while some may use recollection of their own experience to produce an emotional response, others (as Shakespeare vividly reminds us through Hamlet's response to the Player King's 'Hecuba' speech) can create what seem to be equally convincing performances in a very technical manner and on demand. Thomas Wright agreed with Horace that the *orator* who 'will make me weep must first weep himself', but distinguished this from the practices of *actors*, for whom 'the perfection of their exercise consisteth in imitation of others, so they that imitate best, act best' (1971: 172, 179). As a character in Thomas May's *The Heir* observes of the actor who 'personates Hieronimo', he portrays grief:

In such a lively colour, that for false
And acted passions he has drawn true tears
From the spectators. Ladies in the boxes
Kept time with tears and sighs to his sad accents,
As he had truly been the man he seemed.

(1.1.19–23)

In other words, a clear distinction must be recognised between recorded audience response and the actor's means of eliciting that response, and on the latter, as I commented at the beginning of this chapter, Elizabethan and Jacobean actors have left no direct statement. Nor can the ability to produce emotional responses in an audience be used as evidence of 'naturalistic' performance: Arthur Symons, for example, commented of Sarah Bernhardt that her 'very artificial acting . . . mesmerised one, awakening the senses and sending the intelligence to sleep'.[8] Indeed, while some contemporaries may have found it difficult to separate action and actor, the performers themselves were clear on the distinction. Burbage, playing Ferdinand in *The Duchess of Malfi*, observed, 'a good actor many times is cursed / For playing a villain's part' (4.2.289–90), and Joseph Taylor, playing Paris in *The Roman Actor*, responding to Domitia's claim that he must personally possess the heroic qualities he presents onstage, explains:

The argument
Is the same great Augusta, that I acting
A fool, a coward, a traitor or cold cynic,
Or any other weak and vicious person,
Of force I must be such. O gracious Madam,
How glorious soever, or deformed,
I do appear in the scene, my part being ended,
And all my borrowed ornaments put off,
I am no more, nor less, than what I was
Before I entered.

(4.2.43–52)

In shifting between 'inward' and 'outward' action, each (however created) equally powerfully charged, it seems to me that when necessary actors could produce performances that resulted in a pattern of engagement and detachment, a depth and intensity of contrast equivalent to the striking chiaroscuro of contemporary painting and characteristic of the general collisions of moods and tones in contemporary drama.[9] This pattern may also offer a clue as to how Elizabethan actors – partly by constantly shifting the 'depth of focus' – sought to control audience response, something early experiments with a mercurial, actively participatory standing audience (itself exploring a new role) have raised as a particularly important – and testing – task for the performers at Globe 3.

> *. . . and putting himself off with his clothes, as he never (not so much as in the tyring house) assumed himself again until the play was done.*

Flecknoe here suggests that although Burbage could transform himself from one role to another (and undoubtedly shift focus within a single role in the ways referred to earlier) he was always fixed on the particular part he was playing, maintaining his concentration on the part at all times, on or offstage. The late Robert Stephens, on the other hand, who played King Lear (a role first performed by Burbage) for the RSC in 1993–4, was willing to be interviewed for a TV documentary about his career in general, and the part of Lear in particular, apparently actually during a performance, but still received reviews paying tribute to the emotional force of his acting.[10]

> *. . . there being as much difference betwixt him and one of our common actors as between a ballad singer who only mouths it and an excellent singer, who knows all his graces and can artfully vary and modulate his voice, even to know how much breath he is to give to every syllable.*

References to the 'tunefulness' of actors' voices are common in the period and the comparison between Burbage and a ballad singer is also made in the

Character of 'An Excellent Actor' – almost certainly modelled on Richard Burbage – and written in response to J. Cocke's less-than-flattering Character of 'A Common Player' (quoted *ES*, IV: 255–7). The author (probably John Webster) observes that the actor 'adds grace to the poet's labours: for what in the poet is but ditty, in him is both ditty and music', using the word 'grace', I think, in the sense of an 'embellishment of additional notes introduced into vocal or instrumental music not essential to the harmony or melody' (*OED*). In words more appropriate to the art of acting, Webster is pointing out that each actor makes a part his own through his individual interpretation, voice, intonation and personality. There are many references to Burbage's vocal skills, virtually all of which invoke a musical comparison, which was a long-established analogy to describe a good orator or actor. If we could hear a recording, the actual sound Burbage made would strike our modern ears as oddly, no doubt, as would his 'lifelike' performance, but as far as Burbage's delivery of the language was concerned, we can only assume from references elsewhere that he was light, fast and tuneful, knew exactly how to control his breathing and how to stress his lines to match rhythm and sense – all the qualities, in fact, that actors aim for now when working on Elizabethan and Jacobean texts.

> *He had all the parts of an excellent orator (animating his words with speaking, and speech with action) his auditors being never more delighted than when he spake, nor more sorry than when he held his peace . . .*

Thomas Heywood, an actor and playwright who estimated that he had, in his own words, 'either an entire hand or at the least a main finger' (*JCS*, IV: 555) in 220 plays, performed in a range of playhouses, summed up in his *Apology for Actors* what was expected of actors. They should, he believed, 'be men picked out personable, according to the parts they present' who, as well as the range of vocal skills already referred to, needed:

> a comely and elegant gesture, a gracious and bewitching kind of action, a natural and a familiar motion of the head, the hand, the body, and a moderate and fit countenance suitable to all the rest . . . [the actor should not] use any impudent or forced motion in any part of the body, no rough or other violent gesture, nor on the contrary to stand like a stiff starched man, but to qualify everything according to the nature of the person personated.
>
> (1841: 43)

Texts throughout the period confirm the importance of the actor's physical and gestural performance. The majority of gestures (implicit and explicit) are easily read by us, such as the 'natural and familiar' actions suggested by the stage direction from *A Woman Killed With Kindness*, 'Enter Frankford, as it were brushing the crumbs from his clothes with a napkin, and newly risen from supper' (scene 8, s.d., l.21) or the direction 'as if groping in the dark' in the *Second Part of the Iron Age*, a gesture clearly illustrated on the title-page of the 1632 edition and seemingly demonstrating a mimetic performance (Foakes 1985: 135). Other examples, however, suggest that a code of conventional gestures that were readily associated by the audience with specific *emotional* states was also available to the actors when necessary – what David Bevington calls a 'theatrical sign system' (1984). Many of these gestures, too, are unsurprising and fairly compatible with our own social and theatrical conventions. Other instances are more obscure, however, and it becomes difficult – even impossible – to reconstruct the implied gestural performance, either because there is simply too little to go on or because reference is made to a code about which we may speculate but the details of which we cannot ascertain. In 5.2 of Massinger's *The Unnatural Combat* (Globe, *c.* 1624–5), for example, Malefort addresses the ghost of his son 'naked from the waist, full of wounds' and 'the shadow of a Lady, her face leprous' who, 'deprived of language' (276), both communicate with Malefort only with 'several gestures' and 'signs'. Exactly what (if indeed anything specific) the playwright had in mind, or the actors actually did, is irretrievable.

Such a 'sign system' might have embraced an actor's total performance. In the opening scene of *The Changeling*, following Alsemero's explanation to the audience that he has, at first sight, fallen in love with Beatrice-Joanna, he is joined onstage by his servant/companion, Jasperino. Eager that they should take advantage of a long-awaited fair wind and set sail for home, Jasperino is frustrated by his master's apparently motiveless refusal to leave. Listing possible reasons for delaying, Jasperino dismisses any romantic attachment: 'Lover, I'm sure y'are none' (36). Alsemero has confided his reasons to the audience in his opening soliloquy, but from Jasperino's point of view the remark (at least on the page) comes out of the blue. Jasperino may simply be tracing various reasons why a man might behave irrationally, but perhaps on the Phoenix stage he was prompted by Alsemero's physical appearance and performance. In Nathan Field's *Amends for Ladies* (1616), a character, Ingen, observes that his mistress won't take him seriously because he does not fit the typical image of the lover and:

> Lay mine arms o'er my heart, and wear no garters,
> Walk with mine eyes in a hat, sigh, and make faces.
> (1.1.91–2)

Such actions were perhaps precisely those Jasperino and the audience saw Alsemero perform. Indeed, Jasperino's lines were possibly addressed, in effect, to the spectators, advising them (mistakenly as it turns out) not to believe what they see, and so carrying a dominant theme of the play into the interaction of stage and audience.

In his book *The Passions of the Mind in General* (1604) Thomas Wright observed:

> The internal conceits and affection of our minds are not only expressed with words, but also declared with actions, as it appeareth in Comedies [plays generally], where dumb shows often express the whole matter.
>
> (1971: 124)

The prevalence throughout the period, indoors and out, of dumb-shows and other forms of wordless action that frequently convey complex narrative and character detail, confirms that actors needed well-developed gestural skills: indeed, Fynes Moryson reported seeing a company of English actors using those skills to enable them to perform successfully abroad:

> I have seen some straggling broken Companies that passed into Netherlands and Germany, followed by the people from one town to another, though they understood not their words, only to see their action . . .[11]

Among Burbage's roles was probably the eponymous lead in *Pericles*, published in 1609 and, I assume, first performed at the Globe during 1607–8. Scene 18 (Act 4, scene 4 in some editions) opens with a dumb-show:

> Enter Pericles at one door with all his train, Cleon and Dionyza at the other. Cleon shows Pericles the tomb, whereat Pericles makes lamentation, puts on sackcloth, and in a mighty passion departs.

For any leading actor in the period, a major test of his professional expertise – and of his capacity to express emotion in particular – was his ability to act a passion well: it is, for example, the first thing Hamlet asks the First Player to do in order to demonstrate his skills. A 'passion' in Jacobean terms was a heightened emotional state (Thomas Wright calls it a 'perturbation', 1971: 124ff), positive or negative, which produced specific and observable emotional and physiological effects in the person concerned and possibly, in performance, in the spectator too. In plays, expression of a passion generally takes the form of 'passionate speeches', set-pieces of heightened language perhaps accompanied in performance by appropriate action – 'good accent and good discretion' to use the First Player's terms (2.2.462–3). Such speeches are often likened to operatic arias. The comparison is valid, but particularly so if *aria* is understood in seventeenth-century terms where, in the work of Purcell, for example, the term is used to describe a passage where the music is dominant, as opposed to sections of *recitative*, where the words are the more important element: passionate emotion as opposed to narrative dialogue.

Here, the passion is to be expressed without words from the character, but although 'mighty', Pericles' performance is clearly not forced. Indeed, in his commentary on the action, Gower identifies the difference between Pericles' behaviour and the evidently feigned expressions of emotion of Cleon and Dionyza, who significantly do not vary their costume. As always, it is hard to establish exactly what the actor did, but clues from this and other plays help to build up some idea of the elements that Burbage might have included. Gower refers to 'sighs' and 'biggest tears': the former an audience would have heard, the latter they might have to take on trust unless, like the 'seeming late fallen, counterfeited tears' Paris affects in *The Roman Actor* (3.2.151), Burbage faked them or, like the First Player in *Hamlet* and many modern actors, he could produce them at will. Thomas Wright considered 'a pitiful weeping eye and a fainting lamentable tune' ('tune' probably referring to the tone of voice employed) as 'always' necessary in the presentation of grief (1971: 181). The phrase 'makes lamentation' is presumably shorthand for specific gestures that would have seemed appropriate to the audience. Andrew Gurr argues that overly pantomimic action would, by the early years of the seventeenth century, be seen as indicative of old-fashioned excess, and he suggests that while the Player Queen in *Hamlet* 'makes passionate action' of grief during the dumb-show (3.2.134) it was extremely unlikely that the actor playing Gertrude did the same 'in the play proper' (1992: 102). But the fact that it is a *dumb*-show is the key point. The actor playing Gertrude could 'suit his action to the *word*': in the dumb-show the actor would very likely have needed recourse to a range of readily understood gestures. In this case, for example, the 'sorrow' with which Pericles is 'all devoured' might have involved the actor beating his breast, wiping his eyes, wringing his hands, weeping, sighing, 'wreathing' his arms across his chest, even falling prostrate on the ground – actions denoting grief and distraction specified in a range of plays, children's and adults', across the period. The gesture of crossed arms was undoubtedly used by Elizabethan and Jacobean actors to help suggest despair: for example, Ariel tells Prospero that he has left Ferdinand 'cooling of the air with sighs / In an odd angle of the isle, and sitting, / His arms in this sad knot' (*The Tempest*, 1.2.223–5). Conversely, the *absence* of arms with which to make expressions of grief is specifically referred to in *Titus Andronicus* when Lavinia, whose arms have been severed, and Titus who has cut off one of his hands, 'cannot passionate our tenfold grief / With folded arms' (3.2.6–7). To these gestural elements we should add the signifiers of the sackcloth Pericles puts on and the action of his onstage costume change itself, the *absence* of a costume change by Cleon and Dionyza and, presumably, appropriate music. It is easy (and common) for such gestures to be derided as overly 'pantomimic' or melodramatic. Watching actors in 'silent' movies (with and without musical accompaniment) cope with similar problems, however, I have been repeatedly struck by the restrained delicacy with which such gestures can be delivered, and how clearly such performances may be distinguished from those of less skilled film actors whose gestures are excessive, and evidently not grounded in any reality whatsoever.

The use of conventional gestures has been a key point in the argument for a consistent link between the art of acting and that of oratory, in which there is firmer evidence of a fixed correlation between speech and gesture. When Muriel Bradbrook wrote her seminal book *Themes and Conventions of Elizabethan Tragedy* she could justifiably claim that 'the nature of Elizabethan acting has never been considered in any detail' (1935: 20). Her own conclusion was that it was essentially 'formal' rather than 'natural', closely aligned to oratory, producing a style of acting 'probably nearer to that of the modern political platform or revivalist pulpit than that of the modern stage' (21), an opinion endorsed by Alfred Harbage in an influential essay published in 1939.[12] Their views were upheld or refuted in further studies during the 1950s and 1960s, a debate mirrored at the time by that between advocates of Brecht and Stanislavsky – Alienation versus the Method – and discussions of Renaissance acting style still invoke (as I have already done) these two modern theorist-practitioners. In both debates the terms themselves were (and still are) frequently used vaguely and randomly – 'formal' being distinguished from 'natural' as if 'naturalism' itself were not a highly conscious style of presentation. Such distinctions are in fact rather pointless, since not only do the playtexts themselves contain a range of physical and verbal languages that must have demanded a variety of responses from the actor but, as I pointed out earlier, concepts of what is natural or formal shift with time; indeed, the acting of Bradbrook's 'modern theatre' would undoubtedly seem stilted and artificial to us now.

Thomas Wright observed that actors and orators both aimed 'to work wonders among a multitude of men' (1971: 183) and actors could certainly adopt an oratorical mode within their performances when the writing required it. In *The Roman Actor* (Blackfriars, 1626), at the end of the actor Paris's defence of the theatre – a speech that demands specific techniques of persuasion in the formal setting of the Senate – Latinus, one of his fellow actors, notes with admiration:

> Well pleaded, on my life! I never saw him
> Act an Orator's part before.
>
> (1.3.143–4)

Another actor, Aesopus, compares Paris's performance favourably with that of Regulus, who was in reality a lawyer in first-century Rome famous for his persuasive oratory in defence cases. Paris was played by Joseph Taylor, the King's Men's leading actor, and these comments imply some clear distinction between the way he handled this particular speech – gesturally and vocally – and the rest of his performance. Significantly, however, although the speech itself is rhetorical, suiting its purpose and formal situation, the cornerstone of

Paris's defence of his profession rests precisely on the ability and duty of an actor, when necessary, to present the actions of men 'done to the life, *As if* they saw their danger' (emphasis added). It is a phrase that prefigures Stanislavsky's 'magic If', and indeed, Paris's acting elsewhere in the play produces performances which convince at least some in his audience that what they see is not illusion but reality (see Case Study, pp. 100ff).

Gesture, and how it was integrated with language, was therefore (as it still is, of course) a key element in an actor's performance, and Burbage apparently fulfilled Hamlet's advice to 'suit the word to the action, the action to the word', where (as in Flecknoe) 'action' means the actor's whole performance – physical and vocal. In other words, Hamlet (Shakespeare) is advising a coherent performance (body, gesture, intonation, etc.) but not necessarily a consistent one, since actors could undoubtedly move between 'naturalistic' gesture to accompany their words and more conventional gesture, for example in the dumb-shows. To conclude this section on gestural performance, it is perhaps worth noting that even use of conventional gesture by an actor is not in itself necessarily evidence of formal performance. The following lines from *Henry VIII*, for example, performed at the Globe in 1613, in which one character describes the physical actions another is making (or has just made), may seem to indicate a mannered, patterned performance, and, indeed, the speaker describes them as 'most strange postures':

> he bites his lip and starts,
> Stops on a sudden, looks upon the ground,
> Then lays his finger on his temple; straight
> Springs out into fast gait; then stops again,
> Strikes his breast hard; and anon he casts
> His eye against the moon. In most strange postures
> We have seen him set himself.
> (3.2.114–120)

The implied performance is certainly not 'formal' in comparison with, say, that of a Japanese Kabuki actor, who expresses intense internal turmoil by crossing one eye while holding the rest of his body absolutely rigid, a gesture which can *only* be interpreted by a spectator who understands the particular codes of performance. The component actions in the example from *Henry VIII* (lip-biting, erratic gesture and movement, staring, touching the head and striking the breast) were presumably considered by contemporaries (and some may still be thought by us) to be actions appropriate to an expression of emotional conflict, and to that extent they were conventional, part of a social and theatrical sign system. If synchronised with the lines the *effect* might be considered formal – and rather striking when set against the urgent whispered language of the other characters onstage. Alternatively, if the six component actions were employed in various combinations throughout the scene the *effect* derived from the employment of these conventions might well be of a 'natural' performance, just as any 'naturalistic' performance today is constructed of gestures an audience will recognise and accept as appropriate to certain states of mind or feeling.

> *. . . yet even then, he was an excellent actor still, never falling in his part when he had done speaking, but with his looks and gesture, maintaining it still unto the heighth, he imagining 'Age quod agis' only spoke to him . . .*

In *The Antipodes*, the amateur director Lord Letoy complains of one of his own acting troupe that 'when you are / To speak to your coactors in the scene, / You hold interlocutions with the audience' (2.1). Burbage, on the other hand, knew that acting is reacting, and appears to have sustained his part at all times, directing the audience's attention to the focus of the action onstage rather than merely to himself. Apart from when the text demanded direct interaction with the audience, Burbage evidently played with his fellow actors, unlike the 'base and artless' player satirised by J. Cocke as a mere crowd-pleaser who 'when he doth hold conference upon the stage, and should look directly in his fellow's face, he turns about his voice into the assembly, for applause sake' (*ES*, IV: 255–7). The Latin tag, 'age quod agis' can be translated as 'Do what you do', meaning, I think, 'do it as you would in life', which suggests to me that Burbage tried always to let his performance be informed by what Stanislavsky termed the 'given circumstances', letting the 'truth' of the fictional events define his character's actions and responses.

> *. . . so as those who call him a player do him wrong, no man being less idle than he, whose life is nothing else but action; with only this difference from other men's, that as what is but a play to them is his business, so their business is but a play to him.*

Even though Flecknoe's report can tell us nothing in any real detail about how Burbage achieved the impact on an audience that he clearly did, this and other descriptions of him portray an actor who sustained his concentration, inhabited imaginatively the role of the character and circumstances of the play, had the physical and vocal skills to give life and excitement to his performances, and the indefinable 'star' quality that set him apart from virtually all his contemporaries. Burbage appears to have been the complete professional, reflecting and animating, as closely as his evidently considerable skills allowed him to, the life and actions of the wide range of very different characters he played and their counterparts in the world of his audience. His death on 13 March 1619 occasioned an 'outburst of eulogy and sorrow that surpassed the grief for Queen Anne' who had died a fortnight earlier (Nungezer 1968: 73). The shortest but most appropriate elegy for the great actor read simply, 'Exit Burbage.'

*

But Burbage cannot be used as a template for all Elizabethan and Jacobean actors. Just as now, different actors had different ways of acting which pleased some and infuriated others. Edward Alleyn, reputed to be a man of imposing stature, was especially noted for playing majestic parts, and is often considered to have been more expansive in style than (certainly the mature) Burbage – more Albert Finney than Kenneth Branagh, perhaps. Nevertheless, despite (or maybe because of) their differences, Alleyn and Burbage were still paired together as 'the best actors of our time' (Sir Richard Baker, *Theatrum Redivivum*, 1662: 34). Moreover, styles of acting, both individual and general, undoubtedly (and unsurprisingly) changed between the opening and closing of the commercial playhouses. Andrew Gurr has observed that around the start of the seventeenth century the word 'personate' begins to be used to describe acting, and that this may suggest the development of a more 'naturalistic' style of performance, of which Burbage was the prime exponent.[13] The shift would have been stimulated by a number of factors including changes in those material factors that shape an actor's craft in any period: the spaces in which he performs and the texts he is given to act. Patrice Pavis argues that 'once a text is uttered onstage, it is no longer possible for the spectator to imagine the time span between text and performance, since both are presented simultaneously, even if the rhythm of each is peculiar to its own signifying system' (1992: 26). However, though audiences today may not consciously note the original venue where an Elizabethan or Jacobean play was presented, nor precisely when in the period it was written and performed, the performance space would have had a – arguably *the* – defining impact on acting style. Actors inevitably had to adapt to (and make the most of) the demands made by different playhouses and audiences: stepping out onto the vast stage at the Fortune, for example, would have been a very different experience from entering onto the compact stage at the Rose. The Red Bull, home of the Queen Anne's Men, was famed for presenting noisy and exuberant dramas, and actors there were described as 'tear throats' given to exaggerated playing – a charge that carried enough weight for other companies who performed there to begin the afternoon's entertainment by denying it. The King's Men, on the other hand, who performed the 'terser Beaumont's or great Jonson's verse' were described as 'Men of grave and sober behaviour', a 'true brood of Actors' whose 'natural unstrained' acting set them apart. That may have been true as far as their work at the more intimate, indoor Blackfriars was concerned, but at the larger Globe they undoubtedly varied their performance style in keeping with the demands of that particular space: in his Prologue to *The Doubtful Heir*, James Shirley specifies that he wrote it for the Blackfriars since 'we have no Heart to break our Lungs at the Globe', and the volume with which Histrio, the public playhouse actor, speaks, is a gag in Jonson's *Poetaster* which, like all good jokes, must have some basis in truth; a review of an early performance at Globe 3 noted that 'this space demands some real chest-heaving in the rhetoric' (*Observer*, 25 August 1996). Nevertheless, actors at Globe 3, as they become accustomed to the space, comment on how easily focus is lost if they 'push' too hard vocally, and how the theatre allows intimate speeches to work. The impact of space on performance would, of course, have been most acute when moving between outdoor and indoor venues, with some aspects of performance essential outdoors being simply inappropriate or unnecessary in the claustrophobic intimacy of a private playhouse. An analogy with early screen acting may again be useful here, in which many have observed a transition (to use Roberta E. Pearson's terms) from 'histrionic' to 'verisimilar' performance, a change Pearson attributes in part to the increasing use of the 'close up' in the pioneering films of D.W. Griffith, whom she quotes:

> We were striving for real acting. When you saw only the small, full length figures it was necessary to have exaggerated acting, which might be called 'physical' acting, the waving of the hands and so on. The close-up enabled us to reach real acting, restraint, acting that is a duplicate of real life.
>
> (Pearson 1992: 93)

As well as fitting their performances to the spaces in which they perform, actors must respond to the demands of the text, and those demands also inevitably changed during the seventy years between the opening and closing of the professional playhouses. This was something of which playwrights were themselves aware. Thomas Heywood's play, *The Four Prentices of London*, was first performed around 1600, evidently with great success. When it was published in 1615, however, Heywood thought it necessary to append an apology pointing out that although 'some fifteen or sixteen years ago it was in the fashion', the printed version would reveal that 'it comes short of that accurateness both in plot and style that these more censorious days with greater curiosity acquire'. Sometime before 1616 Ben Jonson wrote of Edward Alleyn that 'others speak, but only thou dost act'.[14] Twenty-five years later, apparently referring to Alleyn's great success in the roles of Tamburlaine and Tamar Cam, he wrote:

> the true Artificer will not run away from nature, as he were afraid of her; or depart from life and the likeness of Truth; but speak to the capacity of his hearers. And though his language differ from the vulgar somewhat, it shall not fly from all humanity, with the Tamerlanes and Tamer-chams of the late Age, which had nothing in them but the scenical strutting, and furious vociferation, to warrant them to the ignorant gapers.[15]

It has been suggested that this rather more disparaging criticism, written in the private setting of Jonson's *Discoveries*, and after Alleyn was dead, is a truer reflection of his opinion of the actor's style.[16] But even though, no doubt,

Jonson was articulating his own and others' changing tastes in performance he was more specifically criticising the *language* of the earlier plays that had required actors to respond with appropriate performances – both of which seemed to later tastes outmoded. It is a recurring response. Peter Hall, writing of Richard Burton, observes:

> Every generation has its new actor, somebody who redefines to his own age what acting is all about. He is usually thought of as more 'real' than the previous generation, who suddenly appear old-fashioned and stagy. Richard Burton in 1951 was, for me and countless others, that new actor. He spoke 'true'; but he still spoke Shakespeare. The critics of the time were greatly struck by his charisma and his obvious star quality. But many were disappointed by his understatement, his 'throwaway' naturalness. As members of the previous generation they found him deficient in rhetoric. They were both right and wrong; they were not judging him by the emotional tastes of the new generation, but by the standards of Gielgud and Olivier. I noticed exactly the same response to Gerard Philippe a few years later in France. His performances in *Richard II* and *Le Cid* enraged the French critics. But neither he nor Burton denied the form; they simply adjusted the emotion, so that the rhetoric seemed less. Today, he and Burton would seem artificial.
>
> (1993: 78)

If Renaissance audiences were clear about what constituted 'good' acting, they seem to have been equally certain in their view of what constituted 'bad'.[17] While Webster, in his Character of 'An Excellent Actor', used an analogy with music to define the positive contribution the actor made to a performance, Thomas Dekker, in his Preface to *The Whore of Babylon* (1606), employed a similar comparison to describe how a poor cast could ruin a playwright's work:

> in such consorts [casts], many of the Instruments are for the most part out of tune, and no marvel, let the poet set the note of his numbers, even to Apollo's own lyre, the player will have his own crochets, and sing false notes, in despite of all the rules of music.

Criticism occasionally focused on those actors who did nothing but 'stand like a stiff starched man' (Heywood, 1841: 29) but was most commonly directed at those who 'over-act in beaten satin' (Jonson, *The Staple of News*, Induction, 45–7). I define 'over-acting' as a performance in which the gap between the thing represented and its representation is perceived by the audience to be too great, where one becomes aware of an inappropriate level or manner of expression. However, an actor may vary considerably the *scale* of a performance without over-acting. Contemporaries referred to Edward Alleyn 'strutting' and 'stalking' as Tamburlaine, and the terms have subsequently been interpreted pejoratively to conjure up a bombastic acting style. To Elizabethans, however, 'strut' meant 'to march proudly' or 'to behave proudly or vaingloriously'. Thomas Wright claimed that 'To walk majestically (that is, by extending thy legs forth, and drawing thy body back, with a slow and stately motion) in all men's judgement usually issueth from a proud mind' (1971: 134), while Cotgrave's 1611 *Dictionary* defines a man who 'stalks' as one who 'swaggers, brags or struts it mightily'. Alleyn was presumably expansive in the role of Tamburlaine (it would be odd to play the part otherwise) and to me these terms indicate a physical performance appropriate to the role, matched no doubt by a vocal performance that was also suitably 'heightened' to harmonise with the lines Marlowe had given him to speak. (Interestingly enough, one reviewer of Toby Stephens's generally highly praised performance as Coriolanus for the RSC in 1995, wrote admiringly that he 'struts and swaggers with an electrifying physical presence' in a performance of 'charisma and courage'.)[18] I am equally certain, however, that the *scale* of Alleyn's performance was deftly tuned to the intimate nature of the Rose playhouse where he first played the part: as Ian McKellen remarked while visiting the excavations in 1989, 'Well, I don't need to over-act here.' In a recent production in the similarly intimate Cottesloe Theatre of *Titus Andronicus* (1995), another Rose play in which the leading actor is required to deliver heightened speeches from a character driven beyond the limits of pain and suffering, Antony Sher, playing the title role, demonstrated exactly how a skilled actor governs his performance to match the character's words and actions but still fit the scale of the performance space. The result was a powerful but controlled physical and vocal performance, as no doubt was Alleyn's, and both performances could be easily distinguished from the 'stentor-threated bellowings' (*ES*, IV: 254) of an inferior actor, 'hamming it up':

> Whose conceit
> Lies in his ham-string, and doth think it rich
> To hear the wooden dialogue and sound
> 'Twixt his stretch'd footing and the scaffoldage.
> (*Troilus and Cressida*, 1.3.153–6)

Mark Rylance, while acknowledging the many lessons actors have to learn about the vocal and physical aspects of performing in the space, observes that while many people had predicted the reconstruction would see a return to grand gestures, experience had shown that 'naturalness' worked well.

Around 1613–14, the King's Men presented John Webster's *The Duchess of Malfi*. Webster's play makes much of 'heightened' language that demands an appropriate level of acting, but it also has dialogue (such as that in

1.1.360–415, for example) which is so fast and conversational that a modern audience may think the actors are improvising. The play contains observed action and formal staging, but the text at times also gives guides to the actor for delicate and detailed physical gesture and opportunities for apparent engagement with the character's emotions. This mixture of styles of dramatic and theatrical languages is typical of Elizabethan and Jacobean drama in which the acting unit was at most the scene, not the act (let alone the play). Indeed, the plays are characterised by their (often abrupt) shifts of mood and tone. As the printer of the early play *Promos and Cassandra* (1578) noted, it was 'full of variety, both matter, speech and verse'. As the period progressed new modes of expression developed which added to, rather than superseded, existing modes. Inevitably, the demands on the actors kept pace, requiring them to display great adaptability. 'Consistency', 'through line' and other terms appropriate to naturalistic performance are rarely applicable to the roles Elizabethan and Jacobean actors played, in which narrative demands often take precedence over 'character logic'. As in the cinema in the early years of the twentieth century, it was clearly not only acceptable but inevitable and desirable that a range of acting styles should coexist within a single performance, and John Russell Brown's description of the acting style as 'Epic-natural-romantic-virtuoso-formal' neatly catches the variety and flexibility demanded of actors (Brown 1966: 39).

Two aspects of Elizabethan and Jacobean acting practices in particular are remote from our own experience: the companies of child actors and the use of male actors to play female roles. Both conventions are prevalent in Eastern theatre, but while studies of the Kabuki *onnagata*, or Chen Kaige's film, *Farewell My Concubine*, which traces the rigorous and often brutal training regime of the child transvestite performers of the Chinese Peking Opera, are illuminating, they nevertheless refer to a theatre culture remote from the experience of most Western audiences (Hyland 1987).

Child, or boy actors

If it is hard for us to recapture a sense of adult performance it is even more difficult where the children are concerned. Distance from our own experience, however, and a response perhaps clouded by exposure to child-stars such as Shirley Temple or the uneven quality of a school play, should not cause us to underestimate what was clearly perceived by hard-nosed adult professionals as a threat to their livelihoods and supremacy.

The boys of the children's companies were well trained, evidently often physically attractive, and provided with tailor-made plays by young, avant-garde playwrights such as Marston, Middleton and Jonson. They performed in comfortable indoor playhouses closer to the city centre and attracted a much narrower social range of audience. Their plays were supplemented by excellent music and singing – before, during and after the performances – and those audience members who wished and could afford to, could (except at Paul's) even bring a stool from the tiring-house and sit on the stage itself, smoking, chatting and generally showing off in the music-drenched atmosphere. The plays performed by the children were often strikingly innovatory and frequently made reference to other plays – taking it for granted that the audience were fully aware of the contemporary theatre scene and practice. In other words, and commercially most important of all, they offered a theatre-going experience that was distinctive and different from that offered by the adults outdoors.

The success enjoyed by the Children of Paul's (re-formed as a commercial company in 1599 following a decade in which there was no children's company operating in London) led just a year later to the formation of the Children of the Chapel at the Blackfriars. Their repertoires were distinctive. Whereas the Paul's Boys moved from Marston's urban satire to Middleton's city comedy, the Blackfriars Boys, cultivating a particular and narrow clientele of youthful gallants, courtiers and wits, developed a risky repertoire of sharp satirical 'railing' plays. They interspersed these with broader but no less provocative comedies such as *Eastward Ho!* and *The Isle of Gulls* and downright dangerous tragedies such as Chapman's *The Conspiracy and Tragedy of Byron* (Shapiro 1977; Gair 1982).

The Induction of *Antonio and Mellida*, with which the Children of Paul's possibly opened their new playhouse in 1599, brings the boys onstage to prepare for the play to come, scripts in their hands and cloaks over their costumes. Within the play that follows (and in children's plays generally) much is made of the discrepancy between the actors' physical appearance, language and role, and so it is here as the boys discuss the physical gestures that might suit the styles of language they must speak, often parodying the styles of language and delivery they associate with the adult companies:

ALBERTO: Whom do you personate?
PIERO: Piero, Duke of Venice.
ALBERTO: O, ho! Then thus frame your exterior shape
 To haughty form of elate majesty,
 As if you held the palsy-shaking head
 Of reeling Chance under your fortune's belt,
 In strictest vassalage. Grow big in thought
 As swoll'n with glory of successful arms.
PIERO: If that be all, fear not, I'll suit it right.
 Who cannot be proud, stroke up the hair and strut?
ALBERTO: Truth! Such rank custom is grown popular.
(5–15)

The 'difference' of the boys and youths who played female roles in the adult companies could be accentuated not only by costume but by juxtaposing them with the physical and vocal presence of adult male actors, while the apprentices' subservient position within the theatre company itself was commensurate with (or strikingly different from) that experienced in real life by many of the women they represented. The boys in the children's companies, however, with only other boys to play against and be compared to, were frequently furnished with styles of language and gesture directly associated with adults. The outcome was the opportunity for parody and this, clearly, was a major element in their appeal. In 3.4 of *Poetaster* the Chapel Children give a series of parodic speeches – one in 'King Darius's doleful strain', another (from *The Spanish Tragedy*) in an 'amorous strain' and one as the 'horrible fury soldier'. All the originals have not been identified, but even allowing for the satirical heightening that parody requires, the boys' performances in each instance must have reflected with some accuracy what audiences saw when they went south of the river.

Their skills did not stop at parody, however. Marston's Prologue to *Antonio's Revenge*, a tragic sequel to the comedy *Antonio and Mellida*, appeals to the audience for empathetic involvement in the action:

> But if a breast
> Nailed to the earth with grief, if any heart
> Pierced through with anguish, pant within this ring [i.e., playhouse],
> If there be any blood whose heat is choked
> And stifled with true sense of misery,
> If ought of these strains fill this consort up,
> Th'arrive most welcome.
>
> (Prologue, 21–7)

The play, like many adult plays, frequently utilises the analogy between over-acting and insincerity, and the young actors are at points in the action clearly expected to be able to express emotion in an appropriately convincing manner. In 1.5, for example, Pietro greets the news of Andrugio's death with an aside to the audience, 'Fut, weep, act, feign' followed by the stage direction (perhaps authorial, almost certainly derived from playhouse practice) 'Gives seeming passion'. Such directions are not uncommon and must indicate a distinction between the actor's performance at that moment and his performance in 2.3 where, within the performance conventions of the time, the expression of passion is clearly meant to be deemed 'genuine' by the audience.

Like their adult counterparts, the children surely employed a range of performance styles appropriate to the character, language and action that is indicated by the text at any particular moment. (Again I should stress, however, that we have no way of establishing what this range of acting styles actually looked like.) As the demands implicit in the texts of the plays they performed illustrate (Marston's *The Dutch Courtesan*, for example, written for the Chapel Children has been described as 'a play about language'[19]), they also undoubtedly displayed considerable prowess in handling complex, rhetorically figured language. In a word, they were good. Histrio, the adult actor in Jonson's *Poetaster*, is as enthralled by the Boys' performances ('Oh, admirable good, I protest') as was Jonson himself, as his epitaph to Solomon Pavey (who specialised in playing old men) shows:

> Years he numbered scarce thirteen
> When Fates turned cruel,
> Yet three fill'd zodiacs had he been
> The stage's jewel.[20]

No wonder the adults were worried. In *Hamlet*, Shakespeare refers to the adult actors' concerns about the 'little eyases' (young hawks) north of the river (2.2.337). The lines in the 1603 so-called 'bad' quarto are even more sharply focused and suggest the seriousness of the competition. In answer to Hamlet's query about why the players should be on tour rather than performing in their own playhouse, Gildenstern replies:

> Yfaith my Lord, novelty carries it away,
> For the principal public audience that
> Came to them, are turned to private plays,
> And to the humour of children.[21]

Nevertheless, there is no doubt that however good they were the children's companies were a fad and, like all fashions, could not survive without varying what they offered. Some of the children, such as John Underwood and Nathan Field (who had been impressed to join the Chapel Children at the Blackfriars in 1600, when he was thirteen) graduated successfully to become leading actors in adult companies. Others, such as Ezekiel Fenn, evidently found their talents unequal to that task and faded from view. The adults were soon providing a range and variety of dramatic performance that the boys could not hope to emulate. The boys, on the other hand, were limited by the very quality that made them attractive to audiences – their youthfulness – and that situation itself may have been changing. In 1606, when the Paul's company performed at Greenwich for King James and his brother-in-law, Christian IV of Denmark, a document refers to them as 'the Youthes of Paules', which suggests to Reavely Gair that the boys could no longer be properly described as 'children'. He speculates that 'if the early teenagers of about fourteen who took the major parts in 1599 were still with the company in 1606, they would be over twenty by now' (1982: 154), an age range more comparable with that of the older youths who played female roles in the adult companies. Admittedly, Gair's assumptions are sizeable, but to me, Middleton's city comedies, written between 1602 and 1606 for Paul's Boys and which characterised their repertoire, certainly look increasingly less like specifically children's plays'(White 1992: ch. 2 *passim*).

The Paul's company stopped regular playing in 1606. The closure was a boost for the Blackfriars Boys, as new playwrights brought them their work. But in 1608, following a series of scandals over their repertoire, the Children of the Chapel (renamed the Queen's Revels in 1604) stopped playing at the Blackfriars. The King's Men regained use of the playhouse and the key physical elements of indoor performance that had previously made the children's companies exclusive were for the first time available to paying audiences of an adult company.

Female impersonation

When he might act the woman in the scene
Coriolanus, 2.2.96

Women had appeared in plays in the medieval period, the ladies of the Stuart court did so (in non-speaking roles) in the court masques, and Italian theatre troupes who visited England to perform at court and elsewhere in the country included female performers. Professional French actresses even appeared publicly onstage at the Blackfriars in 1629; they were evidently booed by the audience, but invited later by Queen Henrietta Maria to perform at court. Indeed, soon after Charles I acceded to the throne in 1626, Queen Henrietta Maria had begun not only to commission and perform in court pastorals but, significantly, to *speak* in them as well. No English women appeared publicly on the professional stage in England, however, until after the Restoration of Charles II, when Sir William Davenant obtained the following clause in his patent for his theatre company:

> That, whereas the women's parts in plays have hitherto been acted by men in the habits of women, of which some have taken offence, we permit and give leave for the time to come, that all women's parts be acted by women.

> (*Works*, I: lxvii)

Subsequently, in 1660, a performance of *Othello* was given with, according to Thomas Jordan's Prologue, 'No man in gown, nor page in petticoat'.[22]

Some actors on the Elizabethan and Jacobean stage, such as Alexander Gough, whom James Wright described as 'the woman-actor at Blackfriars', specialised in female roles; others – such as Thomas Parsons, John Shank and Nicholas Tooley – are recorded as playing both male and female parts (Nungezer 1968). Gough played his major roles between the ages of twelve and seventeen, and although most female characters were probably played by teenagers, there were exceptions. Anthony Turner, for example, is first known from a reference to him in 1622 being 'among the chief of them at the Phoenix', and he played a number of mature male characters – such as Justice Lamby in Shirley's *The Wedding* (1626) and Old Lord Bruce in Davenport's *King John and Mathilda* (1629). However, he also took the part of a kitchen maid in Part 1 of Heywood's *The Fair Maid of the West* when it was performed at Hampton Court by Queen Henrietta's Men in 1631–2, though the maid is a minor part, and the casting may have been intentionally comic (Nungezer 1968: 382). It is unclear whether, in addition to boys and young men, companies included mature males (as had been the practice in Tudor Interludes) to play leading roles such as Volumnia, Putana, Livia or Cleopatra, though Davenant's use of the words 'men' and 'women' and Jordan's distinction between 'men' and 'pages' and his references, in the same Prologue, to 'men between forty and fifty' playing women, are interesting in this context. Observing how she will be displayed in Rome, Cleopatra employs a comprehensive playhouse metaphor, embracing both stage and audience:

> Now, Iras, what think'st thou?
> Thou, an Egyptian puppet shall be shown
> In Rome as well as I: mechanic slaves
> With greasy aprons, rules, and hammers shall
> Uplift us to the view. In their thick breaths,
> Rank of gross diet, shall we be enclouded,
> And forced to drink their vapour.
> . . .
>   saucy lictors
> Will catch at us like strumpets, and scald rhymers
> Ballad us out o' tune. The quick comedians
> Extemporally will stage us, and present
> Our Alexandrian revels: Antony
> Shall be brought drunken forth, and I shall see
> Some squeaking Cleopatra boy my greatness
> I'the posture of a whore.
>   (*Antony and Cleopatra*, 5.2.203–217)

Shakespeare's characteristic (but to contemporaries striking and innovative) use of a noun ('boy') as a verb (especially placed in the line where it is most heavily stressed) would undoubtedly have caught the audience's attention, though to what purpose we cannot be certain. If Cleopatra was played by a teenager this was a daring moment of theatrical self-reflexivity, whereas if the lines were spoken by an older actor it would have sustained the appropriateness of the *character's* image. It may also have been a direct reference to the rival children, the terms 'squeaking' and 'posture' intended to suggest the perceived vocal inadequacies and licentious physical mannerisms of those performers compared with the adults.

But as Stephen Orgel reminds us, even though 'the English stage was a male preserve . . . the theatre was not', since in addition to the offstage tasks fulfilled by women attached to the company, women attended the playhouses as members of the audience:

> The fact of the large female audience must have had important con-
> sequences for the development of English popular drama. It meant
> that the success of any play was significantly dependent on the recep-
> tiveness of women; and this in turn meant that theatrical
> representations – whether of men or women or anything else – also
> depended for their success to a significant degree on the receptiveness
> of women.[23]

Views differ on how audiences might have responded to these transvestite performances. Some critics (such as Kathleen McLuskie and Jean Howard) suggest that the convention, especially in serious drama, seems to have been generally either invisible and unquestioned or visible but still unquestioned, unless drawn to the spectators' attention. For Phyllis Rackin, the representation onstage of female characters exercising power 'radically subverted the gender divisions of the Elizabethan world' (1987: 38), while others have argued that the performances touched specifically homosexual desires in men in the audience who perceived 'the boy beneath the woman's costume' (Zimmerman 1992). Marjorie Garber, however, considers the range of responses to have been yet more complex:

> What . . . if the 'boy' of 'boy actor' fame, appropriated by some recent
> historicist critics as a sign of the homoerotic subtext of Renaissance
> theater, and by some feminist critics as a sign of female power and
> agency – what if that 'boy' were to be taken seriously as what it most
> disturbingly represents: the figure of the transvestite? . . . a destabi-
> lizer of binarisms, a transgressor of boundaries, sexual, erotic,
> hierarchical, political, conceptual.
>
> (1992: 90)

Contemporary descriptions of boys acting women are rare. In *Urania*, a lengthy prose romance published in 1621, Lady Mary Wroth used a description of an audience member's response to a boy player's performance as a woman in order to illustrate the response of one of her characters to an obvious piece of seduction:

> there he saw her with all passionate ardency, seek, and sue for the
> stranger's love; yet he [the stranger] unmoveable, was no further

wrought than if he had seen a delicate play-boy act a loving woman's part, and knowing him a Boy, liked only his action.

(Quoted in Shapiro 1989: 187)

Lady Mary seems to be a reliable witness. Ben Jonson dedicated *The Alchemist* to her, she performed in court entertainments and watched the King's Men when they played at court, and her observations presumably reflect her reaction to the professional actors she saw there or at the playhouse. Her words seem to assume that a spectator is aware of the discrepancy between the sex of the actor and the gender of the assumed character and therefore simply concentrates on the representation of action rather than of character. Furthermore, although she uses the analogy with acting to criticise her female character, Lady Mary appears in no way worried that a boy should play a woman's part. Others were less sanguine, however, and among the many charges levelled at the playhouses by their opponents, the impact of transvestite performance on both actor and spectator was the most fiercely articulated. In Stephen Gosson's pamphlet, *The School of Abuse* (1579), he asserted that theatres 'effeminated' the mind: indeed, according to Gosson, dressing like a woman was bad enough, but adopting also 'the gait, the gestures, the voice, the passions of a woman' put the actor in danger of actually becoming a woman. Four years later, Philip Stubbes repeated the charge, claiming that male actors who wore female clothing could actually 'adulterate' male gender (Levine 1986: 121). Stubbes viewed the practice with the same abhorrence as he and others did that of women dressing as men in everyday life, both practices being seen as evidence of corruption and social disorder. Stubbes wrote:

> Our apparel was given us as a sign distinctive to discern between sex and sex, and therefore one to wear the apparel of another sex is to participate with the same, and to adulterate the verity of his own kind.[24]

More worrying still for anti-theatre campaigners than the consequences for the (presumably already degenerate) female impersonators, was the possible impact on male spectators who, seduced by the performance, might lust not after the female characters portrayed (which would be bad enough), but after the boy actors who played them, therefore either transforming themselves into women or, worse, tempting them to give in to homosexual desires (Orgel 1989). The last major anti-theatre tract of the period, William Prynne's *Histrio-mastix* (1633), which was prompted by rumours of women – including the Queen – acting at court, also fulminated against the moral dangers in the boy actors playing women, listing examples of transvestism as a stimulus to homosexual acts. This, Orgel suggests, was the dominant model its opponents offered of the commercial theatre experience – that it was uncontrollably exciting and erotic, and, for male spectators, provided an erotic excitement

that was essentially homosexual. Many in the contemporary audience undoubtedly responded in such a manner to performances, but apart from the women
in the audience there were undoubtedly many adult males who either did not
note or, if they did, did not respond sexually to the boy actor, but interpreted
the convention differently. In other words, as one would expect, different
groupings in an audience would have focused on different readings of single
actions or recognised the particular significance of those actions for sections of
the audience other than themselves.

In an unpublished continuation of *Urania*, Mary Wroth made a second
reference to female impersonators. Describing a woman 'dangerous in all kind,
flattering, and insinuating abundantly' she depicts her as:

> being for her over-acting fashion, more like a play-boy dressed gaudily
> up to show a fond loving woman's part, then a great Lady, so busy, so
> full of talk, and in such set formality, with so many framed looks,
> feigned smiles and nods, with a deceitful down cast look.
>
> (Quoted in Shapiro 1989: 188)

The references to 'over-acting' and gaudy costume seem to suggest something qualitatively different from her previous description of a 'delicate'
performance, where although the spectator may have been conscious of the boy
actor's skill, identification with the reality of the dramatic situation could still
be intense. Different levels of representation, from impersonation to demonstration, such as seem to be implied by Lady Wroth, are employed by a single
actor in Jonson's *The Devil Is an Ass* (Blackfriars, 1616). The part of Wittipol,
'a young gallant', was originally played by Richard Robinson, also well known
as a player of women's roles. In Act 1, scene 6, Jonson presents an extraordinary
scene where, in return for an expensive cloak, Squire Fitzdottrel gives Wittipol
ten minutes in which to try to seduce Fitzdottrel's wife, Frances. Prior to the
meeting, however, Mrs Fitzdottrel has been ordered by her husband (who is to
be present though silent) not to reply. As soon as he realises this, Wittipol gets
his friend, Manly, to stand in his place while he, Wittipol, performs what he
thinks Frances's reply should be. Jonson's marginal direction (to aid the reader)
indicates simply that Wittipol 'speaks for her', but it would seem likely that
the actor would copy closely the gestural and vocal performance given by the
actor playing Mrs Fitzdottrel. Given that the role of Frances Fitzdottrel 'marks
a transition towards the more rounded and empathetic female representations
that were to characterize Jonson's Caroline playtexts',[25] it seems likely that the
performance of the actor playing Frances, and Robinson's imitation of that,
were both in keeping with how the part is written. In the second act of the play,
Meercraft, the duplicitous Projector, finds himself in need of someone to impersonate 'An English widow, who hath lately travelled, / But she's called the
Spaniard, cause she came / Latest from thence' (2.7.27–9). His crony, Ingine, a
secondhand clothes dealer, recommends the actor Richard Robinson ('a very

pretty fellow') and recounts the time that Robinson was brought to a feast:

> Dressed like a lawyer's wife, amongst em all;
> (I lent him clothes) but, to see him behave it;
> And lay the law, and carve, and drink unto em,
> And then talk bawdy, and send frolics! O!
> It would have burst your buttons, or not left you
> A seam.

MEERCRAFT: They say he's an ingenious youth!
INGINE: O Sir! and dresses himself the best! beyond
  Forty o your very ladies. Did you neer see him?
MEERCRAFT: No, I do seldom see these toys.

(2.8.70–8)

Consequently, in 4.3, Wittipol (Robinson) appears dressed as the Spanish Lady, wearing raised shoes to increase his height (he is announced as 'the very Infanta of the giants'). The verbal and physical performance he gives is considerably heightened in comparison with that suggested in his earlier impersonation of Mistress Fitzdottrel. Whereas that was presumably as close an imitation as possible of the 'straight' performance given by the boy playing Mistress Fitzdottrel, the performance that Wittipol/Robinson gives as the Spanish Lady seems more similar to the 'performance' described by Ingine or the second of Lady Wroth's examples. It appears that in addition to adopting a range of conventional looks and gestures, he allows his male persona to show through: both Mrs Fitzdottrel and Manly think they recognise him, though Squire Fitzdottrel is too daft to notice – to him, speaking more accurately than he knows, she is 'all her sex in abstract!' (243), a phrase further suggesting the surface nature of a performance made up of selected, stereotypical elements. In this respect, Robinson's performance as the lofty Spanish Lady resembles that referred to by Thomas Jordan in his Prologue for the 1660 performance of *Othello*:

> For, to speak truth, men act that are between
> Forty and Fifty, wenches of fifteen;
> With bone so large, and nerve so incompliant,
> When you call Desdemona, enter Giant.

This description, and the hints in Jonson's text, invoke for me a performance similar to that of a drag-artist today in which exaggeratedly female clothes are matched by masculine behaviour and voice that call attention to the actual sex of the performer. Certainly, Wittipol's dismay at the prospect of having to kiss either the decrepit Lady Tailbush (played, of course, by another youth – or perhaps an older man) or Fitzdottrel (who has fallen for 'him') derives much of its comedy from that gender confusion.

*

The transvestite performers evidently impressed the playwrights, given the number of female leading roles written for them. Some among the scores of boy players who must have worked in London during the years 1590–1642 went on to play adult male roles: Richard Sharpe, for example, the first actor to play the Duchess of Malfi, became a successful adult actor, as did Richard Robinson, while Stephen Hammerton, wrote James Wright, 'was at first a most noted and beautiful Woman Actor, but afterwards he acted with equal Grace and Applause, a Young Lover's part'.[26]

The satirist J. Cocke sourly claimed that if an actor married 'he mistakes the Woman for the Boy in Woman's attire . . . But so long as he lives unmarried, he mistakes the Boy or a Whore, for the Woman.'[27] Generally, however, audiences praised the skill of these female impersonators. When the King's Men toured their production of *Othello* to Oxford in 1610, forty years before a woman played the role, one of the spectators was struck above all by the moving performance of the actor playing Desdemona, even referring to the actor as if he had, indeed, been female:

> They also had tragedies, well and effectively acted. In these not only by their speech but by their deeds they drew tears. – But indeed Desdemona, killed by her husband, although *she* always acted the matter very well, in *her* death moved us still more greatly; when lying in bed *she* implored the pity of those watching with *her* countenance alone.
>
> (Quoted in Gurr 1992: 226; emphases added)

CASE STUDY: HARRIET WALTER ON PLAYING THE DUCHESS OF MALFI

Masks and curtains

An artist friend of mine once produced a series of drawings in which he depicted single objects in three different ways, respectively entitled Imagined, Observed and Remembered. A map of Madagascar, the lymph gland, Karl Marx's bust, etc., etc. These drawings built up into a sort of catalogue of detailed miniatures, wittily commenting on our ways of seeing. Now that I am trying to describe the process of approaching, preparing and then playing *The Duchess of Malfi* I am reminded of these drawings. At the risk of being too artificially schematic, I shall find it helpful to untangle the subjective strands of remembered experience, wishful thinking and contradictory feedback which is now my perception of the work and divide them into separate categories: the imagined Duchess of pre-rehearsal preparations, the observed Duchess as tried and tested during rehearsals, and the remembered Duchess, as called up and re-created in performance.

Imagined

Torture. Suffering. Hollow eyes. Vein-bursting grief. Children. Sacrifice. Invasion. Sexual abuse. Martyrdom. I am trying to remember my very first impressions of the role, drawn predominantly from the few productions I had seen. Unavoidably there is also a physical image in my mind of another actress playing her. She looks like Helen Mirren, Judy Parfitt, Peggy Ashcroft, Eleanor Bron. etc. [All of whom had previously played the role.] (When does a part begin to look like me? Possibly not until I stand up in rehearsals without book in hand and look into the eyes of a fellow actor who is looking at me as the Duchess.)

Another list of words: Womanly. (Up until this point I had mainly played girlish maidens in the classical repertoire.) Mother. Lusty. Reckless. Courageous. Honourable. Autocratic. Wilful. Democratic. Deceiving. Beautiful. Cunning. Dazzling. Wise. A healthy set of contradictions, but you see how hard it is to avoid value judgements? Try again. Italian. Dark eyed (I've got that bit anyway). Flared nostrils. Thoroughbred horse. Active not pensive. Hot blood. Dark, from the same crucible as her brother. During rehearsals, some of these qualities are to be clung to fiercely when all around you would drown them, others are later proven embarrassingly wrong, yet others are tantalisingly out of reach, remain beyond your scope, goading the imagination.

The pictures of other characters in the play begin to form before I know of the cast. Like people you know in a dream they are a blurred form, a presence, an effect upon you – a spirit. You cannot see their face or the colour of their eyes but you are sure you know who they are. (The process of shifting from the imagined physical presence of a fictional man or woman to accepting the actual actor playing the role is familiar to anyone who has read a novel and later sees it filmed or dramatised on TV). As news of the casting dribbles through, I begin to accommodate them in my imagined projection. The flesh and blood is getting more substantial.

Observed

Who is the play's Duchess of Malfi? The data: aside from the givens that she is sister to the Duke of Calabria and the Cardinal, of the house of Aragon in Spain, who ruled in the south of Italy, we know that she was widowed one year ago, when her husband the Duke of Malfi died, and is now ruling as Regent for her only child, the present Duke. In addition to these and other calculable or historical facts there are the hidden data within the play – John Webster's data. These can be looked for in three areas. What she says, what she does, and what others say of her. In the first category, there is a wealth of information, both direct (through her own 'deliberate' words) and indirect (the revelation of mood and motive through her subconscious imagery and rhythms). Her words become the iceberg tips, by means of which I can infer what lies beneath the surface, and negotiate the currents of her emotions.

Then there is what she does. It takes discipline strictly to separate actions from judgements – the 'what' stripped of the 'how' and 'why', but it can be very revealing of things easily overlooked. She marries her steward in secret, she lies to her brothers, she trusts Bosola. She plans an escape. Then it gets harder as after her arrest she *does* less and less, and more and more is done to her. That in itself is a clue, or at least a pointer to a possible dramatic problem to be compensated for. It is also difficult to separate actions from words. Increasingly, as her power to act diminishes, so her words become her actions. She resists, protests, punishes and stokes courage with speech and only speech, until in the final act, she is a disembodied echo.

The third area of research from the data is what other characters say of her. This is more puzzling and shifting ground since each character has a vested interest in describing her the way they do, which must be seen through and taken into account. This involves working out whether they are lying or exaggerating or telling the truth as they see it, and also considering whether that person is in love with her, or threatened by her, or in awe of her, or has any other attitude which might distort or colour their view. Is she 'an excellent hyena' or Ferdinand's 'dearest friend'? Is she 'a lusty widow' or does her particular worth 'stain[s] the time past and light[s] the time to come', as Antonio insists? These descriptions probably tell us more about the speakers than the Duchess herself, but they cannot be altogether dismissed. And what of Cariola's opinion? Yes, she's loyal and possibly biased, but Webster makes her circumspect. Her telling aside after the wooing scene seems to be the steadfast point of view of someone able to love and criticise at the same time. 'Whether the spirit of greatness, or of woman reign most in her, I know not, but it shows a fearful madness. I owe her much of pity.' Webster seems to be urging the audience to look with Cariola's eyes.

Whether the Duchess is selfish, reckless and over-sexed, or on a mission of piety and integrity is not the point. Webster seems more concerned to force us to examine the sexual hypocrisy and misogyny lying behind the male rules of society. When the Establishment is represented by an incestuous quasi-lunatic and a power-crazed prelate, we can take it that the established order is being questioned.

Learning the lines and scrutiny of the text go hand in hand. The one helps the other. I spent a fortnight prior to rehearsals familiarising myself with the words rather than learning them. I hoped thereby to absorb into my subconscious something of the world of the play, and unlock some of the Duchess's person by soaking up some of the imagery and music of her speech. Inevitably at this stage, there was much I did not understand. But then came rehearsals, discussions with other actors and the unravelling of knots. Some untie swiftly and flow into new insights, others simply get moved further down the piece of string and crop up later, more intricately tied. It's hard because you need to lay down some tent pegs or you cannot begin, but you must try and be open to admit failure and rethink things. Your developing theories may thwart someone else in theirs and vice versa. You have to stop and talk; but too much talk can lead you round in circles, and then it's time to get up on your feet again and see what happens. Nine times out of ten, practice yields more answers than discussion, however fascinating. Some of Webster's more obscure imagery must be chipped away at until, even if you haven't thoroughly 'cracked it', you have a workable *actable* possibility. Then, as in life, the inter-action with other characters modifies your behaviour. Motivations clash and the only true guide through the maze is the ever-important slogan TELL THE STORY.

For actors to maintain the inner fabric of a play over a long run it is necessary to agree on a coherent storyline, even though, like Jacobean plays generally, *The Duchess of Malfi* contains many anomalies and inconsistencies of plot and character. There can seldom be a 'correct' answer to these problems, and to demand too logical a framework can, I think, be a weakness in our response to the plays. Nevertheless, it is hard in rehearsal to avoid entirely this nit-pick-ing, since an audience may well be troubled by what may appear unconsidered loose ends: 'Why did Ferdinand wait three years before taking his revenge?', 'Did Antonio and the Duchess have three children?', and so on. In fact, how-ever hard cast and director work to find *a* coherent logic, it is almost impossible to demonstrate this clearly so as to satisfy an audience. Indeed, many of the issues it seems so necessary to disentangle may not in fact trouble an audience at all. When I saw another production of the play, after I had fin-ished my own production, I saw how little of the play's impact depends on the tying up of loose plot ends. The language of the play is its strength, it seems to me. Surrender to the sensation of that dark language (as actor or audience) and one understands with the instinct, the imagination and the emotional memory, and in this way one comes closer to the essence of the play than ever one can by intellect alone. But for the actors in rehearsal all these questions must be addressed. The resulting coherence (or agreement of incoherence) between those who inhabit the onstage world gives the actors inner clarity and conviction, and is vital in the communication of the play to its audience.

In the opening scene of the play, we learn that Antonio Bologna, the master of the Duchess's household, has just returned from a spell in the French court. We understand that some contests of horsemanship and 'chargeable revels' have been taking place. We know we are in the Duchess's court at Malfi, that her brothers are visiting and that some visitors are departing. We also discover Bosola and a bit about his history, witness his rebuttal by the Cardinal, and his acceptance of Ferdinand's bribery to spy on the Duchess. We are let in on Antonio's adoration of the Duchess. We see a polite exchange between sister and brother in which Ferdinand approaches with a 'suit to you' and 'pray let me entreat' in outward deference to her position as Prince of that territory, and with breathtaking speed we arrive at a point where the Duchess and her steward have clandestinely become man and wife despite the 'frights and threatenings' dished out by her departing brothers to deter her on pain of death from ever remarrying.

Fairly late on in rehearsals, having worked in a certain amount of detail within the scene, we realised that there was an essential factor in the story which underpinned and precipitated all the above events. A widow in those days would mourn her husband for one year, and at the end of that period of mourning, break out into society again with feasts, revels and celebrations. Webster kicks his drama off at that point of the Duchess's re-emergence into the world, when she is a prize to be won and consequently a possible temptation to Antonio, and a terrible threat to her brothers' hold over her. Webster's audience would presumably have had no difficulty in recognising the situation, but how to explain this vital context to a modern audience when the text does not provide the means? Given that later in the play there is an investiture ceremony at which the acceptable face of the Church (i.e., the Cardinal's robes) is exchanged for the less commendable military one, we hit on the idea of an opening tableau presenting the acceptable image of widowhood, i.e., a woman in a black hooded cloak which on the clash of a cymbal gets whipped off to reveal a sparkling bespangled woman bestowing a generous and life-hungry smile on her guests. At that point we would show the brothers' dismay and a sober-suited Antonio bowing in dutiful deference. Well *we* enjoyed it, but still I fear those who do not know the story may not realise the Duchess is a widow at all, until it is mentioned 175 lines in.

The Duchess gives little away in her first interchange with Ferdinand. Her speech is short and polite. However, she could be said to be asserting her authority and will in the gesture of offering personally and with a sense of fun to accompany Silvio to the Haven. Next, knowing now that they have set Bosola to spy on her, we see the brothers' two-pronged assault on her, warning against the pitfalls of any second marriage. The Cardinal laying down his will as if it were law, Ferdinand the uncool letting the paranoid misogynist cat out of the bag.

With one-liners the Duchess attempts to throw back in their faces the reflection of their hypocrisy, and at one point says 'I'll never marry'. In the text, this is a cut off line. Is this deliberate on Webster's part, or just the result of haphazard typesetting? The former could suggest that the Duchess was going on to say '. . . anyone you could disapprove of', the latter allows for the possibility that it is a bold-faced lie.

In a few exchanges we see the first clues to this complex brother–sister relationship. Ferdinand tells us they were twins, but it is so late on in the play that it can only help the actors rather than the audience. Could we use the possibility that they were super-finely tuned into one another, as twins can be? After all, when Ferdinand draws his father's poignard and threatens the Duchess with it, her silence implies she knows he means business. With poetic (or actors') licence we tentatively agreed on the following scenario:

The Duchess and Ferdinand had been reared closely until puberty. The Duchess had then been whisked off to Malfi where her husband had ruled her. Suppose she married at twelve or even sixteen and her son is of an age that he will be able at least to read a letter by Act 3, scene 4, is it not possible that but for a few fleeting visits the brother and sister have had little to do with one another for some ten years? We hear of no women in Ferdinand's life and he has an extremely jaded and vicious view of female sexuality. When they are reunited by her husband's death, she is ignorant of Ferdinand's dark feelings, but anxieties begin to creep in.

In our production, at the end of their first scene, alone together, she tried an affectionate kiss on 'farewell' ('Are we still friends?'). Ferdinand dodged it, then on second thoughts sharply returned it in the manner of a woodpecker pecking a tree. He makes a lewd remark which tricks her into laughter. Of course, 'Fie, sir!' could just as validly be said with prudish shock, but as I have said, I was trying to concentrate on the sensual woman in her. He then swings round on her – 'Nay, I mean the tongue' ('What else *could* you have been thinking of?').

When Ferdinand is gone, and the Duchess is left alone with her confidante, Cariola, the mask is dropped. I felt that the more I played the scene with the brothers with cool command, wit and the occasional unruffled smile, the more her private revelation that she had indeed experienced 'this hate' and 'frights and threatenings' would show the high stakes and need for deceit, and would also quickly tell us how shrewdly she sees through their charade. Most important of all, we get a glimpse of the scale of her courage. They more or less say 'marry and you die' and she seems to reply 'never mind them. I shall marry my steward in secret.' Mad!

'Is Antonio come?' she asks Cariola. If you don't give it away in the playing, there's no reason why an audience member who doesn't know the play should connect 'this marriage' with her steward. That then can be excitingly revealed as the wooing scene unfolds. The Duchess sets up a conversation in *double enten-dres* which she later becomes exasperated with. The situation forces her into it. She must test Antonio's willingness and his mettle and leave him the option of seeming to misunderstand her and thereby escaping his fate. The scene is delightful and dangerous both for the actors and the characters.

The marriage achieved, we are precipitated into a relentlessly fast chain of events. The Duchess gets pregnant and has a child, and throughout seems to enjoy flouting Fate. In the scene when she is given apricots to eat (Act 2, scene 1) she plays upon a knife-edge, publicly flirting with Antonio. It is as though she wants the rumour to spread. I took her line to Antonio, 'But you will say love mixed with fear is sweetest', to be a projection, a clue to her own charac-ter. This and the wilful optimism expressed in her line to Antonio in the wooing scene, 'Time will easily scatter the tempest', must carry her through the next succession of reckless actions. For Webster then throws us forward three years or so – or at least enough time for the Duchess and Antonio to have had another two children – and surely the Duchess has some inkling that rumours of her marriage might spread to her brothers in all that time?

When indeed Ferdinand does come to visit her and surprises her in her chamber, she boldly outfaces him, and her plan for Antonio's escape seems to have been up her sleeve for some time. Again in Ancona, she puts all her energies into preserving her family, and defying what is increasingly becoming inevitable – namely, her captivity. Only at this turning point does a kind of resignation set in, and as I said before, she maintains her position at the centre of the play through words and spirit rather than actions.

What can we find out about the power balance between Antonio and the Duchess? We can find in the Duchess's speeches plenty of genuine and self-explanatory statements indicating her longing for and belief in equality in love. For example 'This goodly roof of yours is too low built. I cannot stand upright in't, nor discourse without I raise it higher. Raise yourself (here a pause, hoping he would, then . . .) or if you please my hand to help you so.' And 'the misery of us that are born great, we are forced to woo because none dare woo us'. Antonio has more of a problem to surmount: fear of ambition, indoctrination, etc., but he enters into the marriage on equal grounds and thereafter is never seen to revert to old attitudes. Nevertheless, in public he is forced to continue playing out a subservient role, while at night behind closed doors he is 'Lord of misrule', father and husband. In rehearsals we looked at the possibility that this double game was creating stress and resentment within the marriage. Thus lines like 'Indeed my rule is only in the night' became invested with a certain bitter complaint. However plausible a scenario this was, we had to drop it in the interests of the more important depiction of delightful, loving intimacy, a glimpse of their rare and painful pleasure.

As the plot continues the Duchess increasingly calls the shots. 'You get no lodging here tonight'; 'you must instantly part hence, I have fashioned it already'. And later, 'I do conjure you to take your oldest son and fly towards Milan.' These are the data. Webster gives her this to say, but we also needed to draw out those moments when Antonio asserts his control over the Duchess, and there are many. In the wooing scene, for example, he passionately argues for her not to waste her life but to remarry (and in our production Mick Ford did this with what I found an almost frightening anger). When the Duchess, in a near feverish state of pregnancy, seems to be skating on dangerously thin ice, commanding Antonio to put on his hat in her presence as a bared head was a mark of subservience, he checks her with a cleverly authoritative *double entendre*.

She is better acquainted with her brothers and with what is at stake than he is, by virtue of being born and bred into their world, so it is understandable that she takes charge and fashions the plans once the heat is on. However, to the accusations some have made that Antonio too readily leaves her to her fate at Ancona, I'd say that like in the original true story it was expected that Antonio as the outsider would receive the brunt of the punishment – the Duchess being somewhat protected by her noble blood and kinship. Therefore, having boldly outfaced Bosola and refused to go with him to the brothers, Antonio takes the Duchess's suggestion with 'you counsel safely', soothes her tears, shakes her out of her despondency (it is she whose thoughts have turned to death), gives her courage and finally leaves with their eldest son believing that they are only being parted in order, like a dismantled clock, later to be brought 'in better order'.

In the scenes after her death we see him acting with courage and initiative, his only weakness being a certain innocence of the worst workings of the politician's mind. In the same way as Posthumus's and Imogen's relationship is described in *Cymbeline* ('her own price proclaims how she esteem'd him; and his virtue by her election may be truly read what kind of man he is'), I think we must believe Webster has painted in Antonio a perfect match for the Duchess, and a Duchess who would not be interested in a weak and colourless husband.

How do Bosola and the Duchess connect? With hindsight, I would say that the Duchess acts as a trigger to Bosola's conscience – but it is unfortunately a conscience that for various reasons he does not heed until she is dead. For the Duchess, Bosola comes most into focus in his various roles after her captivity – as gaoler, tomb-maker, etc. He becomes increasingly her intimate, a kind of guide through purgatory, culminating in the ultimate intimacy of engineering and witnessing her death. During early rehearsals however, we worked through more or less chronologically, and, until the final scenes, the relationship between Bosola and the Duchess is elusive and oblique. We had inklings but no theories, and as in all the best rehearsals, we learnt more from what we had not planned; not from endless theoretical discussion, but from a kind of 'truth' tested out by the actors' sensibilities and instincts *in action*.

One intriguing and memorable day's rehearsal comes to mind. We were working on Act 3, scene 2, after Antonio has left, and Bosola and the Duchess are alone together. What is Bosola's aim in this scene? For a long time we pursued the idea that he came into the Duchess's chamber having just seen a furious Ferdinand leap into the saddle and thunder off to Rome without stopping to explain anything to Bosola. Bosola, the 'speculative man', proceeds with an impromptu test of the Duchess, feeling his way. He sees through part of her 'noble lie' about Antonio's false accounting ('This is cunning') but falls for the dismissal itself, believing the Duchess was getting rid of Antonio because the game was up for him as her bawd.

With this interpretation, Bosola's speeches praising Antonio after he has left, are aimed at forcing from the Duchess some clarification of the situation and with luck the name of her husband. They are deliberate lies therefore. But there is a problem with an actor lying. It is hard to sustain a lie if the audience are not let into the secret. If it is made too obvious to them, the other characters onstage can appear foolish dupes. In Bosola's case if he is subtle enough for the Duchess, how can the audience distinguish between the actor acting well, and the character lying well? Something was sticking in Nigel Terry's (playing Bosola) craw. Our hypothetical scenario held up less well for him every time we rehearsed it. Suddenly he called a halt, saying this version was too subtle and too complicated to play. So let us try another tack: Ferdinand tells Bosola she's married and her husband's somewhere in there with her, find out who it is. Bosola enters, asks what the matter is and the Duchess instantly jumps to a fabrication concerning Antonio fiddling her accounts. Bosola knows that whatever else he is, Antonio is no cheat. Puzzled but with a hunch, he then perhaps understands some of the double-meaning in Antonio's and the Duchess's interchange, even sniffs out some of the chemistry between them, and becomes more convinced.

While he defends and later eulogises over Antonio, does he begin to mean bits of it? Which bits does he mean and which not? How easily does he suppose he can convince the Duchess of his sincerity? By raising all these questions and by trying various experiments, we learnt something important about the characters. The Duchess and Bosola are set up as having opposite attitudes to the world, based on their different experiences of it. She having had a blessed life, expects the gods to be in her favour, expects good to triumph. He, having suffered hardship, punishment and betrayal is a disillusioned man, whose low expectations of himself and of his fellow man become a self-fulfilling prophecy. But this does not make him a conniving Iago. Webster depicts a potentially good man corrupted. Why should not such a man truly see good in Antonio?

We pursued the idea that Bosola fuelled his 'performance' with genuine feeling, much as an actor does; that he identifies with the social standing and ambitions of Antonio and that this lends him a mixture of envy and approval. Spying the way into the Duchess's heart, and genuinely impressed by what he has learnt, Bosola provokes the Duchess's confession and has to feign total surprise. As I saw it, his speech after the Duchess's confession comes so close to the manifesto she would have written herself in order to justify all her actions, that it either suggests a similar credo deep within him, or that his insight into her is inspired. Either way she cannot resist him and puts total trust in him.

This scenario worked much better for both of us. Just taking the evidence of the printed page, Bosola has long, long speeches and the Duchess the intermittent line. A man interrogating a woman would allow her to speak more; but a man deliberately setting up conditions for a woman to confess what he already knows may resort to lengthy speeches to gain her trust. In bringing his problem out into the open, Nigel helped me to see that Bosola was not the only one doing the testing. All the Duchess's lines can be said as simple, defensive cover-ups or else as tests of Bosola's unconventional opinion, leading to the certainty that she need hold back no longer. Thus each character thinks (s)he is in charge of the scene. The Duchess is fatally wrong. (Curiously, when the Duchess next meets Bosola, Webster gives her no comment on what she must now know to be his betrayal. All I could do was glower at him on reading 'I stand engaged for your husband for several debts at Naples'. This had been her own invention and could only have been thrown back at her via Bosola's espionage.)

Several weeks into rehearsal a rule was emerging. Where several things could be said to be going on at once, don't try and play them all. Play each scene for its face value and Webster will provide you with a later opportunity to express the under-layer. For example, play a seeming cool when the brothers harangue you in Act 1, scene 2 and only when they have left the room show how deeply they in fact have perturbed you. Another example of this operates retrospectively. When on the point of death the Duchess is asked, 'Doth not death fright you?' she replies, 'Who would be afraid on't, knowing to meet such excellent company in the other world?', a conviction that would seem dauntingly watertight if it were not for the fact that privately to Cariola in the scene before, she has expressed unallayed doubts: 'Dost thou think we shall know one another in the other world?' I took this to be a vast clue as to how to deal with the Duchess's apparent stoicism in the face of death. Not satisfied with the idea that martyrs are somehow just different, made of sterner stuff, or in some way comfortingly reconciled with their fate, I wanted to get behind this image of noble heroine. Unless I was careful, I could be tempted into a generalised portrayal of a saintly woman with her feet six inches off the ground, having almost transcended her human existence. If people achieve this state of mind it is indeed awesome, but if unrelieved by more human touches, the character is in danger of losing us. The empathetic connection is severed, just when we should be most challenged.

But what if we follow Webster's clues? Bosola describes her as suffering 'nobly', the 'loveliness' of her tears as she seems to welcome death. But this description need not be an indication of fact. Bosola is by now attempting to sway Ferdinand from his course, to evoke pity for the Duchess. Perhaps also he has discovered his love for her and genuinely sees beauty in her now she is completely a victim. (It is not until she is truly dead and no danger that he can release his compassion – the only good Duchess is a dead Duchess?) Bosola also needs to believe in the Duchess, to recognise good in someone else is to find some good in himself. She mustn't let him down. He needs her to act according to his iconic picture of her. When during Act 4, scene 1 both Duchess and actress exercise their autonomy and become an ugly, cursing 'thing so wretch'd as cannot pity itself' it upsets Bosola's interpretation. 'Fie despair! Remember you are a Christian', is perhaps said as much for himself as for her.

By contrast to Bosola, Ferdinand reads 'a strange disdain' in the Duchess's bearing. She seems to be a canvas on which each man paints a different picture. Bill Alexander, our director, demonstrated this during one rehearsal. He got me to sit in a chair and wear as neutral an expression on my face as possible. While I thought my own thoughts, Bill asked Nigel and Bruce Alexander (Ferdinand) in turn to speak their speeches about me to my impassive mask. In this way it was clearly demonstrated how each man's projection of the Duchess was equally believable. What she is really thinking, is my job.

In seeking a logically progressive line in her attitude to death I was confounded. In the wooing scene her references to death are prettily entwined with her sexual imagery. When Ferdinand invades her room she volunteers her preparedness to die in a good cause. This is fairly conventional Jacobean stuff, reflecting a society living at constant close quarters with death. From her comment, 'This puts me in mind of death' at Ancona, and thereafter through the rest of the play, I had to confront a few inconsistencies if I was to pick a more specific path through what could become repetitious and generalised.

'I would have my ruin be sudden', she says, when the vizarded Bosola comes with armed men to arrest her. She seems to surrender with 'I am your adventure am I not', and yet in the same scene she expresses a desire to explode like a cannon, and refuses to accept tyranny like 'a slave-born Russian'. She has identified a sense of guilt which bows her under heaven's heavy hand, and yet at the end of the scene she dares to hope that 'there's no deep valley but near some great hill'. Confronted with what she believes to be the corpses of her family she expresses only a longing to die. She no longer has any mission but despite her despair, she defies madness and tries to defeat death.

Well, those are the data, and I can only conclude that all of these things are at work within the same woman, and that she swings constantly from acceptance to a frantic defiance of death. In other words she is inconsistent, and all the more human for it.

Remembered

I've tried to separate out the imagined, observed and remembered, but they will keep floating together. In retracing the route towards making choices I can't avoid sometimes describing how we played the scenes. Study and rehearsal help map out turning points and establish an emotional pathway through the play. In performance it becomes a learnt pathway which arguably one could follow on automatic like a modern air-plane following the radar signal. But in live performance, to be on automatic is to deny the enjoyment of acting, the balancing act between technique and spontaneity, and is also to rule out the possibility of the audience and your fellow performers altering your state and your plans.

It is a commonly held delusion that actors throw themselves into a make-believe world and lose themselves in it. On the contrary, to reactivate the memory of all that was learnt and decided in rehearsals and simultaneously respond to the present and actual events happening onstage, requires a super-sensitivity to the here and now and a sharp awareness of what's *really* happening – i.e., a performance to an audience over and above what we are pretending is happening. What the learnt pathway does is release one to think on one's feet; one's senses can be turned outwards to the event that night rather than turning inwards to ask 'How would I/she react to this? What am I/is she feeling now?'

The memory of the learnt pathway can be activated by little triggers both consciously selected and accidentally stumbled on. One cannot actually *feel* the Duchess's shock when one knows what's going to happen. One can't *feel* her grief when one knows it's only a play. We're not paid to feel but to pretend, and with any luck to allow the audience to do the feeling. One must, however, tap a truth, a source of emotion in oneself to fuel the pretence. It is very hard to explain how this process works. Like most actors, I'm reluctant even to try. This is not in order to mystify our 'art', but because the very mechanism we are trying to describe does not work under self-conscious scrutiny. It is a kind of combination of plumbing one's own subconscious fears, tapping a physicality of emotion, letting one's empathetic imagination free, dipping into memories, all in order to induce some kind of parallel state to the one in which one's character finds him- or herself. Therefore, the coded trigger is a very personal one. In my experience, the trigger is never foolproof, and has to be reinvented several times a week, if not daily. Not knowing whether any of it will work on this particular night, is what makes acting frightening. Concentration, energy and alertness are for me the most important requisites for performance. The triggers concentrate the mind in the wings, the energy gives you the drive on the stage when the ball's in your court, and alertness allows you to listen. Listening onstage is a very particular form of listening. Obviously you know already the information being given to you, you know how long the speech will go on for and you've already prepared your response, but some new inflection or music or pace in the delivery of another actor can set up exciting new responses in you and vice versa. A phrase will suddenly spring out at you with a new interpretation. A longer pause or a more quick-fire retort will alter the balance of a scene or jolt you out of a habit. You start twiddling the knobs: 'I was a bit quick in there . . . makes her seem too prepared, too glib. Build in some hesitation later on.' Or, 'Ferdinand said that line with a smile, maybe I should return it or he'll be suspicious.' Constantly monitoring.

To write about the past is easier than writing about the present, so it is hard to write about performance which of its nature deals with the here and now, the ephemeral. Alterations and developments are happening all the time and are too innumerable and infinitesimal to record, as well as subsequent performances of the role by other actors whose work raises more questions, opens different routes. Some obvious things changed during the run of the play, as one would expect. Fotini Dimou adapted her set from the Swan at Stratford for which it was conceived, to the Playhouse in Newcastle, a completely different layout, and radically altered it again to fit The Pit at the Barbican in London. In Stratford the wax figures presented to the Duchess were of her entire family. In Newcastle we could only hire one child, so of necessity only Antonio and the eldest son were portrayed. Various editions of the play have presented Antonio in the morbid tableau with three children or with one. In Stratford we decided to have all three. I myself had argued that I couldn't get behind 'There is not between heaven and earth one wish I stay for after this' if two of Antonio's and the Duchess's children remained alive. On the other hand, where would that leave me when I come to say 'Look thou giv'st my little boy some syrup for his cold', etc.? Well, we rather feebly put that down to a momentary mental aberration *in extremis*. With only one child in Newcastle, I felt my earlier reservation about the Duchess's suicidal impulse could be dealt with as coming at the deepest point of despair, and was more than compensated for by the pay-off in her last words being urgent practical instructions to Cariola to stay alive and look after the children she is forced to desert. From this new perspective I suddenly heard 'The apoplexy, catarrh or cough o'the lungs would do as much as they [her executioners] do' as a reminder that the child's cold could be a killer in those days.

So, a closing thought. *The Duchess of Malfi* is not the tragedy of the Duchess of Malfi for she does not need to learn the lesson of the play. Ferdinand and the Cardinal die in the dark. The play is perhaps the tragedy of Bosola. For me, anyway, he emerged as a kind of Everyman, who undermines his own capacity for good through cynicism, and comes to enlightenment too late. It is his story, it seems to me, that must arouse our pity, terror and moral anger.

CASE STUDY: JACOBEAN METATHEATRE – *THE ROMAN ACTOR*[29]

> He that will behold these acts upon this true stage, let him look at that stage whereon himself is an actor, even the state he lives in, and for every part he may perchance find a player . . .[30]

In these closing lines to his appreciation of his lifelong friend, Sir Philip Sidney, the poet and playwright Fulke Greville expressed a commonplace of Renaissance thought: 'all the world's a stage' – *theatrum mundi*. To give the metaphor theatrical life requires the acts of performing and spectating to be foregrounded and in outdoor and indoor plays from the late Elizabethan period to the closure of the playhouses it finds practical expression through a range of metadramatic and metatheatrical strategies such as dumb-shows, prologues, choruses, commentator figures and plays-within-plays. The playhouse building itself (especially outdoors) presented a physical, three-dimensional emblem of *theatrum mundi*: actors stood on the 'promontory' of the world below a 'canopy of air' and a heavens 'fretted with golden fire' and above the ghosts and demons in the 'cellarage' beneath the stage (*Hamlet*, 2.2.295–303; 1.5.159). Upon this stage-play world, playwrights explored notions of 'game' and 'earnest', illusion and reality.[31] They shifted between the double-meanings of words such as *act, stage, tragedy, play* and *perform* and, through various forms of direct address (in powerful contrast to the moments of emotional empathy between actor and spectator that made possible such a strategy), ensured that audiences were alert both to the nature of the fiction presented before them and its correspondences to their own world – to the theatricality of everyday life.

> ARETINUS: Are you on the Stage
> You talk so boldly?
> PARIS: The whole world being one
> This place is not exempted.
>   (*The Roman Actor*, 1.3.49–51)

As well as exploring philosophical notions of the 'world as a theatre', plays-within-plays offer useful insights into methodologies of performance. In order to separate them from the surrounding macro-play, the process of constructing a performance (preparing and rehearsing, the use and nature of props and costumes, the business of acting, and so on) which is normally concealed, is foregrounded. A.R. Braunmuller, commenting on the purposes of such self-conscious theatricality and its metaphorical implications, suggests that:

> Commonly, when the audience witnesses the preparations for a masque or playlet, the subsequent dramaticule (Samuel Beckett's term) appears bracketed or in quotation marks, emphasizing its own theatricality, duplicity, insubstantiality, and – by extension – that of the larger play, and – by further extension – that of the audience's own extra-theatrical existence, which might indeed be a theatre of the world or a theatre of God's judgements.
>   (Braunmuller and Hattaway 1990: 86)

It may also be argued, however, that highlighting the obvious theatricality of the play-within-a-play serves to heighten the apparent 'reality' of the surrounding action and so stimulate the audience's awareness of the way that that too has been created. As Erving Goffman puts it:

The study of how to uncover deception is also by and large the study of how to build up fabrications . . . one can learn how our sense of ordinary reality is produced by examining something that is easier to become conscious of, namely, how reality is mimicked and/or how it is faked.[32]

The Roman Actor was first performed in 1626 by the King's Men at the Blackfriars, with Joseph Taylor in the title role as Paris, John Lowin as the Emperor Domitian and John Thompson as Domitia. Taylor (?1586–1652) had joined the Company in 1619, succeeding Burbage as its leading actor, and was also a sharer in the Company. Lowin (1576–1653) was another leading actor, and Thompson was the King's Men's leading boy player. Others in the cast included Richard Robinson and, playing Domitilla, the Emperor's cousin, John Honyman, who was sixteen years old and evidently not that tall since references to Domitilla's small stature are made twice in the play.

The opening scene, set in a theatre, presents a discussion between a group of actors about the problems they face in the current political climate. Massinger had been in trouble with the authorities on a number of occasions before *The Roman Actor* and would be so again in the future.[33] In 1619, the Bishop of London intervened to delay performance of his play *Sir John van Olden Barnavelt*, written in collaboration with Fletcher, and in 1631 the Master of the Revels refused to license the original text of *Believe As You List* (Massinger rewrote it). In 1638, the censor required *The King and the Subject* (now lost) to be altered, and King Charles himself, incensed at a passage in the play referring to the contentious issue of ship money, wrote on the manuscript in his own hand, 'This is too insolent, and to be changed.' It may be, as Douglas Howard suggests, that 'changes in the political climate after the coronation of Charles . . . helped shift Massinger's attention . . . towards tragedies of power' (Howard 1985: 118): whatever the cause, there can be little doubt that this opening scene, in which a group of very well-known actors, members of the King's Men, discuss the problems they face with the ruler, must to many in the audience at the Blackfriars have thrillingly blurred the boundaries between life and art.

The Roman Actor includes three plays-within-a-play, each staged to make a particular point within the narrative, and, more generally, to comment on the contemporary theatre and its power to affect behaviour. In his *Apology*, Thomas Heywood challenged the claims of men like Gosson and Munday who saw the playhouse as an incentive to vice. Heywood recalled the story of a woman who, seeing the enactment onstage of a crime, broke down and confessed to a similar offence, and the first play-within-a-play – *The Cure of Avarice* – is cast in similar mould (1841: 57–8). Its aim is to correct the miserly behaviour of Philargus. The play is recommended to Philargus's son,

Parthenius, who despairs of his father's behaviour, by the actor, Paris, who has heard a story similar to that recounted by Heywood: as he tells Parthenius, 'Your father . . . shall be so anatomized in the Scene, / And see himself so personated . . . that I much hope the object / Will work compunction in him' (2.1.103–8).

The text of *The Cure of Avarice* gives a number of hints about its performance. Paris enters dressed 'like a Doctor of Physic', and Latinus, the actor playing the Miser (presumably dressed and made up to resemble Philargus) is 'brought forth asleep in a chair, a key in his mouth.' The setting is completed by the addition of a money-chest. The onstage, fictive audience (sitting close to, even in amongst, the Blackfriars stage-sitters, of course) behave very much as their real-life counterparts, offering comments on the action and the performers and presenting the Blackfriars audience with, in effect, an image of itself. As I noted above (pp. 62–6), audiences often found themselves engaged within the action of a play (hence the effectiveness of the controlling 'distancing' devices). Philargus, however, is characterised partly through his constant interruptions to comment on the action and by his inability to balance fiction and actuality. As Aristotle argued, in an aesthetic situation an audience may indeed be caught up in the events portrayed onstage (he actually uses a picture as his trigger-example), but their judgement impedes physical action resulting. Sane spectators are, therefore, 'at once moved emotionally by the fiction and not moved by it to act' (Belfiore 1992: 245), and only those whose judgement is impaired try to intervene physically in the action onstage. When the actors, playing a Doctor and the miser's son, try to wake the sleeping miser, first by noisily opening the chest and then by pouring cascades of gold coins (331–44), Philargus annoys the Emperor by insisting he intercede to 'defend this honest thrifty man' from the 'thieves [that] come to rob him' (337–9). Domitia, Caesar's mistress, on the other hand, is more captivated by the attractiveness of the leading actor, Paris:

> 'Tis a cunning fellow.
> If he were indeed a Doctor as the play says,
> He should be sworn my servant, govern my slumbers
> And minister to me waking.
>
> (327–30)

These lines are obviously an aside to the real-life audience, not overheard by Caesar, and mark the first step in Domitia's fateful passion for Paris. At the conclusion of the performance, although she dismisses the play ('it was filch'd out of Horace') she expands upon Paris's skill as an actor, extolling his 'tunable tongue and neat delivery'.

The actors round-off their performance with a confident couplet:

To this good end, it being a device
In you to show the *Cure of Avarice*.

Their play, however, fails totally in its purpose. Indeed, its intended subject, Philargus, criticises the play precisely because it makes the Miser see the error of his ways:

                                        had he died
As I resolve to do, not to be altered,
It had gone off twanging.

(407–9)

Pressed by Caesar to answer whether he will 'make good use of what was now presented' (431) Philargus begs to be left alone since he is 'past cure' (436). Art having failed, Caesar imposes a harsher remedy:

No; by Minerva, thou shalt never more
Feel the least touch of avarice. Take him hence
And hang him instantly.

(437–9)

Jerzy Limon has drawn attention to the close affinity between this play-within-a-play and an emblem in Whitney's *Choice of Emblems*.[34] Equipped with the motto 'Ex morbo medicina' ('The cure from disease'), the icon and epigram echo the dialogue and the implicit/explicit stage directions in the text of *The Roman Actor* concerning the pouring of the gold. As Limon observes, not only is the affinity between emblem and play 'yet another example of the impact Renaissance emblem books had on drama and literature in general in the Elizabethan and early Stuart periods', but it suggests a guide to the creators of the stage production to stress the likeness. Such a link will, however, be almost certainly lost on a modern audience (see Chapter 1 and Case Study, p. 133ff.).

The second play-within-the-play (in 3.2) is staged at Domitia's request. Not only has she taken up directing ('I have been instructing / The players how to act') but has also involved herself in preparing the performance text and, in order 'to cut off / All tedious impertinencie', has 'contracted / The tragedy into one continued scene' (131–4). Domitia's aim in staging the story of Iphis (with Paris in the lead role and the Emperor's cousin Domitilla as Anaxerete), is to humble Domitilla for refusing to acknowledge her own position as Caesar's mistress.

As in the earlier play-within-the-play, the behaviour of the onstage fictional audience reflects that of the actual one, and Domitia's comments provide a gloss on what is performed: she refers to Paris's 'shape', his 'most suitable . . . aspect' of a 'despairing lover' and the 'seeming late fall'n, counterfeited tears' on his cheeks that were her idea (149–52). She praises his opening speech for the 'feeling' with which it is delivered; indeed, (though she is a somewhat biased critic) Domitia notes that 'he weeps' (either forgetting the fake tears she herself contrived, or suggesting the actor's ability to produce real ones) and admits that she too is close to tears. In fact, like Philargus earlier, Domitia finds it difficult to keep from intervening in the action. When the Porter, played by the actor Latinus with a 'churlish look', berates Iphis, Domitia interrupts, and Caesar has to remind her that the action is 'in jest' and the actor is merely playing 'his part'. When Domitilla, Caesar's cousin, enters as Anaxerete, however, Domitia identifies a very close resemblance between Domitilla's everyday behaviour and her role: 'That's her true nature, / No personated scorn' (246–7). As the play proceeds, Domitia becomes still more engrossed, particularly when Iphis threatens to hang himself and she calls on the others to restrain him. This interruption, unsurprisingly, brings the play to a halt. Caesar reminds her again that it is only a play, while Paris, stepping out of character, points out that 'I ne'er purposed, Madam, / To do the deed in earnest' (285–6). Distraught, Domitia leaves the stage.

The third inset-play is performed at Caesar's command, following his discovery of Domitia's infidelity with Paris who, though reluctant to succumb to the seduction, is given little opportunity by Domitia to resist. This moment of discovery is itself treated in an overtly theatrical manner. Domitia decides to take on the role of actor as well as that of director, her progress from spectator to author-director to director-performer marking her increasing desire to enact her fantasies and so make them 'real'. She has cast Paris in the role of 'Trojan Paris' opposite herself as Helen, and he and she perform to her instructions: 'Kiss me. Kiss me again. Kiss closer' (4.2.102–3). They are unaware that their rehearsal has an audience, however, and that their actions are observed from the upper level by Caesar (who casts himself as Helen's betrayed husband, Menelaus) and other courtiers, whose location on the balcony reflects that of high-paying members of the actual audience. Caesar's descent to the main stage is covered by seven lines, the stage direction that Domitia is 'courting Paris wantonly' indicating the stage business that occupies the audience's attention until Caesar is ready to appear. Seven lines (about twenty seconds) provides about the minimum time (by my calculations using the Inigo Jones reconstruction) to cover a descent and so, if the text matches performance closely, the length of the speech may reflect the speed and energy of Caesar's move to the lower stage to make his entrance. Caesar's lines 'While Amphitrio / Stands by, and draws the curtains' (112–13 – which refer to another mythological story of adultery), are evidently spoken as Caesar draws back a hanging as he enters. This entrance was presumably through the central door, which was used, I suspect (indoors and out), less often than the two flanking doors, and usually for particularly significant entries. The stage direction that Paris 'Falls on his face' both enforces the impression of surprise caused by Caesar's entry and further strengthens the sense of the terror the Emperor exerts.

Caesar's response to the discovery of this 'base act' (125) is to have Aretinus strangled, Domitia conveyed to her chamber and the other three women (Julia, Caenis and Domitilla) who, with Aretinus, told him of Domitia and Paris's assignation, imprisoned for what he assumes to be their complicity in the deception. Caesar then orders Paris to present a performance of a further play from the actors' current repertoire, *The False Servant*, in which Paris plays the title role. Three actors enter – 'Aesopus, Latinus, a Boy dressed for a Lady'. Only four boy actors are listed in the cast list attached to the published text, and so this is presumably one of those, doubling a part. Domitia exits 13 lines earlier than the other three female characters, which may suggest that it is Massinger's aim that the actor who played Domitia should now return to play the Lady (Fotheringham 1985). Caesar immediately relieves Aesopus of his part as the 'injured Lord', husband of the Lady, claiming he did not 'perform it to the life' and that he 'can perform it better' himself. Removing his robe and laurel wreath Caesar puts on his (clearly non-Roman) costume:

> This cloak, and hat
> Without wearing a beard or other property
> Will fit the person.
>
> (226–8)

Aesopus reminds Caesar that he will in fact need one prop – a sword – and bids him lay aside his own and use the stage weapon provided:

> a foil,
> The point and edge rebutted, when you are
> To do the murder.
>
> (228–30)

Caesar refuses, on the grounds that 'in jest or earnest' his own sword never parts from him. This ominous moment, with its repetition of these particular terms, recalls the fatal blurring of fiction and actuality that has characterised the previous inset-performances, and signals the climax to the play as a whole. The Lady and her Servant act the seduction scene (imitating very closely, I imagine, but still being distinct in manner from, the physical actions of Paris and Domitia), watched by the cuckolded Lord (played by Caesar). If the Lady *is* played by the boy who played Domitia, therefore, the same actors in effect play out the seduction scene again. The first time it was ostensibly in game but actually (certainly for Domitia) in earnest; now it is ostensibly in game, but a game completed in earnest when Caesar – prompted by Aesopus ('Now Sir, now') – enters into the action and (despite his earlier claims that he will prove a competent actor, and overcome presumably by the repetition of the earlier scene) forgets his lines – but not his actions:

CAESAR: O villain! thankless villain! I should talk now,
But I have forgot my part. But I can do,
Thus, thus, and thus.
PARIS: Oh! I am slain in earnest.

(281–3)

Caesar's speech over Paris's body completes the theatrical image:

but as thou didst live
Rome's bravest actor, 'twas my plot that thou
Shouldst die in action, and to crown it die
With an applause enduring to all times,
By our imperial hand.

(296–300)

The scene concludes with 'A sad music, the Players bearing off Paris body, Caesar and the rest following.'

For the performance of these plays-within-a-play at the Blackfriars, the central entrance and an area of the stage immediately in front of it may have been used as a distinctive performance-space-within-a-performance-space. This stage space, in conjunction with the upper level (jointly occupied by audience and actors and, when used for acting, frequently associated with 'observations') and the presence of the onstage audience must have been a further means of 'placing' the inset play within, but separate from, the macro-play/performance surrounding it. Such a use of a stage-within-a-stage (wherever and however configured) would echo back to similar tactics in earlier plays and carry appropriate resonance: the revenger in *The Tragedy of Hoffman* (c. 1602; revived in the 1620s) who rigs up a small stage space in which to hang the corpse of his father and his killer, Otho, for example; or further back to *The Spanish Tragedy* in which Hieronimo 'knocks up a curtain' before mounting his final, fatal show (4.3).

In Act 1, scene 3 of *The Roman Actor*, Paris provides a spirited defence of the theatre and acting, arguing that plays deter audiences from licentious acts by the portrayal of the terrible consequences, inspire them to acts of virtue by the presentation of heroic deeds, and never allow villains to escape unpunished. To what extent the three playlets support these arguments is questionable. The first fails to affect Philargus at all, the second reveals both Domitia's failure to distinguish the performer from his role and her sensual response to the actor, and the third not only proves an incitement to violence, but as Paris has apparently learned nothing from playing the part on numerous occasions it, like the preceding playlets, seems to question the power of the theatre to affect behaviour for the better. Indeed, Martin Butler describes the play as 'the most anti-theatrical play of the English Renaissance', in showing the effects of play-acting to be 'disruptive, mischievous and downright subversive' (1985: 160, 159).

It seems to me possible, however, that what Massinger is trying to say to a state censorship wary of the influence of the theatre is that it should not overestimate that influence; that Philargus and Domitia are both clearly reprobate and obsessive characters, whose behaviour and attitudes have clearly not been created by exposure to plays, and who are unable to benefit from the opportunity to learn from what they see performed. They *know* that what they see is an enactment (the point stressed by Domitia's role in setting up performances) but, unlike others in the audience who watch in turn transfixed by what they see (Paris *must* be convincing) and yet alert to its nature as a play, they become so immersed that they fail to maintain a sense of the event for what it is. The actions of these characters further demonstrate that if vice is so deeply embedded it cannot be supplanted through the agency of theatrical performance and that, by logical extension, neither can true virtue. In respect of the final playlet, Paris *is* aware of the implications of his actions. It is clear that it is Domitia who forces the issue. Paris, as his speech to Caesar reveals (4.2.192–7), has the Emperor's best interests at heart, even when that best interest seals his own fate: the actor is ever the King's man.

4

PALACES OF PLEASURE

Outdoor playing spaces and theatre practice

Playhouses

Drama critics often comment in their reviews on the costume and stage-setting of a production, sometimes remark on its lighting and (more rarely) its sound design.[1] It is unusual, however, except on rare occasions when a new theatre space is being inaugurated, to find much detail given of the larger relationship of stage to audience, or reference to the dynamic relationship between the physical structure of the theatre building and the performance. Yet from the point of view of those engaged in staging plays these issues are of prime importance, whether deciding the nature of a new performance space, how to deal with a fixed space, how best to employ a flexible space where the opportunity exists to make choices, or how to transfer a production conceived for one space to another, possibly very different, venue (Bennett 1990: 136–7). A review of a recent production at the Gate Theatre in London of Hauptmann's pioneering naturalistic epic *The Weavers* referred to its large cast of twenty-five and described how:

> Authentic looms fill the stage, the weavers are herded together like half-starved cattle and we even feel the ground shake as the workers gather outside the factory-owner's house and beat the walls with staves.
>
> (*Guardian*, 30 October 1996)

Theatre historians in years to come who uncover such records are likely to be bewildered if they learn from other sources that the play was performed on a small stage in a theatre over a pub and presented to a capacity audience of under one hundred.

The shape, size and operation of Elizabethan playhouses has received such attention over past years that to rehearse the information here might seem superfluous. Discussion of the performance spaces available to English Renaissance playwrights is essential, however, if we are to explore how a play *might* have been staged and to sharpen the theatrically oriented questions we ask of it. Perhaps the most significant event in a story too complex to be treated adequately here (see Gurr 1996) occurred in 1594, when the Privy Council limited the permitted acting companies in London to those patronised by the Lord Admiral and Lord Chamberlain respectively. From that date these companies became associated with specific playhouses: the Admiral's Men with the Rose (until 1600) and then with the Fortune; the Chamberlain's Men with the Theatre (until 1597) and the Globe from 1599 (and, from 1608, with the indoor Blackfriars, too). Touring consequently became less necessary and records of travelling by the Admiral's and Chamberlain's companies between 1594 and 1603 are markedly thinner than prior to 1594, helped further no doubt by the absence of plague closures between early 1596 and March 1603. From 1594, therefore, a playwright who could for some reason be confident that his play would be performed at the Rose, for example, or subsequently at the Globe or Fortune (and later at the Red Bull or Phoenix) knew not only the particular talents of the likely cast, but the nature of the stage and the audience. As the Printer of *The Two Merry Milkmaids* (1619), staged to mark the arrival of the Company of the Revels at the Red Bull, observed:

> Every poet must govern his pen according to the Capacity of the Stage he writes to, both in the Actor and the Auditor.

Nevertheless, staging arrangements within individual playhouses may have changed from day to day, depending on the requirements of particular plays or which version of a script was being used. With a different play being performed each day, it would seem that effects beyond those that could be easily achieved would have had to be kept to a minimum. Moreover, plays throughout the period were frequently presented in other locations, such as the company's own alternative venue, one of the various royal palaces, an Inn of Court, a civic function, or when the companies were touring away from London and using guildhalls, courtyards and rooms in inns. Such an assortment of venues must frequently have involved practice that diverged to different degrees from usual playhouse custom and have required still further flexibility in attitudes to staging.

In 1576, James Burbage and his brother-in-law, John Brayne (a grocer, who provided most of the capital) opened the Theatre, a polygonal open-air playhouse situated in the suburb of Shoreditch in the north-east of London. The Burbage family made an indelible mark on the history of the English theatre: James, a one-time carpenter turned actor (he appears to have been one of the leading actors of the Earl of Leicester's Men) and his sons Richard – who became one of the two most celebrated actors of the period – and Cuthbert, who succeeded his father as a manager of sorts for the King's Men. The year 1576 has subsequently become a common datum point for books and courses on Elizabethan theatre. But John Brayne's place in the history of playhouses deserves wider recognition, for it was he who, in 1567, paid a carpenter, John Reynolds, to construct a playhouse at the 'farme house called and knowen by the name of the Sygne of the Redd Lyon' in Stepney. Documents published in 1983 revealed that this was not, as had been previously thought, an inn used as an occasional performance space, but a real farm, and that Brayne's project was to erect there the first purpose-built playhouse in London. Fortunately for us, the Elizabethans were zealous litigants, and much of our knowledge of their theatres is derived from legal records. In 1569, Brayne took his carpenter to court, and the case records contain particulars of the proposed building. The details are scanty, but in them one finds the essential characteristics of the open-air playhouse as it existed until an Order of Parliament in 1642 decreed the destruction of these palaces of pleasure (Loengard 1983).

Brayne instructed Reynolds to construct a 'Skaffolde or stage for enterludes or plays'. This platform was to be 'in height from the grounde fyve foot' (the only precise reference to the height of an Elizabethan stage in any surviving document), 'in lengthe . . . fortye [a word deliberately blanked out] foote . . . and in bredthe . . . thirty foot' – dimensions close to those of $43 \times 27\frac{1}{2}$ ft specified in the Fortune Contract (1599; the text is printed in *ES*, II: 436–9). The Red Lion was to have a trap-door in an unspecified location on the stage and, to the rear of the stage, a turret 30 ft high, apparently separate from the stage structure, but secured to it. Puzzlingly, only one floor was to be inserted in the turret, 7 ft below the top – in other words 18 ft above the stage. Why? If it was to house spectators they would not, as Peter Thomson notes, either 'have felt (or been) safe', and he surmises that:

> If the purpose of the tower, as on the face of it must have been the case, was to provide the actors with a 'tiring-house' and privileged spectators with the chance of seeing and being seen, Brayne would have been well-advised to add a lower floor-level, some eight or nine feet above the stage.
>
> (1992: 58)

Scott McMillin sees a further purpose for the tower:

> The turret could also serve for flying effects, and I suspect its primary purpose was to put a flag high in the air on performance days, visible for miles around.
>
> (1992: 164)

There are cheaper ways of hoisting a flag, however, such as the ship's mast Henslowe bought to fly the banner at the Rose. I assume, like Peter Thomson, that one lower level (at least) was planned, but the Red Lion turret, like other aspects of later playhouse design and function, remains a mystery. Indeed, it is useful to encounter early in this discussion the fact that much evidence for the physical characteristics of playhouses appears contradictory, especially when we try to square it with our notions of contemporary theatre practice or even with what the surviving texts seem to suggest. There are still considerable gaps in our knowledge waiting to be filled.

Nine years after he embarked on the Red Lion venture, Brayne, in partnership with his brother-in-law, James Burbage, invested a considerable sum of money in building the Theatre in Shoreditch, no doubt reassured by the royal patent granted to Leicester's Men, Burbage's company, by the Queen in 1574. The substantial financial outlay suggests business confidence, but while the Theatre's three-tiered structure of galleries was permanent, the fact that the stage and turret could possibly be dismantled to clear the space for other entertainments, suggests business caution. With the commercial theatre still in its infancy, such wariness was prudent.

During this period the population of London expanded rapidly (from perhaps 180,000 when the Theatre opened to 350,000 when the theatres were closed) and the popularity of play-going grew equally rapidly, especially among the well-to-do (Salingar 1991: 213). In 1577, two other playhouses opened. One, the Curtain, was built close to the Theatre, while the other was erected in Newington Butts, then a village south of Southwark and the site of butts ('targets') for archery practice, and perhaps too far from the city to attract large enough audiences: no record survives of performances there after 1594 (Ingram 1992: 150–81). The next phase of theatre-building was located in the area close to the southern end of Southwark Bridge (the only permanent crossing over the Thames) and already the site of other entertainments with bull- and bear-baiting arenas as well as a large number of brothels. It was also, like the northern suburbs, in the liberties, and so outside the control of the city authorities. Three playhouses were opened in Southwark before the end of the century: the Rose in 1587, the Swan in 1595 and the Globe in 1599. Steven Mullaney comments on the importance of this marginal location in giving the playhouses:

> a liberty that was at once moral, ideological, and topological – a freedom to experiment with a wide range of available ideological perspectives and to realize, in dramatic form, the cultural contradictions of its age.
>
> (1988: ix–x)

Plays were performed every day except, usually, on Sundays, and (though the constraint was not always fully observed) during Lent.

Written records survive – such as the builder's contracts for the Red Lion, Fortune and Hope, and Philip Henslowe's *Diary* – that document the physical nature and managerial practices of outdoor playhouses. The visual evidence includes maps and panoramas but the most substantial pieces currently available are the De Witt drawing of the Swan and, more significant still, the records of the excavations of the Rose playhouse undertaken in 1989. Indeed, the discoveries at the Rose site transformed thinking about the open-air theatres more than any other single piece of evidence that has emerged since the playhouses were demolished. Rather than clarifying matters, however, the excavations revealed a number of significant differences between the Rose's physical structure and the picture of a generic playhouse that had previously been constructed. In fact, put together, the existing written and visual evidence is frequently contradictory. It denies any notion of *the* Elizabethan playhouse, replacing it with a plurality of structures of different sizes and shapes that presumably reflect changing experience and demands. This inevitably complicates any attempt to draw generalized conclusions about the buildings themselves from the explicit and implicit clues within plays, but there remain enough similarities in staging conventions to allow us to talk, though only in guarded terms, about their theatre practice. Furthermore, although I have separated into two chapters the theatre practice of open and indoor playhouses (by which I mean the ways they used music, properties, stage effects, costume, conventions of lighting, and the deployment of the stage space), and although towards the end of the period clear distinctions were observed between the two kinds of venue, at no time was an absolutely exclusive line drawn between them. Actors and plays moved between the two types of playhouse (though the considerable implications of this remain largely unexplored), and parts of my discussion could sit with equal ease in this or Chapter 5. But the existing evidence suggests there *were* different emphases and opportunities – more spectacle, battles and processions in the open air, fewer large scenic constructions but more intimate scenes and experiments with light indoors, for example – and I shall flag these where necessary.

Johannes De Witt was a Dutch visitor to London in 1596, who sent a sketch of the Swan in a letter to a friend, Arend Van Buchell, who copied it into his commonplace book (see Figure 1). Only the copy survives. The information the drawing contains, therefore, is not only secondhand but mediated by the level of skill De Witt and Van Buchell might or might not have possessed as artists, and by whatever changes might have been introduced during the copying.[2] There is also only one extant text of a play – Thomas Middleton's city comedy, *A Chaste Maid in Cheapside* (1613) – known to have been performed at the Swan against which to test the illustration, though the play's demands are entirely consistent with those features illustrated in the drawing.

A few years before De Witt visited the Swan, the English writer George Puttenham described Roman theatres in his study of rhetoric, *The Arte of English Poesie* (1589).[3] Puttenham identified the key elements of the ancient theatre as 'scaffolds or stages of timber, shadowed with linen or leather', with 'sundry little divisions by curtains as traverses to serve for several rooms where

Figure 1 Johannes De Witt's sketch of the interior of the Swan playhouse, *c.* 1596, as copied by Arend Van Buchell. Mark Rylance observes: 'the sketch . . . gives a clear impression of the actors' physical presence on and around the bench. Indeed, it might be said that the actors' expressive gestures are the real focus of [the] drawing' (1997: 170). (Reproduced by kind permission of the University Library, Utrecht, Ms. F.132r.)

[the actors] might repair unto and change their garments and come in again'; there was a 'place appointed for musicians to sing or to play' and 'benches and greeces [steps] to stand or sit upon, as no man should impeach another's sight'. Puttenham noted that the 'great magnificence of the Roman princes and people' led to their theatres being 'sumptuously built with marble', and that they were also used for displays of fencing, 'digladiations of naked men', 'practices of activity and strength' and 'baitings of wild beasts' (1938: 36–7). Apart from a few details, anyone reading Puttenham's description could easily take it for that of a London public playhouse, such as the Theatre, Rose or Curtain, which he might have visited. De Witt clearly saw the similarity: 'its form resembles that of a Roman work', he wrote of the Swan (quoted in Gurr 1992: 132), and accordingly labelled the different parts of his drawing of that playhouse in Latin.

The drawing shows a circular building (probably, in fact, a twenty-four-sided polygon) with a tiled roof, largely open to the sky. At the rear is the tiring-house (*mimorum aedes* = house of the actors) in front of which a platform stage juts out into the yard. What appears to be a lean-to roof, supported by pillars, covers part of the stage. The audience at an outdoor playhouse either stood in the yard (or possibly sat on the ground when it was not crowded or wet), entry to which cost one penny; the spectators for whom Shakespeare invented the term 'groundlings'. Those who could afford it paid extra to enter the galleries that surrounded the yard and stage. The excavations of the Rose (a fourteen-sided polygon, about 74 ft in diameter) revealed a particularly unexpected feature: its yard was flat in the area closest to the stage, but from a point about midway between stage and galleries sloped upwards at an angle of about fourteen degrees. The gradient presumably provided a run-away for rain water but must also have helped those at the back to get a better view. The De Witt drawing's label *planities sive arena* ('flatness or arena'), however, may suggest that the yard at the Swan was level:

> *Planities* is a neutral word, without theatrical reference in the Roman world, whereas *arena* is associated with the most violent and the most acrobatic of Roman entertainments. There is just a hint in the pairing of the two words that the flatness of the yard was, during De Witt's visit, used by the actors as well as the spectators. We do not know that the yard was ever used during performances, but the possibility that it was is strong.
>
> (Thomson 1983: 40)

Early performances at Globe 3 (like its predecessor, a twenty-sided polygon, 99 ft in diameter) have demonstrated how easily and effectively the actors can employ the yard and interact with spectators there (though views among the performers themselves differ on this point, some finding, for example, that it diffuses focus too much). Despite the absence of hard evidence either way, I cannot believe that a desire for novelty and the players' inventiveness would not have resulted in the area being used as a further performance space.

De Witt shows three galleries for spectators. He labelled a section of seats near the stage in the lowest gallery *orchestra*, defined in Cotgrave's 1611 dictionary as the place reserved for the most important in the audience 'between the stage and the common seats', a term used of the Roman theatre but not found in any other contemporary description of an Elizabethan playhouse. De Witt's use of the word seems to indicate that these seats, away from the bulk of the standing crowd and near the stage, were among the most expensive, and probably the 'Gentlemen's rooms' noted in the Fortune and Hope contracts. Early experiences at Globe 3, however, have found this a less than satisfactory vantage point. This may have much to do with the differences between the original actors and their modern counterparts in their use of the stage space, or it may be because the seating arrangements themselves are not differentiated in terms of space and level of comfort from those elsewhere in Globe 3. If the location were to be distinguished in terms of its facilities (and clearly seen to be so by the rest of the audience, as it is in the equivalent position immediately above in Globe 3's middle gallery) the trade-off between position and conspicuous privilege might be more understandable and attractive.

The middle gallery in De Witt's drawing is labelled *sedilia* ('seats') which clearly indicates a seated section, though possibly a less desirable one than that below, contrary, however, to my own spectating experience at Globe 3. The upper gallery is labelled *porticus* ('walkway'). De Witt illustrates the facilities here in the same way as he does the degrees (tiered benches) in the lower galleries, but it may be that he wishes his caption to indicate that here spectators might stand on the benches (Puttenham's 'greeces') to get a better view: there are a number of references that suggest there was provision for both standing and seated spectators in the covered galleries. It is also possible, however, that the label refers to the access passage behind the seats at second and third gallery levels.

The stage

The surviving evidence suggests that the stages at the Red Lion, Boar's Head, Fortune and First Globe were rectangular and possibly of similar size – approximately 43 ft × 27½ ft (13 m × 8.4 m).[4] The Rose stage, however, was revealed as an irregular hexagon, like two trapezoids joined along their longest sides, one trapezoid projecting into the theatre's yard and tapering from a width of about 36 ft 9 in. (11.2 m) where it intersects the playhouse frame, to 26 ft 10 in. (8.2 m) at the front edge and (following Henslowe's alterations in 1592) intruded about two-fifths of the way into the yard (18 ft 4 in.; 5.6 m) as opposed to the 'middle of the yard' for the Fortune stage (and possibly others, too). What the Rose excavations did not show, however, was whether its tiring-house wall was built straight along the centre of the hexagon, or if it followed the angled line of the rear bays to produce three walls, each presumably with an entrance in it. It has been suggested that the wording of the Fortune contract leaves open the possibility that the stage there (and therefore by implication at the Globe) was also not rectangular: having instructed the builder, Peter Street, that the stage should be 'in length Forty and Three foot of lawful assize and in breadth to

116

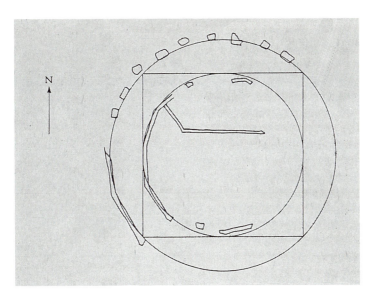

Figure 2 Simplified diagram by John Orrell of the 1587 Rose playhouse. Excavations in 1989 revealed the yard, which sloped towards the stage, was covered in mortar, on top of which was a thick layer of clinker – mixed with hazel-nut shells (a popular snack with audiences). Note the tapered stage and (possibly) angled walls of the tiring-house. (Reproduced by kind permission of John Orrell.)

extend to the middle of the yard of the said house' (i.e., 27 ft 6 in., 8.4 m), the contract adds that the stage should be 'in all other proportions contrived and fashioned like unto the stage of the said playhouse called the Globe', a phrase which seems to include more than just the height of the stage. Michael Holden believes that the Globe stage (certainly the Second Globe stage) also tapered towards the front edge, since the 'vertical sightlines made the downstage corners of the square stage invisible to the upper tiers at the side', a view supported by many theatre practitioners with experience of thrust stages and the problems they present with sightlines.[5]

The size of the stages at the Boar's Head, Globe and Fortune (and perhaps other playhouses such as the Swan), around 1,200 sq. ft (111 sq. m.) in area, made them eminently suitable for large-scale scenes of battle, or processions, or for showing multiple locations, but they also had to accommodate more intimate scenes for two or three people. This might have been achieved by locating such scenes near a space-defining element of the permanent setting – doors, pillars, balcony – or the action might be focused around a scenic item introduced for a particular scene, such as the bench shown in the De Witt drawing, one of the booths or tents to which reference is frequently made, Dido's tomb listed among the properties of the Admiral's Men, or the Arbour probably used in *The Spanish Tragedy* (see Case Study, p. 133ff.). Green rushes were strewn on the stage, indoors and out.

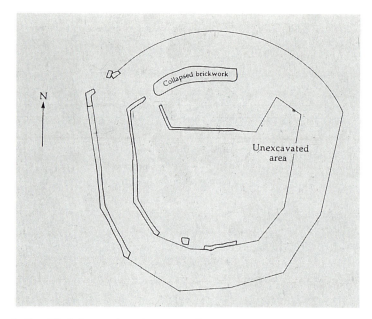

Figure 3 Simplified diagram by John Orrell of the alterations made to the Rose in 1592, to extend the yard and side galleries and enlarge the stage (which was painted, though it is not known in what colours). It appears likely that the yard was levelled also. The changes appear to have increased the Rose's capacity from around 2,000 to 2,400. Evidence seems to indicate the presence of a roof over the stage, but it is unclear whether the 1592 alterations included posts to support such a roof, since plays performed at the Rose before 1592 seem to require stage posts (see Gurr 1992: 124–31). (Reproduced by kind permission of John Orrell.)

Entrances and exits

The De Witt drawing shows two entrance doors in a flat tiring-house wall. Stage directions such as 'Enter at one door . . . at another door' are common, suggesting the effect of balanced or opposed stage images that could be created by the use of two entrances, and would sustain the antithetical structure common to the language and action of many plays. The majority of other commercial playhouses (such as the First and Second Globes, the Rose, the Fortune, the Blackfriars and Phoenix) appear to have had an additional central opening. This might have been closed with a curtain that could be drawn, a fixed hanging, even doors, or perhaps each of these at different times: the curtains at the rear of the stage in Kirkman's *The Wits* look to me from the drawing to be folded over at each corner as if temporary (Foakes 1985: 160). Whether the central entrance was used for entrances and exits of specific importance (such as the comings of kings or the goings of couples at the ends of comedies) and whether, as Andrew Gurr speculates, the evident use of hangings in the central entrance throughout the period as part of the Clown's appearance may be a carnivalesque inversion of their normal use, or, indeed, whether there was any consistency in their use at all, is unknowable (Gurr 1992: 146–7).

Stage directions indicate that some kind of concealment and discovery of characters and objects was at times required: Dekker's *Whore of Babylon*, for example, written for the Fortune, has an opening dumb-show in which the Prologue, 'draws a curtain, discovering Truth in sad abiliments [clothes], uncrowned, her hair disheveled and sleeping on a rock'; Volpone's stash of gold (Globe) or Faustus's study (Rose/Fortune). None of the contracts, however, specifies the provision of an 'inner stage', a feature which is more the product of a nineteenth-century, proscenium-focused imagination than actual contemporary practice. The instances of use for a 'discovery' (at outdoor and indoor playhouses) are limited, for obvious reasons. Not only does it go against theatrical common sense to play scenes too often within the *frons* (and commercial common sense, too, if it puts them out of sight of high-priced ticket holders), but the energy of a thrust stage is to take the actor forward into the midst of the crowd: actors at Globe 3 talk of feeling as if an invisible hand is pushing them forcefully out from the rear doors towards the audience. Only sixteen out of 519 scenes known to have been performed at the Globe required any kind of discovery space. These scenes are found in nine out of twenty-nine plays, and of those seven require the space only once.

Above the stage

De Witt's drawing shows a gallery occupied by eight figures, situated above the doors in the tiring-house wall. At the time De Witt visited the Swan it seems likely that the gallery was used predominantly as a place for privileged members of the audience – known as the Lords' rooms and accessed via the tiring-house. It would also have provided an acting area. Evidence indicates that the Rose had such a playing space, and 45 out of 276 extant plays written during the period the Swan was in use require a performing area 'above'. An upper level not only provided variety and flexibility by adding a vertical dimension to the horizontal and lateral movement on the main stage, but could also be used symbolically in a fusion of 'game' and 'earnest', ascent and descent, that matched the vertical sociology of the playhouse building itself. In 2.2 of *Women Beware Women* (?1621, ?Globe/?Blackfriars) the combination of levels provided a simultaneous image. On the main stage, Livia and the Widow, Bianca's mother-in-law, play chess, a game in which the aim is to 'mate' the King by means of strategy. At the same time, the 'earnest' is enacted on the upper level as the Duke/King, in a display of strength, rapes the pawn, Bianca, protected by the queen/quean/whore Livia. This elevated position is frequently used as one from which characters observe the main stage action as part of the metatheatrical structure of many plays (as in *The*

Roman Actor) and, throughout the period, in plays such as *The Spanish Tragedy* (*c.* 1589) and *The False One* (1620), it is the position from which characters watch the plays and masques within plays. In *Women Beware Women*, it is from this vantage point that the Duke and Bianca view the final masque before, symbolically, descending to the main stage, where they meet their deaths, joining the tableau of dead 'wretched things' with which the play concludes. The distinction between upper and lower levels therefore frequently carries hierarchical connotations, and there are obvious political and satirical implications in the association of characters operating from the balcony with those members of society who normally occupied the same or adjacent seats in the playhouse.[6]

In effect, therefore, the Elizabethan and Jacobean actors (in the private playhouses even more than in the public) performed in the round, if a numerically unevenly distributed one, and the vast majority of references to theatre spaces are couched in terms of circles and spheres. Such a configuration of the audience has implications for the staging of action right at the rear of the stage, whether above or below, though for only a very small percentage of spectators for a very small percentage of a performance. This is particularly true if the rear wall is flat as in the De Witt drawing; if the *frons* at the Rose was angled, those seated in the side bays of the tiring-house would have had a better (though still poor) chance of seeing. At the same time, a position for an actor close to the *frons* wall, centre stage, has proved a strong one at Globe 3. Perhaps those who placed themselves in seats on the stage balcony (like those in the bays closest to the tiring-house) were prepared to trade off the very occasional annoyance of not seeing short sections of the performance for the benefit of being close to the stage and actors and the privilege of being seen themselves? Such a deployment of audience might, however, suggest an entirely different attitude to stage positioning from our own, and grouping actors at the 'front' of the stage, playing directly towards the Lords' and Gentlemen's rooms, might reflect more closely the staging imperatives of a hierarchically configured audience.

The roof over the stage

De Witt shows a roof covering part of the stage, supported on two pillars, which playtexts seem to suggest were often directly employed in staging: in *King Lear* (Globe, 1606) Edgar tells his blind father to sit in 'the shadow of this tree' (5.2.1), and they could also be used to represent the distant ends of a bridge (anon., *Thomas, Lord Cromwell*); as places to hide (Barnes, *The Devil's Charter*, Globe, 1607); the masts of ships; trees to climb or on which to pin love-letters (*As You Like It*, Globe *c.* 1599). According to Will Kempe the pillars were also used to tether pickpockets (a major problem at the playhouses) 'for all people to wonder at, when at a play they are taken pilfering' (*ES*, II: 545–6), and an echo of the leashed bear in the baiting-houses may possibly be found, too, in the image of Flamineo bound to a stage pillar and taunted by his killers in the final scene of *The White Devil* (Red Bull, 1612). The pillars do, however, at Globe 3, present problems in terms of sightlines. The contemporary attitude to sightlines is almost impossible to establish. A tourist who visited Bankside in 1600 recorded that he 'heard an English play' in a playhouse that 'was so built that spectators could very easily see from every part' (*ES*, II: 366). The word 'heard' should alert us to possible differences in our own notion of good sightlines from those of the Jacobeans, though as anyone knows who has worked, or watched a performance, on a thrust stage or in the round, there is no way that each member of the audience can be assured a consistent view of the action. The constantly shifting perspective is one of the excitements of this form of staging that the unifocal end-stage lacks, and the pillars present much less of a problem to the standing, mobile audience in the yard than to those who are seated. Indeed, it is clear from the Prologue to Jonson's 1616 comedy *The Devil Is an Ass*, performed to an all-seated audience, that contemporaries *were* alert to the problems of sightlines. Staged at the Blackfriars where, in Jonson's opinion, the stage space was already reduced by the stage-sitters to the 'compass of a cheese trencher', the Prologue suggests that the presence of fourteen actors onstage in the final scene will lead the frustrated audience to wish the actors were made of 'muscovy glass'. Following an analysis of plays by Shakespeare and other contemporary dramatists, Warren D. Smith (1975) noted that the indications for stage business contained within the text outnumber explicit stage directions by a ratio of ten to one. Furthermore, according to Smith, most of the directions suggest the playwrights' concern to keep the audience informed of gestures, even facial expressions, that might not have been immediately visible. Michael Holden, a design consultant to Globe 3 and the project's chief executive, believes the pillars will seriously obstruct the audience's view of the actors and – as important – vice versa. They will, Holden concludes, 'form an acting constraint, as marked at times as that of a proscenium', and certainly, in the early workshops and productions exploring Globe 3, it seemed to me that problems were caused for both actors and audiences by the shape, size and position of the pillars. How actors and audiences develop their responses to this feature of the reconstruction will, I suspect, remain a key element in the exciting investigations of staging this building encourages.[7]

The roof supported by the pillars was known as the Heavens or Shadow (the latter term used by Puttenham, too). It helped to protect the actors (and particularly their expensive costumes) from rain, to shade them from the sun, and to act as a sound-board to improve the acoustic. At the Hope the roof covered the whole stage; whether it did at all other playhouses (or should at Globe 3 where it does) is a matter of some conjecture. Some actors who have worked on Globe 3 seem to prefer that it should not, being willing to trade the possibility of getting wet for the openness of the frontstage position. The underside of the canopy at the Globe was probably decorated with cosmological symbols, painted or moulded – signs of the zodiac, sun, moon, and planets. It is not certain whether the Rose had a roof over the stage when it opened in 1587 or whether Henslowe installed it (or modified the existing one) as part of the extensive building works carried out in 1592 at the not inconsiderable cost of £105. In Act 4, scene 3 of *Titus Andronicus* (first performed at the Rose on 23 January 1594) the actors enter with bows and arrows and proceed to shoot. As they do so, they comment that their arrows – aimed at Jove, Minerva, Mercury, Mars, Apollo and Saturn – have not always hit their intended target:

TITUS: Ha, ha! Publius, Publius, what hast thou done?
   See, see, thou hast shot off one of Taurus's horns.

                              (68–9)

The editor of the New Cambridge edition speculates that during this scene the actors actually fired through the open top of the playhouse with no regard for any injury done to innocent passers-by, but if there *was* a roof over the stage when the scene in *Titus* was played, it seems to me more likely that the shooting was mimed and that the lines spoken referred directly to the signs of the zodiac, if indeed the underside of the roof was so decorated.

Although it is not certain whether the Swan possessed the necessary machinery, the roof at other playhouses contained a trap-door through which a chair could be flown down to the stage, an effect decried by Ben Jonson in 1616 as a mere crowd-pleaser (Prologue, *Every Man in His Humour*). It seems from the evidence of plays known to have been staged at the Rose that following the 1592 alterations some kind of hoisting gear was available. Instances of flying are, however, comparatively rare, perhaps because while the descent to the stage may well have been spectacular, the ascent was possibly less impressive. A stage direction in a Rose play, *Alphonsus, King of Aragon* (1594), has the opening stage direction:

> After you have sounded thrice, let Venus be let down from the top of
> the stage.

During the play, Venus enters and exits, like the other characters – mortal and mythical – through the stage doors. At the close, though alert to the desirability of ending as he began, the playwright is equally aware of possible technical difficulties:

> Exit Venus. Or if you can conveniently, let a chair come down from
> the top of the stage and draw her up.

It was from high up in the playhouse's superstructure that cannon were fired and fireworks let off to represent the 'exhalations in the sky' (thunder and lightning) to which playtexts frequently refer. From here, too, a flag was flown, and a trumpet blown, both to attract audiences and, presumably, to make the three 'soundings' that initiated the performance.

Beneath the stage

It has been suggested that the De Witt drawing shows either gaps in the hangings round the edge of the stage, drawn back to illustrate places from where devils might run into the crowd, or the bases of the columns supporting the roof above the stage. Of these I favour the former possibility, since at those playhouses with a trap (there is no evidence either way for a trap at the Swan) it would have been necessary to conceal both its operation and the actors getting to and from it. The stage at the Fortune was 'paled in below with . . . oaken boards', and the excavations of the Rose suggest to some that the stage was closed in with a brick wall (it is made to look like dressed stone on a brick base at Globe 3). In *News from Hell* (1606) Thomas Dekker referred to 'hell being under every one of their stages' and together with the Heavens and the platform the cellar completed the 'great stage of the world'. The use of the space beneath the stage varied, but was usually associated with the underworld: in *Hamlet* (Globe) the Ghost of Hamlet's father speaks from under the stage, the Folio text of *Antony and Cleopatra* (Globe) specifies that music was to be played beneath the stage, and fireworks were often let off from there during devil scenes. The trap itself seems to have been specifically associated with the way to and from hell.

Capacity

Johannes De Witt claimed the capacity at the Swan to be some 3,000, though it is unlikely that it was very often full. (Perhaps the actors even preferred rainy days if it meant more of the higher-priced, covered seats were taken up.) An exercise carried out at Alleyn's School in London following the discovery of the foundations of the Rose in order to try to establish the capacity of its yard in 1587 came up with a suggested figure of 533, which, added to Andrew Gurr's calculation of 1,404 for the audience in the galleries, gives a total of 1,937, rising to 2,395 following Henslowe's alterations in 1592, although a study of receipts suggests 600 was a more typical audience size (Eccles 1990: 136; Thomson 1983: 30). Despite the radical differences of shape and size of playhouses, their audience capacity may have been similar: Alfred Harbage calculated the capacity at the Fortune to have been 2,340 and Richard Hosley, basing his calculations on the same assumptions as Harbage, estimates the capacity at the Swan to have been 2,730 (Hosley 1975: 142–3). The capacity of the original Globe was probably close to that of the Swan, possibly as many as 3,000, while that of Globe 3 is in the region of 1,500 spectators. The differences in audience capacity between Elizabethan and Jacobean playhouses and modern theatres of comparable dimensions are due to a number of factors – safety regulations that specify aisle widths, the number of exits, the fact that everyone is seated, the numbers of seats per row, widths between seats, and so on. In addition, according to Iain Mackintosh, not only are modern audiences generally unwilling (and not required) to stand for theatre performances, but the average Elizabethan theatregoer was also 'on average 9 per cent smaller than his London counterpart today'. Putting all these factors together Mackintosh concludes, 'the differences in density and hence seating capacity between a conventional modern theatre and an Elizabethan playhouse of the same area is 1:3 or even 1:4', which gives a useful equation for assessing the characteristic crush of a Renaissance playhouse (1993: 14, 22).

Theatre practice

Costume

> . . . I fear in time
> All my apparel will be quoted by
> Some pure instructor.

Elizabethan and Jacobean society was very conscious of the significance of particular clothes. A series of sumptuary laws, first passed in Henry VIII's reign and reaffirmed on numerous occasions during Elizabeth's (the last being in 1597) regulated who could wear what. The laws were repealed in 1604, but if their influence and the tradition of appropriateness in dress was no longer reflected in the audience, onstage it would have provided a useful code for signalling a character's status and other information, signals to which, when they are referred to in playtexts, modern readers are invariably blind. Henslowe's *Diary* lists a number of costumes purchased for the plays performed in his playhouses, the records indicating that predominant colours were red, black, white and gold, with further substantial sums paid to the 'Lace man'. These extremely expensive costumes reflected the sumptuousness of much contemporary fashion: as one observer noted in 1605, 'When your posterity shall see our pictures they shall think we were foolishly proud of apparel' (Verstegen 1605, quoted in Ashelford 1988: 7). In October 1598, Henslowe records the astonishing sum of £19 for a 'Rich Cloak', possibly in preparation for a (lost) play by George Chapman, *The Fount of New Fashion*. For writing it the author received a fee of £3 (Foakes and Rickert 1961: 99).

Costume (or 'apparel' as it was called) was frequently used to define a particular character. Stage directions indicating an actor appears 'in the habit of a scholar', 'as a beggar' or 'as a soldier' are common, and figures listed in dumb-shows as, for example, Midwife, Master of a ship or Nurse, suggest audiences were able to read the significance of particular clothes without verbal explanation. Costume also functioned, on the virtually bare stage, as a means of defining place: the appearance of a gaoler signifying a prison, a sailor a ship, a huntsman a forest, and so on. At times very specific costume details are given ('Enter two druids in long robes; hats like pyramids, branches of mis-letoe', *The True Trojans*, 2.3 s.d.0). In many instances, however, such as the 'habit of a conjuror' required in *The White Devil*, 2.2, we do not know precisely what the costume comprised, and while illustrations on title-pages and other pictorial evidence can provide some information, they must be used cautiously.

The majority of records, written and pictorial, indicate that the plays were largely performed in contemporary English dress (Shakespeare refers to Julius Caesar's doublet, for instance). It should be remembered, however, that these were generally clothes rather than 'costumes', a fact explored in the work of designer Jenny Tirimani for Globe 3's 1997 production of *Henry V*, for exam-ple (in which the actors also had authentic underwear). There is also evidence that costumes to represent figures from other countries ('like an Italian', 'Turks') were employed. For the details, companies possibly drew on one of the popular volumes of national costumes, especially those published by Jean and Robert Boissard, such as *Habitas Variarum Orbis Gentium* (1581) and their later collection of specifically theatrical costumes, *Mascarades recueillies*, published in 1597. A painting in the National Gallery in London shows William Feilding, First Earl of Denbigh, who had visited India and Persia in 1631–3, dressed in Indian costume, and a picture of Captain Thomas Lee, painted in 1594, shows him in the guise of an Irish foot soldier, his costume identical to that of a char-acter in Jonson's Irish masque. Some attempts at historical costume may not have resulted in a high degree of authenticity or, perhaps more accurately, con-sistency. The drawing on a manuscript of lines from *Titus Andronicus* suggests an attempt at appropriate costuming in terms of the individual characters, but, in the mix of styles and periods, also implies that the overall effect was rather random (Foakes 1985: 48–51). Perhaps this was at times deliberate; Philip Massinger points out in the Prologue to *Believe As You List* (rewritten and reset in a new location to satisfy the censor who had banned the first version) that although his play is set in the ancient world he is a 'stranger to Cosmographie, and may err in the countries' names, the shape and character of the person he presents', which is undoubtedly as much to hint to his audience that the set-ting is a cover and that the action still refers to contemporary events in Europe.

The colour of costumes could also carry particular meaning. In Jonson's *Cynthia's Revels* (1601) one character instructs another in the language of colour:

> Or if you can possess your opposite [convince your rival] that the green your mistress wears is her rejoicing or exultation in his service; the yellow, the suspicion of his truth, from her height of affection; and that he, greenly credulous, shall withdraw this, in private, and from the abundance of his pocket to displace her jealous conceit steal into

his hat the colour whose blueness doth express trueness, she being nor so, nor so affected, you give [show] him the door.

(5.2.28–35)

Specially made costumes were employed for specific effects. The frontispiece to *Nobody and Somebody* (Queen Anne's Men, 1606) for example, shows the central character whose costume is 'all breech' (l. 376) and 'no body'. Somebody's costume, on the other hand, was all body and no breeches. Animal costumes were needed too: a dragon in *Dr Faustus*, a cat in *The Witch*, a dog in *The Witch of Edmonton* (Foakes 1985).

Costumes were also created (or acquired) to help simulate specific contemporary figures. Much of the fun for the audience at performances of Middleton's *A Game at Chess* (Globe, 1624) no doubt stemmed from the considerable care the actors took to reproduce the figures they represented, even, in the case of the Black Knight – who stood for the Spanish Ambassador Gondomar – going so far as to acquire a suit of Gondomar's clothes and the litter in which he rode through London (Foakes 1985: 122–5). In street pageants and masques, the majority of which were provided by the same men who produced the plays for the commercial theatre, costumes were not only elaborate, but frequently carried complex emblematic iconography. Figures in plays, too, may well have been costumed in ways that allowed their roles to be 'read' by the audience, such as Rumour's cloak 'painted full of tongues' (*2 Henry IV*). At times these meanings may not be immediately obvious to us, and while some (such as the figures of History, Tragedy and Comedy who enter at the start of the anonymous tragedy *A Warning for Fair Women*) may be guessed at from other sources, the exact nature of other costumes (such as 'the robe for to go invisible' included in Henslowe's 1598 inventory, and used presumably in *Dr Faustus* where Faustus is 'invisible to all') remains unclear.

Stage dressing

Working on a three-sided stage or (with the audience in the stage balcony) in the round, presents particular problems of blocking and in the use of large properties, and consequently the plays generally require very little in the way of set dressing. The staging more often employs the flexibility of focus provided by the permanent playhouse structure – different levels, a stage capable of expansive, intimate or even split locations, flying gear, pillars, closed doors, curtained or large open entrances – or perhaps its resemblance to specific locations such as the deck of a ship or a shop-front.

Furniture was clearly kept to a minimum, employed only when needed for specific purposes. The modern German playwright Peter Handke once remarked that a chair on a stage is not just a chair but a chair on a stage. In other words, just as everything an actor does on a stage is open to interpretation and will inevitably be interpreted, so is and will everything placed upon

126

the stage, especially when it has no extraneous set dressing, makes little attempt at visual illusion, and self-evidently contains only those things that are essential. In the opening scene of *Women Beware Women* (?1621, ?Globe/Blackfriars), the difference between Bianca's and Leantio's social positions could have been conveyed by the contrast between the quality of fabric and style of her costume and one or two items of simple furniture (possibly the *absence* of chairs),[8] the evident disparity calling in question her protestations that she feels at home in her new husband's house. Hand properties, too, are generally few in number and so become equally key elements in the action, especially if their significance changes throughout the action of the play as a means of defining characters' shifting positions. In *Arden of Faversham*, for example, the silver dice that Alice Arden gives to her lover Mosby (I, 123) are no doubt those used to play the fatal game of backgammon that heralds her husband's murder, and if (as I believe) Mosby attacks Arden with a pressing-iron rather than a dagger (XIV, 235; see note in White 1982) the prop itself underlines the class as well as sexual competitiveness between landowner and lover. In *Women Beware Women*, the shift in Bianca's and Leantio's relationship is exemplified by the comparison of their sparse belongings at the beginning of the play and their later competition for who has gained the most in terms of objects and clothes (4.1). Conversely, the unusually large number of properties needed for *A Chaste Maid in Cheapside*, set in the commercial heart of London, is in itself a sign of the store its characters set by material possessions.

At times, larger scenic items would be brought on to the stage, presumably through the wider central entrance where there was one. There is no hard evidence for the size of this opening, but a gap of about 8–12 ft (2.4–4 m) would more than allow for fast scene changes in keeping with the unbroken flow of action: directions for banquets, for example, often involving table, stools, lights, food and drink are common, suggesting they presented no staging difficulties (in *The Duke of Milan* a banquet is set within the space of ten lines). Large items would be set by the Stage Keeper's assistants dressed in their blue coats, but undoubtedly, as now, other items were brought on by the actors themselves. Not only do planning, practice and discipline enable quite complex scene changes to be effected smoothly and speedily (of particular importance in daylight), but such changes in themselves can be part of the pleasure of the audience's experience.

Lighting: 'day for night'

Before the Rose excavations revealed that its stage faced almost due south, it was generally thought that outdoor playhouses were built with their stages facing north, as the Hollar 'Long View' suggests. John Orrell's detailed examination of the Hollar drawing revealed that it placed the Globe stage facing 48° east of north, and by shining a light on a model of the Globe placed on a table that could be revolved and tilted, he showed that between the hours of two and five in the afternoon, between March and September, some of the audience – especially those in the galleries facing the stage – would have looked directly into the sun, while the actors (with the added protection of the stage canopy) and the high-paying audience above the stage and in the galleries closest to it, would have been in shadow (Orrell 1988: ch. 6 *passim*). If the stage was indeed in the shade, the employment of lit torches, which may initially seem redundant in an open-air playhouse, may have had some impact. Although it is possible that the author of *The Revenger's Tragedy* had an indoor playhouse and a boys' company in mind when writing his play, it was, for whatever reason, first performed at the open-air Globe in 1606. If, in this respect, the printed text reflects the production, it was evidently thought worthwhile to stage the opening procession in daylight with torches (presumably lit ones), and to employ the same device during the scene of the Duke's murder: interestingly enough, Henry Machyn's report of a daytime Corpus Christi procession in 1554 refers to lit torches being carried.[9] Generally speaking, however, lighting states, like all changes in atmosphere, were achieved through a combination of language and action. In *Arden of Faversham* the villain Shakebag, employing a poetic expressiveness totally out of keeping with his normal speech, conjures a mood and a setting with his words:

> Black night hath hid the pleasures of the day,
> And sheeting darkness overhangs the earth.
> And with the black fold of her cloudy robe
> Obscures us from the eyesight of the world,
> In which sweet silence such as we triumph.
> (Scene V, 1–5)

Texts indicate that such language was often supported by the use of a signifying property such as a taper, torch or lantern, and enforced through costume (a nightshirt or gown, perhaps with a nightcap), stage action and the actor's behaviour. In Act 4, scene 4 of Thomas Heywood's *A Woman Killed With Kindness* (Rose, 1603) for example, Frankford, returning in secret to his house to observe his wife and his guest, tells his servant, Nicholas, to make less noise ('Soft, soft.' 1), informs the audience of the time ('So, now my watch's hand points upon twelve, / And it is dead midnight.' 5–6), before asking Nicholas to 'reach me my dark lantern' (20) and telling him again to 'Tread softly, softly' (20). The combination of direct information, stage whispering, appropriate physical action (Nicholas's line, 'I will walk on eggs this pace' gives us a very clear idea of the implicit performance) and the signifying costume and property, matched by the audience's willingness to suspend their disbelief, can create perfectly satisfactorily the appropriate mood, atmosphere and stage state: indeed, the line 'A general silence hath surprised the house' (22), may well describe the atmosphere in the playhouse during the scene.[10]

The play in performance

What particularly struck Johannes De Witt about the Swan playhouse was its size and the magnificence of its columns 'painted in such excellent imitation of marble that it is able to deceive even the most cunning'. The impact of entering the Globe with its decorated *frons scenae*, and the underside of the heavens painted with astrological emblems and picked out in gold, was undoubtedly even more breathtaking, just as the experience of walking into Globe 3 is an arresting one today. Add magnificent costumes such as those suggested by Henslowe's inventory of 1598; possibly 'painted cloths' hung round (as a cheaper alternative to woven tapestries) or the more sombre but equally striking practice of draping the playhouse in black for a tragedy; thrilling language and acting; and the sheer energy and excitement of the entertainment – and its popularity – become clear. It was an enthusiasm matched only, perhaps, by that for talking pictures from the late 1920s onwards, the cinema buildings themselves often being referred to as 'pleasure palaces'. The grandeur (or semblance of grandeur) of the playhouses was seized upon by their opponents, who regularly berated the sumptuousness of the decoration.

In a sense, however, the physical details of playhouses are less revealing than the contemporary cast of mind that could envision the activities of acrobatics, music, dancing and jigs, martial arts (even, in the case of the Hope, animal-baiting) and theatre in one venue. Add to these the practice of selling food and drink during performances (a man at the burning of the first Globe in 1613 had his flaming trousers extinguished by bottled beer); fireworks during and after performances; a virtually unbroken performance with a large proportion of the audience standing, mobile and no doubt vocal; an evident willingness for actors and audience to interact; a heterogeneous audience, divided in terms of class and income, with such divisions clearly reflected in their clothing and location in the playhouse; a thriving trade in prostitution and pickpocketing – and we have a mixture of tones and energies that we must bear in mind when thinking of the nature of the open-air theatre event itself, and the distractions from the onstage action that a playgoer (not to mention a player) had to negotiate.

Different playhouses would have appealed to different kinds of audience, and as the period progressed the divisions between who went where appear to have become more distinct (Gurr 1987). In any public playhouse, however, the range of tastes and attitudes within a single audience would have been considerable, and the prologue to Thomas Middleton's 1612 comedy, *No Wit, No Help Like a Woman's*, probably performed outdoors, refers to the difficulty of pleasing such a spectrum in one event:

> How is't possible to suffice
> So many ears, so many eyes?
> Some in wit, some in shows

Take delight, and some in clothes:
Some for mirth they chiefly come,
Some for passion – for both some;
Some for lascivious meetings, that's their errand -
Some to detract, and ignorance their warrant.
How is't possible to please
Opinion toss'd in such wild seas?
Yet I doubt not, if attention
Seize you above, and apprehension
You below, to take things quickly,
We shall both make you sad and tickle ye.

The ticket prices at the public playhouses ensured that its entertainment was available virtually to all. The precise composition of these audiences, however, has been the subject of much investigation, though we remain far short of any authoritative notion of their social mix and attitudes. Ann Jennalie Cook (1981) asserts that the largest percentage were drawn from the privileged classes, Martin Butler that 'the underprivileged [went] to plays in quantities, and that at least some of the time or in some theatres they constituted the principal audience' (1984: 300), while Andrew Gurr concludes that 'citizens were the staple, at least of amphitheatre audiences, throughout the period (1987: 64). More recently, and interestingly, Thomas Cartelli has observed that contemporary descriptions of the English temperament and behaviour offer the image of:

> a volatile populace at virtually every stratum, sudden and extravagant in its expressions of anger and pleasure; highly susceptible to suggestion; haughty and anti-authoritarian; and strongly responsive to novelty and changes of fashion.
>
> (1991: 52)

He quotes Keith Thomas's description of church-going as a possible analogy with theatre-going:

> Members of the congregation jostled for pews, nudged their neighbours, howled and spat, knitted, made coarse remarks, told jokes, fell asleep, and even let off guns.
>
> (1971: 161)

Attendance at church was, of course, both compulsory and free, and behaviour at an event anyone chooses to pay to go to may be more attentive than this description suggests. But Cartelli's image of a 'receptive auditory', with the ability to respond to the wide 'variety of provocations' offered it from the stage and 'capable of entertaining irreverent attitudes, skeptical opinions, and the most worldly of material ambitions and aspirations' (1991: 64, 61) closely matches the audience implied by the texts and performance strategies suggested by those texts and, indeed, by the anti-theatre tracts. Certainly, the most striking aspect of early performances at Globe 3, and what distinguishes performances there from all other venues (many of which share some of the Globe's physical characteristics) has been the impact on the performances of a *standing* audience, which has released a sense of audience energy, mobility and involvement more akin to that experienced at a soccer match – or, perhaps, Brecht's boxing match. Watching the moving mass of this audience from the vantage point of an upper gallery I have been repeatedly struck by the sense of a crowd with the power to shape and influence the action onstage – a trace, perhaps, of the popular force that the Elizabethan and Jacobean authorities were fearful the theatre could incite.

Although William Poel never fulfilled his ambition to replace his 'Fortune fit-up' replica stage with a permanent, full-scale reconstruction of the Globe (and to have that accepted as England's National Theatre) the Elizabethan playhouse has been a major influence on modern theatre-building. Tyrone Guthrie first became convinced of the appropriateness of the open-stage to Renaissance plays in 1936. His production of *Hamlet*, with Laurence Olivier in the title role, was due to be performed in the open air at Elsinore and in the presence of the Danish royal family to inaugurate an annual festival of drama, when a storm forced the production inside at the last minute. The impromptu performance took place in a hotel ballroom, with the audience seated virtually in the round. Its impact convinced Guthrie that a proscenium staging was fundamentally wrong for Elizabethan plays, in that it placed the audience and the stage action in the wrong relationship to each other. This led Guthrie to create a thrust stage in the Assembly Rooms in Edinburgh, followed by similar stages at Stratford, Ontario, in 1953 and ten years later at Minneapolis. His description of the Assembly Rooms theatre is reminiscent of the Elizabethan model on which he based his ideas:

> The audience did not look at the actors against a background of pictorial and illusionary scenery. Seated around three sides of the stage they focussed upon the actors in the brightly lit acting area, but the background was of the dimly lit rows of people similarly focussed on the actors. All the time . . . each member of the audience was being ceaselessly reminded that he was not lost in an illusion . . . but was in fact a member of a large audience taking part [at] a performance.[11]

In one key respect, however, Guthrie diverged from the original Elizabethan and Jacobean playhouse: in neither of the theatres he built at Stratford, Ontario, and in Minneapolis is there provision for audience seating at the rear of the stage. Others, such as Bernard Miles at the Mermaid Theatre, experimented with audiences surrounding the stage, and in the 1970s, galleries were built at the rear of the main stage at Stratford-upon-Avon. Invariably, however, the fourth wall of audience was missing.

Leaving aside the unique environment of Globe 3 (and the incipient Inigo Jones theatre adjacent to it) there is no doubt in my mind that Elizabethan and Jacobean plays work best in appropriate spaces such as the Swan at Stratford-upon-Avon, the Cottesloe at the Royal National Theatre or the Royal Exchange, Manchester. In the majority of theatre buildings in this country the audience are still divided from the stage, often by a proscenium arch, and more often than not sit in darkness directly facing the action on a lit stage. This runs counter to the active relationship and physical proximity of actor and audience required by Elizabethan and Jacobean plays, and actors who perform in the main house at Stratford regularly express their frustration at battling with an intractable and inappropriate theatre space. Even the Olivier Theatre, while superficially reflecting the open-air Elizabethan stage, lacks some essential qualities of the earlier stages. Most significantly, Laurence Olivier's edict that on no account should audience members be able to see each other across the stage removed precisely that sense of a shared experience, of direct interaction of stage world and audience world, that is constantly invoked by the playwrights. And although the Olivier auditorium is much larger than that at Globe 3, it actually holds about 300 fewer people. I am not suggesting a return to reconstructed performances such as those of *Hamlet* undertaken at the turn of the last century by George Pierce Baker at Harvard University, William Poel in London, or Nugent Monck at the Maddermarket in Norwich – though I acknowledge their achievements and their (often underestimated) influence on modern approaches to staging these plays.[12] Nor am I claiming that fine and satisfying productions cannot be created by companies working on end-stages or any other configuration. Nevertheless, in such circumstances a major ingredient among those that make up a performance of an Elizabethan or Jacobean text is missing. Indeed, the inappropriate tension between the play and performance space in a proscenium theatre is often revealed by the company's use of the auditorium as an entrance point for actors in order to find something of the implied actor–audience interaction, and Globe 3 may allow actors and audiences to recover notions of performance and spectatorship that currently lie dormant.

At the end of his stimulating book, *Architecture, Actor and Audience*, Iain Mackintosh lists what he sees as the key elements essential to successful theatre design. Interestingly enough, many of these are directly applicable to what we know of the theatre buildings of the late sixteenth and early seventeenth centuries – that it is not necessary 'for all the spectators to see equally and perfectly'; that 'a single-tier auditorium is . . . more difficult for the actor to animate'; that 'a more comfortable audience is generally less alert . . . Hard benches for all'; that there is a need for 'a dynamic space animated by cross-currents of energy' (1993: 171–2). Similarly, many contemporary stage designers, responding to spaces sympathetic to the plays, or to production styles that (even in unsympathetic spaces) seem to recognise the nature of the original staging practice, have produced work that would not have looked out of place on the stage at the (Elizabethan) Swan. Just as screen representations of the plays have to deal with the disparity between a generally 'realist' medium and metaphoric and theatrically self-reflexive texts, so stage representations must beware of overriding, or making redundant, the visual content of the stage language. In the early 1960s, Sean Kenny, one of the most influential modern theatre designers, argued that the combination of the open stage (then still a fairly new – or, more accurately, yet-to-be-revived – concept in Britain) and Shakespeare's plays offered designers the most testing and exciting challenge of 'visually supporting' drama in which so much visual detail is contained in the language. It remains, I think, equally true today despite the various experiments in stage languages in the intervening years. Nick Ormerod's design for Cheek by Jowl's 1994 production of *Measure for Measure* provided a simple space that could be transformed by the positioning of a dozen chairs and a desk, a single red banner, hung from flies to floor, signifying the political, public, aspect of the play. This, like his equally simple design for the 1995–6 production of *The Duchess of Malfi* (also for Cheek by Jowl) was for a touring production; perhaps the requirements of touring to a range of very different venues (an experience any Elizabethan actor would have shared) has the very beneficial effect of forcing concentration on essentials.[13] As we have seen in this chapter, the Elizabethan and Jacobean open stage was by no means an empty space, but it was not an illusionistic or cluttered one either. As Webster observed, the 'centre is the actor' – his words, his gestures, his relationship to other figures onstage, to properties, furniture, and to the physical structure of the playhouse and its audience, played out in constant and full light. These are the key factors, that were swamped by the fussy elaboration of nineteenth-century productions, and are still obscured by visually overstated productions such as Philip Prowse's *The Duchess of Malfi* (National Theatre 1985) or *The White Devil* (National Theatre 1990), where in each case the stage design succeeded in dominating the stage language and action rather than enlivening it, or the production of *Macbeth* at the Birmingham Repertory Theatre in 1995 where the scene changes resulted in a running-time of nearly three and a half hours for what is Shakespeare's shortest tragedy.

CASE STUDY: *THE SPANISH TRAGEDY*, ACT 2, SCENE 4

Thomas Kyd's play *The Spanish Tragedy* ushered in the genre of revenge tragedy that was to prove remarkably popular with audiences for the next twenty years or so. Kyd established many characteristics and conventions that were repeated and reshaped by succeeding playwrights. He also demonstrated an awareness of the possibility of enmeshing the perennial theme of revenge with areas of contemporary interest such as madness, and with issues of topical political concern. *The Spanish Tragedy*, with Edward Alleyn first taking the star role of Hieronimo, was an enormous and immediate success. It appears that Richard Burbage may also have played the part. Henslowe's *Diary* indicates that between 1592 and 1597 only Marlowe's *The Jew of Malta* and a lost play called *The Wise Man of West Chester* were performed more often. Between 1592 and 1633 eleven editions appeared, and the extent to which the play was parodied by later writers and the frequency of references to it further indicate the hold it gained in the popular imagination. Kyd's role in developing dramatic verse writing is well established, but as Michael Hattaway has demonstrated in his study of the play, Kyd also 'along with Marlowe and the young Shakespeare had a sense of basic stagecraft that far exceeded that of their predecessors' (1982: 101), and the play in total rewards careful study of its theatrical strategies. A scene which justifies perhaps more attention than Hattaway gives it is 2.4, an example of a scene that demands a complex mix of responses from the spectator.

The story so far: Bel-Imperia, daughter of the Duke of Castile, has vowed to take revenge for the death of her lover, Andrea. In part to further this she develops a romantic relationship with Andrea's best friend, Horatio. When her brother Lorenzo learns of this liaison, however, he determines to prevent it, since it is his intention that Bel-Imperia should marry Don Balthazar, the captured son of the King of Portugal, and through the marriage forge a political alliance between the two countries. The scene opens as Bel-Imperia and Horatio, accompanied by the (unknown to them) treacherous Pedringano, seek privacy in the garden.

In the moments before the scene begins, a bench and a structure representing the bower referred to in 1.4 are brought onto the stage. It is possible that the property was a tree rather than a bower. Exactly when stage posts were originally installed at the Rose is unclear, though they were definitely in place after 1592. But possibly there, or when the play was performed at the Fortune, one of the stage posts may have been employed in this scene, with a bench placed somewhere near it (as in the unidentified activity De Witt records in his drawing of the Swan), leaving the actors' words to interact with the audience's imagination to create the scene. My own view is that a bower closely resembling the title-page illustration of the 1615 Quarto is a vital element in the complex mix of image/sound/language/action that the ensuing scene develops. (See Figure 4.)

Enter HORATIO, BEL-IMPERIA, and PEDRINGANO

HORATIO: Now that the night begins with sable wings
To overcloud the brightness of the sun,
And that in darkness pleasures may be done,
Come Bel-Imperia, let us to the bower,
And there in safety pass a pleasant hour.

As always on the stage at the open-air public playhouses any state, such as day and night, hot or cold, had to be established through the language – one of the actors (perhaps Pedringano) might carry a torch or lantern. An Elizabethan audience would undoubtedly have noted the irony of invoking darkness, invariably associated with danger and evil, at the beginning of what promises to be a love scene.

BEL-IMPERIA: I follow thee my love, and will not back,
Although my fainting heart controls my soul.

The stage direction is implicit in the language here, suggesting that the keener, less wary Horatio is leading the way. Bel-Imperia's lines further enforce the sense of foreboding Horatio has (unconsciously) introduced at the scene's opening.

HORATIO: Why, make you doubt of Pedringano's faith?
BEL-IMPERIA: No, he is trusty as my second self.
Go, Pedringano, watch without the gate,
And let us know if any make approach.
PEDRINGANO: [Aside] Instead of watching, I'll deserve more gold
By fetching Don Lorenzo to this match.

Exit PEDRINGANO

The reference to 'the gate' is to one of the doors in the rear wall of the stage, while Pedringano's comment about getting 'more gold' may indicate that Bel-Imperia has paid him to watch (and, perhaps, to make amends for seeming to doubt his trustworthiness).

HORATIO: What means my love?
BEL-IMPERIA: I know not what myself.
  And yet my heart foretells me some mischance.

> The clues given to actors by the form of the verse are always impor-
> tant. This is the only example in this scene of a line being shared
> between the two characters, and in general the verse forms are not as
> varied and flexible as one finds later in the period. Here the divided
> line serves two particular purposes; it enables the scene to pick up its
> pace after the aside and departure of Pedringano, and draws Horatio
> and Bel-Imperia together, if not physically (though it may) certainly
> emotionally.

HORATIO: Sweet say not so, fair fortune is our friend,
  And heavens have shut up day to pleasure us.
  The stars thou see'st hold back their twinkling shine,
  And Luna hides herself to pleasure us.
BEL-IMPERIA: Thou hast prevailed, I'll conquer my misdoubt,
  And in thy love and counsel drown my fear.
  I fear no more, love now is all my thoughts.
  Why sit we not? for pleasure asketh ease.

> The language continues to enforce the image of night and of the plea-
> sure they both anticipate. Here however (for performances following
> the likely installation of a roof over the stage at the Rose in 1592) the
> words might refer specifically to the underside of that roof above the
> stage, known as the Heavens, possibly decorated with stars, moons
> and signs of the zodiac as the later Globe's definitely was.

HORATIO: The more thou sit'st within these leafy bowers,
  The more will Flora deck it with her flowers.
BEL-IMPERIA: Ay, but if Flora spy Horatio here,
  Her jealous eye will think I sit too near.

> At this point, the actors now seated together on the bench, the lan-
> guage moves into rhyming couplets, the formal patterning intended
> to chart the increasing intimacy of the characters.

HORATIO: Hark, madam, how the birds record by night,
For joy that Bel-Imperia sits in sight.
BEL-IMPERIA: No, Cupid counterfeits the nightingale,
To frame sweet music to Horatio's tale.

There are many instances in plays performed outdoors where music/sound is used to intensify the dramatic moment. Whether or not some imitation of a nightingale was used (not difficult on a wind instrument; the word 'record', here meaning sing, may also be a concealed play on the word 'recorder') or whether the references to 'sweet music' are to be taken more literally, I do not know. I am convinced however, that the language is being enriched by the addition of sound. Certainly, both indoor and outdoor theatres were able to reproduce bird-song. *Blurt, Master Constable* (a play sometimes attributed to Thomas Middleton and performed by Paul's Boys in 1601) has the stage direction 'Music suddenly plays and Birds sing', while the text of John Marston's *Dutch Courtesan*, performed by the rival boys' company at the Blackfriars in 1603 specifically indicates that 'the Nightingales sing'.

HORATIO: If Cupid sing, then Venus is not far:
Ay, thou art Venus or some fairer star.
BEL-IMPERIA: If I be Venus, thou must needs be Mars,
And where Mars reigneth, there must needs be wars.

On one level, the exchange is straightforward; at least it is for those members of the audience who know that Venus is the Goddess of Love and Mars the God of War. The exchange contains a further level of ironical reference, however, in that Venus was unfaithful to her husband in having a sexual relationship with Mars. Although Bel-Imperia is not strictly guilty of adultery (her affair with Don Andrea having been only a clandestine one), the hint here reminds us that this relationship with Horatio lacks any parental approval and needs to be kept secret from those who would consider it illicit. The reference to Cupid may have reminded the audience of the story in Homer's *Odyssey*, where Mars and Venus, observed by Cupid, were caught under a net while making love. If the bower had a lattice structure, echoing the net, such as is shown in the 1615 frontispiece, the visual stage image may also have suggested the reference, especially if the figure of Pedringano is still visible by the rear door.

Figure 4 Illustration from the title page of the 1615 edition of *The Spanish Tragedy,* by Thomas Kyd. The illustration conflates three moments in 2.4 and 2.5 – the hanging of Horatio in the 'arbour', Lorenzo and Balthazar dragging Bel-Imperia away, and the discovery by Hieronimo of his son's body. Note Lorenzo's vizard (mask), the shirt and nightcap Hieronimo wears (as specified in the text) and the torch he carries to signify night-time. (By permission of the British Library.)

HORATIO: Then thus begin our wars: put forth thy hand,
That it may combat with my ruder [coarser] hand.
BEL-IMPERIA: Set forth thy foot to try the push of mine.
HORATIO: But first my looks shall combat against thine.
BEL-IMPERIA: Then ward [shield] thyself: I dart this kiss at thee.
HORATIO: Thus I retort the dart thou threwst at me.

As a sign of their increasing intimacy, not only the content of the language (continuing the imagery of battle and of Cupid and his arrows) indicates their initial physical contact, but the form itself does too: they move from separate couplets to completing each other's couplet, an effect similar to the sharing of half-lines by two characters.

BEL-IMPERIA: Nay then, to gain the glory of the field,
My twining arms shall yoke and make thee yield.

138

HORATIO: Nay then, my arms are large and strong withal:
Thus elms by vines are compassed till they fall.

> At this point, as the text makes clear, Bel-Imperia first embraces Horatio, and then he her, until they are wrapped in each other's arms. The moment provides a good example of a stage image reflecting an established emblem, therefore providing at least some of the contemporary audience with a further layer of meaning than will not be immediately apparent to a modern spectator. The relevant emblem here can be found in Geoffrey Whitney's *Choice of Emblems*, and, like the stage image / dialogue, takes the form of a picture/text: it is an emblem signifying friendship and for those who recognise it will further enforce the growing amity and closeness of the two characters. See Figure 5.

BEL-IMPERIA: O let me go, for in my troubled eyes
Now mayst thou read that life in passion dies.
HORATIO: O stay a while and I will die with thee,
So shalt thou yield and yet have conquered me.

> The scene has traced the lovers' gradual convergence and their progressive enjoyment of the senses of sight, hearing and touch as they move towards the fusion of such physical pleasure in a sexual union. Bel-Imperia's line indicates a movement away, just as his reply suggests he stops her from going. Picking up the notion of the elm 'dying', Horatio puns on the word's double-meaning – to ejaculate. His logical development of a war of love resulting in the 'death' of the lover is about to become fact rather than verbal conceit.

BEL-IMPERIA: Who's there? Pedringano! We are betrayed.

Enter LORENZO, BALTHAZAR, SERBERINE, PEDRINGANO, disguised

> The frontispiece suggests Lorenzo and his companions are wearing full-face masks: as Supervacuo says in the later play, *The Revenger's Tragedy*, ''Tis murder's best face when a vizard's on' (5.5.181).

62 *Amicitia, etiam poſt mortem durans.*

To R. T. and M. C. Eſquiers.

A Withered Elme, whoſe boughes weare bare of leaues
  And ſappe, was ſunke with age into the roote:
A fruictefull vine, vnto her bodie cleaues,
Whoſe grapes did hange, from toppe vnto the foote:
    And when the Elme, was rotten, driie, and dead,
    His braunches ſtill, the vine abowt it ſpread.

Which ſhowes, wee ſhoulde be linck'de with ſuch a frende,
That might reuiue, and helpe when wee bee oulde:
And when wee ſtoope, and drawe vnto our ende,
Our ſtaggering ſtate, to helpe for to vphoulde:
    Yea, when wee ſhall be like a ſenceleſſe block,
    That for our ſakes, will ſtill imbrace our ſtock.

Figure 5 Emblem of the vine and the elm from Geoffrey Whitney's *Choice of Emblems*,
1586.

140

LORENZO: My lord, away with her, take her aside.
O sir, forbear, your valour is already tried.
Quickly despatch, my masters.

> The scene's pattern of two characters converging and meeting, a pattern encoded in forms of language, overall stage action and detailed gesture (all clearly revealed by the text) is now thrown into reverse. Lorenzo's opening two lines, spoken presumably to Balthazar and evidently in response to the Portuguese prince's keenness to get in on the action, are cast in a couplet. This is partly because they deal only with one other character, but partly I suspect to afford the greatest contrast possible with his next line, which is only seven beats long, its shortness helping to stress its bluntness.

They hang him in the arbour

HORATIO: What, will you murder me?
LORENZO: Ay, thus, and thus; these are the fruits of love.

They stab him

> At this moment the stage direction indicates Horatio is 'hung' by the two servants in the arbour property, the bench probably being used to get him up there and support his weight while the actor is attached. Horatio's line helps cover the action. The bench is then possibly kicked away leaving Horatio suspended in an image similar to that in the frontispiece of the 1615 edition (see Figure 4). In this way, the stage image mirrors the earlier one of Horatio (the elm) entwined with Bel-Imperia (the vine), and prompts Lorenzo's reference to the 'fruits of love', a cynical joke referring back to that image and to the image of Horatio's body now suspended and surrounded (as the frontispiece shows) with leaves or flowers. Lorenzo's line indicates he stabs Horatio twice. It is possible, of course, that the arbour was set in a central rear opening, especially if the line of the Rose tiring-house were angled, making the rear opening more visible than in a flat tiring-house wall.

BEL-IMPERIA: O save his life and let me die for him!
O save him brother, save him Balthazar:
I loved Horatio, but he loved not me.
BALTHAZAR: But Balthazar loves Bel-Imperia.

LORENZO: Although his life were still ambitious proud,
　　Yet is he at the highest now he is dead.
BEL-IMPERIA: Murder! murder! Help, Hieronimo, help!
LORENZO: Come, stop her mouth. Away with her.

Exeunt

> With Bel-Imperia pulled away to another point of the stage while
> Lorenzo (making another macabre joke) apparently remains near the
> body, the stage focus is split, contrasting with the single focus of the
> majority of the scene. The effect of the intrusion onto the stage and
> into the scene of the physical violence and fractured language pro-
> duces a tangible contrast with what has gone before. After a scene in
> which the patterning and self-consciousness of the spoken language
> has played so significant a role, Lorenzo's exit line is grimly apt.
> Given the Elizabethan/Jacobean theatre's awareness of the dramatic
> possibilities of 'convergent' and 'discrepant' music, it is tempting to
> think that the 'nightingale music' continues playing throughout the
> violent conclusion of the scene, providing a sharply ironic counter to
> the image of Horatio's corpse hung in the bower.

In the years following the play's first performance the text was altered many
times, presumably to take account of changing tastes and attitudes. The
edition of 1602 includes five 'additions', which some critics believe are the
'adicions in geronymo' (the play was generally referred to by the name of its
central character) that Henslowe paid Ben Jonson to write in 1601–2. Others
doubt this, finding no similarity of style between the additions and Jonson's
other writing. Whatever the truth, the matter need not concern us here, since
it is the actual content of one of the additions, printed between 3.12 and
3.13, which is of particular interest. In total the addition runs to some 170
lines (printed in the Revels edition, 127–33) and contains the following conversation between Hieronimo and a painter, Bazardo:

HIERONIMO: Bazardo! afore God, an excellent fellow! Look you sir, do you see,
　　I'd have you paint me in my gallery, in your oil colours matted, and draw
　　me five years younger than I am – do you see, sir, let five years go, let them
　　go like the marshal of Spain – my wife Isabella standing by me, with a
　　speaking look to my son Horatio, which should intend to this or some
　　such purpose: 'God bless thee, my sweet son,' and my hand leaning upon
　　his head, thus sir, do you see? May it be done?
PAINTER: Very well sir.

HIERONIMO: Nay, I pray mark me sir. Then, sir, would I have you paint me this tree, this very tree. Canst paint a doleful cry?

PAINTER: Seemingly, sir.

HIERONIMO: Nay, it should cry: but all is one. Well, sir, paint me a youth, run through and through with villains' swords, hanging upon this tree. Canst thou draw a murderer?

PAINTER: I'll warrant you sir: I have the pattern of the most notorious villains that ever lived in all Spain.

HIERONIMO: O let them be worse, worse: stretch thine art and let their beards be of Judas his own colour [i.e., red] and let their eye-brows jutty over: in any case observe that. Then sir, after some violent noise, bring me forth in my shirt, and my gown under mine arm, with my torch in my hand, and my sword reared up thus: and with these words: 'What noise is this? Who calls Hieronimo?' May it be done?

PAINTER: Yea sir.

HIERONIMO: Well sir, then bring me forth, bring me through alley and alley, still with a distracted countenance going along, and let my hair heave up my night-cap. Let the clouds scowl, make the moon dark, the stars extinct, the winds blowing, the bells tolling, the owl shrieking, the toads croaking, the minutes jarring, and the clock striking twelve. And then at last, sir, starting, behold a man hanging, and tottering and tottering, as you know the wind will weave a man, and I with a trice to cut him down.

Michael Hattaway suggests that the addition might be a 'digression apologetical for the nature of the play' to a later audience with more sophisticated tastes (1982: 105). Nevertheless, I think the scene gives a vivid impression of the effect Kyd imagined performance would give to his text through the juxtaposition of such heightened moments, their energy being sustained by an appropriate level of 'passionate' acting (see Chapter 3).

5

CHAMBERS OF DEMONSTRATIONS[1]

Indoor playing spaces and theatre practice

Before playing became institutionalised through the building of permanent outdoor playhouses the traditional working environment for adult actors had been predominantly an indoor one. In London, although a Privy Council ban of 1594 prohibited the use of inns for theatrical performance, a range of other indoor spaces were used, the most important of which was, of course, the royal court. Away from the city, as Alan Somerset has shown in his analysis of the forty-two playing spaces known to have been used by companies on provincial tours, only two venues were indisputably outdoor, whereas thirty-three were definitely, and seven probably, indoor spaces:

> Travelling players may have had to contend with rain and mire on the road . . . but at least they acted, most often, in dry and warm conditions while on tour.
>
> (Somerset 1994: 59)

Indeed, it was playing outdoors in London to which they may have been required to adapt, and during the period adult companies, even after they acquired permanent outdoor playhouses, looked increasingly to secure regular indoor venues in the capital.

TRUMAN: The Black-friers, Cockpit, and Salisbury-court, were called Private Houses, and were very small to what we see now. The Cockpit was standing since the Restauration, and Rhode's Company Acted there for some time.

LOVEWIT: I have seen that.

TRUMAN: Then you have seen the other two, in effect; for they were all three Built almost exactly alike, for Form and Bigness. Here they had Pits for the Gentry, and Acted by Candle-light. The Globe, Fortune and [Red] Bull, were large houses, and lay partly open to the Weather, and there they always Acted by Daylight.

> (James Wright, *Historia Histrionica*, 1699)

144

This exchange sums up the features that distinguished private from public playhouses: they were roofed; they were smaller; the pit immediately next to the stage was a desirable and pricey place from which to watch; and the stage and auditorium were lit by candles. Moreover, the whole audience was seated.

The capacity of the smallest indoor playhouse – St Paul's – has been estimated to have been between 100–200, the Phoenix (or Cockpit) about 700, and the Blackfriars possibly about 800, rather fewer than the 1,000 claimed by Francis Beaumont in 1609 (Orrell 1983: 129; Gurr 1987: 22). Iain Mackintosh's 1:4 calculation of relative audience volume (see p. 124) reduces these figures for an equivalent modern theatre to approximately 25–50, 175, and 200, figures that give an even sharper sense of the private playhouses' sense of intimacy, even claustrophobia. Although the theatre practice of adult companies was in many respects broadly similar in both outdoor and indoor theatres, there were clear distinctions. Indoors, there was not only more music, but different instrumentation and greater variety in its use; artificial light; and different acting demands and opportunities afforded by the smaller, more intimate performance spaces. At first, there was an overlap between repertoire choices indoors and out; when the King's Men first added the indoor Blackfriars to the outdoor Globe, it appears that they intended to play very much the same range of plays at both venues. Indeed, plays continued to be transferred between indoor and outdoor venues, and for the actors, the experience of moving between very different spaces must have been similar to that of actors of the Royal Shakespeare and Royal National companies, for example, who can find themselves performing turn and turn about in large, medium and small theatre spaces. Then as now, however, different spaces not only attracted different audiences but also became associated with different types and scales of entertainment, distinctions which became more marked as the period progressed and the indoor playhouses became more court-dominated.

The widely used term 'private' to describe indoor playhouses is misleading, since they were, in fact, no less public than those in the open air. They did, however, charge substantially higher ticket prices: sixpence for a seat in the top gallery, one shilling and sixpence for a seat in the pit facing the stage, and two shillings and sixpence for a side-stage box. This price structure (approximately £18 to £99 in modern currency, and more like today's price range for opera than for theatre) inevitably narrowed the social range of the audience. Even allowing for flattery, John Marston's description of those gathered to watch his play *Antonio and Mellida* at the playhouse in St Paul's as 'Select . . . auditors', is a fair guide to the composition of an indoor playhouse audience at any time in the period.[2] Andrew Gurr, whose *Playgoing in Shakespeare's London* specifically addresses the 'question of a division between the popular and the privileged . . . and what playhouses it separated people into', logically reasons that as a result of the higher prices at the indoor playhouses 'the main clientele must have been the privileged, principally gallants, law students, the wealthier citizens and the nobility' (1987: 67, 26); at the nearby Lincoln's Inn, for example, there were 800 trainee lawyers in 1610, many of whom were undoubtedly more intent on fun than study. However, while Ben Jonson's description of those in the Blackfriars top gallery (paying six times the basic price of admission to the public playhouses) as 'sinful, sixpenny mechanics' is probably a typical overstatement, it does suggest some range within the indoor audience. But as the period progressed, and the indoor playhouses became increasingly court-dominated, the division between those who attended open-air and indoor playhouses, like the repertoires played in each, widened until:

> the social range branched from the boxes at the Blackfriars, which might contain the Countess of Essex, the Duke of Lennox or the Lord Chamberlain himself, to the nameless chimney boys and apple-wives in the yard of the Fortune or the Red Bull.
>
> (Gurr 1987: 79)

The audience at the Blackfriars, Salisbury Court or Phoenix could choose to sit in the pit in front of the stage, in boxes to the side of the stage at stage level or in a gallery that ran round the auditorium and the rear and sides of the stage at first-floor level. At Blackfriars and Salisbury Court the audience could also pay two shillings for a stool and enter through the tiring-house to sit on the stage itself. Jonson, never much impressed with audiences' intelligence or behaviour, claimed that the presence of stage-sitters at the Blackfriars left no more space to perform in than the 'compass of a cheese trencher' (*The Devil Is an Ass*, Prologue), and satirised the banality of the stage-sitters' comments in the Induction to *The Staple of News* (Blackfriars, 1626):

> You come to see who wears the new suit today, whose clothes are best penned (whatever the part be), which actor has the best leg and foot, what king plays without cuffs and his queen without gloves, who rides post in stockings and dances in boots?

At the St Paul's playhouse, where the stage was much smaller, the spectators realised that sitting on the stage would 'wrong the general eye . . . very much'. Whether or not the audience sat on the stage at the Phoenix is not known for certain, but the action of 3.7 of *'Tis Pity She's A Whore* seems to suggest that they did (see Case Study, p. 156ff.). Undoubtedly, actors were used to an audience very much more responsive than those to which we are accustomed today. While I suspect that audiences indoors, with fewer of the distractions experienced outdoors, were less volatile, they were by no means passive. In particular, those who sat on stools or sprawled on the floor of the indoor stage (usually young men out to make an impression) could at times be a nuisance to the performers. They were, however, also a significant source of playhouse income, and when (in 1639) the stage-sitters were removed by royal decree from the stage at the Salisbury Court playhouse, the actors were reimbursed 'in consideration of the want of stools on the stage'.[3]

Playwrights, aware that audience members would be seated onstage at indoor playhouses, frequently made direct use of their presence within the action of the play itself. The opening of John Fletcher's comedy, *The Humorous Lieutenant* (King's Men; Blackfriars 1619), replete with easy jibes against citizens who presumed to attend the private theatres – invective that was evidently enjoyed by those among the Blackfriars audience who considered themselves superior to the merchant classes – demonstrates the fluid but sometimes tense interaction between stage and audience. The play begins – presumably while the audience are still settling into their seats – with two Ushers and an unspecified number of 'Servants, with perfumes, &c.' setting the stage (exactly *what* they are setting is unclear). Their activities are interrupted by the arrival of '2 or 3 Ladies' accompanied by ambassadors who have come to see the play. After carefully flattering the visitors, the First Usher encourages them to find seats in the 'upper lodgings' (the Lord's Rooms, presumably) where they may 'see at ease'. The First Usher then turns back to his preparations but is almost immediately interrupted by the arrival of 'diverse Citizens and their wives'. This time the Usher is appalled at the intrusion (1.1.26):

FIRST USHER: Why, whither would ye all press?
FIRST CITIZEN: Good master usher –
SECOND CITIZEN: My wife, and some of my honest neighbours here –
FIRST USHER: Prithee, begone, thou and thy honest neighbours:
    Thou lookst like an ass: why, whither would you, fish face?

Insults quickly turn to blows:

FIRST USHER: . . . here's no place for ye –
    Nay, then, you had best be knocked.

It is interesting to speculate how the sight of the Usher (essentially a servant whether in his actor's or his character's persona) cuffing a merchant around the ear would be received by the latter's real-life counterparts (and critics) in the audience. It certainly seems to demonstrate the willingness of playwrights and players to stimulate confrontation between actors and audience and between different social groupings in that audience, and Augusto Boal's term 'spect-actor' seems particularly apt in the context of Jacobean theatre-going.[4]

There were two particular production opportunities available indoors that were not open to the actors in the public playhouses: variable lighting and increased use of music.

Stage lighting

The indoor playhouses, like those outdoors, opened in the afternoons, (barring closures for Lent, Sunday and the plague) but with, in some instances, slightly later performance times (Gurr 1996: 78–81). As a result they relied predominantly on artificial light provided by candles, lamps and torches. Although neither Jones's designs for an unidentified indoor playhouse nor those for the Cockpit-in-Court show the lighting facilities, the candles were undoubtedly placed in chandeliers above the stage and auditorium, and in brackets along the front of the galleries. The records of payments made in respect of the Cockpit-in-Court (converted into a playhouse *c.* 1629–30) suggest that performances employed about 150 candles placed in gilded candelabra of which 'ten smaller and two greater than the other' were placed 'about and before the stage' (quoted in Wickham 1959–81, II, ii: 236). The frontispiece to Francis Kirkman's *The Wits*, a 'curious collection of several drols and farces' published in 1673, shows a stage with two chandeliers above the stage, each holding eight candles, and a row of 'footlights' – candles or possibly oil-lamps placed along the front edge of the stage (see cover illustration). The plans of the Cockpit-in-Court, however, show that it had rails along the front edge of the stage, a feature that the plan of the stage for the unidentified Jones theatre also appears to indicate. Stage rails are shown on the *Messalina* and *Roxana* vignettes, though whether the Blackfriars had rails or not is unknown. (All illustrations in Foakes 1985.)

Any performance lit by candles is today likely to generate in an audience an emotional response similar to that provoked by eating by candlelight, lights on a Christmas tree, or the blaze of a bonfire. To the Jacobeans, however, it was presumably different, their delight arising not from seeing a candle-lit performance as such (for which there was a long-standing tradition and which was in any case the norm in indoor theatres), but for the ways in which the production might employ this theatre technology. It has been suggested that the low level of illumination (by modern standards) provided by candle-light may have created difficulties in actually seeing actors' faces and that this would have made listening more difficult (Sturgess 1987: 57). As Samuel Pepys informs us, however, in a report of a seemingly under-prepared performance by William Beeston (Christopher's son), the light level was sufficient to enable the actor to read:

> It was pleasant to see Beeston come in with the others, supposing it to be dark, and yet he is forced to read his part by the light of the candles.
>
> (*Diary*, 2 February 1668–9)

Of course, compared to modern expectations, visibility would be much less good, but (although we should always remember the importance of listening in Elizabethan and Jacobean playhouses) my own experiments with candle-light have presented no significant problems of visibility or audibility (see pp. 170–3).

Whereas today the lighting design of any stage production is a central element in its preparation and performance, it was obviously much less so in the Jacobean theatre. The quote from Pepys suggests a constant stage state, with the illusion of darkness being achieved by actors and audience 'supposing it to be dark', a contract of imaginations comparable to that at the outdoor playhouses. However, as far as the open-air playhouses were concerned (apart from those occasions when a darkening afternoon light might be cannily referred to by the playwright), dark rooms or night-time could only be evoked by this willing interaction between actors and audience, aided by the use of language, costume, properties and action. A dramatist writing for an indoor playhouse, on the other hand, knew he had the facility to adjust the lighting states, if only to a limited degree, and there is substantial evidence in the texts of indoor plays performed by both children and adults that variations in mood were effected, or at least supported, by appropriate changes in the light levels.

In a modern production lighting states can be varied extremely speedily, but it takes time to extinguish and relight candles. Consequently, lighting changes that involve such operations tend to be grouped around clusters of scenes, and often precede an act interval or lead into a scene where relighting can be part of the onstage action. The action of *Antonio's Revenge* (Paul's), for example, takes place over a period of two days, and the passage of time is very clearly marked, most notably by the use of light and dark stage states. Comparatively significant changes in the illumination levels on a candle-lit stage can be effected through the use of supplementary light brought onto and then removed from the playing area, and each act except the fourth begins with a torch-lit scene. More substantial changes require time, time provided by the act intervals; Marston's fourth act, for example, has all its scenes in 'day light' and is preceded and followed by acts in which the action takes place at night.

Rather than reducing the general lighting state, a common technique seems to have been to *add* lights shortly before a scene intended to be 'dark', so that the removal of these lights would give the impression that the stage had, in fact, been darkened. This is similar to the technique employed by modern lighting designers, where the light levels are subtly raised in advance of a 'dark' scene, then lowered to their original level; the eyes of the audience, slow to respond to the change, perceive the scene as darker than it in fact is, allowing the effect of darkening the stage to be achieved while still allowing the action to be visible.

Although a director today obviously has considerably more flexibility of choice where lighting is concerned than the Jacobeans, in deciding how to stage a scene set in darkness he or she (or the lighting designer) may wish to consider the impact it might have had in terms of its likely original staging. Although *The Duchess of Malfi* was written with indoor performance in mind, Webster undoubtedly anticipated that the King's Men would, if it proved popular, also perform the play outdoors, and the scenes of darkness – central scenes in terms of the play's impact – provide a useful point of comparison of indoor and outdoor practices. At the opening of Act 4, Bosola reports to Ferdinand on the condition of the imprisoned Duchess. Ferdinand exits and the Duchess enters, to be informed by Bosola that she is to be visited by her brother Ferdinand who:

> 'Cause once he rashly made a solemn vow
> Never to see you more, he comes i'th' night;
> And prays you, gently, neither torch nor taper
> Shine in your chamber.
>
> (4.1.23–6)

The Duchess orders the lights to be removed. When performed at the Blackfriars, I believe that the preceding act interval would already have been used to extinguish a number of the candles near the stage, an appropriate change of mood as the play moves towards the murder of the Duchess at the end of the fourth act. If Ferdinand and Bosola (who begin the scene) entered carrying torches, and assuming that the Duchess was accompanied by Cariola (though this is not indicated in the text) or by other servants, or that she carried a light herself, further lights may have been brought on to the stage at line 17. The subsequent removal of all these portable lights at l.29 would have given a fairly realistic impression of the room darkening. At the end of the section between Ferdinand and the Duchess, when Ferdinand, exiting, calls for lights (53), the return of torches would have created sufficient illumination for the audience and the Duchess to see the severed hand he has left with her, especially if a light was held directly by it. The torches or lanterns brought on to the stage at that point would also perhaps have been used to illuminate the tableau of the figures of Antonio and the children that immediately follows, while the generally lower level of light throughout the remainder of the act would have been appropriate to its further horrors. Furthermore, the relighting of candles in the break between the fourth and fifth acts would chime with Antonio's arrestingly optimistic opening line of 5.1: 'What think you of my hope of reconcilement / To the Arragonian brethren?' and have ensured the fates of the surviving characters were played out in full view of the audience.

In performances of this scene at the Globe, however, the torches would have acted only as signifiers of darkness, aided by the verbal references to listening and to the difficulty the characters have in seeing each other. The language would have been supported (in either venue, no doubt) by appropriate gestural and physical performances by the actors (such as those in *A Woman Killed*

With Kindness described earlier, or those illustrated on the frontispiece of Heywood's *The Second Part of the Iron Age,* 1632; see Foakes 1985: 135), and by the willing imaginations of the audience. The difference between the versions of the staging centres, therefore, on how each positions the audience. In the Blackfriars staging (certainly for those not immediately next to the stage) it seems likely that the audience would have been as uncertain as the Duchess as to what was going on, and hence have been as surprised and horrified as she at the revelation of the 'dead man's hand' (55). In other words, the audience would have experienced Ferdinand's act from the Duchess's point of view. At the Globe, however, where presumably the audience might have seen what Ferdinand was doing, they could observe the cruelty enacted upon the Duchess. As the varying approaches taken to this moment by modern directors illustrate, it is a difficult decision. The 'Blackfriars option' might increase empathy for the Duchess, whereas the 'Globe option' maintains Webster's dramatic strategy of allowing the audience at times to observe the Duchess as an object of male manipulation and oppression – a strategy that other devices (such as characters observing and commentating on other characters and their actions, *sententiae*, interruptions of the action, self-reflexive references) seem designed to establish.

Music

John Marston's play, *The Malcontent*, was originally written for and performed by the Children of the Queen's Revels, based at the Blackfriars. When, some time later, possibly through devious means, it came into the possession of the King's Men at the Globe, John Webster added an Induction which includes the following exchange between Richard Burbage (as himself) and another actor as William Sly – supposedly a member of the audience more used to the theatrical conventions of the private theatres than the public:

SLY: What are your additions?
BURBAGE: Sooth, not greatly needful, only as your sallet [salad] to your great feast, to entertain a little more time, and to abridge the not-received custom of music in our theatre.

(78–81)

The custom to which Burbage refers was the use in the private theatres of music between the acts, specifically to allow time to trim the candles. With no act breaks (and obviously no lights to attend to) the King's Men presumably felt the need to add more dialogue to fill out the text. Music, however, was by no means unknown in the public playhouses prior to the King's Men's takeover of the Blackfriars (at which point they installed a Music Room above the stage of the Globe) though with a different configuration of instruments. The Admiral's Men inventories of 1598, for example, include three trumpets and a drum, a treble viol, a bass viol, a bandore, a cittern, one chime of bells, three timbrels and a sackbutt.[5] The number of instruments available to a company may have been even greater since actors frequently bequeathed instruments in their wills. Outdoors, music tended to be introductory to the overall event (to announce the Prologue, or provide a kind of overture to the play), to herald processional entries within the action of the play, to accompany songs within the action and to provide music for the jig or dance with which performances – of tragedies as well as comedies – were (in the earlier years of the period) commonly concluded. This is what Mary Chan calls 'representational' music; in other words, the replication onstage of musical activity found in everyday life.[6] In Elizabethan and Jacobean society, all meetings between nobles, all important receptions, processions and progresses, were supported and enhanced by music. When Henry VII sent his daughter, Margaret, to Scotland in 1503 to marry James IV, her entourage included 'Johannes and his company, the Minstrels of Music, the trumpets in displayed banners, in all the departings of the towns, and in the entering of the same, playing on their instruments to the time that she was passed out'.[7] Choral singing, too, was a feature of such royal entries.

There are also numerous examples of 'mood' music being used to enforce stage atmosphere in outdoor playhouses. The power of music to affect an emotional response was well known; to some, music provoked licentiousness and was therefore potentially dangerous. Sir Francis Bacon noted that 'the sense of hearing striketh the spirits more immediately than the other senses', and in his treatise *The Passions of the Mind in General* (1604) Thomas Wright (echoing Orsino in *Twelfth Night*) observed that:

> . . . just as certain foods delight the palate, so in music diverse consorts stir up in the heart diverse sorts of joys, sadness or pain.
>
> (1971: 166)

Although music and songs were used in outdoor performances to enhance the action, their use in indoor theatres was still more extensive. *The Tragedy of Sophonisba*, or *The Wonder of Women*, for example (also by John Marston), performed by the Children of the Queen's Revels at the Blackfriars in 1605, opens as 'Cornets sound a march' to announce the procession of the Prologue. At the end of the Prologue the cornets play again while some of those onstage exit and others take up positions for the opening scene; in 1.2, cornets play a 'phantastique measure' and then join with the organ and voices to accompany Sophonisba's song; in the same scene the cornets again herald a formal entry and, with the organ once more, play 'loudfull music' to conclude the act and span the act change. While the music plays, action is performed onstage in dumb-show:

Whilst the music for the first Act sounds, HANNO, CARTHALO,

BYTHEAS, GELOSSO enter: they place themselves to counsell; GISCO, the impoisoner, waiting on them; HANNO, CARTHALO, and BYTHEAS setting their hands to a writing, which being offered to GELOSSO, he denies his hand, and, as much offended, impatiently starts up and speaks.

If the music ended as abruptly as Gelosso's speech began, it would have marked the beginning of the scene and given it a very up-beat start. This pattern in the first two acts – music between acts, as accompaniment to songs, backing for dumb-shows and to announce processional entries – is repeated throughout the play, with instruments playing in various combinations either with or without voices and perhaps, in Act 4, wordless vocal music. Music more specifically to establish a mood in the theatre is used in 4.1, where 'Infernal music plays softly' (101, s.d.) to conjure up 'Dreadful Erictho', the 'great soul of charms' who, like a kind of demonic cuckoo, lives in 'graves and tombs' having forced their ghostly inhabitants to flee. It is possible that the infernal music was played from beneath the stage (there is no specific direction here, but Erictho makes her exit in Act 5 via the stage trap) and that it was played on an *hautboy* (though again there is no direction to that effect). However, this ancestor of the oboe was generally associated with the supernatural or with foreboding. As Warwick Edwards writes:

> In the theatre, where consort music was often played, instrumentation would often be determined by the symbolic associations of particular instruments. Strings, whether viols or violins, represented harmony, unity or agreement; oboes had magical associations and were often called for in connection with evil portents; the soft sound of flutes or recorders, sometimes referred to as 'still music', tended to symbolize death.[8]

In *Sophonisba*, whatever the particular instrument used to produce it, the infernal music is soon challenged by altogether more gentle sounds emanating from 'within the canopy'. This direction may refer (as it appears to do in references at the Paul's playhouse) to hangings at the rear of the stage, but in this instance may possibly refer to the hangings of an onstage bed:

A treble viol, etc., a base lute, play softly within the canopy

SYPHAX: Hark! hark! Now softer melody strikes mute
    Disquiet Nature. O thou power of sound,
    How thou dost melt me! Hark! now even heaven
    Gives up his soul amongst us. Now's the time
    When greedy expectations strains mine eyes
    For their loved object; now Erictho willed,

Prepare my appetite for love's strict gripes.
O you dear founts of pleasure, blood and beauty,
Raise active Venus worth fruition
Of such provoking sweetness. Hark, she comes!
                                              (4.1.199–208)

At this point is sung 'A short song to soft music above' (208, s.d.). Songs were a major part of indoor performances, such as social or political satires to match the content of the acerbic comedies in which the children excelled, bawdy songs or, as here, songs intended both to deepen further the stage atmosphere and advance the action (Shapiro 1977: 233–55). The word 'above' in the stage direction is a reference to the position of the musicians above the stage (though whether the singers were also to be on the upper level or on the main stage is unclear), and indicates that at this point – perhaps with instruments also within an onstage bed – Marston has brilliantly utilised all levels of the stage space and characterised the action through music and song.

The music indoors was normally played by a mixed ensemble, sometimes also called a 'broken consort', possibly because it included only a selection of the instruments found in a full consort. The ensemble would probably have comprised six musicians, playing lute, bandora, base-viol, cittern, treble-viol and flute – the combination of instruments for which Thomas Morley's influential *Consort Lessons* (1599) were written – though clearly the combination could be varied if desired: *Sophonisba*, for example, specifies organ, cornet, recorder, viol and base-lute. The standard of playing was evidently, but unsurprisingly, high: the orchestra at the Blackfriars theatre was 'esteemed the best of common musicians in London' by Bulstrode Whitelocke in 1634. The musicians – perhaps seated round a square table on which would rest a book with each part facing the instrumentalist – would have either played music composed especially for a particular play, or drawn from a repertoire of stock tunes that could be applied as necessary to the onstage action.

After experimenting extensively with music, language and action in a range of plays (and indoor plays performed by the adults in particular), I am certain that music would have been used even more regularly and extensively than is indicated in playtexts, in a manner not dissimilar to the way it was used to accompany action in early cinema and in film scores today. Such music would not only have affected the audience's responses but would also have aided the actors, especially in passages of wordless action: D.W. Griffith, the pioneer film director, for example, had a small band play while he filmed actors performing for his silent movies, to help them generate and sustain the required level of emotion. David Mann argues that Jacobean music is too narrow in range to provide the necessary variety to match a wide range of onstage moods (1991: 114), but Wilfred Mellers describes Tudor and Stuart music as '*emotionally* descriptive', often with 'elaborately contradictory rhythms' and 'dissonant harmony to reinforce verbal pathos' (1964: 393–4; emphasis added). Furthermore, in addition to scored music, musicians no doubt improvised when necessary, as is suggested by the frequency of stage directions for music that is 'sad', 'dreadful', 'loud', 'soft', 'out of tune', and so on. As Edwards notes, the range of effect could be further varied through the choice of particular instruments:

> A rigid choice of performing medium is alien to 17th-century and earlier music [and] the *function* of the music, rather than the music itself, tended to govern the instrumentation.[9]

In practical exercises and performance – using period instruments, contemporary music and appropriate improvisation by the musicians – I have found it perfectly possible to match contemporary music to the shifting moods of individual speeches and complete scenes, to coordinate gestures and speech, and to explore how a musical accompaniment can enable an emotional moment to be 'held' by the actor. The anonymous play *The Second Maiden's Tragedy* (probably by Middleton) has been woefully neglected in terms of professional performance since the King's Men performed it at Blackfriars in 1611. The third act is one long scene, set in a house in which Govianus, the rightful ruler, and his betrothed – known only as the Lady – are confined. The usurper of Govianus's throne, known only as the Tyrant, sends his men to bring the Lady to him. She, rather than submit to the Tyrant's lust, persuades Govianus to kill her. As he runs to her with his sword drawn he falls to the ground, apparently dead, leaving her to kill herself, which she does. Govianus, however, has only fainted, and coming to his senses, finds the Lady dead beside him. The play as a whole is theatrically self-conscious, commenting on the acts of play-making and watching, and referring to other well-known plays. For a contemporary audience, this particular scene would have had at least two celebrated Shakespearean antecedents: the climactic scene in *Romeo and Juliet*, and the deaths of the lovers in the Mechanicals' playlet, 'Pyramus and Thisbe' in *A Midsummer Night's Dream*. In other words, the scene contains, with equal force, the twin poles of tragedy and comedy characteristic of the Grotesque in general and Middleton's work in particular. To a modern audience, possibly unaware of these antecedents, the moment Govianus faints may shade into slapstick, since his swoon is something of a pratfall and likely to provoke laughter. Working on the play, however, I found that by setting the whole act to music that enhanced the tragic mood, the comic element in the action could be very productively strengthened, creating a tension of moods and responses while still maintaining the shape of the scene.[10]

CASE STUDY: *'TIS PITY SHE'S A WHORE* IN ACTION

The title-page of the first edition of *'Tis Pity She's a Whore*, published in 1633, states that the play was 'Acted by the Queenes Maiesties Servants, at The Phoenix in Drury-Lane'. This playhouse was owned by Christopher Beeston, who started his career as an actor and was, by 1616, both member and manager of Queen Anne's Men, based at the Red Bull. In that year, Beeston leased the site of a cockpit built in 1609 by John Best, and began to convert it to a playhouse. Audiences at the Red Bull, infuriated at the prospect of losing their entertainment, attacked the indoor playhouse and inflicted severe damage upon it. Beeston rebuilt it, after which ascent from the ashes it was widely known as the Phoenix.

In 1969, two sheets of drawings by Inigo Jones of the elevation and plan of an indoor playhouse were discovered in the Library of Worcester College, Oxford, by Don Rowan, though he was unable to identify the specific playhouse. There has subsequently been widespread speculation about which playhouse (if indeed it *is* a specific playhouse) the drawings represent, and though no unanimous view prevails, many (including me) believe it possible that they show the Cockpit, or Phoenix in Drury Lane. Whatever the truth, the drawings depict in more detail than any other visual source yet discovered the spatial arrangement of a Jacobean indoor commercial playhouse, and provide the basis for the reconstruction – to be known as the Inigo Jones playhouse – that stands alongside the reconstructed Globe at the International Shakespeare Globe Centre in London.[11]

The drawings show a theatre building 55 ft long and 40 ft wide (16.9 m × 12.3 m) in its external dimensions. At its widest point the stage is 23 ft 10 in. across, slightly narrower (22 ft 4 in.) at its front edge, and 15 ft deep (7.3 m, 6.8 m, 4.6 m). This gives a total stage area of 360 sq. ft (33 m²), compared with possibly 537 sq. ft (50 m²) at the Blackfriars and a massive 1,182 sq. ft (110 m²) at the Fortune (based on the contract's specifications). As it was the practice at the Phoenix (and at Blackfriars; but not at Paul's, where the stage was too small) for certain members of the audience to sit on stools at the edge of the stage or sprawl on the floor, the usable stage space would have been reduced – possibly by as much as a third. To the rear of the stage are three doors. The central door is the same height as those that flank it, but wider and, as a result of its architectural detailing, visually more imposing. The stage appears to be about 4 ft high (1.2 m), allowing only very limited space beneath for a trap unless the area below the stage was excavated. In fact, no trap is indicated in the plans and none seems to be required for plays known to have been performed at the Phoenix. It appears from the plans that the front edge of the stage was railed; Dungworth, a character in Thomas Nabbes's *Covent Garden*, performed at the Phoenix in the late 1630s, seems to refer to this feature when he asks in the opening scene, 'What are all these things with rails?'. (See King 1992b.)

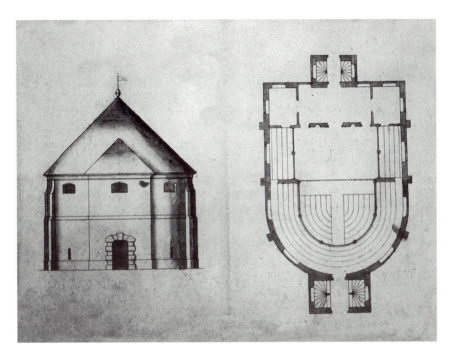

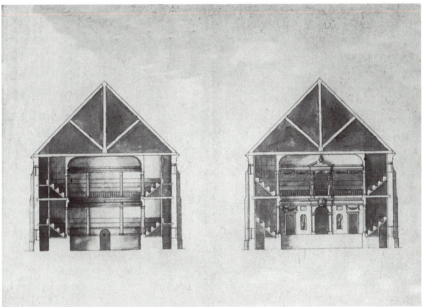

Figure 6 Inigo Jones's Drawings for a conversion to a playhouse, probably the Phoenix (or Cockpit) in Drury Lane, *c.* 1616. (Reproduced by kind permission of the Provost and Fellows, Worcester College, Oxford; 7B and 7C.)

Jones's drawings show a balustraded gallery (which Nabbes refers to throughout *Covent Garden* as the 'balcony') 10 ft 6 in. (3.2 m) above the main stage, a continuation of the gallery that ran right round the playhouse as the view from the stage makes clear. As in the outdoor playhouses (and in the tradition of indoor playing elsewhere) audiences also occupied the seats either side of the central opening, though – perhaps in deference to sight-line difficulties – the plans indicate three degrees of seating rather than four as in the other galleries. The middle section above was used by both musicians and actors. Presumably, the musicians could either play on the front area, visible to the audience (for the music preceding performance or for music which needed to be a part of the onstage action), or retire to the rear, out of sight of the spectators, to provide atmospheric background music and allow the actors to use the balcony space. Some editors are very cavalier in locating scenes 'above', but in both indoor and outdoor theatres the space was in fact used sparingly – usually for short, static scenes involving only one or two performers. (See discussion of 'above' in Chapter 4, pp. 119–20.)

Jones's designs indicate that the auditorium seating in both pit and galleries was curved in a horseshoe shape, a trace perhaps of the earlier cockpit. In the galleries spectators sat on tiered wooden benches (called degrees), steeply raked at an angle of 40°, and shaped to keep the feet of those in one row from kicking the backsides of those in front. Access to these seats at both levels was by passageways behind the seating, the top passage being lit by windows, while the lower was evidently unlit. In the pit, elegantly but somewhat impractically to my mind, the benches repeat the curve of the auditorium, requiring those sitting nearest the stage to turn their faces through 90° to look at the stage. There are six rows of pit benches, rising in a height of three feet and so more shallowly raked than those in the galleries. A central aisle leads to the exit. Audience capacity was probably in the region of 700–750, though as in all playhouses this was probably rarely achieved. The drawings show a solid wall dividing the stage boxes from the auditorium on each side which John Orrell believes would 'almost certainly have been brought up to the full height of the roof trusses' (Gurr and Orrell 1989: 138). If so, the wall would have had a significant effect on sightlines.

The curved shape of the auditorium is usually attributed to the constraints placed on the design by the existing foundations of the cockpit on which Beeston built his playhouse. Bearing in mind, however, that the galleries at the Second Blackfriars were probably also curved, Jones's plans may simply be in keeping with a prevailing roundness in contemporary theatre design. Allusions to the auditorium in a range of plays performed at the Phoenix confirm its curved shape. In Heywood's *Love's Mistress*, for example, which according to its title page was 'Publicly Acted by the Queens Comedians, at the Phoenix in Drury Lane', one character speaks to another, and refers to the audience:

See'st thou this sphere spangled, with all these stars,

Figure 7 Photographs of a full-scale, candle-lit reconstruction of an indoor playhouse, based on the Inigo Jones Drawings, constructed in the Wickham Theatre, University of Bristol, March 1997, for a production of John Ford's *Love's Sacrifice*.

Top The auditorium. It is hoped in future experiments to reproduce the curved seating Jones indicates in the pit.

Bottom The stage. Note the stage height is 2′ 6″, rather than the 4′ indicated in the Drawing, due to restricted headroom. The reconstruction is regularly used in classes on Jacobean indoor theatre and performance. (Photos: John Adler.)

All these Love-arts; nor shall they part from hence
With unfeasted cares.

John Orrell points out that although 'The compliment to an audience as a circle of shining beams is conventional enough', the lines clearly reflect the image of the audience as 'the interior of a sphere as seen from the stage' (1988: 194). To this I would add that the speech may also be referring to the specific effect created by the candles in their holders on the gallery fronts, the decorated ceiling illuminated by the chandeliers, and even the light reflecting from the clothes and jewellery of the audience.

The rear wall of the stage contains arched niches to either side of the central doorway in which are placed (or painted) statues about 4 ft high, too sketchily drawn to be readily identified but almost certainly figures representing the Muses of Tragedy and Comedy (Melpomene and Thalia) stage right and left respectively. The central entrances at stage level and above are decorated. The interior, though made of wood, would be likely to have been painted to resemble stone, with the posts supporting the galleries treated as classical columns. The *frons scenae* was undoubtedly picked out in gold, and possibly given a marbled effect.

The Wickham Theatre in the Department of Drama at the University of Bristol accommodates almost exactly a theatre space with the internal dimensions indicated in the Jones drawings. On the basis of the drawings it has been possible to erect a reasonably complete structure of the playhouse auditorium and stage, and to apply to that space playtexts known to have been performed at the Phoenix – specifically *'Tis Pity She's A Whore* and *Love's Sacrifice* (both by John Ford) in full performance, and a number of others in extensive workshop exercises. The discoveries made inform the following analysis.

The 1633 Quarto divides the five acts of *'Tis Pity* into twenty-seven scenes. Of these, as in indoor plays generally, the majority (twenty) are clearly designated in the text as interior scenes, only six as specifically exterior. Only one (3.1) is left uncertain, but since scenes are located with such care in the play, I think it evident that it is set in the street outside Florio's home which Bergetto and Poggio have just left. The twenty interior scenes may be further subdivided into specific locations: the Friar's cell; Florio's house; Soranzo's house. Exterior scenes are precisely placed, too. 1.2, for example, is set immediately outside Florio's house ('What mean these sudden broils so near my doors'), at which point the central stage doors become specifically *his* doors and the upper level represents the window or balcony of his home from which Annabella and Putana observe the scene. Obviously the street in 3.9 is immediately outside the Cardinal's house and so the central entrance way and balcony then become his. In all plays performed at the Phoenix the location of the upper level changes during the course of the play, and the same is true of the doors. I presume, however, that individual productions applied some logic to indicate where the doors led to as seen, for example, in the detailed stage directions contained in Thomas Nabbes's *Covent Garden* (King 1992b: 185–202). Entering through one side stage door and exiting through the other (the move indicated, I believe, by the common direction to 'pass over the stage') could presumably be used to indicate the actors' passage along the length of a street (as in 1.2 and 3.7; see discussion below).

In its arrangement and division of scenes the play is predominantly interior, while the exterior scenes are generally located outside specific buildings (whose interiors we often visit too) and involve tightly grouped action. The physical use of the stage is therefore consistent with its dimensions and physical features, and an analysis of the opening scenes illustrates how Ford has related stage space, audience and action.

Act 1, scene 1

The play opens in mid-debate. In a theatre with no curtain to raise and no lights to bring up, it is left entirely to the actor to harness the audience's attention. It is noticeable, too, especially in indoor plays, how the opening lines or dialogue are often more concerned to establish the dynamic of relationships between specific characters and circumstances than the place of the action. The location is described so far as is necessary, but the setting is not painted through words (see, for example, the opening speeches in *The Witch* or *The Changeling*). In this instance, the Friar's arresting opening line – 'Dispute no more in this' – suggests an action being brought onto the stage in mid-flow, so engaging the audience in trying to latch on to the cause of the argument. The scene is an intense two-hander between Giovanni and the Friar and sets up the structure of opposition between personal desire and the pressures and constraints of Church and society that informs the play as a whole. The scene is aptly suited not only to the intimacy of the playing space but to the high percentage of educated young men in the audience. Many of these would themselves have had personal tutors in the not-too-distant past, and be likely therefore to be immediately interested in the role of a character who challenges received opinion. Young lawyers, who comprised a large proportion of the audience, may have been particularly attracted to a 'dispute' (one of the exercises in their training), while older members of the audience were perhaps reminded of their own collisions with youthful certainty. The way in which the play is targeted at specific groups within the audience is particularly striking, as we shall see. Ford rapidly sets out and develops the tension that exists between the two characters in terms both of what separates them – age versus youth, received ideas versus personal desire – and of what holds them together – long and close friendship, the Friar's sacrifice of his Orders to follow Giovanni back to Parma as his tutor and his admiration of his pupil's skill and intelligence.

The content and the form of the text suggest that neither character is as confident as he might wish to appear. Giovanni searches for intellectual arguments to justify his passion and still remain within the social frame, which of course he cannot do without resorting to false logic – 'nice points' as the Friar calls them. Consequently, as the play progresses, Giovanni increasingly sheds the social and spiritual restraints to which he is still at this moment in thrall. For his part, the Friar is torn between his love for Giovanni and his genuine fear for his pupil's soul. A major task for any modern production, especially in these opening scenes, is to establish the power of the temporal and – more difficult in our essentially secular society – spiritual forces in the play, particularly where the complex relationship between Giovanni and the Friar is concerned. In this, the production team faces a problem posed by almost all Elizabethan and Jacobean plays: how not merely to present but arouse a modern audience's interest in ethical and moral issues that are couched in specifically seventeenth-century terms.

The surface certainty and the underlying doubt, the division and conjunction that simultaneously exist in the characters, are embodied in the structure of the language and in the pattern of separation and union in the stage action:

GIOVANNI: It were more ease to stop the ocean
    From floats and ebbs, than to dissuade my vows.
FRIAR: Then I have done, and in thy wilful flames
    Already see thy ruin: Heaven is just.

              (64–7)

These are two absolute, seemingly final statements, suggesting characters at a physical and intellectual distance. Their separation, however, is immediately challenged in the following line, where the shared desire for reconciliation is expressed by the equal sharing of a perfect metrical line and undoubtedly – for the first time in the scene – by physical contact between the actors:

FRIAR: Yet hear my counsel –
GIOVANNI: As a voice of life.

It is, to repeat a point made in Chapter 1, a good example of the form of the text guiding staging.

Act 1, scene 2

The second scene widens the play's perspective and introduces the public, social world that collides ferociously and fatally with the individual, private desires raised in Giovanni's debate with the Friar. It is a much longer scene than the first (263 lines to 84) and may be divided into twelve separate units. Subdividing a complex scene in this way is often done in rehearsal to help the actors avoid 'playing the whole play at once'. Moreover, each unit requires a different pace and tone, and analysing them separately enables the director and actors to avoid blurring their edges. It is a particularly useful approach with Jacobean plays in general where the shifts of tone and mood within scenes are often rapid and marked, as analysis of 1.2 shows. The scene is also revealing in that it utilises all aspects of the Phoenix playing space and its actor/audience relationship.

Unit 1 (lines 1–19)

The energetic verbal sparring of the opening scene, and the comparative physical stillness of the implied staging which focuses the spectator's attention on the opposing arguments expressed, is matched now by violent physical energy and movement onto the stage. The opening is a mirror of the start of the first scene: two characters enter, again presumably both from the same side door, and again the dialogue suggests ('Come, sir, stand . . .') that this, as in 1.1, is not the first line of the exchange. Grimaldi's movement may be towards the other side door before Vasques's words pull him up – the stage movement suggesting passage along a street. Their costumes would readily distinguish the characters as being from different social classes. The stage direction indicates they are 'ready to fight', though the subsequent dialogue suggests that only one, if indeed either, has yet drawn a weapon, since the other is very keen to avoid a skirmish. The stage direction may, therefore, refer to their physical and vocal manner.

Superficially, the exchanges between Vasques and Grimaldi (as the dialogue soon identifies them) can appear as simply generalised abuse that forms the preamble to a fight. In fact, their lines comprise a very precise sequence of insults that would be read as such by a Jacobean audience, especially one with the social composition of the Phoenix. In order to provoke a fight, Vasques, Soranzo's servant, first accuses Grimaldi of being a coward if he will not fight. Grimaldi attempts to deflect this challenge on the grounds that he and his opponent are mismatched both socially and in terms of skill. Vasques retorts by calling him a braggart. Grimaldi now develops his original response by identifying in more detail the difference between them in terms of social standing, claiming that his reputation as a gentleman would be damaged if he were to fight with an inferior, a 'cast suit' – one whose clothes are passed on to him by his employer. (There is a theatrical in-joke here, since the clothes worn by actors were sometimes sold to them by the servants of wealthy benefactors or acquired second hand.) Vasques responds by upping the level of his insults, calling Grimaldi a cot-quean (a whore), accusing him of 'scolding' and 'prating' (words frequently applied to women; Annabella rebukes Putana for 'prating' later in the scene), and claiming Grimaldi is in fact inferior even to Soranzo's servants. Grimaldi attempts once again to assert his social superiority: not only is he 'a Gentleman', but one from Rome, not this out-of-the-way provincial town, and one who has, he repeats, won his 'honour' in battle. Vasques's retort is the turning point in the exchange:

VASQUES: You are a lying coward and a fool. Fight! or by these hilts
    I'll kill thee. Brave, my lord. You'll fight!

Duelling was forbidden by law, but the code of honour for a Jacobean gentleman was of greater force: Caesar in *The Roman Actor*, for example, argues that 'cruelty of honour' (4.2.289) prevents him from forgiving Paris, of whom he is truly fond, and demands that he kill the actor for betraying him. In such situations, as Richard Braithwaite explained in *The English Gentleman* (1630: 43):

> Can any Gentleman suffer with patience his Reputation to be brought in question? Can he endure to be challenged in a public place, and by that means incur the opinion of a Coward? Can he put up disgrace without observance, or observing it, not revenge it, when his very Honour (the vital blood of a Gentleman) is impeached?

At this moment, evidently tired of Grimaldi's stalling, Vasques uses the insult that no gentleman could ignore without losing face: he calls Grimaldi a liar. The fact that playwrights could be certain that their audiences would recognise the significance of this moment is clear from the number of plays – for both indoor and outdoor theatres – that refer to the codes of insult and duel. Often (as in Middleton and Dekker's *A Fair Quarrel*) the niceties of these codes provide key points in the plotting and characterisation, with satiric jokes being made at the expense of those who followed the complex rules of insult and duel. Shakespeare is sufficiently certain that enough people in the audience at the Globe would understand the code to make it the basis of a comic exchange between Jaques and Touchstone, the clown, in *As You Like It*:

TOUCHSTONE: I did dislike the cut of a certain courtier's beard. He sent me
    word, if I said his beard was not cut well, he was in the mind it was. This
    is called the Retort Courteous. If I sent him word again it was not well
    cut, he would send me word he cut it to please himself. This is called the
    Quip Modest. If again it was not well cut, he disabled my judgement.
    This is called the Reply Churlish. If again it was not well cut, he would
    answer I spake not true. This is called the Reproof Valiant. If again it was
    not well cut, he would say I lie. This is called the Countercheck
    Quarrelsome. And so to the Lie Circumstantial and the Lie Direct.
JAQUES: And how oft did you say his beard was not well cut?
TOUCHSTONE: I durst go no further than the Lie Circumstantial, nor he durst
    not give me the Lie Direct, and so we measured swords and parted.

(5.4.68–85)

Even the foolish Bergetto understands the significance of this potentially deadly procedure. As he tells his uncle, recalling an experience not unlike Grimaldi's:

> As I was walking just now in the street, I met a swaggering fellow who needs would take the wall of me, and because he did thrust me, I very valiantly called him rogue. He hereupon bade me draw; I told him I had more wit than so, but when he saw that I would not, he did so maul me with the hilts of his rapier that my head sung whilst my feet capered in the kennel.
>
> (2.6.69–75)

Perhaps chastened by this experience, Bergetto is wary of doing anything other than agreeing when Florio identifies the young woman Bergetto has fallen for as 'the doctor's niece' even when he has no idea whether that's right or not, since 'if I should have said no, I should have given him the lie, uncle, and so have deserved a dry beating again' (2.6.99–101).

Once this pattern of insult is understood, we will be able to read and perform the section as not merely a bluster of invective, but a conscious and deadly strategy on Vasques's part in keeping with the rules of combat. Having established that Vasques's accusation that Grimaldi is a liar is the crucial and climactic moment in the exchange, the section can be paced accurately. Placing a pause before the deliberate delivery of the line 'You are a lying coward and a fool' and the way Grimaldi's reception of the insult is played, will ensure that we register its significance. A further bonus may be that the audience laughter that most certainly erupted in the Jacobean playhouse on Grimaldi's response 'Provoke me not', may also be raised in ours.

Unit 2, stage direction: They fight

Stage fighting was a popular element of performances outdoors but (unsurprisingly given the more limited stage space available) much less frequent at indoor playhouses. Care was no doubt given to the staging of a fight, not only because of the proximity of those members of the audience seated on the stage, but because further information regarding a character's personality could clearly be revealed through the manner in which he fought: Grimaldi's back-stabbing attack on Bergetto in 3.7 is an extension of this.

Unit 3 (lines 20–29)

The rapid pace of the scene continues through the fight into lines 20–62 and the emergence onto the stage of Florio and Donado, whose opening lines indicate that they physically pull the two fighters apart, Florio going to Grimaldi, Donado to Vasques, and dragging them, I imagine, into diagonally opposite corners of the stage. Their lines are basically a series of rhetorical questions couched in fast-moving regular iambics designed to be spoken quickly and vehemently – the repeated 'ee' sound on the stressed words in 'As not to eat or sleep in peace at home', for example, driving the line and the character's energy.

Like the exchanges in the opening scene, these between Grimaldi and Vasques also seem designed to appeal to different factions. They are written in such a way as to encourage the actors to play to the audience, and for their characters to seek support among different groups among the spectators. Vocal interjections by early audiences at the Globe 3 reconstruction have tended to be rather indiscriminate, and clearly both they (and actors) need to learn how to balance different kinds and levels of engagement. The actors, for their part, need to be able to control audience response and there are clues in texts as to how this might operate. Florio's speech when he enters, for example, is made up of three repeated statements all saying basically the same thing:

> What mean these sudden broils so near my doors?
> Have you not other places but my house
> To vent the spleen of your disordered bloods?
> Must I be haunted still with such unrest
> As not to eat or sleep in peace at home?
>
> (20–5)

If I am right in thinking that the audience have been encouraged to engage directly in the scene so far (and it is difficult to imagine that the fight at least will not have generated some excitement) then it is possible that this speech is intended as much to quieten them as the characters. This is no doubt further achieved by the crucial question 'What's the ground?', and Soranzo's promise to all the 'signors' in the house that he will answer it.

Unit 4 (lines 30–62)

Soranzo's convoluted speech, however, is in marked contrast. Full of parenthetic remarks and multiple-clause sentences, it *cannot* be spoken quickly, and pulls the vocal and physical dynamic of the scene up short. The measured pace of the lines and, possibly, a later entry point, allow the stage focus to move entirely to Soranzo and change the pace of the scene completely. These shifts establish Soranzo's control of the stage, and the hierarchical structure of the play's world begins to emerge more clearly. No one interrupts Soranzo: he saunters, he addresses whomever he wants however he wants. It is a speech that swaggers.

On l.33 Soranzo apparently draws the attention of the characters onstage and of the audience to the arrival of Annabella on the upper level where she has entered accompanied by Putana. Annabella's presence performs a number of functions: at last we see the woman who is, we know now, sought after by three men (Giovanni, Grimaldi and Soranzo), and who is the focus of the verbal and physical disputes we have witnessed in the opening two scenes. Soranzo, meanwhile, can use the fact that she witnesses Grimaldi's humiliation to demonstrate further his own superiority. Furthermore, the actors' position on the upper level frames the female character as an object of the gaze of the main-stage audience of characters and stage-sitters (all male) and of the men in the audience proper (and exercises on the reconstruction have demonstrated the potency of this stage location). It is a perspective emphasised by Soranzo's implied gesture (on line 33) towards 'Signor Florio's daughter', further defining Annabella in terms of her relationship to her father rather than by her name. There is, in fact, a double perspective at work: the audience observe Annabella from their position as audience ('so this is the woman over whom everyone in the play so far seems to be quarrelling!') but, in the following unit (if there has been the interaction with the stage I believe Ford intended) the spectators are also made aware of themselves by Annabella's companion, Putana, as participants in the preceding action. It is another example of how audiences of these plays are shifted between engagement and detachment.

Unit 5 (lines 63–99)

Putana is rather like the only member of the audience with a programme, or one who has seen the play before, as she fills in the details on characters and events for everyone in the playhouse. It should be noted that Putana speaks in prose, Annabella in verse, not because of their different status, but because of their very different viewpoints on the events and characters they have been watching. It is important also to note that Putana and Annabella are placed close to members of the audience, visually virtually indistinguishable from those seated either side of them on the upper level. Putana's remarks are those of anyone commenting on what they have just seen and heard: 'here's threatening, quarrelling and fighting on every side' (63–4). The phrase 'on every side' confirms, I think, that the play so far has been concerned to arouse partisan and opposing views in its audience – between those of different classes, ages and allegiances – divisions that might be enforced by the stage rails and (possibly) walls dividing the boxes from the auditorium. Indeed, the play up to this point has introduced a student, his tutor, a foreign nobleman (Grimaldi makes much of the fact that he doesn't come from Parma), an aristocrat, his servant, two merchants, a young female and her chaperone – precisely those sectors of society we might expect to have found represented in a private theatre audience.

Unit 6 (lines 100–125)

Putana directs Annabella's (and the audience's) attention back to the main stage on the entrance of Bergetto and Poggio. Her commentary from the balcony, mixed with the onstage dialogue, ensures that the audience concentrates in turn on each of the protagonists, and that the foundations of the narrative are well laid.

Unit 7 (lines 126–138)

The entrance of Giovanni offers an interesting example of an issue regarding performance that I raised in Chapter 3. Annabella actually describes the physical performance she and the audience witness:

> this is some woeful thing
> Wrapped up in grief, some shadow of a man.
> Alas, he beats his breast, and wipes his eyes,
> Drowned all in tears: methinks I hear him sigh.
>
> (131–4)

As I pointed out in Chapter 3, it is evident that certain gestures signified distinct states of mind, and that to beat the breast, weep and sigh were conventional expressions of grief: as John Bulwer noted, in the theatre (as opposed to oratory) 'the Breast stricken with the Hand is an action of Grief, sorrow, repentance and indignation'.[12] While many Jacobean acting signifiers may not match our own and may, consequently, prove difficult for an actor to utilise convincingly, Jonathan Cullen, who played Giovanni in the 1991 RSC production (in which the lines were cut), always repeated these precise actions offstage before he entered, finding they helped generate the physical and emotional energy he needed for the scene.

It should be noted that Putana, in response to Annabella's remarks, also speaks verse. Such shifts are usually for a dramatic purpose; here, I think, it is intended to effect a change in the energy onstage as we move from the mundane, social (prose) world we have just observed, to the intense personal (verse) relationship of Annabella and Giovanni.

Unit 8 (lines 139–158)

The first soliloquy of the play. It performs two functions – it allows time for the two actors on the upper level to descend to the main stage via the stairs at the rear of the musicians' space; secondly, in being addressed directly to the audience, it allows Ford to present the change in Giovanni that has occurred since his exit in scene 1 when he vowed he would conquer his sexual desire for his sister. Soliloquies enable the actor to forge an empathetic relationship with the audience or seek to engage them emotionally and imaginatively in the stage action. They may also challenge the hearer to take a critical attitude to the speaker, and here Giovanni continues to factionalise those listeners: 'I find all these but dreams and old men's tales / To fright unsteady youth (151–2). This aspect of the soliloquy is especially important in those cases (Beatrice-Joanna is another good example) where the actions of a character in a play seem designed by the author to demand an increasingly objective assessment by the audience. In this play, although Giovanni begins with the audience's sympathy on his side, our attitude to him at the end is radically different. Ron Daniels, who directed a production for the RSC in 1977, saw Giovanni as a radical, a revolutionary – an interpretation, in my view, that makes the mistake of seeing Giovanni as he sees himself. More accurate, I believe (and much braver) is the line played by Jonathan Cullen, who saw Giovanni ultimately as a butcher, a 'sexual terrorist' who denies Annabella any of the 'freedom' Giovanni trumpets (private letter).

Unit 9 (lines 158–170)

Annabella and Putana join Giovanni on the main stage. Annabella's act of sharing his line indicates the energy with which she enters, while Giovanni's completion of that shared line as an aside suggests his difficulty in encountering her face to face. The 'shape' of the text on the page (in this and the following unit) indicates a further change in rhythm of the scene, as it moves into dialogue, with a mixture of short, full-length and shared lines.

Unit 10 (lines 171–202)

Following Putana's exit, a section of rapid exchanges (too short to be identified as either verse or prose) shifts into obvious verse for Giovanni (reflecting the emotional level of his expression) intercut with short exchanges from an apparently bewildered Annabella.

Unit 11 (lines 203–240)

At line 202 a weapon is drawn for the second time in the scene. The sexual imagery is clear – in Guiseppe Griffi's 1973 film version of the play, the lovers grasped the knife together before letting it fall; in a production directed by Jerry Turner for the Oregon Shakespeare Festival in 1981, Giovanni held it erect between them as they knelt (Wymer 1995: 133). It seems likely, too, that for some in the audience the action would have echoed (and still may for an audience today) the moment in *The Duchess of Malfi* when Ferdinand threatens his sister with a dagger. In Webster's scene (3.2), while the sexual imagery is as clear as it is in Ford's, Ferdinand's act of tempting his sister to suicide aligns him 'with the diabolical agents of the morality plays whose attempts to damn the Mankind figure frequently culminated in a temptation to that despair of God's mercy which suicide was thought to indicate' (Wymer 1995: 63). This reading is not wholly applicable to this moment in *'Tis Pity* (though Giovanni is encouraging his sister to perform an act that will damn her) but the action of this unit must be recalled in 5.5 when Giovanni again produces a dagger, but this time murders his sister. This powerful gesture prompts Annabella to recognise a move from apparent 'game' to 'earnest' in her brother's behaviour. She apparently takes the knife (if his line to her, 'Why d'ee not strike', 215, is to make sense) and that enables the shift to the next unit at line 240 to come as a surprise to the audience.

Unit 12 (lines 240–263)

Interestingly, the line on which she articulates her decision is a shared one:

GIOVANNI: Must I now live or die?
ANNABELLA: Live. Thou hast won . . .

   Shared lines should be seen as acting guides, indicating here that there should be no pause before Annabella answers his question. In practice, I have found and observed that actors like to take a pause at this moment while they seemingly make up their mind. If the line is played seamlessly, however, it suggests that Annabella has, in fact, come to a decision earlier as, indeed, she proceeds to explain she has. The preceding dialogue is used by Annabella to realise not that her brother loves her but that he feels the same as she does, demonstrated in action by the fact that it is she who first kneels to begin their 'betrothal' ceremony. In other words, the language and action in this short section enable the actor playing Annabella to match, as it were, the aims and energies that, so far in the play, Giovanni has been given more lines and time to express. It enables Ford, in the closing moments of the scene, through a pattern of mirrored gestures and lines, to present an image of two figures equally engaged in thought and action. The physical acts of kneeling, kissing and embracing (plus the possible translation of dagger into cross) are mediated by Ford's insistence on underlining the familial relationships in the spoken dialogue (the repetitions of 'brother' and 'sister' in particular). The result is a compelling tension between the image and its possible interpretations – betrothal and incestuous union – a tension that in various forms (see the discussion of 3.7 below) informs the entire play.

In his commendatory verses to Massinger's *The Great Duke of Florence*, Ford wrote that 'Action gives many poems right to live', and the text of *'Tis Pity* and other plays indicate how conscious he was of the visual dynamic of the stage image, gesture and grouping. Among the effects he could utilise were those involving the playhouse's candlelight, and Ford was clearly alert to the mood-inducing, expressive use of light and the psychological and emotional impact of the relationship of light and action. In *Love's Sacrifice*, for example, one finds the stage directions:

   Enter Colona with lights, Bianca, Fiormonda, Fernando and D'Avolos;

Colona places the lights on a table, and sets down a chessboard.

(2.3)

and, in the following scene:

Enter Bianca, her hair about her ears, in her night mantle; she draws
a curtain, where Fernando is discovered in bed sleeping, she sets down
the candle before the bed, and goes to the bed side.

(2.4)

It obviously took time to extinguish and relight candles, and it is significant
therefore that (as in *Love's Sacrifice* and other indoor plays by other writers) the
scenes in *'Tis Pity* in which candlelight plays a key role in establishing place
and mood are grouped together in a specific sequence. The first indications of
impending darkness are given in 3.5 where, in the space of a few lines, three
references are made to the onset of night: 'this very night' (8), 'this night' (13),
'a night' (14). This is not dissimilar to the technique in the open-air playhouses, but I suggest it may be preparing for a short break between 3.5 and 3.6
in which some alteration is made to the lighting state as indicated by the
detailed stage direction that heads 3.6:

Enter the Friar sitting in a chair, Annabella kneeling and whispering to
him; a table before him and wax lights; she weeps and wrings her hands.

The implied stage image, with its obvious representation of an altar table,
clearly aims to demonstrate the spiritual pressures being brought to bear on
Annabella. In my experience, it is unwise to carry onstage a table with the candles already lit (curtains and breeze have a habit of extinguishing them), and it
seems to me likely that the table was placed and then the candles placed and lit.
Indeed, this action would repeat in miniature the procedure of lighting the playhouse's candles at the start of the performance, and enable the sequence of
scenes in which the artificial light plays a key role to be firmly established as virtually a separate inset play. Dekker refers to the shutters on the windows in an
indoor playhouse being 'clapped up' and if this were done, perhaps with some
accessible candles being extinguished at the same time, it would further darken
the auditorium.[13] In experiments in our reconstruction at Bristol we found
that even a slight reduction in the (admittedly already quite dim) light effected
a substantial change in the stage atmosphere, and that this change could be
swiftly achieved by snuffing the wall-mounted candles on the side boxes and on
the rear facade. The removal of the 'wax lights' at the end of 3.6 will make the
stage darken further, especially as the candles have been the focus point of the
audience's eyes, while the change of scene may allow time for more candles to be
extinguished in further preparation for the following scene which needs to
replicate a street at night.

171

Ford makes very careful use of the stage space and lighting in 3.7, and the text allows us to reconstruct the staging with some precision. Grimaldi enters carrying a 'dark lantern' – that is, one with a device for obscuring its light. His opening lines are obviously addressed to the audience, and it seems likely to me that the best place for an actor playing a well-dressed young man-about-town to conceal himself (the stage direction is *He lies down*), is among those well-dressed young men-about-town sitting or sprawling at the sides of the stage. Once Grimaldi extinguishes his lantern at the end of his opening lines, the stage will again seem even darker than it actually is, since, as modern day lighting designers know, adding a light onstage and then removing it has the effect of making the previous state seem dimmer, even though it has not in fact changed at all, especially when Grimaldi's lantern (like the 'wax lights' in 3.6) will have been a focus of the audience's attention.

Bergetto and Philotis enter from one of the side doors (bearing in mind the possible convention for moving along a street employed in 1.2) with Richardetto and Poggio some distance behind; perhaps they do not actually enter until Grimaldi has finished his lines. It is important that none of the other characters sees Grimaldi actually stab Bergetto, and that Bergetto himself has no idea what has happened to him. This is perfectly feasible. In an article in the *Guardian* (28 December 1992) on street violence, 'Blooding of the New Blades', the author wrote:

> Young men stabbed in the chest or the back, often unaware of the extent of their injuries until they reach the hospital, are brought in on an alarmingly regular basis.

It is clear from the text that Richardetto dispatches Poggio for help and lights (back through the door from which they entered) before he moves to Bergetto. It is equally clear that Richardetto's doubt over the extent of Bergetto's injuries results from the fact that neither he nor the audience can see very well. The tone of the scene is as important here as it is in the scene of the death of Mercutio (*Romeo and Juliet*, 3.1) on which it is obviously based. Bergetto, presented from the outset as a buffoon is still, from the point of view of his companions, playing the fool, and it is vital that the actor's perfor-mance allows this interpretation to be placed upon it. It is not until Poggio returns accompanied by Officers with lights, and a torch or lantern is either passed to Richardetto or held near him, that the truth of the situation dawns on them. Following the exit of the Officers (the departure of their lanterns again darkening the stage) the mood switches once more, and the rapidity with which the tone changes from one extreme to another, from laughter to sym-pathy to sorrow, all within the space of only 38 lines, is characteristic of the Grotesque (see Chapter 6). The creation of this sense of disruption and confu-sion is aided by the constant shifting of the light as the characters (and audience) try to work out what's going on.

Philotis starts to tear her petticoat to make bandages, while Richardetto comforts Bergetto. In a play rife with selfish and self-seeking men, especially in their attitudes to women, the poignancy of this innocent's death is underlined by his concern for Philotis, and the final image (Richardetto perhaps having led Philotis away) of Poggio cradling his dead friend is a deeply moving one, the more so because of its contrast with the mood of the earlier part of the scene.

The hand-held lanterns or torches illuminate the stage action more precisely than is usual under the even candle-light, producing an effect not dissimilar to the chiaroscuro (strongly contrasted light and shadow) seen in Caravaggio's or Rembrandt's work, and matching the similarly distinct tones and moods of the action in general in this and other plays. Now suddenly an expression or gesture (such as Richardetto looking at the blood on his hands) can be caught, as it were, in startling close-up.

Scene 3.8, a short scene between Vasques and Hippolita, is not specifically located. As it is placed between two scenes which are clearly exterior, both of which trace the single narrative of the death of Bergetto and the search for his murderer, it may be that it is intended to be played on the upper level (although in all other instances in the play scenes placed there have *above* specified in the printed text's stage direction). The scene's function is to act as a kind of commentary on other plot lines to keep them alive while the death of Bergetto strand of the narrative is played out. Furthermore, if placed on the upper level, and particularly if the actors carry lights, the effect will be to draw the focus away from the main stage. Bergetto's body can then be removed before 3.9, when the central doors become those of the Cardinal's palace. The Cardinal may enter through these doors (perhaps with servants with lights) but it is also possible that the Cardinal and Grimaldi also appear on the upper level (they do not enter until l.27, which means there is plenty of time for Vasques and Hippolita to vacate the space). In that case, the physical positioning would again embody the hierarchical structures of power in Parma and underline the Cardinal's remoteness. The fact that Grimaldi kneels, however (at some point between l.39 and the Cardinal's 'Rise up, Grimaldi' at l.50), may argue against this. The upper level had a balustrade and it might be thought that a character would be unlikely to kneel while speaking. References to characters kneeling, or even lying down, on the upper level are not unknown, however, and that may be explained by the fact that they would still be partially visible and perfectly audible through the rails of the balcony, especially as the instances are invariably short in duration.

Scene 3.9 concludes the third act. The fourth act opens with a feast to celebrate the marriage of Annabella and Soranzo, and the music between the acts will not only establish that festive atmosphere, but the interval, used to trim the candles, would provide ample opportunity to relight those that had been extinguished and, if necessary, un-shutter the windows.

Analysis of the Quarto text in the light of the Jones drawings raises further questions concerning the use of the main stage and the upper level. Apart from my speculation concerning its use in 3.8 and 3.9, three scenes, or parts of scenes, in the play are clearly marked in the text to be played 'above': 1.2, where Annabella and Putana observe the quarrel between the suitors in the street below; 3.2, where Giovanni observes Soranzo's wooing of Annabella; and 5.1, where Annabella's repentance is observed by the Friar. All these scenes are linked, therefore, by acts of *observation* and *commentary*, both characteristic of the use of the upper level, and which allow the dramatist to control the audience's perception of the action.

Some scenes are more difficult in terms of reconstructing possible staging. For example, the stage direction at the start of 4.1 reads:

> A Banquet. Hautboys. Enter the Friar, Giovanni, Annabella, Philotis, Soranzo, Donado, Florio, Richardetto, Putana and Vasques.

The New Mermaids editor suggests that the Friar's lines (1–6) indicate 'a more formal feast', but if that were so it raises the question of whether there is sufficient stage space, especially following the stage direction at l.36:

> Enter Hippolita and Ladies in white robes, with garlands of willows. Music and a dance.

Assuming even merely two Ladies the stage now has to accommodate thirteen characters and the dance, as well, presumably, as the stage-sitters. During experiments on the reconstruction at Bristol I have been struck by how precise and formal the staging needs to be (even if one relaxed normal expectations in terms of sightlines), particularly because of the presence of audience members seated on each side of the stage itself and of the need to satisfy the reasonable demands of all sections of the audience, especially those seated above the rear wall of the stage. In this particular instance, I think it most likely that the characters stand onstage or sit (some perhaps using the rails and again, possibly, making use of the stage-sitters to help create the scene), with some characters perhaps positioned upstage in front of the side doors, allowing Hippolita and her Ladies to enter through the central opening. Exactly how these staging problems were resolved at the Phoenix cannot be determined, though it may be worth noting that with any performance on a thrust stage, and even more so in-the-round, a spectator spends (or should spend) equal amounts of time seeing characters' faces and backs, or reading scenes from the expressions and actions of those addressed or from listening to what is said: indeed, Flecknoe's praise of Burbage's 'reaction' acting may reflect this fact (see p. 73). Furthermore, as I observed in Chapter 4, the social deployment of the audience may have influenced staging decisions in ways that would seem unacceptable to us.

However, large numbers of people onstage and substantial items of furniture (usually beds or tables) do cause more difficulties, partly because of the space the furniture takes and partly because it renders the actors more static and the sightlines therefore more fixed. In 5.6., for example, the stage direction indicates that the characters enter and 'take their *places*'. T.J. King (1964–5) supposes that these words refer to seats onstage, and it may be that Soranzo's lines (2–3) do refer to some sort of formal arrangement. As with the earlier banquet scene, the numbers onstage are high – reaching eleven in this instance (assuming two attendants and two Banditti). In addition, a fight is called for which, even if it is not so formal a sword fight as in 1.2, will still occupy a significant amount of space. (Always remember the presence of the stage-sitters.) Giovanni's lines suggest that he is mobile in the scene, and able to confront particular characters with the heart on the dagger, though this is not necessarily inconsistent with a table placed onstage. If it is meant to be a formal set-piece the setting may be reasonably complex. The stage directions in 3.3 of Thomas Drue's *The Bloody Banquet* (Phoenix, *c.* 1639, are precise instructions for setting up a banquet scene using four stagehands/servants: the opening stage direction – 'Soft music, a table with lights set out. Arras spread' [as a tablecloth or a carpet on the stage floor]. – is followed a few lines later by 'Loud music. Enter 2 with a Banquet; other 2 with lights; they set 'em down and depart' – and, after further lines, 'Loud Music, Enter Roxano, Mazeres and the 4 Servants, with dishes of sweet meats, Roxano places them: each having delivered his dish makes low obeisance' and exits.

There is, however, a potential stage-management problem caused by the fact that the bed (an essential item in the preceding scene) will have to be struck through the central doorway. So perhaps no table was used in 5.6, the actors entering through the side doors carrying stools while Giovanni carried the body of Annabella out through the central exit followed by the bed – this would provide a smooth overlapping scene change (added to which there might be some changes to the level of light onstage in the manner suggested in *The Bloody Banquet* example). Or perhaps no furniture at all was used in 5.6: in Thomas Goffe's *The Raging Turk*, for example, performed by students of Christ Church College, Oxford, probably in the early 1620s, a stage direction reads 'Enter a banquet, all kneel' (E 903) and a cup is passed round between seven characters.

The frequent references in stage directions to beds being 'thrust' onto the stage suggest it was common practice for the stagehands simply to push the bed through the central entrance, frequently with the occupants in place (perfectly easily done on the Bristol reconstruction). That is what might be signalled at the start of 5.5 by the direction 'Enter Giovanni and Annabella lying on a bed'. Or the direction might simply mean that the bed is set and the actors move to it and start the scene. As Giovanni notes, this bed is a symbol of both love and death. It is here, as Giovanni tells us in a chilling phrase, that he 'digged for food' (5.6.25) and, depending on whether a table is used for the banquet in the final scene, the placing of the bed and table in identical positions might be employed to underline the grim parallels between the two scenes.

We should not forget, however, that solutions to staging problems invariably rely on theatrical common sense and the audience's willing acceptance of the demands they can see for themselves to be placed on the performers. On the modern stage one frequently sees actors setting and striking quite elaborate scenes with practised ease and speed or handling large scenes on small stages; I see no reason to suppose that in doing this they are not repeating the actions of their Jacobean counterparts.

6

'POISON IN JEST'[1]
Some comic (ir)resolutions

At the opening of Act 5 of *Hamlet*, the stage direction in the 1603 Quarto reads *enter Clowne and an other*, but the scene's speech headings identify the characters only as 'Clowne' and '2'. It is generally agreed that this Quarto was an unauthorised, pirated edition, possibly based on the memory of one of the actors who took part or on a 'stol'n and surreptitious' copy, and published without the permission of either the Company or Shakespeare himself: a so-called 'bad quarto'.[2] A second Quarto rapidly followed, described on its title-page as 'Newly imprinted . . . according to the true and perfect copy'. Its fifth act opening stage direction specifies *Enter two Clowns*, but the speech headings now identify the first Clown as a Gravedigger, 'a figure who derives in part from the knavish Sexton, a popular character in contemporary farces and jigs, with an ancestry that can be traced to the gravedigging Death of the *danses macabres*' (Neill 1992: 51–2). The second character is still distinguished only as Other, and the common practice onstage of making this Clown a gravedigger too (which originated in the late seventeenth century) is not supported by the dialogue. His role is basically that of the feed to his companion.

After a bit of by-play, some song and comic business, the second Clown leaves. A moment later, Hamlet and Horatio enter. The Clown/Gravedigger (presumably standing in the stage trap) continues to dig Ophelia's grave, throwing up skulls as he does so, while Hamlet speculates with his characteristic witty cynicism on the original identity of the skulls' owners. The Clown/Gravedigger then produces a skull to which he can put a name ('This same skull, sir, was Yorick's skull, the King's jester') and Hamlet's comments move from the general to the particular.[3] The image of Hamlet with the skull (the most celebrated stage image in Renaissance drama) would have been read by the contemporary audience as an emblem of the Melancholic Man (and possibly a self-conscious one), but I assume Shakespeare decided that the skull's owner, Yorick, should have been a jester rather than any other kind of servant, because Hamlet, too, has taken on an 'antic disposition', the word 'antic' being a Jacobean synonym for 'clown'.[4]

Not only the fusion of words, gesture and positioning should be noted, but the 'presence' on the Globe stage of the original actors involved: Richard

Burbage (celebrated tragic actor) playing Hamlet, and Robert Armin (an equally celebrated comic actor) as the Clown/Gravedigger, holding a clown's skull. If, to the contemporary audience, there was a reference through Yorick to the greatest Elizabethan clown of all – Richard Tarlton – who had died only a few years earlier, in 1588 – the image takes on yet a further resonance. In recent times it would be like Laurence Olivier acting alongside Max Miller, or perhaps Ian McKellen (holding the skull supposedly of Max Miller) acting with Tommy Cooper: two great performers, their seemingly opposed energies of tragedy and comedy equally balanced. In fact, Kenneth Branagh's film version of *Hamlet* (1996) includes at this point a flash-back in which the veteran British comedian Ken Dodd plays Yorick. Within the emblem of the jester's skull Shakespeare embodies the twin poles of jest and death between which fluctuate the action of the play overall and the behaviour of its central character in particular. The stage image as a whole – created by a complex compound of action, language, properties and actor identity – establishes a further emblem that characterises much Elizabethan and Jacobean drama: the jester in the graveyard.

In mixing 'Kings and Clownes', 'hornpipes and funerals', Shakespeare was directly contravening the critical precepts of Sir Philip Sidney who had decried such 'mongrel' practices in his *Defence of Poesy*.[5] But as Michael Bristol has argued, Sidney's 'fundamental distrust of ludicrous situations and the complex attitudes of shared pleasure and derision experienced in viewing such situations' was the exception rather than the rule and out of kilter with the time (1985: 127). Indeed, other theoretical opinion supported combinations of apparent opposites: Erasmus, for example, had argued in *The Praise of Folly* that 'Truth is grasped as a mingling of joy and grief'. It is precisely 'this linking of strong contrary feelings' that connects Erasmus's ideas with the most systematic of Renaissance theories of laughter, Laurent Joubert's *Treatise on Laughter*, published in 1579. According to Joubert:

> laughter is made up of the contrariety or battle of two feelings, holding the middle ground between joy and sadness.
>
> (Bristol 1985: 133)

Contrasts and contradictions are defining characteristics of the work of many Elizabethan and Jacobean dramatists, and virtually all the plays discussed in this book are built up of strongly opposed moods and modes of expression within the same play, scene, speech, or, on occasions, even the same line. It is a stylistic strategy with which all who work on these plays in practice must engage, but is also, as Nicholas Brooke notes, one that not only intrigues but sometimes alienates performers, audiences and students alike, and for which the dramatists have 'come in for some hard treatment' (Brooke 1979; Hoy 1973: 50).

In recent years, critics who have turned their attention to the incongruity that characterises so much of the drama of the period have found in it close similarities to the work of Mannerist artists. They have compared the playwrights with painters such as El Greco, Pontormo, Parmigianino, Fiorentino and Tintoretto, sculptors such as Michelangelo, and writers such as John Donne and Montaigne (who described his own writings as 'monstrous bodies, patched and huddled together of diverse members, without any certain or well-ordered figure'). The work of these artists is linked by a desire to contain contrasting, often contradictory, modes of expression within the same frame, or to collide apparently irreconcilable elements of content and form. They seek (to borrow Dr Johnson's famous definition of metaphysical poetry) 'to yoke heterogeneous elements . . . by violence together' (Wain 1973: 254), and so create a tangible, palpable experience for the spectator of the tension that exists in the subject matter itself.

One example of Mannerist art has been widely drawn on to illustrate this comparison: El Greco's *The Burial of the Count of Orgaz*, painted between 1586 and 1588 for the parish church of Santo Tome in Spain.[6] The contract signed by the artist lists the principal elements that were to be included in the picture:

> On the canvas he is to paint the scene in which the parish priest and other clerics were saying the prayers, about to bury Don Gonzalo de Ruiz, Lord of Orgaz, when Saint Augustine and Saint Stephen descended to bury the body of this gentleman, one holding the head, the other the feet, and placing him in the sepulchre. Around the scene should be many people who are looking at it and, above all this, there is to be an open sky showing the glory of the heavens.

The two-storey composition of the finished painting was nothing new. Nor, taken separately, were the style and arrangement of the heavenly figures in the upper section or the 'naturalistic' portrayal of the mourners (dressed in sixteenth-century clothes to witness a fourteenth-century event) in the lower. El Greco's innovation lay in juxtaposing these elements within the same 'frame' – an antithesis of styles (*contraposto*) characteristic of Mannerist art. Mannerism is a highly self-conscious form that employs a number of stylistic devices by which it calls attention to itself as a work of art. Among these is the presence in the painting of the figure of a *Sprecher* ('speaker'), in this instance a young boy (thought to be El Greco's son, Jorge Manuel) who stands in the foreground, his feet clearly set at a level below those of the other figures, looking out at the spectator and gesturing towards the scene behind him. The sprecher's function parallels that of dramatic characters such as Bosola, Flamineo or Vindice, whose role is in part to bridge the gap between the play world and the world of the audience and to comment on the stage action. (See Pentzell 1986; Greenwood 1988.)

In its component parts and overall effect El Greco's painting operates in a fashion similar to much Elizabethan and particularly Jacobean drama: it is antithetical in structure, inviting the viewer to engage but prepared to hold him or her at arm's length; it is clever, intriguing and disturbing – all at the same time. Arnold Hauser's comments on the relationship of the two halves of El Greco's painting are equally applicable to plays:

> It is only a half-truth to describe mannerism as unnaturalistic and for-malistic, or irrational and bizarre, for it possesses as many naturalistic as unnaturalistic features, and its rational are no less important than its irrational elements . . . its essence lies in this tension, this union of apparently irreconcilable elements.
>
> (1965: 12)

In other words, the impact on the viewer is created not merely by the pres-ence in the work of strange or unexpected elements, but by the radical contrast within the same work of one mode of presentation with its opposite.[7] The most common contrast in Elizabethan and Jacobean plays is of comedy with violent action (such as in the Agincourt sequence described by Matthew Warchus), but it should be emphasised that this is only one possibility: the key point is the contrast itself. Linda Murray describes her response to Mannerist architecture as one of 'unease', brought about by its 'confusion between forms', its 'distor-tions' and 'surprises'.[8] As the analysis of specific texts that follows will illustrate, these terms could as easily and accurately be applied to the dis-turbing responses these plays can arouse in an audience in the theatre.

There is, however, an aesthetic of dissonance more immediately applicable to the Elizabethan and Jacobean period than Mannerism, and one that can be applied uncontentiously and productively to both literature and the visual arts. Furthermore, it is an aesthetic that in illuminating the late sixteenth, early sev-enteenth and twentieth centuries helps further to establish reasons for our current excitement in these plays. It is the concept of the Grotesque. The ori-gins of the Grotesque in the visual arts lie at least as far back as the early Christian period of Roman culture, where there evolved a style of combining human, animal and vegetable images, intricately interwoven, in a single paint-ing. The Roman writer Marcus Vitruvius Pollio, writing in the age of Augustus, described the new style in which:

> contemporary artists decorate the walls with monstrous forms rather than reproducing clear images of the familiar world.
>
> (Quoted in Kayser 1968: 20)

The term Grotesque was first applied to this kind of mixed decoration fol-lowing the discovery in 1480 of the Domus Aurea, the home of the Roman

Emperor Nero. After Nero's time the villa had been incorporated in the foundations of the Baths of Trajan, and its rooms filled in with earth. Because the
buried rooms had to be entered through the vaults of the Baths and excavated
downwards through the earth, the discoverers believed they had found a series of
artificial caves, or grottoes, and they called the decorative work they found
grottesca, 'grotto work': interestingly, the word chosen in England to describe such
features was 'antic', which, as we have seen, was also another term for clown.

Vitruvius identified two key elements in the Grotesque style, which are
repeated, if in different terms, by virtually all subsequent writers on the genre –
the sense of confusion experienced by the viewer, caused by the presence of
incompatible elements, and secondly, the artist's refusal to reproduce 'clear
images of the familiar world'. In other words, Vitruvius characterised the
Grotesque as transgressing the classicist's notion of order in both the world and
the artistic representations of that world, finding the artist's work at one and
the same time monstrous and ludicrous (Thomson 1972). It is a criticism that
prefigures the charges levelled against much Elizabethan and Jacobean drama.

English Renaissance artists did not need classical or continental precedents
for examples of what St Bernard of Clairvaux had described as 'deformed
beauty and beautiful deformity'. Willard Farnham has illustrated how English
medieval art – painting, architecture and decoration – was suffused with
Grotesque images struggling with what he terms 'non-grotesque' images to
create a tension in the spectator, seen, for example, in the mix of idealised and
distorted human figures, natural and fantastic animals and plant forms commonly found in contemporary illustrations.[9] In his detailed study of the
Grotesque, David Evett argues that as far as visual and literary artists of the
Tudor and Stuart periods were concerned the Grotesque mode was both more
extensively used and more significant than has been recognised:

> Grotesque features, singly or in groups, constituted the most striking
> class of decorative elements on the possessions of well-to-do
> Elizabethans – their houses, their furniture, their lingerie.
>
> (1990: 132)

In other words, everything that surrounded them. It is, Evett suggests, 'just
such stylistic mongrels that ultimately prove to be the most satisfying Tudor
works of art' (77), and he sees in the Grotesque a challenge to order, stability
and control similar to that located by Hauser in Mannerism:

> We can therefore consider the Grotesque as a style in which
> renascence artists could express some of the tensions that arose from
> the incompatability between the ideals espoused and imposed by
> government, by church, by university, by all the agencies of institu-
> tional culture, and the actualities of individual experience.
>
> (1990: 138)

That they should have sought such 'exploratory, critical, sometimes even subversive' (Evett 1990: 140) aesthetic forms, capable of embodying such ideas is hardly surprising. As Cyrus Hoy writes:

> It would be odd if so thorough-going a revolution in man's conception of himself, his world, his relation to deity – all accomplished within the limits of a single century – had not left its impact on the art of the sixteenth and seventeenth centuries and of course it has done so, both on the art of literature, and on the arts of painting, architecture and sculpture.
>
> (1973: 49)

Evett's discussion, however, is not confined to the Renaissance, and he argues that the Grotesque mode has given the same opportunity to artists of all places and periods. In the light of that claim it is interesting to note that a resurgence of interest in El Greco and John Donne early in the twentieth century coincided with the modernist spirit in theatre that sought to hold elements of naturalism and various forms of non-naturalism within a single work and with a growing interest in Renaissance, especially Jacobean, playwrights. Philip Thomson has summarised the role of the Grotesque in twentieth-century art and literature:

> Where previous ages had seen in it merely the principle of disharmony run wild, or relegated it to the cruder species of the comic, the present tendency . . . is to view the grotesque as . . . an appropriate expression of the problematical nature of existence. It is no accident that the grotesque mode in art and literature tends to be prevalent in societies and eras marked by strife, radical change or disorientation. Although one runs the risk of succumbing to clichés when one regards the past forty or fifty years as just such an era convulsed by momentous social and intellectual changes, it can nevertheless be fairly said that this is an important contributing factor in the present artistic situation, where the grotesque is very much in evidence.
>
> (1972: 11)

Thomson is writing from the perspective of the early 1970s, but his description of the upheavals of the preceding fifty years could easily have been written by someone in 1640 looking back over the same period of time. Thomson's list of modern exponents of the Grotesque in drama include Pinter and Orton, to whom I would add Nikolai Erdman from the early years of this century (his plays *The Suicide* and *The Mandate* are exemplary Grotesque texts) and, more recently, Dennis Potter (the disturbing *Brimstone and Treacle* in particular), virtually anything by Howard Barker (whose work reveals a vision of a world that is 'vile, well no, it's pretty . . . vile and pretty – at the same time', *The Castle,*

Act 2, scene 2), and Terry Johnson's *Hysteria*.[10] Thomson cites Fellini's *Satyricon* as an example of a grotesque film, an assessment that students watching it now are often at a loss to understand, beyond the incongruity implicit in the figure of the hermaphrodite, or the disparity between the physical beauty of the young heroes and the ugliness and corruption of their world and behaviour. What was shocking in the mid 1960s no longer disturbs or challenges the viewer; the extremes are no longer at the edge. For modern examples of the Grotesque in film, I would suggest Peter Greenaway's *The Cook, The Thief, His Wife and Her Lover* (with its startling collisions of sound and image and its cannibalistic climax), David Cronenberg's *Crash* or (with reservations) Quentin Tarantino's *Pulp Fiction*. Alejandro Jodorovsky's *Santa Sangre* – which the director summed up in a speech at the 1989 London Film Festival as containing 'Violence. *Yes!* Poetry. *Yes!* Tragedy. *Yes!* Madness. *Yes!* Comedy. *Yes!*' – may appear to share some characteristics of the Grotesque. In fact, in its desire to shock with no obvious further purpose, Jodorovsky's film has more in common with a distant cousin of the Grotesque – grand guignol. This term derives from, and describes, a theatre devoted to extreme and realistic portrayals of violence that flourished in Paris from the end of the nineteenth century until the end of the Second World War saw its decline. The theatre finally closed in 1962. (See Emeljanow 1991 and Callahan 1991.)

I began this brief discussion of the Grotesque by referring to the image of 'the jester in the graveyard'. An early Egyptian illustration draws its humour from the chaos of a collision of funeral barges.[11] In similar fashion Grotesque plays in all periods frequently employ graveyard settings and funerals, the conventional expectation of mood and behaviour in such an environment providing a strong base from which to challenge those expectations. Comic and tragic plays alike explored the humorous potential of the social and dramatic conventions associated with funerals, including *Summer's Last Will and Testament* (1592), *Antonio and Mellida* (c. 1599), *The Honest Whore* (Part 1; 1604), *The Widow's Tears* (1605), *The Knight of the Burning Pestle* (c. 1606) and *The Wits* (1634) (Neill 1992). Later Grotesque texts, such as Frank Wedekind's *Spring Awakening*, Nikolai Erdman's *The Suicide* and Joe Orton's *Loot*, have also productively exploited the funeral/graveyard. To the Russian director, Meyerhold – probably the greatest exponent of the Grotesque onstage in the twentieth century – the Grotesque 'forces the spectator to adopt an ambivalent attitude towards the stage action' and preserves this ambivalence 'by switching the course of the action with strokes of contrast. The basis of the Grotesque is the artist's constant desire to switch the spectator from the plane he has just reached to another which is totally unforeseen.' Meyerhold, too, uses the example of a funeral to illustrate the impact he sought in the theatre:

On a rainy autumn day a funeral procession crawls through the streets;

the gait of the pall-bearers conveys profound grief. Then the wind snatches a hat from the head of one of the mourners; he bends down to pick it up, but the wind begins to chase it from puddle to puddle. Each jump of the staid gentleman chasing his hat lends his face such comic grimaces that the gloomy funeral procession is suddenly transformed by some devilish hand into a bustling holiday crowd. If only one could achieve an effect like that on the stage![12]

CASE STUDY: *THE DUCHESS OF MALFI*, ACT 5, SCENE 2

I've never laughed so much as when we rehearsed *The Duchess of Malfi*
Judi Dench[13]

The notion that laughter was incompatible with serious subject matter would have baffled Elizabethan and Jacobean dramatists. Like so many elements of the Elizabethan and Jacobean world, the roots of the practice lie further back. Critics who have explored links between rituals, rites and drama have written illuminatingly on the structure of inversion they display (Woodbridge and Berry 1992), and while Cyrus Hoy may be right to suggest that nothing in medieval plays 'prepares us for the grotesque discontinuities' (1973: 54) of Jacobean drama, plays such as the *Second Shepherd's Play* in the Townley Cycle (which parallels finding a stolen lamb with the birth of the Lamb of God) illustrate how such strategies were embedded in indigenous theatre practice. Some medieval plays (the York play of the Crucifixion and the various versions of the Slaughter of the Innocents, for example) also mixed violence with gruesome and cruel humour:

> the unique force and dramatic effect of the role [of Herod in the Townley Slaughter] are rooted in the tension and interaction of the horrible and the comic.
>
> (Weimann 1978: 68)

Such strategies may be uncomfortable for an audience, but, also, as Thomas Cartelli observes, 'freed of normative constraints by the dependence on theatrical convention, the play-goer is able to turn the occasion of someone else's suffering into an occasion of pleasure' (1991: 35). He quotes John Ellis:

> It is equally possible for pleasure to be gained from scenes of humiliation and defeat as it is from scenes of success and victory. In both cases the pleasure comes from the fulfilment of a wish (for we wish what we fear as well as what we desire), and from seeing the fulfilment of that wish in the other.[14]

It is an observation that we may wish to resist, but the Grotesque depends precisely on our readiness to allow such responses to surface or, conversely, to acknowledge what we are doing when we choose to suppress them.[15]

In her pioneering study *The Jacobean Drama* (1936 [1958 edn: 144]) Una Ellis-Fermor offered an analysis of the opening scenes of Jacobean plays. It is, however, the climaxes of Elizabethan and Jacobean tragedies that often prove more problematic to actors and audiences. The number of deaths, and the speed with which they occur, invariably provoke laughter, and it is not uncommon for productions to seek to control this response in an audience, presumably for fear of upsetting the mood of tragic seriousness they believe *should* dominate. Though not referring specifically to the play's ending, Bernard Levin's review of the 1978 RSC production of *The Changeling* (which Levin, echoing William Archer, dismissed as 'a fairly bad play' – a judgement I hope haunts him) sums up this attitude:

> . . . it is naughty of Terry Hands to mock it . . . He does not mock it throughout, but this actually makes things worse, since it seems he is laughing at the play only when he feels he cannot stop the audience doing so; surely the right course for a director as gifted as this one is either to refuse to take the play seriously at all or to ensure, by iron control, that the audience does not feel inclined to laugh even at the most dangerously risible moments.
>
> (*Sunday Times*, 22 October 1978)

Such control works against the dynamic of *The Changeling* and a large number of Elizabethan/Jacobean plays.[16] *The Duchess of Malfi*, for example, concludes with four deaths (a servant, Bosola, the Cardinal and Ferdinand) in the space of about 70 lines (5.5.35–105), although the three main characters actually receive their fatal wounds between lines 45 and 74. The dead body of Antonio (killed in the previous scene) is onstage throughout. The scene is in many ways typical of Jacobean endings (though the body-count is lower than average) and has – also typically – 'continually attracted unfavourable criticism and taxed actors' ingenuity' (McLuskie and Uglow 1989: 197).

The Phoenix Society production in 1919 seems to have cared little whether an audience laughed or not:

> They interrupted the rolling period of the dying speeches made by each of the eight (sic) persons who are murdered onstage by realistic splutters and gurgles. They tried to individualise every 'item' in the massacre by each dying in a different attitude. Having exhausted every other possible posture, the Duke Ferdinand was reduced to expiring upside down, his head on the ground and his feet over the back of an arm-chair.
>
> (*Spectator*; quoted in McLuskie and Uglow 1989: 197)

It is not only the physical action that might lead to laughter in an audience. The lines of the text are obviously designed to elicit just such a response, mainly through the contrast achieved by juxtaposing their self-referential nature and deflationary tone with the heightened drama of the action: as Mike Gwilym (who played Ferdinand in the 1980 Royal Exchange production) points out, Ferdinand's line 'I do account this world but a dog kennel' (5.5.67), delivered by a character who thinks he's a wolf, seems designed to get a laugh.[17] Some productions, fearful of such laughter, have made a number of cuts to remove the possibility. The RSC 1987 production, for example, cut Antonio's lines in the following exchange (5.4.57–9), removing the jolt that Webster clearly intended:

BOSOLA: Thy fair duchess
    And two sweet children –
ANTONIO: Their very names
    Kindle a little life in me.
BOSOLA: Are murder'd.

Such tampering seems to me unjustified. Why should there be a problem with audience laughter at such moments? The Cardinal and Ferdinand may be awesome in their cruelty, but, as the play as a whole seeks to demonstrate, their efforts to kill the Duchess and Antonio – or more precisely the values they represent – are ultimately futile and arrogant. The Duchess and Antonio ('natural democrats' in Adrian Noble's neat phrase[18]) survive embodied in the figure of their son who outlives them. Those productions that seek to undercut this optimistic ending in some way (such as at the Bristol Old Vic in 1976 where the surviving Prince was dressed as a replica of his uncle Ferdinand rather than his father) wilfully distort Webster's point. Ferdinand and the Cardinal are violent men who meet violent deaths; they are men to be despised, their vanity seen as ludicrous. It is appropriate, therefore, that Webster should seek to achieve a tension of responses at this moment. A dashing sword fight is obviously wrong: Ferdinand's references to 'struggling / Here i'th' rushes' suggest a clumsy and messy brawl on the floor. Laurent Joubert theorises the idea thus, pointing out that people who are 'unworthy of pity or compassion' constitute the domain of the ludicrous (Bristol 1985: 134). Antonio is absolved from such criticism, the Aragonian brothers fully absorbed by it. That Bosola, despite his growing conscience, is placed within the orbit of laughter, albeit on the periphery, is a tangible sign of the tension between his self-awareness and his actions – 'an actor in the main of all / Much 'gainst my own good nature' (5.5.85–6) as he describes himself – perhaps matched by a sense on our part that he only partially deserves to be treated comically at his death.[19]

In the light of these points, it is hard to understand to what or to whom the mood of sombre loss should refer. As Michael Bristol points out: 'Renaissance theories of laughter all posit a human collective as the precondition for laughter', and the shared laughter of an audience at such moments as these is the public demonstration of a shared response to the action onstage – a response of power over such creatures that shows itself in deriding them (Bristol 1985: 137). It is also a tangible demonstration that it is the public performance more than the text of a play that 'may be dangerous' and most difficult to control: as Francis Bacon wrote, 'the minds of men in company are more open to affections and impressions than when alone'. A production of *Malfi* at the Bristol Old Vic in 1994 was criticised for allowing the ending to be 'farcical rather than tragic', and specifically for the laugh raised by Malateste's line on viewing the corpses: 'O sad disaster' (5.5.80), which was delivered sardonically. Such criticism must rest on the idea that the deaths of the Cardinal and Ferdinand are indeed a 'sad disaster' and tragic – an odd reading of the play, and one that is entirely based on a 'respect for tragedy' and, more significantly, respect for 'great' men, whatever their actions.[20] Joubert is again relevant here. In a section discussing his second category of laughing matter – 'seeing someone fall in the mire', he observes that our response is heightened if it is focused on the fall of 'a great and important personage'. It will also, he continues, be a particularly harsh and unpitying laughter:

> if this same personage is unworthy of the rank he holds and of the honour one gives him, if he is hated for his pride and excessive arrogance, resembling a monkey dressed in crimson, as the proverb has it.
> (Bristol 1985: 135)

The aim for a production should therefore surely be to sustain contrasting responses from an audience: dismay at the violence but ridicule of its perpetrators. This balance was achieved, I think, by Adrian Noble's revelatory production, first staged at the Manchester Royal Exchange in 1980, and later at the Roundhouse in London. Much of the physical and mental cruelty meted out to the Duchess in Act 4 was staged for maximum emotional impact on the audience: the 'bodies' of Antonio and Giovanni (the other two children were omitted) were pushed in on hospital trolleys; the madmen (confined in a metal cage borrowed from Manchester's Piccadilly Station) were genuinely disturbing; and the Duchess's death was a grimly realistic and terrifying execution. The deaths in the final scene, however, were (in the early performances) enacted with weapons and the predominant audience response was laughter. Then a change was made that involved Ferdinand (played by Mike Gwilym, dressed in modern hospital clothes) jumping on Bosola's (Bob Hoskins) back and biting out his jugular vein. The action – aided by an effective prosthesis of a throat and substantial amounts of stage blood – was so effective that it took the audience by surprise. Of course there was still laughter (and some faintings) but the action had the effect of shifting the audience response very sharply between laughter and shock. This was, indeed, a world gone mad, into which the arrival of Delio and the young Prince Giovanni – surviving emblems of

187

Antonio and the Duchess – intruded as potential saviours, effecting yet another radical contrast of tone and mood.

CASE STUDY: *TITUS ANDRONICUS*, ACT TWO, SCENE 4

> Why dost thou laugh? It fits not with this hour.
>
> (3.1.266)

Titus Andronicus, too, ends in a whirlwind of killing (four deaths in the last scene, three of them in the space of five lines). Apart from the difficulties modern performers (and hence, perhaps, their audiences) encounter with the speed of such sequences, the actual representation of violence onstage itself presents considerable technical problems. This is especially true if audiences measure the stage business against the realism of effects that can be created on film and television. When successful (as in Adrian Noble's *Duchess of Malfi*) the results onstage can be genuinely shocking, but they are often less than convincing, and Alan Hughes is right to raise the possibility of laughter stemming merely from the audience 'ridiculing an inadequate illusion'.[21] Though his point is generally applicable, Hughes is commenting specifically on Shakespeare's *Titus Andronicus*, a play that deliberately generates laughter in response to violence. Much of the laughter derives from 'sick' jokes: for example, the series of puns (terrible or wonderful, depending on your taste) that the characters seem unable to avoid following the severing of Titus's hand ('O handle not the theme to speak of hands'), or the shocking hairdressing puns in the description of Lavinia's mutilation:

AARON: They cut thy sister's tongue and ravished her
    And cut her hands and trimmed her as thou sawest.
LUCIUS: O detestable villain, call'st thou that trimming?
AARON: Why, she was washed and cut and trimmed, and 'twas
    Trim sport for them which had the doing of it.
LUCIUS: O barbarous, beastly villains, like thyself.

(5.1.92–97)

The actor Alan Howard (who played Lussurioso in the RSC 1966 production of *The Revenger's Tragedy*) catches the dislocating effect of such moments when, talking of his performance as Richard III, he said:

> the laughs that one wants are sick laughs, followed by appalled reflection – the thing you get in Jacobean plays: 'God, what am I laughing at? That man has just pulled somebody's guts out through his bottom' . . . something like that.[22]

In *Titus Andronicus*, laughter in the face of violence is not confined to the audience. Gazing on his 'mangled daughter' and on the severed heads of his two sons, sent in return for the severed hand he sent for their release, Titus himself finds laughter the only possible response to the catalogue of disasters that have befallen him and his family. To his brother, Marcus, ever one for decorum, who believes the moment calls for towering rage, this response is inappropriate: 'it fits not with this hour.' To Titus, however, with 'not another tear to shed', no other response is left. His laughter stifles ours. It is a moment which intensifies rather than diminishes our sense of the terribleness of his situation (3.2).[23]

Titus Andronicus, however, contains many other collisions of forms and contents that are equally exemplary of the Grotesque in operation. That the play has, until recent years, been widely condemned by critics will therefore come as no surprise. Dr Johnson, whose description of metaphysical poetry as 'heterogeneous elements . . . yoked by violence together' provides such an apt definition of the Grotesque, was less convinced when it came to such stylistic conflicts being put into practice onstage, claiming that in *Titus Andronicus* 'The barbarity of the spectacles, and the general massacre which are here exhibited, can scarcely be conceived tolerable to any audience.'[24] T.S. Eliot, more tersely, dismissed it as 'one of the stupidest and most uninspired plays ever written' (1932: 82). Recent, more admiring critical evaluations, however (as in the case of *The Revenger's Tragedy* and *The Changeling*), have been refashioned to a great extent by critics' experiences of seeing the play in performance. Alan Dessen has traced the twentieth-century stage history of *Titus Andronicus*, and in doing so has revealed how directors in Britain and other countries have sought to control the audience's response to this complex text.[25] Here, however, I want to concentrate on how stage productions (in particular those at Stratford-upon-Avon in 1955 and 1987) and one for BBC television, handled the particularly tricky section of the play that presents the rape, dismemberment and discovery of Lavinia. Within this sequence I want to focus even more precisely on the confrontation in 2.4 between Marcus and the mutilated Lavinia.

At l.186 of 2.3, Chiron and Demetrius toss the body of Bassianus into the pit (presumably the stage trap) and drag Lavinia offstage. Tamora follows almost immediately. At l.191, Aaron enters with Quintus and Martius. As two young men exit, therefore, two others enter, also 'hunting' their prey, a visual parallel that announces a link between the action that follows onstage and off, and which is sustained by the central association between the pit and vagina. The language with which Quintus and Martius describe the pit/vagina is resonant with male fear of women's sexuality: it is a 'subtle hole', 'whose mouth is covered with rude-growing briers / Upon whose leaves are drops of new-shed blood'; 'this unhallowed and bloodstained hole'; 'this detested, dark, blood-drinking pit'; 'this fell devouring receptacle', and so on.

Scene 2.4 opens with the stage direction: *Enter the Empress's sons with Lavinia, her hands cut off, and her tongue cut out, and ravished.* For readers and critics, but most of all for performers and audiences, the problem of the scene that follows centres on the relationship of language and spectacle. In an influential essay published in 1957, 'The Metamorphosis of Violence in *Titus Andronicus*', Eugene Waith analysed the scene in detail, drawing attention to the echoes in Marcus's speech (and the play as a whole) of Ovid's *Metamorphoses* and, in particular, the story of Philomel, who was raped by Tereus, her brother-in-law, who then cut out her tongue in order to prevent her accusing him of the crime. Unable to speak, Philomel embroidered her story on a cloth which she sent to her sister, Procne, Tereus's wife. In revenge, Procne stabbed her son, Itys, and Philomel slit his throat. While the boy was still breathing the women dismembered him, cooked him, and served his flesh to Tereus in a banquet at which Philomel presented Tereus with his son's head. Tereus pursued the two women and all three were metamorphosed into birds – Philomel into a nightingale, Procne a swallow and Tereus a hoopoe.[26]

The scene cannot be fully explored, however, without reference to how it operates (or has been allowed to operate) in performance.[27] In Peter Brook's 1955 production, Vivien Leigh, as Lavinia, entered with her 'right arm outstretched and head drooping away from it, left arm crooked with the wrist at her mouth', her hair 'in disorder over face and shoulders' and 'scarlet streamers, symbols of her mutilation' trailing from wrists and mouth (a device repeated in John Barton's heavily cut 1981 production and again in Abacus Theatre's production at the Edinburgh Festival in 1993). Brook cut Marcus's speech completely (ending the scene at line 10), but something of the contrast of its tone with the object it describes was achieved by the music (written by William Blezard) that accompanied Lavinia's entrance. According to Richard David (1957: 126) 'a small stylized tune was played on harp harmonics followed by piano' which produced 'an eloquent, not a horrific moment'. It has frequently been argued that in this scene, and throughout the play, characters (more specifically male characters) resort to ritualistic action or language in order to find coherence in a rapidly fragmenting world. By removing the 'ritual' of Marcus's rhetorically figured speech, however, and transferring its quality to replace the 'realistic' visual image presumably intended in the original, the production denied the scene the dynamic of dissonance which it was evidently designed to have. Shakespeare clearly aims at a moment that is simultaneously both verbally eloquent *and* visually horrific, a point to which I shall return. To Brook, the play was about 'the most modern of emotions – about violence, hatred, cruelty, pain', but his textual surgery (650 lines were cut) was nevertheless extensive; the deaths of Chiron and Demetrius took place offstage, Lavinia did not hold the bowl of blood in her stumps, Titus's severed limb was instantly concealed, and so on. J.C. Trewin summarised the director's approach as having 'manipulated the text so that his actors could let fly without dread of mocking laughter; whenever he spied a possible laugh, he either cut the offending phrase or unmasked his protective atmospherics'.[28]

Other productions have followed Brook's lead. According to Gerald Freedman, his 1967 New York production used 'music, mask and chorus in order to make the violence, gore and horror . . . more meaningful and emotional to a contemporary audience' and to enable them to 'accept the mutilations and decapitations and multiple deaths with belief instead of humour'. The severed heads of Titus's sons were represented by 'empty half-masks on visibly empty wire frames'; as a result, according to Freedman, the audience were 'properly horrified and disgusted without being led to reflect on mundane and natural-istic detail'.[29]

Trevor Nunn directed the play at Stratford in 1972 as part of a season in which he staged all of Shakespeare's Roman Plays. The production was noted for its restraint where the acts of violence were concerned but Nunn, unlike Brook, presented the results of that violence as realistically as he could: Chiron and Demetrius's severed heads were accurately modelled and the sound of a saw cutting through bone accompanied Titus's act of severing his own hand. Janet Suzman (as Lavinia) entered in 2.4 like 'a pitiable, hunched grotesque crawl-ing out of the darkness like a wounded animal' (*Guardian*). Twenty-nine lines were cut from Marcus's speech. Two years earlier, the first production of the play in South Africa had taken the realistic approach to even greater lengths:

> In one scene the twice ravished Lavinia staggers on to the stage with her hands severed and her tongue cut out. Pointing her bleeding stumps at the audience she tries to speak, but blood froths from her mouth. Behind me a young man groaned, and clutching his stomach, rushed out of the theatre.[30]

In 1987, Deborah Warner directed the play for the RSC at the Swan in Stratford, a production widely described as 'definitive', and the first time since Buzz Goodbody's production of *Hamlet* at The Other Place in 1975 that a woman had directed Shakespeare at the RSC. Characteristic of Warner's approach to Shakespeare the text was uncut and, as a result, parts of the play that had become established not only as 'unplayable' but literally 'unspeakable' were given the opportunity to be tested in performance (see pp. 219–20 below). In Warner's production, Lavinia was carried off bodily by Tamora's sons, Chiron (having savagely kissed her and spat out a piece of her tongue) shoving his hand violently between her legs. The section following Martius's fall into the pit was played for its tension, Quintus prowling around the open-ing of the pit. Trying to help his brother out, he tumbles in on top of him:

QUINTUS: Reach me thy hand that I may help thee out,
  Or wanting strength to do thee so much good,
  I may be plucked into the swallowing womb
  Of this deep pit, poor Bassianus's grave.
  I have no strength to pluck thee to the brink.

MARTIUS: Nor I no strength to climb without thy help.
QUINTUS: Thy hand once more; I will not loose again
    Till thou art here aloft or I below.
    Thou canst not come to me; I come to thee. *Falls in.*

At this point, Warner shifted the tone (rightly in my view) into broad physical comedy, the more to contrast the action of these youths falling into Tamora's pit with the unseen (but clearly audible) actions of Tamora's sons off-stage forcing themselves 'into the swallowing womb' of Lavinia. Heather James has commented on this parallel action, referring to a production at Santa Cruz, California, in 1988:

> audiences . . . had no trouble in grasping either the humor or the horror of the scene, precisely because the production did not attempt to efface the specter of *vagina dentata* that looms over Martius' and Quintus' pathetic fall into the pit.
>
> (1991: 139)

At the opening of 2.4, in Warner's production, Sonia Ritter (as Lavinia) entered crawling, tried to stand, but fell to the floor. Her appearance, so different from the vibrant young girl presented by Ritter in the first act, produced on both occasions I saw the production a palpable response from members of the audience, and heightened further the contrast with the response of her abusers, who mimicked her actions and derided her with jokes. Finally, Chiron sat astride her, spat in her face, and the men exited. Her stumps were not symbolically treated, nor realistic open wounds, but looked as if the severed ends had been wrapped in linen (a recurrent material in the production) and then, like her dress, covered in what appeared to be mud to staunch the bleeding. Donald Sumpter, as Marcus, entered cheerfully whistling. Lavinia immediately ran away DSR (I am using the positional terms of the prompt-copy), turning to face Marcus on his line 'Where is your husband?'. Marcus's speech, left intact, had the rare opportunity to demonstrate why it is so long. Indeed, with 47 lines it is the longest speech in the play; significantly, Titus's 40-line speech (5.2.166–205) before he murders Tamora's sons in revenge for the rape, is the second longest. Jonathan Bate suggests that 'Marcus needs a long speech because in it he has to learn slowly and painfully to confront suffering' (1995: 62), though his crass comments in the following scene might suggest the lesson isn't that successful; as Gillian Kendall writes, 'Marcus, of all the characters, seems to have an ear for the inappropriate and grotesque' (1989: 308). More pertinently, I believe, the *audience* need time to confront the image of the mutilated woman and to respond both to her and Marcus's description of her. Marcus remained CS before moving towards her on 'Why dost not speak to me?' At that point the actress let a trickle of blood spurt from her mouth, prompting Marcus's eloquently poetic response: 'Alas, a crimson river of warm blood, / Like to a bubbling fountain stirred with wind, / Doth rise and fall between thy rosed lips' (22–4). This moment, possibly because it was the only blood used in the scene, 'elicited shocked gasps from the audience' (Dessen 1989: 60) and produced an effective tension between language and image. At this point, Lavinia moved USC where they embraced and, on line 38, they sank to the floor. Marcus cradled Lavinia in his arms and held that position until he carried her off at the end of the scene. It was, Dessen claims, to many observers 'the strongest single moment in the show' (1989: 60).[31]

I, too, admired and enjoyed this production, and agree that it successfully handled many of the problems identified or assumed by previous directors. As well as opening up perspectives on the play ignored or overlooked by previous (male) directors, Deborah Warner also displayed a willingness to take considerable theatrical risks, such as having Titus, 'like a cook', wear a tall chef's hat (an idea used ten years earlier in Adrian Noble's vivid Bristol Old Vic production) and have the banquet of boys carried in to a whistled dwarves chorus of 'Heigh Ho!' from Disney's *Snow White*. In 2.4, however, it seems to me that the production solved the problems by reconciling rather than highlighting the conflicting elements and as a result, for some viewers at least, there was 'none of the dislocation or indecorum that Waith finds' (Bate 1993: 112) nor that, in my view, Shakespeare created. I think it is worth considering, therefore, how the scene might work if 'dislocation' and 'indecorum' were actively sought – not merely by making no effort to reconcile the language and image, but by consciously trying to keep them apart.

Although Jonathan Bate vividly describes the 'black comic theatricality' in *Titus Andronicus*, and discusses how Shakespeare blurs 'the conventional distinctions between comedy and tragedy' (Arden ed. p.11) neither he nor the writers of other perceptive stage-centred studies of the play – such as Dessen and Hughes – seeks to contextualise or conceptualise the question of the contrast of tones in text or performance through reference to the Grotesque. As I noted earlier, English medieval drama provided later playwrights with a tradition of representing onstage acts of dismemberment and violations of bodies, and similar acts are common in Renaissance plays throughout the period. In his influential study, *Rabelais and His World*, Mikhail Bakhtin emphasises that the body, and especially the distorted or violated body, is a characteristic feature of the Grotesque. He also points out the frequency with which, in Grotesque literature, a link is made between dismemberment of the body and of society (1968: 351), which is an emblematic connection common also in Elizabethan and Jacobean drama (*Arden of Faversham, Richard III, Julius Caesar, Coriolanus, The Roman Actor, The Virgin Martyr*, etc.). The mutilation or, more specifically, rape, of a woman was a common trope for conquest, and one that further explains the violation of Lavinia as not only a personal tragedy but one that is symbolic of the centrifugal forces of male violence in the society Shakespeare portrays (Tennenhouse 1989). As Peter M.

Daly observes, in Renaissance drama 'the corpse is an emblem that instructs' (1979: 147).

Not only is the text of *Titus Andronicus* replete with verbal images of violent acts upon the body, but there can be little doubt that those who staged the Elizabethan production at the Rose in 1594 would have presented the wounds visually as realistically as they could. A considerable body of evidence (puns are contagious) exists that demonstrates how assiduously realism was sought in medieval productions, and references such as those to animals' innards in the Plot of *The Battle of Alcazar* (1584) or directions such as 'Sertorio brings in the flesh with a skull all bloody' in *The Bloody Banquet* (1639) or the decapitations in *The Insatiate Countess* (1607) and *Sir John Van Olden Barnavelt* (1619), make it clear that Renaissance actors throughout the period followed suit. Nor were such displays mere flourishes of *grand guignol*, shock-horror devices to thrill audiences. Thomas Platter observed that 'At the top of one tower almost in the centre of the [London] bridge, were stuck on tall stakes more than thirty skulls of noble men who had been executed and beheaded', while contemporary accounts of tortures, punishments and executions stress the significance of the removal of limbs and organs in public and the symbolic weight the spectators were meant to attribute to those acts.[32] The violence enacted on Lavinia is extreme (a version of the exaggeration of acts on the body characteristic of the Grotesque) and (again typically in the genre) Shakespeare – through the contrast of language and image – stresses the disparity between what she was and what she now is (Bakhtin 1968: Introduction *passim*). Bakhtin – in common with all writers on the Grotesque – notes that the genre depends upon 'combining in one image both the positive and the negative poles' (1968: 308). In the *Titus* example, if the image of the mutilated woman is one pole, then the language used by the male character to describe her is the other. The degree of separation between language and image is crucial and must be sustained in performance. This means keeping the contrasting elements hard-edged, not allowing them to blend together to produce what Trevor Nunn calls a 'lugubrious wash',[33] but holding both (and therefore the viewer) in suspension. To return to Warner's production. Stanley Wells thought Donald Sumpter's delivery of Marcus's lines, in 'hushed tones', reshaped into a 'deeply moving attempt to master the facts' a speech that might 'read like a heartless verbal exercise by a bright boy from the local grammar school' – the kind of rhetorical exercise described in Chapter 1 (1988: 179). But what if that exercise is exactly what it was meant to remind the original audience of? Even modern listeners, though they may not recognise the rhetorical exercise referred to, are likely to find Marcus's images and expression incongruous, and may be more inclined to share Gillian Kendall's view of the moment than Wells's:

> Seldom if ever has such a description of violence been juxtaposed with a vision of that violence itself. This juxtaposition – and this

imposition of idealized imagery of Lavinia onto her mutilated body –
is grotesque.

(Kendall 1989: 307)

In other words, the inappropriateness is all. The result of the actor playing
the speech as a 'heartless exercise' (or with something of the attitude implied
in that phrase) rather than as a slow, gentle attempt to reconcile and grieve at
what he sees and condition the audience, too, to the event, will not, I suspect,
provoke laughter (though laughter is unpredictable; Freud identified contrast
between words and meaning as a key characteristic of joke-making).[34] But,
precisely because the scene will be more difficult for the spectator to receive,
and because the spectator will have to formulate a more adequate response than
Marcus's, the scene may result in a greater recognition of the appallingness of
human actions.

Productions of *Titus Andronicus* are still comparatively rare events, and so
anyone who wishes to explore their own reactions to the scene in performance
should try to see Jane Howell's excellent production, made by the BBC in
1985, and available on video.[35] Perhaps unsurprisingly for an essentially 'naturalistic' medium, and given that it was entirely studio-based, the production
was set within a 'realistic' world – walls, stairs and smoke for interior scenes,
trees, leaf-covered ground and mist for outdoor scenes – so rendering, as in any
naturalistically conceived production of an Elizabethan play, the image-setting
language a mere descriptive adjunct. At the same time, however, in keeping
with the Elizabethans' confident use of mixed conventions, the production also
effectively utilised effects not available to stage directors, such as slow-motion
and separation of voice and image. Furthermore, by letting much of the action
be seen from the point of view of Lucius (and stressing his youthfulness)
Howell achieved something of the same complicity between the action and the
viewer provided by the bridging function of the *Sprecher* in paintings and
onstage, a relationship of viewer to screen not characteristic of television generally. Lavinia's mutilations were extremely convincing, the stumps clearly
showing the severed bones and sinews of her arms (all the severed heads and
limbs were authenticated by the Royal College of Surgeons). At Marcus's
query why she did not speak, a spurt of blood shot from her mouth, globules
of it remaining dangling from her lip throughout the scene.

Marcus's speech – apart from the omission of one and a half lines – was left
intact. From line 25 until the end of the scene, Marcus and Lavinia were held
in the frame at all times: even when the camera moved to a close-up of Marcus,
one of Lavinia's stumps was kept in the foreground of the screen. Marcus
(with the ultimate in rhetorical questions, 'Shall I speak for thee') offers to act
as Lavinia's voice. Unlike Warner, who (dealing with the multiple perspective
of a theatre audience) midway through the scene fused the contrasting elements in the act of the embrace, Howell placed the two contrasting elements
within the same frame but kept them separated from each other (recalling the

organisation of El Greco's *Burial of Count Orgaz*). The viewer is able, therefore, in addition to listening to Marcus, also to observe Lavinia's response to his words, an aspect of the scene largely overlooked by critics: Mary L. Fawcett, for example, believes Lavinia blushes and turns away because of what 'Marcus immediately recognizes as her shame'.[36] Surely, Marcus *interprets* Lavinia's gesture as signalling her shame, a moment which tells us more about his (male) notions of (female) honour and Lavinia's feelings about his response to her fate, than it does about her own attitude to her position. In other words, the moment needs to be played as a critical comment on Marcus rather than as evidence of his sympathy.

Forced to confront image and words simultaneously, even a viewer unaware of the precise Ovidian references in Marcus's speech would find revealed in his poetic images (and Lavinia's reaction to them) not merely the inappropriateness of his language, nor his inability to empathise with Lavinia's predicament but, I believe, the limitations of *all* language to describe such physical actuality. Significantly, in later plays – *Coriolanus*, *King Lear* and *The Winter's Tale*, for example – Shakespeare discovered the power and appropriateness of silence at moments of intense emotional pressure.[37] Alan Dessen found that in Jane Howell's version of the scene 'the artifice of [Marcus's] poetry did not mesh well with the verisimilar stumps and bloody mouth' (1989: 47). I agree with him that they jarred, but found in that uneasy, queasy juxtaposition of language and image precisely the tension and ambivalence at which I believe Shakespeare aimed, the inability of Marcus to find the right words enforcing our own sense of the inexpressible violence of the act. (See also Tricomi 1974.) In other words, the problem of the scene is ours too, not Marcus's alone. If language, the very thing that separates human beings from animals, cannot encompass the terror of an act, what does that say of the inhumanity of that act? As John Ruskin wrote of Renaissance artists who employ the strategies of the Grotesque, 'it is because the dreadfulness of the universe around him weighs upon his heart, that his work is wild'.[38]

7

'A GOOD PLAY GONE WRONG'[1]

Renaissance drama in action 1642–1997

In 1892, *The Duchess of Malfi* was staged using a text that, though considerably altered, was still closer to the original Quarto (1623) than any text employed for any performance since the seventeenth century. It was not a universal success. Reviewing the play rather than the production, William Archer catalogued what he saw as its many faults, describing Webster as 'a great poet who wrote haphazard dramatic or melodramatic romances for an eagerly receptive but semi-barbarous public'.[2] It was a criticism endorsed and amplified by George Bernard Shaw, who dismissed out of hand not just Webster but 'the whole crew of insufferable bunglers and dullards whose work stands out as vile even at the beginning of the seventeenth century'. With a swipe at the scene where the Duchess is confronted with wax effigies of her family (4.1), Shaw (whose exaggeration even Archer found excessive), claimed that:

> When one thinks of . . . the opacity that prevented Webster, the Tussaud Laureate, from appreciating his own stupidity – when one thinks of the whole rabble of dehumanized specialists in elementary blank verse posing as the choice and master spirits . . . it is hard to keep one's critical blood cold enough to discriminate in favour of any Elizabethan whatever.[3]

Less than a century later, in 1980, Robert Cushman, then critic of the *Observer* newspaper, wrote of Adrian Noble's illuminating production of Webster's play at the Royal Exchange theatre in Manchester, that 'the rediscovery of the Jacobeans – and the means to do them justice – has been the most encouraging development in the British theatre in the last couple of years' (28 September 1980). In fact, the reasons for this definite – though limited, faltering and gradual – arc of change in attitudes to Elizabethan and Jacobean plays may be traced back to the closing years of the nineteenth century and through the theatrical experiments of the current century. But first, I want to trace briefly the stage life of the non-Shakespearean plays following the reopening of the playhouses in 1660.

The Restoration

In 1653, in the midst of the Commonwealth ban on public theatre activity, Aston Cockaine wrote a poem to preface an edition of *Five New Plays* by Richard Brome. He anticipated with relish the time when the London theatres would reopen:

> Then we shall still have Plays! . . .
> Then shall Learn'd Jonson resume his seat,
> Revive the Phoenix by a second heat
> Create the Globe anew, and people it,
> By those that flock to surfeit on his Wit.
> Judicious Beaumont, and th'Ingenious Soul
> Of Fletcher too may move without control.
> Shakespeare (most rich in Humours) entertain
> The crowded Theatres with this happy vein.
> Davenant and Massinger, and Shirley, then
> Shall be cried up again for Famous men.
> And the Dramatic Muse no longer prove
> The people's Malice, but the people's Love.

When the theatres eventually did reopen in 1660 there were significant innovations, chiefly the introduction of actresses onto the public stage and the use of painted, changeable scenery. But there were still strong links with the past: actors survived who had direct experience of the performance styles and practices of the pre-Civil War companies, and they initially performed, on a thrust stage, in close contact with the audience at two surviving playhouses, outdoors at the Red Bull or indoors at the Phoenix, lit by candles. According to John Downes, the company at the Phoenix initially included actors who 'commonly acted Women's Parts' in which they were 'very Acceptable to the Audience' (1987: 45–6). Although public performances had officially ceased in 1642, plays from the earlier period had continued to be published during the Interregnum and, with few 'modern' plays yet available, these formed the basis of the early Restoration theatre's repertoire, in part to meet the need for a very rapid turnover generated by the popularity of theatre-going. Of the 959 performances recorded in London between 1660 and 1700, 486 were of 'old' (i.e., pre-Restoration) plays, 473 of new (Vickers 1989: 213). It was a balance that did not meet with universal approval from contemporary dramatists since, according to George Powell (1690) 'a new play cou'd hardly get admittance, amongst the more precious pieces of Antiquity, that then waited to walk the stage' (quoted in Sorelius 1966: 202). Many plays were performed in more or less their original form, but others – for a variety of reasons – were adapted, often radically. Sara Jayne Steen notes that Middleton's plays, for example, 'were raided by dramatists scurrying to keep the playhouses supplied and only performed in adaptations with someone else's name on the playbill'. As Gerard Langbaine observed in 1668, only because audiences were so unfamiliar with the originals were the adapters able to get away with so much unacknowledged plagiarism from writers such as Middleton, Massinger and Marston (Steen 1993: 10–11). Shakespeare presented a more particular problem. His plays were generally better known and adaptations therefore more obvious, and for twenty years following the Restoration Thomas Killigrew's King's Company (one of two granted a monopoly by Charles II in August 1660) performed their Shakespeare plays (except *The Taming of the Shrew*) in more or less their original form. As early as February 1662, however, Sir William Davenant's Duke's Company (the other licensed company) presented the first adaptation of a Shakespeare play – a mixture of *Measure For Measure* and *Much Ado About Nothing* called *The Law Against Lovers*. The following year Davenant presented his version of *Macbeth* resplendent, according to Downes, with 'new Clothes, new Scenes, Machines, as flyings for the Witches; with all the Singing and Dancing in it' (largely Middleton's additions), and in 1667 collaborated with Dryden on *The Tempest; or the Enchanted Island*, which became the most frequently revived play of the Restoration period. Though with different degrees of self-awareness, Shakespeare's Restoration adapters (Davenant, Tate, Dryden) and their successors (Cibber, Garrick, Kemble, Theobald, and so on) all applauded themselves for rescuing Shakespeare's ideas (his genius) from obscurity caused by his inability to construct a play properly, while being careful at the same time to praise his 'immortal fame', 'natural wit', or some such quality. It is common for these – and indeed later adaptations – to be dismissed by critics 'in tones of horror, dismay, disgust or amusement, with very rare touches of grudging praise' (Spencer 1965: 7). In fact, Christopher Spencer argues, 'the best of the adaptations are enjoyable in themselves [and] read as new plays will add to our own understanding of Shakespeare . . . by comprehending their version of the Shakespearean material with which they were working' (1965: 32). And while prevailing aesthetic rules were undoubtedly a major factor in the desire to 'reform' the old plays, Michael Dobson offers a further caution against seeing the Shakespearean adaptations only from this perspective:

> Clearly, Tate's reasons for rewriting Shakespeare have more to do with contemporary politics than with contemporary literary criticism, and any lingering belief in the old story that he gave *Lear* a happy ending because he was some kind of neo-classical cissy who couldn't stand the sight of stage blood can easily be dispelled by a quick glance at the orgy of gratuitous violence with which he chooses to conclude *Coriolanus*.
>
> (1992: 83)

As the seventeenth century drew to a close many of the actors with the King's company, who had provided a link with the earlier theatre, were approaching old age; Davenant died in 1668. Dwindling audiences created a financial crisis for the Duke's company, and in 1682 the King's and Duke's companies amalgamated, and played together until 1695. Opening their first season in November 1682, Dryden's prologue for the occasion set out their new artistic manifesto, promising that:

> Old Men shall have good old Plays to delight 'em:
> And you, fair Ladies and Gallants that slight 'em,
> We'll treat with good new plays; if our new Wits can write 'em.

Revivals were still a key part of the repertoire (indeed, Thomas Rymer could claim that 'Shakespeare, Fletcher and Ben Jonson . . . [are] in possession of the Stage') but new plays were beginning to dominate.[4] Old plays were increasingly seen as antique curiosities which served, in James Wright's words:

> to discover the Manners and Behaviour of Several Ages; and how they Altered: for Plays are exactly like Portraits Drawn in the Garb and Fashion of the Time when Painted.
>
> (*Historia Histrionica*, 1699)

The physical environment of theatre buildings was also changing. Alterations to the Theatre Royal Drury Lane in the 1690s had fundamentally shifted the relationship of actor to audience by shortening the forestage and moving the actors away from the spectators. Colley Cibber's complaint of the result of the alteration (echoing Webster's terms in *An Excellent Actor*) published in 1740, voices an acute awareness of the essential relationship between theatre space and acting:

> when the Actors were in Possession of that forwarder Space to advance upon, the Voice was more in the Centre of the House, so that the most distant Ear had scarce the least Doubt or Difficulty in hearing what fell from the weakest Utterance: All Objects were thus drawn nearer to the Sense . . . every rich or fine-coloured Habit had a more lively Lustre; Nor was the minutest Motion of a Feature . . . ever lost, as they frequently must be in the Obscurity of too great a Distance: And how valuable an Advantage the Facility of hearing distinctly is to every well-acted Scene, every common Spectator is a Judge.
>
> (Cibber 1987: 241)

The eighteenth century

Although the pressure (as Davenant put it) to 'reform . . . ancient plays' and 'make them fit' for performance persisted into the eighteenth century, and meant a number of Elizabethan and Jacobean plays by writers other than

Shakespeare still survived, the decline in the popularity of old plays continued. Downes noted that following performances at the newly opened Haymarket Theatre in 1705 of 'half a score of their old Plays, Acted in old Clothes . . . The Audiences are falling off extremely with entertaining the Gentry with such old ware' (1987: 100), and many Elizabethan and Jacobean plays simply faded from sight. By 1707, for example, Nahum Tate could publish a play titled *Injured Love: or the Cruel Husband* without thinking it necessary to mention that it was a version of Webster's *The White Devil. Injured Love* appears never to have been performed, unlike *The Fatal Secret*, by Lewis Theobald, which was staged in 1731. In a letter to a friend, William Warburton, Theobald described his new work:

> I have applied my uneasy summer months upon the attempt at a tragedy . . . I lay my scene in Italy. My heroine is a young widow duchess who has two haughty Spanish brothers that enjoin her not to marry again. She, however, clandestinely marries the Master of her Household on the morning I open my scene.
>
> (Quoted in Hunter and Hunter 1969: 38)

It is, of course, the plot of Webster's *The Duchess of Malfi*. Theobald's deception, however, was apparently discovered, since he confessed in the Preface to the published edition (1735) that:

> Though I called it *The Fatal Secret* I had no intention of disguising from the public that . . . John Webster had preceded me, above a hundred years ago, in the same story . . . If I have borrowed Webster's matter freely I have taken it up on fair and open credit, and hope I have repaid the principal with interest.
>
> (Quoted in Hunter and Hunter 1969: 40)

The changes Theobald introduced – no children are born; the severed hand Ferdinand presents to the Duchess is replaced by a ring; the Duchess apparently dies offstage but has, it turns out, been saved by a reformed Bosola to emerge and marry Antonio at the end – were all made to bring the play into line with current neo-classic notions of dramatic structure, but arose also from 'a concern to influence a theatre which was turning increasingly to more trivial forms of entertainment' (McLuskie and Uglow 1989: 22). Equally important was the potential Theobald saw for the play to appeal to the contemporary taste for sentiment, and in particular to women in the audience – the 'female Judges' as he calls them. The Duchess is made an exemplary figure and the role of Bosola divided between two characters, the involvement in the Duchess's torture and death being allotted to a new character of Ferdinand's secretary. My interest here, however, is not in the pros and cons of such adaptation; Elizabethan and Jacobean dramatists were themselves very free in adapting and recycling each other's work, and 'creative vandalism' of different kinds is a common, often invigorating feature of the modern theatre's handling of classic plays (see Case Study, p. 217ff.). The point I wish to underline is that these adapters seem to have had no concern that their sources would be identified, even when, as in Theobald's case, Warburton, to whom he wrote, was himself a scholar and future editor of Shakespeare – a tangible sign of just how little-known certain plays had become less than a hundred years after their last recorded performances in the seventeenth century.

The second half of the eighteenth century was a period of considerable interest in the works of Shakespeare's contemporaries. In 1733 Lewis Theobald published an edition of Shakespeare in which he referred to the works of other contemporary dramatists to explain difficult words and phrases, and in 1744 Robert Dodsley published a twelve-volume *Select Collection of Old Plays*. In 1745, Dr Johnson wrote that 'In order to make a true estimate of the abilities and merit of a writer, it is always necessary to examine the genius of his age, and the opinions of his contemporaries', a view he expanded in his *Proposals* (1756):

> he [Johnson] hopes that, by comparing the works of Shakespeare with those of writers who lived at the same time, immediately preceded, or immediately followed him, he shall be able to ascertain his ambiguities, disentangle his intricacies, and recover the meaning of words now lost in the darkness of antiquity.[5]

Gradually, the desire to ensure the 'Regularity and Probability of the Tale' (as Tate phrased it) that had been a powerful influence on earlier critical judgement and adaptation was losing its sway. Nevertheless, the emphasis of literary critics and historians, when not using the old plays as windows on Shakespeare, was still to treat them as texts to be studied, not scripts to be performed. Furthermore, the range of playwrights whose work was published was extremely limited. Apart from Shakespeare, Beaumont and Fletcher and Jonson, Philip Massinger was the only Elizabethan/Jacobean dramatist whose complete plays were published (three times) before 1800. There were those who wished it otherwise, however. Monck Mason prefaced his 1779 edition of the works of Philip Massinger with an essay of 'Critical Reflections on the Old Dramatic Writers', attributed to Colman. The essay is significant not only for its defence of the particular characteristics of Jacobean drama that had been (and continue to be) problematical to readers and spectators (specifically the collisions of styles, moods and tones), but because the essay was addressed to David Garrick, the most prominent actor of his generation. Arguing that plays 'need not be written on the severest plan to please in the representation' the essay writer called on Garrick to influence what was actually being staged in the contemporary theatre, to broaden the repertoire and rescue those Jacobean plays still languishing in obscurity:

In the name of Burbage, Taylor and Betterton I conjure you to do it! –
it is certainly in your interest to give variety to the public taste –
encourage new attempts, but do justice to the old! the theatre is a
wide field; let not one or two walks of it alone be beaten, but lay open
the whole excursions of genius!

(Genest 1832: vol. 6, 119–24)

But despite enjoying 'a position of eminence that would have enabled him
to make the decisive break with the adapters, had he wished' (Vickers 1989:
223) Garrick showed as little inclination to do so as he did to restore
Shakespeare's plays to something more closely resembling their original form,
though he sought to encourage a rather different impression, maintaining in
the Prologue to his version of *The Winter's Tale*, for example, that:

> 'Tis my chief wish, my claim, my only Plan
> To lose no drop of that immortal Man.

In practice, however, Garrick cut three of the original five acts of that play;
his version of *Macbeth* remained closer to Davenant than Shakespeare; and in
presenting his version of *Hamlet* (1772) he claimed (in a letter the following
year) to have 'rescued that noble play from all the rubbish of the 5th act',
which meant saving it from the voyage to England, the gravediggers, Ophelia's
funeral, and contriving for Laertes to survive the sword-fight and replace
Fortinbras as the future king (Dobson 1992: 172–6).

The nineteenth century

Although a new, influential generation of distinguished and passionate defend-
ers of the plays emerged at the beginning of the nineteenth century, a gap still
existed between critical assessment and theatre practice. The conservatism of
audience taste was a further constraint, and plays that did survive in performance continued to do so only in radically altered versions. Even then, the
ever-growing size of theatre auditoria and the poor acoustics they provided
militated against successful productions: Drury Lane in the middle of the
eighteenth century could hold about 1,200 people, by 1794 its capacity had
trebled. The earliest champion of the Elizabethan and Jacobean drama in the
nineteenth century was Charles Lamb, though he despaired of the ability of the
contemporary theatre, with its 'elaborate and anxious provision of scenery' and
audience desiring little but to be 'complimented in their goodness', to stage
the plays satisfactorily (1901: 264, 274). In 1808, he published *Specimens of the
English Dramatic Poets who Lived about the Time of Shakespeare*, in which he
printed 'scenes of passion, sometimes of the deepest quality, interesting situations, serious descriptions'. Lamb's opinionated editorial stance ('I have
expunged without ceremony all that which the writers had better never have

written') resulted in many of the extracts being brief and unrepresentative, some only a few lines long. Lamb, however, was also a fierce opponent of the 'ribald trash' the adapters had 'foisted into the acting plays of Shakespeare', and alert to the dangers of presenting isolated passages: 'I have chosen wherever I could to give entire scenes, and in some instances successive scenes, rather than to string together single passages and detached beauties.' Nevertheless, his work may have contributed to the notion that the plays are a mix of good (to be praised and retained) and bad (to be regretted and cut), an attitude seen in critical practice, for example, in Una Ellis-Fermor's view that *The Changeling* would be improved as a play if it were to be performed without the madhouse plot (1936 [1958 edn]: 144), and in the theatre in productions such as the 1976 version at the Glasgow Citizens which did precisely that. *The Changeling* is not, in fact, one of Lamb's chosen texts; the only Middleton and Rowley collaboration included is *A Fair Quarrel*, later praised by Swinburne for its portrayal of manly virtues – qualities approved of by many Victorian critics. Lamb's treatment of *Women Beware Women*, however, is illustrative of his method. He prints the chess/rape scene, followed by a sequence of six short speeches, all of which are out of sequence, ignore the distinction between different characters' lines, and which are given titles. For example, the following lines between the Mother and Bianca, from Act 1, scene 3, are headed 'Great Men's Looks':

> Did not the Duke look up? methought he saw us. –
> That's everyone's conceit that sees a duke,
> If he look steadfastly, he looks straight at them:
> When he perhaps, good careful gentleman,
> Never minds any, but the look he casts
> Is at his own intentions, and his object
> Only the public good.

This scheme gives speeches the appearance of separate poems, generalised comments devoid of particular character or context. The scope of Lamb's selection is broad, however, and reading the *Specimens* is an excellent way to get a sense of the perception of Elizabethan and Jacobean playwrights at the start of the nineteenth century among Romantic critics (notably Hazlitt, Hunt and Lamb himself), who celebrated the sheer emotional power of the plays and responded to precisely those qualities of dissonance and tension that their eighteenth-century predecessors had resisted.

The change in the fortunes of Philip Massinger's work provides an indicator of this shift in critical taste. Formerly one of the most admired of English Renaissance dramatists, his reputation was to Lamb – who thought his work lacked passion – a result of the limited responses of earlier critics. By setting out examples of Massinger's work in his *Specimens* and comparing them with 'the more impressive scenes of old Marlowe, Heywood, Tourneur, Webster,

Ford and others' Lamb sought to 'shew what we have slighted, while beyond all proportion we have cried up one or two favourite names'. Lamb's list reflects closely those playwrights most frequently performed today but, as Martin Garrett has pointed out, 'most of Lamb's contemporaries . . . were not yet ready for Webster' (1991: 23). Lamb's arguments gradually advanced the claims of dramatists 'next, or equal, or sometimes superior . . . in power' to those few whose plays 'still keep regular possession of the stage'. This transformation in critical acclaim led to a number of new editions of playwrights attractive to the Romantics: Ford (1811 and 1827), Marlowe (1818–20 and 1826), Webster (1830) and Middleton (1840). In 1827, Lamb went still further, having had time since publication of his *Specimens* to explore more of the playtexts in the British Museum. In his comments on Henry Porter's *The Two Angry Women of Abington*, Lamb pleaded for the work of more Elizabethan and Jacobean drama-tists to be published, and raised again the question of comparison with Shakespeare:

> Why do we go on with ever new editions of Ford and Massinger . . .? Not a third part of the treasures of old English dramatic literature has been exhausted. Are we afraid that the genius of Shakespeare would suffer in our estimate by this disclosure? He would indeed be somewhat lessened as a miracle and a prodigy. But he would lose no height by the confession . . . the plays of Shakespeare have been the strongest and the sweetest food of my mind from infancy: but I resent the comparative obscurity in which some of his valuable co-operators remain.
>
> ('Notes on the Garrick Plays', 1901: 287)

In very general terms, nineteenth-century attitudes to Elizabethan and Jacobean drama (attitudes that continued into the twentieth) polarised between Romantics who saw the playwrights, in Edmund Gosse's words, as creators of 'sudden sheet-lightning of poetry illuminating for an instant dark places of the soul', and those who viewed them as ramshackle hacks who occa-sionally turned out some wonderful verse but were generally unable to structure a play to satisfy either moral or aesthetic tastes. It was a view sus-tained to the end of the nineteenth century, when the work of the Elizabethans and Jacobeans was attacked alongside 'decadent' artists such as Oscar Wilde and Aubrey Beardsley. Setting his sights on those critics (especially Lamb and Hazlitt) who advanced Middleton, Webster and Ford above 'Jonson with his laborious art . . . Massinger with his surefooted style [and] Beaumont and Fletcher with their decorative fancy and lyrical grace', William Watson, minor poet and critic, wrote in 1893, that 'Webster and his group . . . had no sober vision of things. Theirs is a world that reels in a "disastrous twilight" of lust and blood', so that whereas 'we rise from Shakespeare enlarged and illumined' these lesser figures have a 'contracting and blurring influence'.[6]

Developments in theatre architecture, too, had moved still further away from the needs of Elizabethan and Jacobean texts. In 1821, the Theatre Royal, Haymarket, London, had been rebuilt, though still retaining its forestage, with proscenium doors and boxes above them, and the stage and auditorium were still both lit by candles and oil-lamps. When it was rebuilt again in 1880, the forestage and proscenium doors were removed, and the proscenium became a frame for the stage pictures, with the auditorium darkened as a result of the installation of gas lighting.[7] The predominant tendency of nineteenth-century staging was to create lavishly detailed settings that evoked as completely and accurately as possible the period and location in which the plays (or productions) were *set*, the apotheosis of which was perhaps Beerbohm Tree's 1900 production of *A Midsummer Night's Dream* complete with real grass, water and rabbits: a production style which, according to Shaw, smothered intelligibility in scenery. In Britain, William Poel led the opposition to such notions, with his ambition to present Shakespeare's work 'under conditions the play was written to fulfil' (or more accurately his conception of those conditions) and attempts to relate the physical characteristics of the Elizabethan/Jacobean stage, and particularly its actor–audience relationship, to modern performance, have been a key factor in the staging of the plays this century (see Chapter 4, pp. 131–3).

Occasional revivals of neglected plays can come about for all kinds of reasons – the impulse of a particular director with access to the means of production; a college-based experiment; an anniversary of a writer or event, and so on. But if the plays from one period are to enjoy an active and sustained stage life in the theatres of another period without being subjected *as a matter of course* to the level of adaptation or critical disenchantment I have been outlining, two conditions in particular must be met, and firmly in place: firstly, the form of the drama must be acceptable to the audience as a means of presenting a true image of experience; and secondly, the plays must present a vision of the world that is immediately recognisable intellectually to, and shared emotionally by, an audience. Interestingly enough, in the history of the theatre plays have probably been rejected by audiences more often because of their form than their content. And not only revived plays have suffered. It has often been argued, for example, that the riot in the audience on the first night of Alfred Jarry's *Ubu Roi* (9 December 1896) was in response to the word *merde* (shit), but as Frantisek Deak has shown, more reliable reports suggest that 'the formal innovations . . . can be seen as the primary cause of the uproar' since 'these were not part of contemporary theatre conventions'. The performance on the following night, to a paying and therefore (Deak believes) more likely a bourgeois audience, passed off quietly, further suggesting that the response at the première 'was in the context of literary discourse . . . rather than in the context of moral or class concerns'.[8] A similar pattern is observable elsewhere; at the Paris première of Ibsen's *The*

Wild Duck (1891) the audience made quacking noises at the stage; the enraged audience of Pirandello's *Six Characters in Search of an Author* (1921) pursued the author to his apartment demanding to know what he thought he was doing; W.B. Yeats criticised the stylistic shifts in Sean O'Casey's *The Silver Tassie* (1928); and when Beckett's *Waiting for Godot* opened in London in 1955 the majority of the critics were completely bewildered because it seemed so different from the 'realistic' drama that dominated the stage at that time. All these are examples of plays that were initially rejected not so much because of the ideas they put forward but for the theatrical means by which those ideas were presented.

In the late nineteenth and early twentieth century the dominant aesthetic against which the work of the Elizabethans and Jacobeans was measured was not neo-classicism, but naturalism. The dramatic and theatrical conventions developed by this aesthetic had far-reaching implications for drama. Characters were given fully-fledged lives, past and present; stage settings attempted to reproduce the real world with a high degree of surface, photographic realism; actors, and the newly emerging directors, worked to develop a performance style with which they could inhabit this new stage world comfortably, and so appear to be unaware of the presence of the audience behind the 'fourth wall', and with whom they would never make direct contact. Towards the end of the nineteenth century, however, a reaction set in against the dominant tenets of naturalism. In Maurice Valency's words:

> The naturalists had thought of themselves as physiologists. The new movement was much involved with psychology, with hypnotism, and the Hermetic [occult] sciences.
>
> (1963: 115)

Evidence of the new spirit was everywhere. Just as the turn from the sixteenth to the seventeenth century saw a surge in studies of the human mind, so did the turn from the nineteenth century to the twentieth: Havelock Ellis produced six volumes of *Studies in the Psychology of Sex* between 1897 and 1910; in 1900 Sigmund Freud published *The Interpretation of Dreams*; in Russia, Stanislavski developed an approach to acting designed to make accessible the actor's subconscious. Theatrical experimentation was vigorous: in Paris, the French director Lugné-Poe presented Maeterlinck's symbolist dramas at the new Théâtre de L'Œuvre, as well, significantly, as an adaptation of Ford's *'Tis Pity She's A Whore* (Deak 1993: 218–20); in 1899, Henrik Ibsen, whose earlier work had appeared to many as the epitome of naturalistic drama, wrote *When We Dead Awaken*, described by Valency as having a 'Maeterlinckian quality that is quite new' in Ibsen's work (1963: 227). Ibsen's play centres on a meeting, after some years of separation, between a sculptor, Professor Rubek, and his former model, Irene. They discuss a statue he sculpted of her in the past, a statue he refers to as his 'masterpiece':

IRENA: 'Resurrection Day' you called it – I called it our child.

RUBEK: I was young then, and knew nothing of life. Resurrection, I thought, would be most beautifully, most exquisitely, personified as a young woman, untouched by the world, waking to light and glory, with nothing ugly or impure to shed.

IRENA: Yes . . . and that is how I stand there now in our work?

RUBEK: Not . . . exactly, Irena.

IRENA: Not exactly? Don't I stand there just as I stood for you?

RUBEK: In the years that followed, I came to know something of the world, Irena. Resurrection Day began to mean something larger, and something – something more complex. The little round pedestal where your figure stood so straight and solitary – no longer had room on it for all that I now wanted to show –

IRENA: What else did you show? Tell me.

RUBEK: I showed what I saw with my own eyes in the world around me. I *had* to show it, Irena, I couldn't help myself. I enlarged the pedestal, made it broader and wider, and on it I placed a corner of the curved and splitting earth, and out of the fissures in the ground there now swarm human figures with secret animal faces – men and women, just as I knew them in life.

(1964: 269)

In this sequence, Rubek identifies the collision of forms he believes necessary to give shape and substance to the totality of his experience. The sculpture he describes is, in effect, a microcosm of the major aesthetic trends that emerged during the forty years from 1880 to 1920 and which, with their various off-shoots, forged the anatomy of dramatic expression then and, to a considerable degree, for the rest of the twentieth century: Naturalism, Symbolism and Expressionism.

The tendency to stretch the boundaries of representation is seen even more radically in the work of August Strindberg, whose later plays (especially *Road to Damascus* and his dream plays, written between 1901 and 1907) embraced a mix of naturalism and distorted exaggeration characteristic of the modernist spirit in contemporary literature, painting and sculpture, which led, in turn, to a revival of interest in the work of John Donne and the seventeenth-century Mannerist painter, El Greco. Some of these strategies were even more forcefully employed by the German Expressionist movement of the 1920s, the impact of which is summed up by Valency:

Once the dramatist felt free of the necessity for preserving the illusion of actuality, it became possible to treat a play as a play, to take direct control of the presence of the audience, and to control, rather than to be controlled by the illusion.

(1963: 397)

Raymond Williams has commented on all this activity:

There has never been, in any comparable period, so much innovation and experiment, and this has been related, throughout, to a growth and crisis of civilisation which the drama has embodied, in some remarkable ways.

(1968: 1)

Both critics are describing events and attitudes around the turn of the last century, but Valency could be describing the relationship of actor, space and audience in the Elizabethan and Jacobean theatre, and Williams could as well be discussing the relationship between theatre and society in the late sixteenth and early seventeenth centuries. It underlines the growing synergy between the two periods, in both of which one finds aesthetics characterised by a mix of (often contradictory) styles employed in an effort to reproduce the artist's experience of the world; the image of Rubek's sculpture is closely matched, for instance, by the stage image of the Duchess of Malfi slowly circled by the dancing madmen in her prison or the extrusions of farce into moments of apparent seriousness (or vice versa) that are common to Elizabethan and Jacobean plays (see Chapter 6). I am not proposing that the links between the periods were immediately productive, or even recognised: for much of the twentieth century audiences continued to be turned off by the violence of the plays and bewildered by their conventions. What I do suggest, however, is that modernist experiments in the late nineteenth- and early twentieth-century theatre that originated with Ibsen and Strindberg and that were developed by influential theorist/practitioners such as Granville Barker, Meyerhold, Brecht and Artaud, contributed to making it increasingly possible for Elizabethan and Jacobean plays at least to stand a chance of being measured sympathetically in the light of aesthetic values of the modern theatre. In other words, when looking for reasons for revival, one must look at developments in the drama and theatre of the twentieth century as well as at the plays of the sixteenth and seventeenth.

The twentieth century

Although vigorous theatrical experimentation was taking place outside England, forces nearer to home were at work, too. Not only were major figures in mainstream contemporary British theatre such as Granville Barker, Shaw and Archer addressing themselves (if not always favourably) to Elizabethan and Jacobean drama, but a number of small theatre groups were established to pursue interests not met by the commercial theatre. In 1891, J.T. Grein had founded the Independent Theatre Society. In March that year the Society staged Ibsen's *Ghosts*, and then, unable to find a suitable contemporary English play, mounted Poel's production of *The Duchess of Malfi* in 1892. In 1895 Poel founded the Elizabethan Stage Society, and in 1899 the Stage Society was founded 'to promote and encourage Dramatic Art; to serve as an Experimental Theatre', with a repertoire drawn mainly from contemporary British and European dramatists. In 1919 an off-shoot of the Stage Society – the Phoenix Society – was formed with the express purpose of reviving neglected Renaissance plays. It survived for six years, during which time it staged twenty-six plays drawn roughly equally from the Renaissance and Restoration periods. Other, similar societies were formed at this time, but the Elizabethan Stage Society and the Phoenix Society deserve to be acknowledged as especially major forces in the twentieth-century revival of Renaissance plays. The critic T.S. Eliot was also attempting to rehabilitate neglected playwrights. His 1919 essay on Jonson, for example, sought to rescue him from a readership of only 'historians and antiquaries', observing that Jonson's work possessed a 'brutality, a lack of sentiment, a polished surface, a handling of large bold designs in brilliant colours, which ought to attract about three thousand people in London and elsewhere' (1963: 81). Eliot was referring to readers, however, not audiences, and the 1919 production by the Phoenix Society of *The Duchess of Malfi* (a play Eliot much admired) prompted him to enquire wryly why 'the revival of seventeenth century drama suggests virtue, vegetarianism and a headache'.[9] Nevertheless, Eliot's criticism no doubt helped prompt Phoenix Society productions in 1921 of *Volpone* and *Bartholomew Fair* after absences from the English stage of 136 and 190 years respectively. Eliot himself described the production of *Volpone* as 'the most important theatrical event of the year' (*Dial*, LXX, June 1921) and, as Gary Taylor observes, 'For the first time in almost two centuries, Shakespeare had company on the Everest of English drama' (1989: 236).

But what of the content of the plays? Serious and comic plays from the period are generally concerned with questions of class, politics, money, sex, death, the roles of men and women in society, and commonly treat these issues with a satiric edge or a mix of seriousness and comedy, the comedy frequently macabre and disorienting. These characteristics are clearly in tune with the interests, attitudes and approaches of modern writers and audiences. As we have seen, however, particularly (though by no means exclusively) in the nineteenth century, major criticism of the Elizabethan and Jacobean plays targeted their supposed preoccupation with violence and cruelty. The plays are still occasionally attacked along these lines today, though events of this century from the First World War to the civil war in Bosnia have made such criticism even less tenable. Indeed, key revivals seem often to have been stimulated by traumatic events: *Troilus and Cressida*, for example, received its first professional production in London for over 300 years just five years after the end of the First World War. In an article published in 1970, when Elizabethan and especially Jacobean plays were particularly popular, S. Gorley Putt attempted to identify the 'many reasons for supposing that the present time is favourable for an appreciation of Jacobean drama'. He suggested that:

We, who have heard of doctors reading by the light of lampshades made of the skin of their human victims need not shudder when the Duke in Tourneur's *The Revenger's Tragedy* is made to kiss a poisoned skull. And before the incineration of Hiroshima, Marlowe's Tamburlaine himself would have turned pale.[10]

The same point had been made fifty years earlier, however, when F.L. Lucas, editing the works of Webster, found an analogy for the horrors of the play-wright's world in the carnage of the First World War:

The most exaggerated fuss of all has been made about the dead man's hand in *The Duchess of Malfi*. Too many of the present generation have stumbled about in the darkness among month-old corpses on the battlefields of France to be much impressed by the falsetto uproar which this piece of 'business' occasioned in nineteenth-century minds.

(I: 33–4)

By chance, the review of the 1945 production of *The Duchess of Malfi* in *The Times* was printed beneath photographs of the victims of Nazi concentration camps. A similar image was invoked in the *New Statesman* review of the same production:

If *Measure for Measure* and *The Winter's Tale* were not known to be by Shakespeare, and were therefore as unfamiliar upon the stage as *The Duchess of Malfi*, some critics would doubtless declare these plays to be of merely antiquarian interest. The plots and the characters, we should be told, are incredible to the modern public. So they are. And so is Buchenwald.

(*New Statesman and Nation*, 28 April 1945, p. 271)

The Times review of the 1960 RSC production reiterated the point:

It may be because we have lived close to violent events that it is easier for us than audiences of the nineties to enter sympathetically into a powerful poetic mind obsessed with violent lives that come to their crises in violent deaths.

(16 December 1960)

This extract from D.H. Lawrence's *Kangaroo* sums up this shift in response:

It was in 1915 the old world ended. In the winter of 1915–16 the spirit of the old London collapsed: the city, in some way, perished,

perished from being the heart of the world, and became a vortex of broken passions, lost hopes, fears and horrors.

(Quoted in Bradbury and McFarlane 1976: 33)

Different writers provide different datum points (for Virginia Woolf 'human character changed' in 1910), but the general argument remains the same – the concerns and atmosphere, 'fears and horrors' of the twentieth century seem to have allowed the Jacobean tragic writers a voice in a way denied them for centuries. At the same time, increasing preoccupation with money and possessions, the fine line between business and crime, the enduring British interest in social status and our obsession with sexual scandals concerning royalty or politicians have enabled many of the comedies (and tragedies) to speak directly, even seemingly topically, to a modern audience. Experiments and developments in theatrical (and literary) forms, too, have made Renaissance plays look increasingly modern, and, indeed, made many more recent plays look naïve.

Many of these points were made by the director Tony Richardson in an article in *Plays and Players* following his 1961 production of *The Changeling*, in which he explained his approach to the play and raised the issues that – though they may result in different solutions – face all those who choose to stage these old plays today (*Plays and Players*, April 1961: 5). Richardson chose *The Changeling* (a play which he had regarded as a 'masterpiece' since first reading it) for a number of reasons: the 'extraordinary existentialism of the theme . . . the idea that you are solely and wholly responsible for your actions'; Middleton's 'understanding of a certain kind of sexual violence, an almost Strindbergian love–hatred relationship'; and the 'curious and ironic mixture of styles within the play, of abrupt switches from farce to thriller, from thriller to tragedy'. All these qualities were, Richardson considered, 'tremendously in tune with the contemporary theatre audience [and] with contemporary attitudes to writing and in the other arts'. In other words, in terms both of form and content the play could hope for a direct response from its modern audience.

Of course, as Richardson points out, while preserving the 'style and period of the play', a production must still communicate its 'relevance and aliveness' through choices in 'staging . . . decor, and a certain approach to the acting': 'We were determined to present *The Changeling*, not as some musty exhibition, a dramatic National Gallery, but as a play that is as vibrantly alive today as it was when Middleton and Rowley wrote it.' Richardson (as a number of subsequent directors have done) chose to transpose the play to Spain in the 'Goya period' to stress its Spanish quality and because 'there is also behind Goya a quality of insanity which finds a direct parallel in Middleton'. Verse speaking began from an understanding of the meaning of the line: 'once [the actor] knows what he is saying the verse will take care of itself'. The intimate nature of the Royal Court suited the 'intimate style' of the play, and the 'direct aside to the audience, a rather awkward melo-dramatic device that one just cannot get out of' but which, 'if tackled bravely and done honestly' can be successful. The madhouse plot was included. Richardson concluded his article with a view of the position of the less well-known playwrights in the English theatre in the early 1960s from the perspective of a theatre-practitioner, linking their viability directly to the state of contemporary drama:

> In presenting plays such as *The Changeling*, the English Stage Company are carrying out the kind of work that a National Theatre [not yet created] should do. Such plays, at the moment, are generally neglected, yet they ought to be constantly and readily available in a National Theatre repertoire. That *The Changeling*, *The Duchess of Malfi* (at the Aldwych) and *The White Devil* (presented for one performance at the Old Vic last month) have all just turned up together is purely fortuitous; whereas such revivals should be planned at regular inter-vals. At the present moment, however, it seems likely that we shall see a number of these minor classics brought out for an airing. Our the-atre has suddenly become tremendously vital and alive, and as a result of this vitality there is a curiosity to see some of the off-beat classics that correspond in a way to the unconventional modern plays we have been seeing.

The range of approaches to Elizabethan and Jacobean plays – especially since the end of the Second World War – has been as diverse as theatrical experi-ment in general during the century, too diverse indeed to trace here. There have been, however, key productions, figures and events, all of which have pro-vided a growing resource on which subsequent generations of directors, designers and actors may draw. The following list (that repeats some examples already given) is offered in no particular order and, as always with artistic activity, there is frequent overlap between different elements and events:

- Granville Barker's productions of Shakespeare at the Royal Court from 1904 and more especially at the Savoy Theatre from 1912–14 that dis-pensed with cumbersome set changes and (influenced by Poel) encouraged the actors to speak rapidly;
- Barry Jackson's production of *Cymbeline* at the Birmingham Repertory Theatre in 1923, the first this century in modern dress, followed by *Hamlet* (seen also in London) in 1925 with jazz music;
- Tyrone Guthrie's innovations with arena staging, aided by Tanya Moiseiwitsch, designer of the Festival Theatre, Stratford, Ontario, built in 1953;
- Gordon Craig's experiments with fluid, kinetic staging sympathetic to verse drama;

- The Council for the Encouragement of Music and the Arts (CEMA) founded in 1939, was jointly funded by private and public money. In 1942 it became entirely state-funded, and in 1947 became the Arts Council of Great Britain, its remit in part to 'develop a greater knowledge, understanding, and practice of the fine arts exclusively, and in particular to increase the accessibility of the fine arts to the public'. Its subsidies have been a major factor in providing theatres with the means to present plays that would not be considered by the commercial theatre. In the late 1950s, for example, the former Shakespeare Memorial Theatre, led by Peter Hall, was awarded substantial funding from the Arts Council, resulting in a change of title to the Royal Shakespeare Company in 1960: an example of the 'combination of state funding and the powerful influence of scholarly criticism' (McLuskie and Uglow 1989: 49) that has been a key factor in the twentieth-century stage history of classical plays in mainstream theatre. In Stratford-upon-Avon the RSC was constrained by its charter to the production of Shakespeare's plays, but when, in 1960, it opened a base in London at the Aldwych Theatre, it marked the event with a production of *The Duchess of Malfi* with Peggy Ashcroft in the leading role.

Major critical and theatrical influences came from other countries:

- Bertolt Brecht saw in Shakespeare and the Elizabethan drama a model for his Epic theatre, and the visit of his company, the Berliner Ensemble, to London in 1956 was a major influence on subsequent stagings of Elizabethan and Jacobean plays and on directors who sought to stress their social and political aspects.
- Antonin Artaud saw in English Renaissance drama, and in Ford's *'Tis Pity She's A Whore* in particular, an image of his notion of the Theatre of Cruelty, a vision that strongly influenced the work of Peter Brook, Charles Marowitz and a range of other practitioners and productions.
- Jan Kott's *Shakespeare Our Contemporary* (1961) was a profound influence on theatrical interpretation, most notably Brook's *King Lear*.
- Peter Brook's work in general has itself been a major force in rethinking approaches to Shakespeare – his productions of *Titus Andronicus* (1955) and *A Midsummer Night's Dream* (1970), for example, challenged conventional views of those plays. Ruby Cohn observed (1976: 295) that Brook's production of *The Tempest* at the Roundhouse, London, in 1968:

> predates most of the New Theater experiments [and] several of its experimental procedures were to become customary in a relatively short time – emphasis upon the physical as opposed to the verbal, and upon the spontaneous as opposed to the structured, free use of playing space rather than traditional actor-audience

separation, absence of set, costumes and props, story line blurred in favour of images emerging from actors' improvisations, ready eruption of the violent and the sexual.

- Peter Daubeny's World Theatre Seasons, that ran annually from 1964 until 1973 brought to London the experience and ideas of international theatre artists, many of whom, less 'constrained' by the original language of the plays, demonstrated a stimulating originality in terms of staging. At the Edinburgh Festival and elsewhere, there have been opportunities more recently to see the work of a number of theatre practitioners from abroad in productions of Shakespeare by, for example, Robert Lepage, the Japanese Ninagawa Company, Giorgio Strehler, Peter Sellars, Heiner Müller, Peter Zadek and Jürgen Flimm.
- The emergence of studio theatre spaces enabled experiments with language and action in spaces often more sympathetic to the texts of the plays. The first wholly flexible studio theatre was built by the University of Bristol in 1951 followed by a number of open-stage playhouses (at Sheffield and Bolton, for example) and the opening of the Other Place (originally known as The Studio Theatre) at Stratford in 1973 that became a venue for key work such as Trevor Nunn's 1976 *Macbeth* with Ian McKellen and Judi Dench.
- University drama has played its part, too. The Oxford University Dramatic Society and the Amateur Dramatic Club at Cambridge began in the 1880s to stage revivals of Shakespeare's plays, since when universities have often provided a site for less well-known texts on which the commercial and even the subsidised theatre could not take a chance. University-educated directors have helped both to expand the repertoire and maintain links between academic scholarship and theatre practice. The first university Department of Drama in Britain was founded at Bristol in 1947 and, following in the footsteps of pioneers such as Nevill Coghill, E.K. Chambers and Muriel Bradbrook, scholars such as Gerald Bentley, Glynne Wickham (the first Professor of Drama in this country) John Russell Brown, R.A. Foakes, Bernard Beckerman, Peter Thomson and Andrew Gurr have stimulated discussion and experiment of the texts in the theatre context of their own time. Since the 1980s, the emergence of performance-based critical approaches have further strengthened the links of scholarship and theatrical performance, connections the reconstructions of outdoor and indoor playhouses at the International Shakespeare Globe Centre in London should foster even more strongly.
- Specific companies apart from the RSC and the National, such as the English Stage Company, Joan Littlewood's Theatre Workshop at Stratford East and, more recently, the Glasgow Citizens, have broadened the repertoire by staging little-known Renaissance plays, and further developed styles of performance.

- The work of Fringe and Alternative theatre companies in this country (such as Triple Action and Théâtre de Complicité), in Europe (such as the Gruppo Sperimentazione Teatrale) and America (such as Richard Schechner's Performance Group of New York), often less respectful to the source text, have, in developing the ideas of specific theorists or their own methods, further diversified approaches. Other, textually rigorous, productions (such as in the work of Kick Theatre, founded by Deborah Warner, Classics on a Shoestring, founded by Katie Mitchell and Mike Alfreds' Method and Madness) and the work of Northern Broadsides and the Cheek by Jowl Company have offered equally productive and exciting alternatives to the work of larger-scale subsidised companies such as the RSC and National, and have themselves come to influence those companies' own work.

- The work of directors and designers who, working within the mainstream of British theatre, have also consistently developed approaches to presenting the plays, often drawing on experiences in other media (such as opera) and frequently anticipating approaches to staging elsewhere in the world.

- Dramatists who have turned not only to Shakespeare but to his contemporaries as material to rework or as a stimulus to new work.

Events and works such as these (plus others I have undoubtedly omitted) have created a bedrock on which theatre artists consciously or otherwise, in imitation or rejection, build their productions, and on which they set a further layer of their own discoveries and approaches. Even in the seventeen years since Robert Cushman wrote that the theatre had discovered the means to do Jacobean plays justice, those means have developed, as the views and examples contained, for example, in the collection *In Contact With the Gods* (Delgado and Heritage 1996) so clearly demonstrates. That theatre artists continue to apply themselves to English Renaissance texts, and not just to Shakespeare, in ways that range from 'straight' production to inventive interpretation to radical textual adaptation, and that they use the texts freely as sites for experiments in performance, is welcome evidence that the plays sit increasingly firmly in the repertoire. As Richard Eyre has written:

> [classic plays] are our genetic link with the past and our means of decoding the present. Every age sees its own reflection in these plays. We find in them not the past throwing a shadow on the present, but a distorted image of ourselves – our questions, our doubts and confusions. The classics survive not because they are venerated for their age but because of what they mean to us now . . . We have to keep rediscovering ways of doing the classics . . . the life of a theatre should always be in the present tense.[11]

CASE STUDY: NEW PLAYS FOR OLD – RICHARD BROME AND STEPHEN JEFFREYS, *A JOVIAL CREW*

> If all pitch in and argue on the substance of the play, then there's no art.
>
> Stephen Jeffreys, *A Jovial Crew*

Transformation of old plays in the modern theatre, prompted by desires to reshape the texts to sharpen their 'relevance' or suit particular critical or aesthetic viewpoints, takes two major forms – directorial interpretation (which invariably involves cutting and sometimes adding to the text) and textual adaptation of a more extensive kind, usually by a playwright (or, as at times with John Barton, say) by a director acting as one.

Directorial interpretation (and the scenographic or performance tactics often associated with such experiments) frequently bring cries of 'foul!' from reviewers and audiences. Some academic critics, too, who take what might be called a 'purist' approach, often argue that failure to 'respect the text' can result in serious distortions, even of plays that are well known.[12] Many (especially those working in the theatre) find these responses hard to understand, arguing that not only is the text, in Meyerhold's words, merely the 'pre-text' for any production, but that the majority of plays that figure in the accepted classic repertoire (especially Shakespeare's) are performed sufficiently frequently to bear any amount of intervention. In *Performing Nostalgia* (1996), for example, Susan Bennett discusses 'Seventeen Lears', no fewer than twelve of them 'mainstream' productions of *King Lear* between 1980 and 1990 (two on television, the rest onstage), and, as the playwright David Edgar joked, if you went to the theatre in 1989 without seeing a performance of *As You Like It* you were awarded a 'small cash prize'. Commenting on objections to 'tampering' with Shakespeare, Peter Hall has written:

> If I walk into the Louvre and paint a large black moustache on the face of the *Mona Lisa*, it's there for ever, defaced. But if I do *Macbeth* – as I did – in red rugs [RSC, 1967], I make nobody a fool but myself. *Macbeth* is still there at the end – staring at me. I have done nothing to *Macbeth*.
>
> (Quoted in Berry 1981: 10)

Indeed, radical interpretations are dependent to a degree on the audience's knowledge of the 'original' text, and cutting, emendation, unforeseen characterisation or surprising delivery can focus attention on the known rather than the performed text:

> Hamlet's 'To be or not to be' soliloquy would arguably gain maximum impact in a production if it were to be deleted altogether, because its very absence would raise a host of questions concerning

its meaning and importance and the justifiability of its excision.

(Buzacott 1991: 142)

(Though even the omission of that soliloquy would presuppose – unjustifi-
ably – that the majority of those in the audience would know exactly where in
Hamlet it should come.) In the case of less well-known plays, however, the
audience may be totally unaware of the degree to which the production they
are watching diverges from the original text, and so be unable to shape their
understanding of what *is* being performed by a knowledge of what is *not*.
Directorial interventions usually involve cutting, transposing and occasionally
supplementing the source text to allow a particular interpretation to be trans-
mitted. The entry on *The Tempest* in the *Cambridge Guide to English Literature*,
for instance, argues that directors invariably ruin that play by looking for an
interpretation when, in fact, 'None is needed – [it] should be staged according
to the text and the characters allowed to speak for what they are.'[13] There is,
of course, no such thing as an uninflected or 'straight' production: as Peter
Brook has commented, if you let a play speak for itself it may remain silent.
'Characters' do not exist without the actors who play them, and those actors
will inevitably deliver the character to some degree through their individual
personalities and attitudes.

Directors differ, however, in their views on the validity of cutting classic
plays in general and Shakespeare in particular.[14] (I am here distinguishing cutting from what I see as 'trimming' – making slight and occasional cuts to
remove irretrievably obscure references, for example.) Trevor Nunn describes
his attitude to the source text as one of 'loyalty', but claims that it is at times
necessary to remove, telescope or even add text (taken from other plays or written by himself) in order to clarify and focus 'certain things that are intended
in the original text but are presented obliquely' (Berry 1977: 72–3). Peter
Brook balances 'respect on the one hand and disrespect on the other', arguing
that it is to an extent a matter of degree that distinguishes directorial interpretation from what he terms 'exploitation':

> every interpretation if it works in its place and its moment has some
> life. But I think that into that totally permissive view, that every-
> thing is possible, one can introduce a certain scale of values. One can
> ask whether the interpretation takes the smallest or the widest view
> of what the play contains . . . If I *use* the play, the permissive attitude
> is at its worst. Because the play is then no longer a vehicle for a re-
> exploration of truth, it becomes a vehicle for exploitation.
>
> (Berry 1977: 128, 124–5)

A production of *The Merchant of Venice* by the American director Peter
Sellars, staged in London in 1994 as part of the 'Everybody's Shakespeare'
Festival, set the play in modern Los Angeles with a multi-cultural cast (a

black Shylock and a Chinese American Portia, for example), and employed a wide range of the technology – such as hand-held cameras and microphones – that has become a signature of much postmodern theatre performance. The text, however, remained intact. As Sellars says:

> This is the only time I'm sure most people in that audience will have ever seen an uncut *Merchant of Venice* . . . I am scrupulous and go out of my way to give the most complete text possible. I do feel a very specific obligation and if something doesn't fit my conception I leave it there, because I don't wish to pretend that my conception covers, blanket style, everything the author had in mind: of course not.
>
> (Delgado and Heritage 1996: 231)

Deborah Warner is similarly opposed to making cuts, emendations or transpositions in Shakespeare's plays. Referring to her work on *King John* (performed at the Other Place in Stratford in 1988) she observed that she decided not to cut the source text for a number of reasons:

> not least because it has not been performed in the full version . . . for years, in fact I would argue it has never been played uncut. It's popular at the moment to cut the plays but I don't like to do so. I think there is a strong case for those plays which have been cut, or otherwise messed about, to be played as they were originally intended to be. It's because this has not happened that the myths have grown up that they are difficult or unactable or cannot be put across to today's audiences.
>
> (Cook 1989: 105)

Warner thinks the problem lies with the director, not necessarily the script, especially if it is by Shakespeare:

> I feel if you do reach a dead-end, then, as a director, it is your fault. It's no good thinking, oh, well, it's an early play, not one of his best, it's not my fault. I happen to find it hard to believe that this particular author is ever at fault.
>
> (Cook 1989: 105)

She identifies the value of this way of working:

> The most exciting discoveries come in those moments when you have doubted and then you suddenly understand how it should be done. It can come when you wonder if you should cut the play but, as you work on it more and more, you realise exactly why those lines are there.
>
> (Cook 1989: 105)

The results are certainly exciting and illuminating. Her productions of Shakespeare's *Titus Andronicus* (1987) and *King John*, both played totally uncut (except for the removal of three words in Latin from *Titus*), to a large extent rediscovered texts which had in earlier productions been considered in need of directorial help to make them work. By insisting on trying to accommodate all the apparent incongruities, even absurdities, in the texts with which they were working, Warner and her actors produced performances that embraced the plays as complex, difficult and challenging.

The second major form of intervention is authorial adaptation. As Eric Bentley has written, 'All roads lead to Shakespeare, or perhaps it might be more correct to say that Shakespeare leads to all roads.'[15] The directors' views expressed throughout *In Contact With the Gods* reveal 'the dominance of Shakespeare' (Delgado and Heritage 1996: 4) in their work and, as Michael Scott notes in the postscript to his discussion of some plays by Tom Stoppard, Edward Bond, Eugene Ionesco, Arnold Wesker, Charles Marowitz and Harold Pinter (to which list I would add Beckett, Howard Brenton, David Edgar and Barrie Keefe), many authors too 'feed off Shakespeare':

> Some serve as critiques of his drama reacting against the reverence surrounding his 'sacred texts'; some play off Shakespeare helping us to find new insights about him and his work; others find within the Shakespearian dramatic formula new modes of expression pertinent to the modern world.
>
> (1989: 121)

Other writers have adapted Shakespeare's plays more directly: Brecht, Osborne, Dürrenmatt, Jarry, for example, produced versions of Shakespeare's plays, or plays directly indebted to him. But it is not only Shakespeare, and dramatists have also sought to use other Elizabethan and Jacobean playwrights in similar ways: some adaptations, such as Brecht's *The Duchess of Malfi*, Howard Barker's 'collaboration' with Thomas Middleton on *Women Beware Women* (described by Jonathan Dollimore as an act of 'creative vandalism') or Stephen Jeffreys' extensive reworking of Richard Brome's *A Jovial Crew* have radically altered existing texts, in these particular instances to sharpen the plays to fit the modern collaborator's political perspective. Other plays, such as Caryl Churchill's modern city comedy *Serious Money* and Barry Keefe's *A Mad World, My Masters*, take elements of the earlier genre as a model; Stephen Jeffreys' *The Clink* is more an attempt to imitate an earlier style, while entirely original plays such as Peter Flannery's brilliant *Singer*, and many by Peter Barnes, still draw conspicuously and consciously on the dramatic and theatrical conventions of Jacobean drama.

Adaptation of the original text itself at authorial level has prompted strong responses from critics, scholars and audiences, especially when the rewriting, in Robert Cushman's words, apparently 'reshapes the soul of the play'. Adapters themselves have not always found the process straightforward. In 1983, Howard Davies asked the playwright David Edgar to help him prepare the text for a production of Shakespeare and Fletcher's *Henry VIII*. Davies considered it to be 'very much a modern play, dealing with taxes, unemployment and social divisions'. As a well-known author of political plays, whose anti-fascist play *Destiny* had been staged by the RSC in 1976, who had adapted Dickens's *Nicholas Nickleby* in 1979–80 and whose epic play tracing post-war socialism, *Maydays*, was running at the Barbican at the same time as *Henry VIII* in Stratford, the choice of Edgar as collaborator seemed particularly apt. As Robert Shaughnessy observes:

> a 'Shakespeare and Edgar play' might have seemed like an excitingly disruptive, potentially radical proposition, a dialogue between a 'classic' and the present that might have echoed the oppositional interventions of Brecht and Bond.[16]

In the end, however, the collaboration did not materialize. According to Davies:

> I don't think [David Edgar] could quite bring himself to do it. He stayed in rehearsals and was invaluable and did rewrite scenes which we rehearsed, and that was very exciting, but he just felt he didn't have the courage to be that impertinent.[17]

From my own experience of working with David Edgar (directing a rewrite of his and Susan Todd's play *Teendreams*) I know how protective he is of his own work, reasonably asking that no changes to his text be made without his approval, and that any agreed changes not be included until he had typed them out and delivered them to the rehearsal room; perhaps he found it difficult to deny Shakespeare the same rights.

There is a difference, of course, between the work of a dramatist who (like Stoppard in *Rosencrantz and Guildenstern Are Dead*) uses an existing play as a launchpad for what is, in effect, an entirely new work, and the act of adapting an existing text. Christopher Spencer (1965: 7) provides a useful definition of adaptation:

> The typical adaptation includes substantial cuts of scenes, speeches and speech assignments; much alteration of language; and at least one and usually several important (or scene-length) additions.

In the programme for his 1977 version of Jonson's *The Devil Is an Ass*, Peter Barnes set out his attitude and approach to the adaptation of Jacobean plays:

I would prefer to call it 'restoration'. For, I believe, adapting an old play is much like restoring an old painting. Time renders certain areas opaque and words, like protective varnish, go dead and do not refract light. These obsolete words have to be replaced by others of equal precision, beauty and force, but whose meaning is clear. The opaque areas have to be cut . . . or retouched. In certain cases I have added speeches and in one extreme instance, a whole scene in the interest of clarity . . . If the retouching is successful it will be indistinguishable from Jonson. If it is not, it will be glaringly obvious and there will be no need for a programme note to point it out. The only question to ask is, is it true to the original and theatrically alive?[18]

The Devil Is an Ass is an extremely complicated play, even by the standards of Jacobean comedy, and, as with any play with a farce structure, a production needs to ensure that the plot-lines are clear and the action logical. Comedies, especially those that were topical and satirical, present particular problems: as Peter Barnes notes, 'it's important that the jokes are funny and you understand them as they're being said, not with a glossary afterwards' (quoted in Dukore 1981: 90). Nonetheless, the *Sunday Times* critic, Bernard Levin, stung by what he perceived as unacceptable alterations in Jonson's text, became querulous in his review:

The National Theatre . . . appear to have inaugurated Ben Jonson Bugger-the-Text week . . . A few days since, we had the NT's own magnificent *Volpone*, marred by feeble concessions to the groundlings, modern words being substituted for many of Jonson's ancient ones in case somebody in the audience might otherwise be obliged to think.

Turning his attention to Barnes's programme note, Levin continued:

Did you ever see such a gallimaufry of fallacies? Why do 'obsolete' words 'have to be' replaced, and why must 'opaque areas' be 'cut and retouched'? Has Mr Barnes not entertained the possibility that the opaque areas may be in his own brain, and the obsolescence in his belief that audiences are no better educated than he? What work of genius would be safe from this filleting and stuffing if anything not instantly familiar to all 'must be' removed and replaced? . . . Does he not even realise that the patina of an old painting is itself part of its beauty? . . . Or that 'is it theatrically alive' is *not* the only question, for there is also the matter of integrity to be considered?

(*The Sunday Times*, 5 May 1977, p. 37)

Questions surrounding the 'integrity' of the text and the 'rights' of dramatists to adapt old plays surface from time to time in the press, and were raised

recently by the theatre critic of *The Times*, Benedict Nightingale, in response
to Stephen Jeffreys' adaptation of Richard Brome's 1641 comedy, *A Jovial
Crew*, performed in Stratford and London by the RSC during the 1992–3
season. Nightingale's review of the production in Stratford was largely
favourable, but in an article (that echoed the Barnes–Levin exchange) published the week prior to the production's London opening, his attitude
appeared to have shifted:

> At what point does adaptation turn into creation, and a touched-up
> play, like a touched-up painting, become more the work of the
> restorer than the original artist? And are such changes more or less
> legitimate if the piece is an obscure one? . . . Would you like to see
> machine guns inserted into Uccello's Battle of San Romano? Or a psy-
> choanalyst into *Oedipus Rex*? If not, perhaps it is time to insist that we
> see the works of yesteryear with their warts intact.
>
> (*The Times*, 14 April 1993, p. 29)

Jeffreys made his own case in *The Times* a week later, and developed it in the
Introduction to the published text of his adaptation. There, he writes that
although Brome's play 'is powered by a striking and original conceit', 'contains
some brilliantly sustained comic scenes' and is 'a fascinating social document
of a precise historical period', it also 'presents insuperable problems for modern
directors and audiences'. He specifies what he sees as the most significant of
these obstacles: the fact that much of the comedy depends on contemporary
references and analogies; the presentation of the beggars as an 'idealised literary device' rather than a collection of dramatic characters; faults in the play's
structure; a *dénouement* which is 'wildly implausible' and contradicts the psychology of the central character, Springlove.[19]
A further influence on Jeffreys' view of the play was Martin Butler's study
of Caroline drama, *Theatre and Crisis: 1632–1642*, in which Butler argues
that Brome's play is a 'state of the nation' play set (in Jeffreys' words) 'at a
moment of decisive political transformation'. In this respect, the choice (made
before Jeffreys was asked to do the adaptation) of Max Stafford-Clark as director is significant, with his reputation for socially acute productions and his
interest both in the English Civil War period and in exploring bridges
between old plays and the modern stage. Stafford-Clark, then Artistic Director
of the Royal Court, had been responsible for bringing together Howard Barker
and Thomas Middleton's *Women Beware Women*; had directed Farquhar's *The
Recruiting Officer*, alternating the production with a new work by Timberlake
Wertenbaker, *Our Country's Good*, which commented on the earlier play; and
written a book of illuminating essays – *Conversations with George* – based on his
imaginary conversations with Farquhar while directing the latter's play.
Stafford-Clark only accepted the invitation to direct the play on the understanding that he could adapt it with a modern writer, and Jeffreys only

accepted the commission on the understanding that the rewriting could be extensive. Encouraged by the director, Jeffreys aimed to try to 'deliver this hidden play from the conventions and codes of the period and to make Brome's comic conception work onstage'.[20] This statement probably sums up the aim of all adapters (and directors) of English Renaissance plays, but Jeffreys' solution was a radical one, since in seeking to release what he perceived as the 'hidden play', he created what is in effect a new text.

In the same way that directors differ in their views on cutting the texts of old plays, so do those engaged in extensively adapting or rewriting them. Charles Marowitz, who staged a number of 'collages' of Shakespeare's plays in the late 1960s, points out that his work involved 'the re-structuring of a work, the characters and situations of which are widely known', familiarity which enabled the audience to measure the reworking against the original.[21] Peter Barnes takes the opposite approach, arguing that it is precisely the obscure and neglected plays that most need reworking, and that he would not adapt plays such as *The Alchemist* or *Volpone* 'because they are fully realized masterworks'.[22] But does it actually matter? Does an audience really care who wrote what so long as it enjoys itself? Some of the most thrilling productions result from directors, actors and designers overturning our expectations of a play, and, as we saw earlier in this chapter, readings of plays inevitably shift in line with what Stanley Fish terms the 'interpretive community'.[23] Nevertheless, when a play is little known, and even more so if it is getting an airing in effect for the first time (and Brome's play had not been performed publicly for two hundred years)[24] there is perhaps some weight to the argument that audiences should be allowed to judge the source text – at least one not altered beyond the unavoidable changes made in any playtext during rehearsal to aid clarity in language and action, adapt to given circumstances, and so on. In other words, an audience should be allowed to make up their own minds. To repeat Deborah Warner's point:

> I think there is a strong case for those plays which have been cut, or otherwise messed about, to be played as they were originally intended to be. It's because this has not happened that the myths have grown up that they are difficult or unactable or cannot be put across to today's audiences.
>
> (Cook 1989: 105)

Jonathan Miller, too, has argued that working on a little-known play may impose some constraint, if temporary, on a director:

> I don't believe one has any duty or obligation to an author, once he's dead. I think that the concept of the public domain is very important in art, and that when a work in the performing arts has been finished, after the first, second or third try, during which I think one owes it to

the author to honour his explicit conscious intention, and to co-operate with him and try and imagine it as it was when he wrote it, then after that it enters this curious zone of the public arena and his aesthetic rights in it lapse. The play becomes a public object and one should be able to do to it exactly what one wants.

(Cook 1974: 101)

This period in which productions might at least give the writer the benefit of the doubt may be thought to be even more significant when (as is the case with Brome's play at the time of writing) no text of the play is in print. The programme for the RSC production billed *A Jovial Crew* as 'adapted by Stephen Jeffreys' but gave no indication of the nature or extent of the alterations. To an extent, Peter Thomson's comments on the RSC's 1974 production of *King John*, heavily adapted by John Barton, are applicable in this instance, too:

> it cannot be *ignored* that the audience . . . will assume that the *King John* they are seeing is Shakespeare's, and that no amount of programme notes will erase that impression. The free cast list confirmed at the bottom right hand corner that 'the text for this production incorporates lines from *The Troublesome Reign of King John* and Bale's *Kyng Johan*, and some additions by John Barton', but such honesty is like the small-print disavowals in manufacturers' guarantees, which indemnify the deceiver without enlightening the deceived.
>
> (1975: 138)

Indeed, in a programme note, while usefully setting out the social and political context of Brome's play, Martin Butler wrote that 'At the end of the play the beggars return with their Utopian play about the state of England.' In Brome's play they do nothing of the sort (see below), but the note is confusing (the more so as Butler's next sentence praises the 'poignancy and strength of Brome's achievement'), and, by blurring the distinction between Brome's conclusion and Jeffreys', could easily have led an audience to think that what it was seeing was in fact the original text.

In the published text (which makes perfectly clear that it is his adaptation) Jeffreys gives a brief outline of who wrote what, but I want to look in more detail at this adaptation (probably the most extensive of a Jacobean play in recent years) since it not only provides an insight into how a modern dramatist sympathetic to the fabric and texture of the original play deals with occasional obscurities and repetitions but also how he shapes a 350-year-old play to his own ends, and attempts to render it more appropriate for a modern audience. For Jeffreys and the company, the circumstances of writing the adaptation were not unlike those surrounding a new play in the seventeenth-century theatre (see Chapter 2). The text was still being put together while the cast rehearsed what had already been completed; two writers (albeit one of them dead) were 'collaborating' on the text; a number of plays were being mounted within a few days of each other; and the writer had the opportunity to create parts with particular actors in mind and to write for a specific playhouse.

Jeffreys' treatment of Brome's first scene demonstrates most of the approaches he uses throughout his adaptation. Brome opens his play with a conversation between Oldrents and Hearty in which they recall a previous event. In Jeffreys' adaptation this discussion is preceded by the event itself being enacted; some obscure lines are rewritten (for example, 'Am I not bitten to it every day, by the six-footed bloodhounds that they leave in their litter' becomes 'Am I not bitten every day by the lice they leave in their litter? Lice? Six foot bloodhounds, sir'); and the sense of 'these sad and tragic days' to which Brome refers in his Prologue but not his text is reinforced by Jeffreys through the insertion of phrases such as 'these lean times'. The song lyrics are also altered to sharpen the edge on the presentation of the play's world – the line 'Harsh hunger is rife' replaces softer sentiments in Brome's song, such as 'Our bellies are full, our flesh is warm' and 'Let rich men care, we feel no sorrow'. A shift in the presentation of the beggars is the most significant change in the remainder of Brome's opening scene (turned into a separate scene in Jeffreys' version and titled 'Beggars'). Apart from the named Patrico, Brome's speech-headings give them as 1st, 2nd, 3rd and 4th Beggar, but they are more specifically identified in the dialogue: the 1st Beggar is a 'decay'd poet'; the 2nd is a lawyer; the 3rd a 'Netherland soldier', now a deserter; the 4th a courtier, 'a great court beggar'. Jeffreys, too, identifies them partly by number, but makes certain changes. He retains the lawyer, courtier and soldier (though he keeps Brome's lines only for the last), and changes Brome's poet to an actor, partly to lay the ground for the comic section later in the play where the actor's attempt to 'revive my Tamburlaine with the crew in support' is rejected in favour of a more ensemble production: star-vehicles in admiration of great conquerors not being the taste of the time. More generally, the references to acting introduce the device of 'playing-within-the-play' that performs a more substantial function in Jeffreys' text than in Brome's. In addition, Jeffreys invents the characters of Meg O'Malley, a former apple-woman; Liz, a wife; Old Ben Butler, a printer and seller of (presumably politically dissenting) pamphlets. Of Brome's 100 lines (363–460) establishing the beggar crew, Jeffreys keeps only eleven. In other words, whereas (as he states in his Introduction) the adaptation overall contains lines in the ratio of 55:45 (Brome:Jeffreys), for this scene the ratio is 10:90. This is significant, for it is in the presentation, role and emphasis placed on the beggars that Jeffreys' intervention in Brome's text is most evident. As well as individualising and distinguishing the beggars, making them more than the representative types of Brome's four figures, Jeffreys makes them more dynamic dramatically. In Brome's text, each is described by another, while in Jeffreys' play they speak for themselves. In these ways, Jeffreys achieves his aim of 'giving the crew a more realistic social background' and making them more active than reactive.

Obviously, with some scenes undergoing revisions as radical as those in scene 2 (and some even more so), much of Brome's text remains virtually untouched. Scene 3 (2.1 in Brome) is such a case. Indeed, one of the striking things about the adaptation is Jeffreys' preparedness to leave the original language alone. He does at times change words and phrases, and at times writes in a footnote in dialogue, but just as frequently he leaves the sense to be conveyed by the sound of the words, the dramatic context, or the skill of the actor. For example, in 1.1 of Brome's text, Oldrents has the following speech to his Steward, Springlove, in which he questions his promptness in producing his accounts:

> Not common among stewards, I confess,
> To urge in their accompts before the day
> Their lords have limited. Some that are grown
> To hoary hairs and knighthoods are not found
> Guilty of such an importunity.
> 'Tis yet but thirty days, when I give forty
> After the half-year day, our Lady last.

Jeffreys points out how clear Brome's play is in terms of much of its social detail – such as the precise role of the Steward – and accordingly he and the director were keen 'to amplify the social background so that it seemed real'. Having learned (as I just have) from a footnote, that 'The accounting year usually began on Michaelmas Day, the half-yearly accounts being closed on Lady Day, or March 25' which means that 'Springlove presents his accounts only thirty days after the half-year day, or April 25, though he was allowed forty days, or until about May 5', Jeffreys wrote the following lines, unobtrusively incorporating the footnote into the text:

> 'Tis duty to complete our half year's accounts
> By the fifth of May, which date yet stands some ten days
> Off. It is not common among stewards
> To urge in their accounts before the day
> Their lords have limited.

Apart from some very slight rewriting to clarify the occasional word and narrative, Jeffreys reproduces Brome almost exactly in his own third scene, even including passages that might seem prime candidates for translation or excision, such as Rachel's lines:

> We that were wont to see my gossip's cock today, mold cocklebread, dance clutterdepouch, and hannykin booby, bind barrels or do anything before him . . .

Meriel's claim that she would 'rather hazard my being one of the devil's ape leaders than to marry while he is melancholy' was initially removed, but was reinstated at the request of the actor and director.

Adaptation, however, is not a case merely of excision or alteration. A major element is in new additions. Perhaps the most significant of these, and the one that needs most careful examination (see below) is the play's ending, but there are others. Two scenes (4 and 8) are entirely Jeffreys' invention. Scene 4 introduces the character of Justice Clack, who does not appear until near the end of the original play. This earlier entry-point for Clack allows Jeffreys to effect a telling contrast between Clack's mercenary attitude and Oldrents's liberality, and helps to emphasise the reality of the begging life. What the scene shows most clearly, however, is Jeffreys' 'feel' for the period and its language. He is also the author of *The Clink*, closely modelled on a Jacobean comedy, and much of the success of his adaptation stems from his ability to act as a genuine 'collaborator' with Brome.

In the final scene of Brome's play, the beggars perform a play for Oldrents and Justice Clack. The play-within-a-play begins with a scene between Oldrents (played by the beggar Lawyer) and the fortune teller (played by Patrico) who first told Oldrents that his daughters would become beggars. Hearty, who also appears in the first scene of the play proper, is impersonated by the beggar soldier. The following scene has Springlove (playing himself) and 'Oldrents', repeating word for word the exchange between the two characters in scene 1 of the play proper. In the third and concluding scene, Rachel, Meriel, Vincent and Hilliard (as themselves) explain their reasons for absconding. The 'real' Oldrents, watching the play, perceives that:

> The purpose of their play is but to work my friendship, or their peace
> with me; and they have it.

In Brome's text the sequence of events from that point is as follows: Patrico reveals to Oldrents (privately) that Springlove is Oldrents's long-lost son; Springlove announces that he and Amie, Clack's niece, are contracted to be married, and Clack objects; Oldrents grants Springlove £1,000 a year and Clack withdraws his opposition; Oldrents grants Patrico a 'competent annuity' for life, and Clack gives the remaining beggars a 'free pass, without all manner of correction!' The play adopts therefore a structure of closure appropriate to a romantic comedy – Jack has Jill (and an income) and everything ends happily.

Jeffreys' adaptation follows a different pattern. When the actors enter they are 'mostly disguised from head to foot in straw Mummers' costumes' with Amie, who carries a broom to sweep out an acting area, performing the role of Enterer-in. The play that follows is based on the traditional Play of St George, with St George representing an England divided between rival factions:

Oh, George you are a fine hero no more:
For you are vex'd by both the rich and poor:
Parliament and King, the country and the town,
The city and the court conspire to bring you down.

Three figures representing these factions – a city merchant, a courtier and a
country gentleman (who gets Oldrents's vote) – press their case to George, who
fails to recognise that their conflicting claims are breaking his kingdom apart.
Joined by a soldier who also states his intention 'to win this game', all the
characters are quickly engaged first in battle with each other and then all join
against George whom they kill. Although the Lawyer and Priest fail to revive
George, Amie recognises him as Utopia, and calls forward the Short-Haired
Beggar (the Masterless Man). He revives George, newly constituted as a
Commonwealth.

Let old George lie and fine Utopia stand
Let people dwell in freedom through the land:
And nevermore will hunger, lash and pain
Stalk in good old England's land again.

Hearty and Sack are outraged by the play which they see as 'sedition
pure and simple', but the moment is defused by Meriel (who plays St
George) and Rachel revealing themselves. The narrative from this point is a
reshaping of Brome: the children explain their reasons for absconding;
Springlove announces his intended marriage to Amie and Clack objects; at
this point Patrico reveals (publicly) that Springlove is Oldrents's son;
Oldrents endows Springlove with £1,000 and Clack drops his objections.
There is one further change of substance. In place of Brome's harmonious
ending of couples uniting, Jeffreys presents further division. Patrico accepts
Oldrents's annuity, and Rachel happily returns to her father's house and
looks forward to her marriage to Vincent. The Short-Haired Beggar, however, realises that merely representing events does not mean they are enacted
in actuality:

I have tonight acted in a play which I did trust would show the
thoughts that jostle in my head. But I see nothing was done, nothing
shone forth and 'tis already forgot.

Meriel, in fact, has been changed by her experiences:

Beyond our gates
There lies a world where people fight for
What I play'd but now; Utopia
In England.

She breaks off from Hilliard and the Beggars divide into two groups, described by Jeffreys as Comfort Seekers and Radicals, with:

> one faction pursuing the idea that all advances in society are based on domestic security, the other restlessly seeking freedom 'out there' on the road. This split attempts to dramatise Brome's wider theme: at some time in our lives we all choose between security and danger.

The play concludes as the Comfort Seekers exit one way, and the Radicals 'open the door to the outside world. A beautiful England of green foliage and blue sky awaits them', there is the sound of birdsong, and the stage fades to black.

Jeffreys' ending is undoubtedly powerful, its complex resolution having been skilfully prepared for by his interpolations and reshaping of the preceding text. But it is not, of course, Brome's. Jeffreys' justification for the changes is that he believes the original contains many things that are no longer acceptable to us and that if the play were able to sustain itself without adaptation it would have been performed before. Benedict Nightingale took Jeffreys to task, claiming that his ending 'very nearly turns Brome into a twentieth-century socialist' (not, I suspect, intended as praise). What I found more interesting, however, given the evident desire of both writer and director to stress the social realism of the play and address the 'two-nation' identity of post-Thatcher Britain, was that the production did not take *further* the notion of beggary, especially since it was performed at the Barbican in London, a city that is now only the largest of those in Britain with a vast homeless population. Jeffreys himself observes that 'the play as it stands is rather tasteless in the current context of people begging in the streets of London'[25] and the cast were sent out to experience for themselves the problems of begging in the street (the proceeds being given to charity). In Tony Harrison's play *The Trackers of Oxyrhynchus*, staged at the National Theatre in 1989, itself a new work derived from an old play (in this case the surviving fragment of a Greek satyr play), specific analogies *were* drawn between the 'high' art of the event shared by the National Theatre audience and the proximity to the building and performance of the homeless in 'cardboard city' under Waterloo Bridge. The beggars in the production of *A Jovial Crew*, however, remained very much a theatrical representation far removed from the reality outside the theatre, lessening, in my view, the possible fusion of stage and audience worlds.[26]

In discussing his adaptation of *A Jovial Crew*, Jeffreys described the ending of Brome's play as 'conventional and improbable', in need of change since 'grown ups will not happily sit through such skimble-scamble stuff'. This view was based, however, not only on his own response to the text but the views of those who had worked on or attended a workshop production of the play at the National Theatre studio in 1989. In this instance, therefore, there had been some practical exploration of the text against which the impression gained from reading alone could be measured. Not only the endings of Jacobean plays seem regularly to pose problems, and too often, it seems to me, plays may be rejected without the chance to prove themselves stage-worthy. Middleton's *The Witch*, for example, may appear on reading to present a range of problems resulting from what can seem clumsy plotting, outdated conventions, loose ends, impenetrable period-specific detail and, in particular, a 'conventional and improbable' final scene. All, or some, of these perceived 'blemishes' may account for its having been totally ignored by the professional theatre since 1616 and, if it were to be considered for production, might lead a director to begin to cut and emend it or to send for an adapter. In performance, however, I found (and so far as I could establish members of the audience did too) that the strategies of Middleton's play became clear and that what initially may seem inept craftsmanship, lazy writing or slavish adherence to the largely lost conventions of Jacobean tragicomedy, became thrilling and entirely workable on its own – and a modern audience's – terms. In other words, if plays are to be tested they must be staged, and if they are to be staged they should – at least initially – be trusted.

In many ways, the actions of skilful and sympathetic adapters such as Barnes and Jeffreys are in line with Elizabethan and Jacobean practice. Collaboration between playwrights was common, though we do not know exactly how such collaborations were undertaken in practice and so cannot be certain how closely the different writers worked. Plays were not owned by their authors but by the company who commissioned the play, and were only published when they had ceased to be a box-office draw, or when the theatres were closed because of a plague outbreak or some other prohibition and the company needed to raise some cash. Even then, the published texts did not always acknowledge the author(s); Shakespeare's name, for instance, did not appear on a printed version of one of his plays until the publication of *Love's Labour's Lost* in 1598 and only half of his plays were even published in his lifetime. Indeed, at times when Shakespeare's name does appear – such as on the title-page of the anonymous *A Yorkshire Tragedy* – one suspects it might be the act of a canny publisher cashing in on an illustrious reputation.

Thomas Heywood's claims in his preface to *The English Traveller* that 'It was never any great ambition in me to be in this kind voluminously read', or in his note to *The Rape of Lucrece* that 'It hath been no custom in me . . . to commit my plays to the press', were largely typical of Elizabethan and Jacobean playwrights as a whole. Publishers, moreover, did not consider it necessary to print everything written in a manuscript. The printer's Preface to Marlowe's *Tamburlaine* plays, for example, states that:

> I have (purposely) omitted some fond and frivolous gestures, digressing (and in my poor opinion) far unmeet for the matter, which I thought might seem more tedious unto the wise, than any way else to be

regarded, though (happily) they have been of some vain conceited fondlings greatly gaped at, what times they were showed upon the stage in their graced deformities: nevertheless now, to be mixtured in print with such matter of worth, it would prove a great disgrace to so honourable and stately a history.

This highlights the difference between a published text and the actual performance given of the play, and should alert us to the dangers of assuming a published text has a particular authority as a record of what actually happened in a theatre. A performance, for example, might well include material other than that provided by the named author. In the Epistle to the 1605 edition of his play *Sejanus*, performed two years earlier by the King's Men at the Globe, Jonson wrote:

I would inform you that this book, in all numbers, is not the same with that which was acted on the public stage, wherein a second pen had good share: in place of which I have rather chosen to put weaker (and no doubt less pleasing) of mine own, than to defraud so happy a genius of his right by my loathed usurpation.

Even when one has a text based directly on a playhouse prompt-copy, there is no clear relation between what was actually said onstage and what was printed when the play was finally published. Plays were cut for performance just as they frequently are today. As Richard Brome explained in a postscript to the published text of his comedy *The Antipodes* (Salisbury Court, 1638):

Courteous reader: you shall find more than was presented upon the stage, and left out of the presentation for superfluous length, as some of the players pretended.

There is also scope for additions through verbal improvisation on the part of actors, whether voluntary or enforced (*Hamlet*, 3.2.38–45). What was *done* onstage is another matter still, as the Plot of *The Battle of Alcazar* reveals – a fact recognised by the Lord Mayor of London in his 1594 letter to Lord Burghley complaining of plans to open the Swan, in which he stresses how plays 'are handled' and 'framed and represented'.

POSTSCRIPT

In 1827 Charles Lamb observed that about two-thirds of extant Renaissance plays were still generally unknown, in print or performance. Even though the number of plays in print has increased, the number performed with any regularity on the professional stage is still comparatively small. The intense financial pressure on all theatres means that the risk of staging a little-known play is almost unthinkable. And it is a risk. Birmingham Repertory Theatre's 1994 production of *The Atheist's Tragedy*, imaginatively staged as what the company refers to as one of its 'discovery pieces', was critically acclaimed, but, unknown to audiences and featured on no school and few university syllabuses, it played to houses only one-third full. Even well-known, theatrically tried-and-tested and widely studied non-Shakespearean plays present a financial risk. In 1991, the Sheffield Crucible replaced a production of *The Revenger's Tragedy* planned for the autumn season with (surprise, surprise) *As You Like It*. The artistic director of the theatre, Mark Brickman, explained that 'all the indications suggested a fairly chilly autumn' and that in the circumstances, the theatre would be 'taking a bit of a flyer with a play which doesn't really exist in the public's consciousness' (*Guardian*, 12 July 1991). With funding and venues for new writing already in short supply, the opportunities to stage obscure Jacobean plays are understandably rare. The determination of the Globe 3 directorate to stage currently neglected Elizabethan and Jacobean plays is an immensely significant initiative. Another source of experiment must lie in student drama productions. Surely it is more inventive and imaginative, in the protected freedom of a college production, to present Middleton's *A Mad World My Masters* or *Hengist, King of Kent*; Massinger's *The Picture* or *The Unnatural Combat*; Beaumont and Fletcher's *A King and No King*; almost any Marston play; or Jonson's *The Staple of News* or *The Magnetic Lady* than another *Midsummer Night's Dream* or even *The Changeling* or *The Duchess of Malfi*, and to present them as work arising from a critical and historical study of the plays, as practical examples of how they relate space and language and action. Furthermore, I should like to see established a closer relationship than currently exists between this work and the needs of the professional theatre, especially the large subsidised companies that have both the responsibility and the resources to extend and develop the classic repertoire. If the professional theatre were to be linked in some way to these test-bed productions, perhaps providing resources that they already possess but which are beyond the means of the stretched budgets of academic departments, these little-known plays would at least be seen by those currently responsible for deciding repertoires and be experienced by some of those who will act, design, direct and watch future productions. With luck, the tiny repertoire of Renaissance plays will, in time, grow. But only if the plays are performed. In 1604 John Marston wrote, 'The life of these things consists in action.' Many plays await resuscitation.

NOTES

1 'Comedies are writ to be spoken, not read'

1 John Marston, 'To My Equal Reader', Preface to *The Fawn*.
2 Konstantin Stanislavsky, 1865–1938, Russian theatre director and theorist.
3 *Guardian*, 27 July 1984, p. 11.
4 Remarks reported at a conference on Ben Jonson, University of Reading, January 1996.
5 Hunter 1994: 116. See also Mack 1994b and Vickers 1994.
6 John Webster, *Works*, ed. F.L. Lucas, vol. IV, 1927: 42–3, emphasis added.
7 The Globe reconstruction in London (known throughout this book as Globe 3) opened its first public season in May 1997 following a number of trial productions in a 'Prologue' season the previous year. Originally the vision of American actor and director Sam Wanamaker (who died in 1993), many issues have been raised concerning the reconstruction project (see, for example Bennett 1996; Holderness 1992; Stewart 1984). Theatre directors have conflicting views; John Barton and Adrian Noble are reportedly less convinced of its value than, for example, Peter Hall who believes that work on the reconstruction will affect the way Shakespeare (and presumably his contemporaries) are presented on the modern stage: 'It will change the way we think about Shakespeare, change the ways we speak his words, stage his plays' (Interview, BBC2, 25 August 1997). In this book, however, I shall concentrate on the opportunities (unique in the UK) it offers for practice-based study of Elizabethan and Jacobean public playhouse plays. As actors discover how to work with the space – and the audience – they express considerable excitement and interest in the opportunities Globe 3 offers, while the precise nature of the director's role in this theatre is seen as an area for exploration.
8 Strong 1969: 30–1.
9 In Dekker's *The Honest Whore*, Part 2 (1604) Matheo, a gallant, explains how he has played 'the gentleman's part' by keeping his tailor waiting for payment. Asked why, he replies: 'To keep the fashion; it's your only fashion now of your best rank of gallants, to make their tailors wait for their money neither were it wisdom indeed to pay them upon the first edition of a new suit; for commonly the suit is owing for, when the linings are worn out, and there's no reason then that the tailor should be paid before the mercer.' (4.1.8)
10 See, for example, the painting by Cornelius Ketel, *Fragment of an Allegory* (1580), Delman Collection, San Francisco. Reproduced in Hearn 1995; Diehl 1986. My thoughts on *The Witch* are informed by my production of the play in Bristol in March 1995. I am grateful to Dr Marion O'Connor for her help in clarifying the emblematic nature of this moment in the play. See Elizabeth Schafer's New Mermaid edition of *The Witch* (1994) for details of the relationship between the play and the 'sensational

events of the scandal involving Frances Howard' (Introduction: xv).

11 Powell 1966: 157.

12 Francis Bacon, *The Advancement of Learning*, The First Book, 1969 edition: 29–30.

13 John Barton calculates that prose accounts for 28 per cent of the language in Shakespeare's plays.

14 Surrey probably wrote his verse translation around 1537–8 or a little later. The translation of Book IV was published in 1554, and again in 1557, this time in conjunction with Book II. 'In this poem we can see the nature of English poetry being transformed in one of the great moments of our history' (Keane 1985: 83).

15 Shepherd 1965:134.

16 It has always been fashionable for each generation to belittle its predecessors' artistic efforts, and the limits of such plays are presumably parodied and ridiculed by Shakespeare when, in the Boar's Head tavern, Falstaff amuses his cronies by performing in 'King Cambises's vein' (*1 Henry IV*, 2.4). Nicolas Brooke, however, offers a useful corrective to any tendency to dismiss *Cambises* too readily (1966: 94).

17 Interview with the author.

18 Interview with the author.

19 Interview with the author. See Wright 1992.

20 An article in *The Times* (9 July 1997) reported criticism of the training provided by some theatre schools in the basic skills required by classic plays (though, as usual, the focus is on Shakespeare). In response, the principal of the Central School of Speech and Drama was quoted as saying that most actors 'go into television and have to be flexible . . . There's not enough Shakespeare around.' The Leader in the same edition observed: 'The challenge is to ensure that the old words dance and the old plays are as fresh for us as they were for our ancestors . . . What is at stake is the very survival of Shakespeare as a living force.'

2 'The life of these things consists in action'

1 John Marston, 'To My Equal Reader', Preface to *The Fawn*.

2 Edward Alleyn 1566–1626. For details of his life and career see Bentley, *JCS*, II: 346–9; Nungezer 1968; Hosking 1952.

3 See Foakes and Rickert 1961: 276–7.

4 Ibid.: 297.

5 Q1607 (Bodleian copy) A2^r; Malone Society Reprint 1963.

6 Philip Massinger, *Believe As You List*. See the Introduction (1976: 298–301) and the illustration of the annotated prompt-copy between pp. 302 and 303.

7 I am grateful to a former student, Lucy Nevitt, for this reference.

8 Letter to the author.

9 Thomas Nashe: 'his very name (as the name of Ned Allen on the common stage) was able to make an ill matter good' (*Strange News*, 1592).

10 Rea 1989: 16.

11 See M. Holden and P. Tucker, eds, *The Folio Shakespeare* series.

12 Master Correction, a character in Edward Sharpham's play *Cupid's Whirligig* (1607), comments of his pupils, 'I have taken as much pains with them as any poet could have done, to make them answer upon their cue with good action, distinction and deliberation.' This may refer only to practice with the Children's company for whom the play was written, but many dramatists were actors as well, and would no doubt have been able and willing (even determined) to offer advice to the adult professionals.

13 Foakes and Rickert 1961: 56–8.

14 Letter to the author.

15 Letter to the author. In 1902, the Russian director, Meyerhold, established a company

of twenty-seven actors in the port of Kherson, on the River Dnieper, close to the Black Sea. Their season opened on 22 September 1902 and closed on 17 February the following year, during which period they presented seventy-nine plays (about a quarter of them one-act) and Meyerhold, in addition to directing, acted in 83 of the 115 performances. Most significantly, despite the enormous workload, the company, according to Meyerhold's biographer, Edward Braun, raised 'artistic standards to a level almost certainly without precedent on the Russian provincial stage' (Braun 1995: 19).

16 Downes 1987: 51–2, 55.

17 The involvement of the writer in production was evidently not invariably welcome. In the Induction to *Bartholomew Fair* (Hope, 1614) the Stage Keeper reports a squabble he had with the playwright for suggesting that a property pump would improve the staging, and that a bit of business with a prostitute and some young lawyers would amuse the audience. The exchange may reflect ironically on a dramatist's (or at least Jonson's) expectations regarding his role in staging his work:

> But these master-poets, they will ha' their own absurd courses; they will be informed of nothing. He has, sir reverence, kicked me three or four times about the tiring-house, I thank him, for but offering to put in, with my experience.
>
> (25–9)

18 Gurr 1992: 210. The source was Edward Hall's *The Union of the Two Noble and Illustre Famelies of Lancastre and Yorke*, 1548, and the specific reference is: '. . . the Lord Clifford, either for heat or pain, putting off his gorget [helmet], suddenly with an arrow (as some say) without a head, was stricken in the throat, and incontinent rendered his spirit' (Clxxxvjᵛ).

19 See Rasmussen 1989, p. 5, who argues the change was made because 'the exit and re-entry of the same characters . . . violated the "law of re-entry" or the "principle of the open stage"'. I prefer my own pragmatic reasoning.

20 Bentley 1986, ch. 6, 'Managers', especially pp. 157–60.

21 See note 6 above.

22 This version of *Troilus and Cressida* (now lost) was by Thomas Dekker and Henry Chettle.

23 See Bradley 1992 for illustrations of the *Orlando Furioso* Part and of Plots. It is perhaps worth pointing out, too, that sheets of paper containing information on who does what are not uncommonly pinned up backstage in theatres today, especially when actors are out of communication with stage-management staff.

24 Matthew Warchus began his professional career as a director in 1988, following a Degree in Drama and Music from the University of Bristol. His productions of English Renaissance plays include *Sejanus* (Edinburgh Festival), *Much Ado About Nothing* (winner of the 1993 Shakespeare's Globe Classic Award for Most Promising Newcomer), *Volpone* (Royal National Theatre), *The Devil Is an Ass*, *Henry V* and *Hamlet* (RSC).

25 Holland 1995: 211. This is a detailed and sympathetic account of the production and also includes a review of Katie Mitchell's production of the *Henry VI* plays. See also *Theatre Record*, XV, 1995, pp. 1213–14, for reviews of *Henry V*.

3 'Speeches well pronounced . . .'

1 Richard Edwards, *Damon and Pythias*, 1564, Prologue.

2 See Nungezer 1968: 67–79.

3 Interview with the author.

4 Brecht 1964: 137. See also sections 10, 13, 24, 31, 34, 38 ('A Short Organum for the Theatre') and 47; Krause 1995: 262–74; Mitter 1992.

5 *The Works of Beaumont and Fletcher*, ed. Alexander Dyce, vol. I: lvi.

6 Stanislavsky 1967, 1980, 1983. See also Braun 1984; Magarshack 1967; Mitter 1992; and Peter Holland's eminently sensible discussion (1984).

7 Roach 1985: 23–4 and Chapter 1 *passim*. Interestingly, three hundred years before Stanislavsky, Ignatius Loyola, founder of the Jesuits, set out a system of devotional practices that included exercises requiring those at prayer first to imagine in detail places and people central to the planned devotion in order to generate actual and appropriate feelings. See Tetlow 1987.

8 Quoted by States 1995: 27.

9 Elly Konijn reaches a similar conclusion in her survey of 114 professional Dutch actors, in whose 'theatre practice detachment and involvement are not mutually exclusive, but aspects of both styles are used simultaneously by the actors in performing character-emotions.' Indeed, she also notes that, according to her survey results, 'Even for actors with an involvement strategy, no correspondence between actors' emotions and characters' emotions is found, which indicates that while becoming involved in their character they do not participate in the same emotional experiences as the presupposed character-emotions' (1995: 138). See also Mack 1962: 275–96.

10 See *Theatre Record*, XIII, 1993 for press reviews of *King Lear*.

11 Hughes 1967: 476. Orators' gestures in themselves (like many of those referred to in playtexts) were not necessarily 'stylised': as Bertram Joseph rightly pointed out (1964: 16) John Bulwer, whose manuals for teachers of the deaf, *Chirologia* and *Chironomia*, published in 1644, have been used to elucidate the orator's skills, found many of the 120 gestures he illustrated in the marketplace, of which perhaps only a fifth are likely to be obscure to us now.

12 Harbage 1939. As Peter Holland notes, 'the fiercer "formalists" have recanted' (1984: 61).

13 Gurr 1992: 99–100.

14 'To Edward Alleyn', in Parfitt 1975: 62.

15 Ben Jonson, *Timber, or, Discoveries*, in Parfitt 1975: 397–8.

16 Gurr 1963: 95–102.

17 Significantly, 'overacting' was commonly employed in plays as an analogy for insincere behaviour.

18 Review in *Theatre Record*, XV, 1995, p. 1071. Thomas Fuller wrote (*The History of the Worthies of England*, 1662, Fff2ᵛ) that Alleyn was 'the Roscius of our age, so acting to the life, that he made any part (especially a majestic one) to become him'.

19 Hamilton 1972: 75.

20 Parfitt 1975: 81.

21 Holderness and Loughrey, eds, *The Tragicall Historie of Hamlet Prince of Denmarke*, p. 65.

22 Thomas Jordan, 'A Prologue to introduce the first woman that came to act on the stage, in the tragedy called *The Moor of Venice*', probably 8 December 1660. Quoted Nungezer 1968: 212–13, who notes that 'Mrs Coleman had played Ianthe in *The Siege of Rhodes* in 1658, but this was a "quasi dramatic performance"'.

23 Orgel 1989: 8. See also Levin 1989; Howard 1991.

24 Gosson 1841: 19. Philip Stubbes, *The Anatomie of Abuses*, 1583, sig. F5ᵛ. Stubbes's attitude is not confined to the seventeenth century. Marjorie Garber quotes a ruling by the Dean of Yale University in 1915 stating that members of the Yale Dramatic Association could not impersonate female characters for more than one year in succession because continued impersonation tended to make men effeminate (Garber 1992: 63).

25 Julie Sanders, in an unpublished paper delivered at the Ben Jonson Conference, University of Reading, January 1996.

26 Wright, *Historia Histrionica*, 1699, quoted *JCS*, II: 461.

27 'A Common Player', 1615, quoted *ES*, IV: 255–7.

28 Harriet Walter is one of Britain's leading actresses. Her classical roles include Winifred (*The Witch of Edmonton*), Viola (*Twelfth Night*), Helena (*A Midsummer Night's Dream*), Helena (*All's Well That Ends Well*), Imogen (*Cymbeline*) and – on radio – Lady Macbeth. She played the Duchess of Malfi in the RSC 1987 production directed by Bill Alexander.

29 This analysis is informed by my production of the play in the Wickham Theatre, University of Bristol, March 1996.

30 Fulke Greville, *A Dedication to Sir Philip Sidney*, in Gouws 1986: 135.

31 See White 1992, pp. 115–17.

32 Goffman 1974: 251; see also Waugh 1984.

33 See P. Edwards and C. Gibson, eds, *The Plays and Poems of Philip Massinger*, vol. I, 'General Introduction': xv–xlv. Also see Clare 1990 for an excellent discussion of contemporary theatre censorship.

34 Limon 1992.

4   Palaces of pleasure

1 Stage designers, however, are frequently unimpressed with critics' abilities to 'read', evaluate and describe the scenography. See Ellie Parker, 'Design and Designers in Contemporary Theatre Production', unpub. dissertation, University of Bristol, 1997.

2 John B. Gleason argues that Van Buchell was 'unusually capable in drawing' (1981: 329), a view challenged by Johan Gerritsen (1986) who claims that while De Witt was a competent draughtsman, Van Buchell was not.

3 Puttenham 1978: ch. XVII: 36–7.

4 The Hope contract instructed the builder to make it to similar dimensions to the Swan, though with a removable stage (*ES*, II: 466–8). The De Witt drawing appears to show a stage more square than rectangular in shape but this may simply be a result of the artist's (or copier's) ability.

5 Michael Holden, 'Playing Areas: A Theatre Consultant's View', unpublished paper given to the conference 'Within this Wooden O', International Shakespeare Globe Centre, London, 20 April 1995. An enigmatic sketch in a copy of the 1600 Quarto of Shakespeare's *2 Henry IV*, may show a stage – possibly tapered depending on how you orientate the drawing – with, possibly, positional markings for actors. See Foakes 1985: 156–7 for an illustration and fuller discussion.

6 See Hosley 1975, Thomson 1986a and 1986b. Early experiences at Globe 3 have raised the question of the difficulty of focusing on scenes on the balcony, partly because of the absence of specific lighting.

7 Michael Holden; see note 5 above. At the time of writing, Mark Rylance, Globe 3's artistic director, confirms that the size and positioning of the stage pillars have indeed been the subject of more extensive discussion than any other element of the reconstruction. As part of the Globe directorate's admirable commitment to flexibility and exploration, however, they maintain the possibility for changes to be made in this and other aspects of the building in the light of experience.

8 M. Jourdain points out the scarcity of chairs 'due to their rarity during the early Renaissance. Stools and forms outnumbered the chairs in hall and parlour until the Restoration', *English Decoration and Furniture of the Early Renaissance 1500–1650*, 1924: 241; quoted by White 1982: 86fn, in discussion of a scene in *Arden of Faversham* in which the social implications of the stage furniture are significant.

9 Machyn also refers in his *Diary* to various funerals, including a clothworker whose procession was attended by 'four dozen torches' and 'burning tapers' (Nichols 1848: 170–1).

10 The experience of watching plays in the even light of the shaded stage, with no stage lighting to direct the gaze, so requiring the actors to draw the audience's focus of

attention, has been one of the striking elements of early performances at Globe 3, and has underlined, for example, the significance of costume in assisting the actors focus the stage action. See Chapter 5 for further discussion of light in the Jacobean playhouse.

11 Guthrie 1961: 168–72.

12 See O'Connor 1987; Hildy 1994; Hutson 1987; Newlin 1980. I have recently located Poel's (previously unpublished) autographed plan for a scale model of his proposed Globe reconstruction – see 'William Poel's Globe', *Theatre Notebook* (forthcoming).

13 'It's a cliché to say that Shakespeare paints his own scenes and that he doesn't require scenery, but it's true that the word does it in most of the plays we deal with. Nothing more is needed really than the actor and, say, something to sit on – not even that sometimes. So you start off with an advantage that you don't actually need anything', Nick Ormerod, interviewed with Declan Donnellan, in Delgado and Heritage 1996: 80–92, here 86.

5   Chambers of demonstrations

1   I'll ha' you to my chamber of demonstrations,
         Where I'll show you both the grammar and the logic
         And rhetoric of quarrelling.
                    (Ben Jonson, *The Alchemist*, 4.2.63)

2 *Antonio and Mellida*, Prologue, l.3.

3 Thomas Dekker presents a satirical portrait of stage-sitters in his prose pamphlet, *The Gull's Horn Book*, which, though it may be describing practices when the Blackfriars was occupied by the Children, no doubt remains an apt observation of behaviour during the adults' tenancy. A stage-sitter, Dekker reported, could display his clothes, physique and hair-style to the rest of the audience; comment on the performance and the quality of the play; attract the attention of women in the audience or the boys onstage; get a light for his pipe (smoking was very popular) and examine at close quarters (and then no doubt comment audibly on) the quality of the actors' costumes (Dekker 1967: 65–109; especially 98–102). The evidence is rather cloudy, but it seems that sitting on the stage at the public playhouses was, if allowed at all, at least before the 1620s much more an exception than a rule (Orrell 1988: 89–90).

4 See Boal 1995 *passim*. See Case Study, p. 156ff. for further discussion of the 'sectioning' of contemporary audiences.

5 The inventory is printed in Mann 1991 and Thomson 1983.

6 Chan 1980.

7 Stevens 1961: 236.

8 Edwards 1980: 674.

9 ibid.: emphasis added.

10 I am grateful to my friends and colleagues, Simon Jones and Wyndham Thomas, and to those students from the Department of Music at Bristol University who have helped with a number of performance exercises.

11 See Rowan 1970 and 1980; Orrell 1977; Gurr and Orrell 1989.

12 *Chirologia*, 1644. In Ford's *Love's Sacrifice*, 2.2., for example, D'Avolos describes to the audience, and interprets, the actions of an onstage character, Fernando: 'Alone? reading a letter? Good. How now! Striking his breast! What in the name of policy should this mean? Tearing his hair! Passion, by all the hopes of my life, plain passion! Now I perceive it.' Clearly, the actor playing Fernando has to perform the actions described, and do them 'passionately'. He also has to match them in some way to his overall physical performance. See also Hattaway 1982: 76–7.

13 Thomas Dekker, *The Seven Deadly Sins of London*, 1606. See Graves 1982.

6 'Poison in jest'

1 *Hamlet*, 3.2.230.

2 The controversial term 'bad quarto' is frequently used to describe 'piratically published versions based upon the memorial reconstructions of the plays by bit-part actors', Holderness and Bryan Loughrey, eds, *The Tragicall Historie of Hamlet Prince of Denmarke*, p. 8.

3 G.R. Hibbard considers this 'one of the most remarkable moments in the whole play' (*Hamlet*, Oxford edition, 1987, 327fn.) in which the entire perspective of Hamlet's life and death is opened up in a flash-back to his birth and childhood.

4 Gellert 1970: 67.

5 Shepherd 1965:135.

6 The catalogue of an El Greco exhibition seen in Spain and America in 1982–3, and published as 'A New York Graphic Society Book' by Little, Brown & Company, Boston, 1982, discusses in detail the painting (which is described as El Greco's 'greatest work') and the concept of Mannerism. An imagined, yet vivid, description of Grotesque paintings and their impact on the viewer is given by Umberto Eco in ch. 2, 'Sext', of *The Name of the Rose* (1981: 40–45); I am grateful to a former student, Sebastian Khalhat, for drawing my attention to this example. See also Shearman 1967.

7 Seen, for example, in the rapidly shifting tones and energies of the opening act of *The Revenger's Tragedy*, and in the play as a whole. Brian Shelton, who directed the first revival since the seventeenth century (at Pitlochry in 1965) described it as 'pungent, moralistic, melodramatic, comic, allegorical, violent, poetic, bawdy, tragic, absurd, ironic . . . each element is contrasted against the other' (quoted in Scott 1982: 40). A similar pattern is seen in the conflict between the domestic, 'naturalistic' world of the Duchess of Malfi and Antonio and the irrational world of her brothers, or in the contrast between the heightened, allegorical style in which the battle for the soul of the Lady is presented and the sharply drawn psychological, 'domestic' treatment of marital infidelity in the parallel plots of *The Second Maiden's Tragedy*. These contrasts may have been embodied in the original staging. In at least one instance (*Herod and Antipater*) the effect was created by splitting the stage to play contrasting actions simultaneously, an effect employed to great effect by Phyllida Lloyd in her production of *Pericles* (Royal National Theatre, London, 1994). In *Antony and Cleopatra*, described by a number of critics as a 'Mannerist' tragedy, much rests on the contrast of the two worlds that Antony tries to embrace: it seems to me possible that some similar juxtaposed staging might have been attempted in performances at the Globe.

8 Murray 1967: 132.

9 Farnham 1971.

10 'My feeling is that the dramatist must have the right to change formal gear at any time. There's supposed to be a healthy shock, for instance, at those moments in *Loot* when an audience actually stops laughing. So if *Loot* is played as no more than farcical, it won't work' (Orton 1978: 13).

11 This, and other illustrations, can be found in Wright 1865.

12 Braun, 1969: 138; from Meyerhold's essay 'The Fairground Booth', pp. 119–46.

13 Evans 1974: 141.

14 Ellis 1982: 86.

15 A key element of the Grotesque (which adds to the difficulty of grasping its qualities other than in practice) is its impact on the viewer. The question of what Meyerhold describes as the spectator's 'ambivalent attitude towards the stage action' (Braun 1969: 139) is as central to an understanding of the Grotesque in the theatre as to an understanding of the effect on the viewer achieved by paintings such as the *Burial of Count Orgaz* or Michelangelo's Medici tombs. Essentially, the Grotesque requires the viewer to embrace the contradictions presented, to confront the duality of experience, and to

allow the contradictions within his or her responses to be exposed and experienced within the controlled environment of the theatre.

16 Equally – though perhaps more difficult – a *refusal* to allow both responses to emerge has to be acknowledged. In Levin's review of *The Changeling* he noted (approvingly) that the audience at the Royal Court in 1961, unlike that at the Aldwych in 1978, did not laugh at Beatrice-Joanna's line following sexual intercourse with De Flores – 'This fellow has undone me endlessly'. It seemed not to occur to him that this changed response reflected not only a different kind of society but was undoubtedly closer to the response Middleton and Rowley expected. In his seminal book, *The Grotesque in Art and Literature* (1968), the first study to attempt the formulation of a coherent concept of the Grotesque, Wolfgang Kayser found it impossible to avoid the question of audience response in reaching a definition of the Grotesque. For Kayser, the Grotesque possessed the power to stir in the audience or viewer a sense of 'estrangement' with the world, its essential absurdity. Kayser is careful to point out that the Grotesque does not deal in the fantastic: we are at all times alert to the links between our own world and the world presented. Kayser is aware of the importance of the question of the 'anxiety' created in the audience by such alienation but he does not pursue further the issue of psychological impact. This central element of the Grotesque is the subject of Michael Steig's important essay, 'Defining the Grotesque: An Attempt at Synthesis' (1970).

17 Interview with the author.

18 Interview with the author.

19 Bob Hoskins who played Bosola died with the manic laugh that had been the trademark of his performance (McLuskie and Uglow 1989: 201).

20 Directed by Andrew Hay. The review appeared in the University of Bristol *Newsletter*.

21 William Shakespeare, *Titus Andronicus*, ed., Alan Hughes, Cambridge, 1994, Introduction: 43. All line references are to this edition, which has a very good stage-focused introduction.

22 Alan Howard, *Sunday Times* magazine, 11 January 1981, p. 26.

23 Mikhail Bakhtin quotes from *The Night Watches* of Bonaventura, 1804: 'Is there upon earth a more potent means than laughter to resist the mockeries of the world and of fate? The most powerful enemy experiences terror at the sight of this satirical mask, and misfortune itself retreats before me, if I dare laugh at it. What else indeed except laughter does this earth deserve, may the devil take it! (1968: 38). In Deborah Warner's production, Brian Cox as Titus laughed for fully ten seconds, a very long time onstage.

24 Dr Johnson, in Sherbo (1968) *Johnson on Shakespeare, the Yale edition of the Works of Samuel Johnson*, vol. VIII, p. 750.

25 Dessen 1989.

26 Waith 1957; Ovid's *Metamorphoses* (1986: 134–42). See also Brucher 1979.

27 G.R. Hibbard's essay is a good example of criticism offered with no reference to performance. Hibbard sees the juxtaposition of 'the frightful spectacle of the ravished girl' and 'the "favour and prettiness" that Marcus is turning it all into' as an artistic failure on Shakespeare's part to reconcile 'the poet and the dramatist' and 'to bring the two sides of his genius into a proper and fruitful working relationship with each other' (1972: 80).

28 Brook 1961; Trewin 1971: 82.

29 Gerald Freedman, 'Introduction', *Titus Andronicus*, The Folio Society edition, 1970, 3–5.

30 Stanley Uys, quoted by Quince in Redmond 1991: 218.

31 There is no doubt that the particular violence in this scene – the rape – is especially problematic to modern spectators, even leaving aside the dismembering, however terrible that may be. Other difficulties of response are raised, for example, by another Grotesque text – Dennis Potter's *Brimstone and Treacle* – which offers the view that rape can ultimately produce good, a view which may be deemed too irresponsible by any

standards, and which contributed to its showing being prohibited for some years. For Jonathan Bate, the Warner/Ritter version was successful in part because 'rape matters to them as late twentieth-century women more than it could possibly have done for Shakespeare writing for Marcus and to the boy who first played Lavinia' (Arden edition, 1995: 63). Social attitudes to rape were certainly less sympathetic, but I've no more idea than Professor Bate of Shakespeare's or either actor's personal views (though, for the record, there are reports of Elizabethan boys being abused). But that is not the issue. Nor is it a straightforward seventeenth/twentieth-century equation. Thomas Middleton, in *Women Beware Women* (c. 1621), for example, portrayed the Duke's rape of Bianca as a dehumanising act that helps trigger her absorption into the corrupt world of the court. Howard Barker, on the other hand, reworking the play 350 years later, presented rape as a politically liberating act.

32 See Fraser 1996, especially ch. xv.
33 Interview with the author. Trevor Nunn was talking generally, and without reference to this particular play or production.
34 Freud 1960.
35 Available from BBC Educational videos.
36 Fawcett 1983.
37 See Levenson 1972; Luckyj 1993.
38 Ruskin, 'The Grotesque Renaissance' 1904: 135–230.

7   'A good play gone wrong'

1 At the end of the nineteenth century *The Changeling* still remained unperformed in any version since William Hayley's unattributed 1789 adaptation, *Marcella*. William Archer used the play as a basis for his own drama *Beatriz Juana*, and his opinion of the play is set out at some length in his book *The Old Drama and the New*. This book was published in 1923, but contained material drawn from the previous thirty years reviewing and writing about the 'old drama'. The arguments are not only illustrative of Archer's own critical standpoint but typical of a whole range of late nineteenth-century opinion that sought, as much as the neo-classic critics of the previous century, to apply a set of wholly inappropriate criteria to Jacobean plays. After analysing the relationship between De Flores and Beatrice, which he sees as fundamentally illogical, Archer (1923: 100) concludes:

> *The Changeling* is, in fact, a good play gone wrong: it rattles at the joints, and falls to pieces at a touch for lack of thoughtful and rational adjustment. And in this respect it is absolutely typical. The plays of the period which will stand even the least exacting tests of external plausibility or internal consistency are few indeed. What distinguishes *The Changeling* from the general ruck of Elizabethan melodramas is that it more narrowly misses being a good play. We feel that Middleton was a real dramatist, who, in another environment, would have been capable of working up to higher standards.

2 William Archer, *New Review*, VIII, January 1893: 96–106. Reprinted in Moore 1981: 132–43.
3 Shaw 1931: vol. III: 334.
4 See Bevis 1988; Hume 1976.
5 Samuel Johnson, *Proposals for Printing by Subscription Shakespeare's Plays*, 1756, in Sherbo 1968: 56.
6 William Watson, *Excursions in Criticism*, 1893: 1–22, quoted in Moore 1981: 146–51.
7 See illustrations in Wickham 1985: 212–13.

8 Deak 1993: 236.
9 Quoted in McLuskie and Uglow 1989, Introduction: 58. Their Introduction is an excellent survey of shifting attitudes to Webster's play in particular and Jacobean drama in general. See also Steen 1993.
10 Putt 1970: 18.
11 Eyre 1993: 175–6.
12 See Dessen 1985, especially ch. 8, 'Elizabethan Playscripts and Modern Interpreters'. Also Dessen 1987.
13 Stapleton 1983. The comment is not included in the new edition.
14 See Thompson 1991; Wells 1984; Jackson 1986.
15 Eric Bentley, *What Is Theatre?*, New York, 1952: 107, quoted in Cohn 1976: 389.
16 Shaughnessy 1994: 156.
17 Ibid.
18 Directed by Stuart Burge, and performed at the Nottingham Playhouse, opening in March 1973. The production was subsequently staged at the National Theatre in 1977.
19 Richard Brome, *A Jovial Crew*, adapted by Stephen Jeffreys, 1992, 'Author's Introduction'.
20 Ibid.
21 Marowitz 1978: 12.
22 Dukore 1981: 90.
23 Fish 1980.
24 For details of revivals in the seventeenth and eighteenth centuries see Lennep *et al*. 1965.
25 Interview with the author, to whom I am grateful for his help with this Case Study, though the views expressed on the production are entirely my own.
26 McDonald 1992, especially ch. 6.

BIBLIOGRAPHY

Place of publication is London unless stated otherwise.

Primary sources

Plays

All line references are to the following editions unless stated otherwise.

Anon, *Arden of Faversham*, ed. Martin White, 1982.

——, *Alphonsus King of Aragon*, Malone Society Reprints, Oxford, 1926.

——, *The Fair Maid of the Exchange*, Malone Society Reprints, Oxford, 1962.

——, *The Three Parnassus Plays*, ed. J.B. Leishman, 1949.

——, *The Second Maiden's Tragedy*, ed. Anne Lancashire, Revels Plays, Manchester, 1978.

——, *A Warning for Fair Women*, ed. Charles Dale Cannon, The Hague, 1975.

——, *Wily Beguiled*, Malone Society Reprints, Oxford, 1912.

——, *The Merry Devil of Edmonton*, ed. C.F. Tucker Brooke, in *The Shakespeare Apocrypha*, Oxford, 1908.

Brome, Richard, *The Antipodes*, ed. A.S. Knowland, in *Six Caroline Plays*, Oxford, 1962.

——, *A Jovial Crew*, ed. Ann Haaker, 1968.

Brome, Richard and Stephen Jeffreys, *A Jovial Crew*, 1992.

Davenant, Sir William, *Dramatic Works*, 5 vols, 1872.

Dekker, Thomas, *If This Be Not a Good Play, the Devil Is in It*, ed. Fredson Bowers, *The Dramatic Works of Thomas Dekker*, vol. III, Cambridge, 1966.

——, *The Honest Whore*, Parts 1 and 2, ed. Fredson Bowers, vol. II, Cambridge, 1964.

——, *The Whore of Babylon*, ed. Fredson Bowers, vol. II, Cambridge, 1964.

Drue, Thomas, *The Bloody Banquet*, Malone Society Reprints, Oxford, 1961.

Edwards, Richard, *Damon and Pythias*, in *Dodsley's Old Plays* (originally published 1744) ed. W.C. Hazlitt, vol. IV, 1874.

Field, Nathan, *Amends for Ladies*, ed. A. Wilson Verity, in *Nero and Other Plays*, 1888.

Ford, John, *The Broken Heart*, ed. T.J.B. Spencer, Manchester, 1980.

——, *Love's Sacrifice*, ed. Havelock Ellis, 1960.

——, *'Tis Pity She's A Whore*, ed. Brian Morris, 1968.

Fletcher, John, *The Humorous Lieutenant,* ed. Cyrus Hoy, in *Beaumont and Fletcher: Dramatic Works,* gen. ed. Fredson Bowers, vol. 5.

Greene, Robert, *The History of Orlando Furioso,* Malone Society Reprints, Oxford, 1906.

Heywood, Thomas, *Dramatic Works,* 6 vols, 1874.

——, *The Four Prentices of London,* vol. 2, 1874.

——, *Love's Mistress,* vol. 5, 1874.

——, *The Second Part of the Iron Age,* vol. 3, 1874.

——, *A Woman Killed With Kindness,* ed. Keith Sturgess, in *Three Elizabethan Domestic Tragedies,* Harmondsworth, 1969.

Ibsen, Henrik, *When We Dead Awaken,* trans. Peter Watts, Harmondsworth, 1964.

Jonson, Ben, *The Alchemist,* ed. Peter Bement, 1987.

——, *Bartholomew Fair,* ed. G.R. Hibbard, 1977.

——, *Cynthia's Revels,* ed. C.H. Herford and Percy Simpson, Oxford, 1966 (reprint of 1932 edition).

——, *The Devil Is an Ass,* ed. Peter Happe, Manchester, 1994.

——, *Every Man in his Humour,* ed. M. Seymour-Smith, 1966.

——, *The Poetaster,* ed. George Parfitt, Nottingham, 1979.

——, *The Staple of News,* ed. Anthony Parr, Manchester, 1988.

——, *Volpone,* ed. Philip Brockbank, 1968.

Kyd, Thomas, *The Spanish Tragedy,* ed. Philip Edwards, 1959.

Lyly, John, *The Complete Works of John Lyly,* ed. R. Warwick Bond, Oxford, 1942.

Marlowe, Christopher, *Dr Faustus,* ed. John D. Jump, 1962.

——, *Tamburlaine,* Parts 1 & 2, ed. John D. Jump, 1967.

Marston, John, *Antonio and Mellida,* ed. W. Reavley Gair, Manchester, 1991.

——, *Antonio's Revenge,* ed. W. Reavley Gair, Manchester, 1978.

——, *Parasitaster or The Fawn,* ed. David A. Blostein, Manchester, 1978.

——, *The Malcontent,* ed. Bernard Harris, 1967.

——, *The Tragedy of Sophonisba, or The Wonder of Women,* ed. Peter Corbin and Douglas Sedge, in *Three Jacobean Witchcraft Plays,* Manchester, 1986.

Massinger, Philip, ed. Philip Edwards and Colin Gibson, *The Plays and Poems of Philip Massinger,* 5 vols, Oxford, 1976.

——, *Believe As You List,* ed. Edwards and Gibson, vol. III, Oxford, 1976.

——, *The Duke of Milan,* ed. Edwards and Gibson, vol. I, Oxford, 1976.

——, *The Emperor of the East,* ed. Edwards and Gibson, vol. III, Oxford, 1976.

——, *The Roman Actor,* ed. Edwards and Gibson, vol. III, Oxford, 1976.

——, *The Unnatural Combat,* ed. Edwards and Gibson, vol. II, Oxford, 1976.

May, Thomas, *The Heir, Dodsley's Old Plays,* vol. VIII, 1825.

Middleton, Thomas, *A Chaste Maid in Cheapside,* ed. Alan Brissenden, 1968.

——, *No Wit, No Help, Like A Woman's,* ed. Michael Taylor, Oxford, 1995.

——, *The Old Law,* ed. A.H. Bullen, *The Complete Works of Thomas Middleton,* 8 vols, vol. II, 1885–6.

——, *A Trick to Catch the Old One,* ed. G.J. Watson, 1968.

——, *The Witch,* ed. Elizabeth Schafer, 1994.

——, *Women Beware Women,* ed. William C. Carroll, second edition, 1994.

——, *Blurt, Master Constable* (attrib.) ed. A.H. Bullen, vol. I, 1885.

——, *The Revenger's Tragedy* (attrib.) ed. R.A. Foakes, 1996.

Middleton, Thomas and William Rowley, *The Changeling,* ed. N.C. Bawcutt, Manchester, 1958.

Norton, Thomas, and Thomas Sackville, *Gorboduc, or the Tragedy of Ferrex and Porrex*, ed. Irby B. Cauther Jr, 1965.

Peele, George, *The Battle of Alcazar,* ed. John Yoklavich, in *The Dramatic Works of George Peele*, New Haven, 1961.

Preston, Thomas, *Cambises*, ed. Ashley Thorndike, in *Minor Elizabethan Drama, Vol. I: Pre-Shakespearean Tragedies*, 1958.

Shirley, James, *The Doubtful Heir*, in *Dramatic Works and Poems*, ed. W. Gifford and A. Dyce, 1833.

Shakespeare, William – except where stated otherwise, all references are to *William Shakespeare: The Complete Works*, ed. Stanley Wells and Gary Taylor, Oxford, 1986.

——, *Antony and Cleopatra.*

——, *As You Like It.*

——, *Coriolanus.*

——, *Cymbeline.*

——, *Henry IV Part 1.*

——, *Henry IV Part 2.*

——, *Henry V*, ed. Gary Taylor, Oxford, 1987.

——, *Henry VI Part 1.*

——, *Henry VI Part 3.*

——, *Henry VIII.*

——, *The Tragicall Historie of Hamlet, Prince of Denmark,* ed. Graham Holderness and Brian Loughrey, Hemel Hempstead, 1992.

——, *Hamlet*, ed. Harold Jenkins, 1982.

——, *Macbeth.*

——, *A Midsummer Night's Dream.*

——, *Pericles.*

——, *Romeo and Juliet.*

——, *The Tempest.*

——, *Titus Andronicus,* ed. Alan Hughes, Cambridge, 1994.

——, ———————————, ed. Jonathan Bate, 1995.

——, *Troilus and Cressida.*

——, *The Winter's Tale.*

Tomkis, Thomas, *Lingua*, in *Dodsley's Old Plays*, ed. W.C. Hazlitt, vol. IX, 1874.

Tourneur, Cyril, *The Atheist's Tragedy or, The Honest Man's Revenge,* ed. Brian Morris and Roma Gill, 1976.

Webster, John, *The Devil's Law Case*, ed. Elizabeth M. Brennan, 1975.

——, *The Duchess of Malfi*, ed. John Russell Brown, 1969.

——, *The White Devil*, ed. John Russell Brown, 1996.

Other works

Baker, Sir James, *Theatrum Redivivum* or, *The Theatre Vindicated*, 1662, Johnson Reprints, New York, 1972.

Braithwaite, Richard, *The English Gentleman*, 1630.

Bulwer, John, *Chirologia: Or the Natural Language of the Hand*, 1644, ed. J.W. Cleary, 1974.

Dekker, Thomas, *Prose Works*, ed. E.D. Pendry, 1967.

Flecknoe, Richard, *A Short Discourse of the English Stage*, 1674, Johnson Reprints, New York, 1972.

Gosson, Stephen, *The Schoole of Abuse*, 1579, Shakespere Society Reprint, 1841.

Heywood, Thomas, *An Apology for Actors*, 1612, Shakespere Society Reprint, 1841.

Nashe, Thomas, *The Unfortunate Traveller and Other works*, ed. and intr. J.B. Steane, Harmondsworth, 1972.

Ovid, *Metamorphoses*, trans. A.D. Melville with introduction and notes by E.J. Kenney, Oxford, 1986.

Puttenham, George, *The Arte of English Poesie*, 1589, ed. Gladys Doidge Willcock and Alice Walker, New York, 1978. Reprint of 1936 Cambridge edition.

T.G. [Thomas Gainsford] *The Rich Cabinet*, 1616 in W.C. Hazlitt, *English Drama and Stage*, 1963.

Whitney, Geoffrey, *Choice of Emblems*, 1586, ed. Henry Green, 1866.

Wright, James, *Historia Histrionica*, 1699, Johnson Reprints, New York, 1972.

Wright, Thomas, *The Passions of the Mind in General*, 1604; reprint based on the 1630 edition, Illinois, 1971.

Secondary sources

The following works are those I am conscious of having used in writing this book. I also acknowledge the many others that undoubtedly helped shape my ideas but which I am not aware of having used directly.

Archer, William (1923) *The Old Drama and the New*.

Armstrong, Nancy and Leonard Tennenhouse, eds (1989) *The Violence of Representation*.

Ashelford, Jane (1988) *Dress in the Age of Elizabeth I*.

Astington, John H. ed. (1992) *The Development of Shakespeare's Theater*, New York.

Bakhtin, Mikhail (1968) *Rabelais and His World*, trans. Helene Iswolsky, Cambridge, MA.

Barbour, Richmond (1995) '"When I Acted Young Antinous": Boy Actors and the Erotics of Jonsonian Theater', *Publications of the Modern Language Association*, October: 1006–22.

Barish, Jonas A. (1981) *The Antitheatrical Prejudice*, Berkeley, CA.

—— (1988) 'Shakespeare in the Study; Shakespeare on the Stage', *Theatre Journal*, 40:1, 33–47.

Barroll, J. Leeds, Alexander Leggatt, Richard Hosley and Alvin Kernan (1975) *The Revels History of Drama in English*, vol. III: 1576–1613.

Barton, John (1984) *Playing Shakespeare*.

Bate, Jonathan (1993) *Shakespeare and Ovid*, Oxford.

Beauman, Sally (1976) ed. and with interviews, *The Royal Shakespeare Company's Production of 'Henry V' for the Centenary Season at the Royal Shakespeare Theatre*, Oxford.

Beckerman, Bernard (1962) *Shakespeare at the Globe: 1599–1609*, New York.

—— (1990) *Theatrical Presentation*, eds Gloria Brim Beckerman and William Colo, New York.

Belfiore, Elizabeth S. (1992) *Tragic Pleasures: Aristotle on Plot and Emotion*, Princeton, NJ.

Bennett, Susan (1990) *Theatre Audiences: A Theory of Production and Reception*.

—— (1996) *Performing Nostalgia: Shifting Shakespeare and the Contemporary Past*.

Bentley, G.E. (1941–68) *The Jacobean and Caroline Stage*, 7 vols, Oxford.

—— (1986) *The Professions of Dramatist and Player in Shakespeare's Time*, Princeton, NJ.

Berger, Harry, Jr (1982) 'Text Against Performance in Shakespeare: The Example of *Macbeth*', *Genre*, 15, 1 and 2: 49–79.

—— (1989) *Imaginary Audition: Shakespeare on Stage and Page*, Berkeley, CA.

Berry, Cicely (1993) *The Actor and the Text*.

Berry, Herbert, ed. (1979) *The First Public Playhouse: The Theatre in Shoreditch 1576–1598*, Montreal.

Berry, Ralph (1977) *On Directing Shakespeare: Interviews with Contemporary Directors*.

—— (1981) *Changing Styles in Shakespeare*.

—— (1985a) *Shakespeare and the Awareness of the Audience*.

—— (1985b) 'The Reviewer as Historian', *Shakespeare Quarterly*, 36: 594–7.

—— (1989) *On Directing Shakespeare: Interviews with Contemporary Directors*.

—— (1993) *Shakespeare in Performance: Castings and Metamorphoses*, Basingstoke.

Bevington, David (1984) *Action is Eloquence: Shakespeare's Language of Gesture*, Cambridge, MA.

Bevis, Richard W. (1988) *English Drama: Restoration and the Eighteenth Century 1660–1789*.

Blake, N.F. (1983) *Shakespeare's Language: An Introduction*.

Boal, Augusto (1995) *The Rainbow of Desire*, trans. Adrian Jackson.

Bradbrook, Muriel (1935) *Themes and Conventions in Elizabethan Tragedy*, Cambridge.

Bradbury, Malcolm and James McFarlane, eds (1976) *Modernism 1890–1930*, Harmondsworth.

Bradley, David (1992) *From Text to Performance in the Elizabethan Theatre*, Cambridge.

Braun, Edward (1969) ed. and trans. *The Theatre of Meyerhold*.

—— (1984) *The Director and the Stage*.

—— (1995) *Meyerhold: A Revolution in Theatre*.

Braunmuller A.R. and Hattaway, Michael, eds (1990) *The Cambridge Companion to English Renaissance Drama*, Cambridge.

Brecht, Bertolt (1964) *Brecht on Theatre*, ed. and trans. John Willett.

Bristol, Michael D. (1985) *Carnival and Theater: Plebeian Culture and the Structure of Authority in Renaissance England*, New York.

Brook, Peter (1961) 'The Search for a Hunger', *Encore*, July–August: 16–17.

Brooke, Nicholas (1966) 'Marlowe the Dramatist', pp. 87–105 in Brown and Harris 1966.

—— (1979) *Horrid Laughter in Jacobean Tragedy*.

Brown, John Russell (1966) *Shakespeare's Plays in Performance*.

—— (1989) 'The Nature of Speech in Shakespeare's Plays', pp. 48–59 in Thompson and Thompson 1989.

Brown, John Russell and Bernard Harris, eds (1966) *Elizabethan Theatre*, Stratford-upon-Avon Studies.

Brownstein, Oscar (1979) 'Why Didn't Burbage Lease the Beargarden? A Conjecture in Comparative Architecture', pp. 81–96 in Berry 1979.

Brucher, Richard T. (1979) 'Comic Violence in *Titus Andronicus*', *Renaissance Drama*, n.s. X: 71–91.

Burns, Edward (1990) *Character: Acting and Being on the Pre-Modern Stage*, Basingstoke.

Burt, Richard (1993) *Licensed by Authority: Ben Jonson and the Discourses of Censorship*, Ithaca, NY.

Butler, Martin (1984) *Theatre and Crisis*, Cambridge.

Buzacott, Martin (1991) *The Death of the Actor*.

Callahan, John M. (1991) 'The ultimate in theatre violence', pp. 165–89 in Redmond 1991.

Carson, Neil (1988) *A Companion to Henslowe's 'Diary'*, Cambridge.

Cartelli, Thomas (1991) *Marlowe, Shakespeare, and the Economy of Theatrical Experience*, Philadelphia.

Chambers, Colin (1980) *Other Spaces: New Theatre and the RSC*.

Chambers, E.K. (1923; reprt. 1961) *The Elizabethan Stage,* 4 vols, Oxford.

Chan, Mary (1980) *Music in the Theatre of Ben Jonson*, Oxford.

Cibber, Colley (1987) *An Apology for the Life of Mr Colley Cibber, Comedian*, ed. J.M. Evans, New York.

Clare, Janet (1990) *'Art Made Tongue-Tied by Authority'* – Elizabethan and Jacobean *Dramatic Censorship*, Manchester.

Cohn, Ruby (1976) *Modern Shakespeare Offshoots*, Princeton, NJ.

Colley, John Scott (1974) 'Music in the Elizabethan Private Theatres', *Yearbook of English Studies*, 4: 62–9.

Cook, Ann Jennalie (1981) *The Privileged Playgoers of Shakespeare's London*, Princeton, NJ.

Cook, Judith (1974) *Directors' Theatre*.

—— (1989) *Directors' Theatre: Sixteen Leading Directors on the State of Theatre in Britain Today*.

Coursen, H.R. (1992) *Shakespearean Performance as Interpretation*, Newark, NJ.

Crowl, Samuel (1992) *Shakespeare Observed: Studies in Performance on Stage and Screen*, Athens, OH.

Daly, Peter M. (1979) *Literature in the Light of the Emblem*, Toronto.

David, Richard (1957) 'Drams of Eale', *Shakespeare Survey*, 10: 126–34.

—— (1978) *Shakespeare in the Theatre*, Cambridge.

Davidson, Clifford, C.J. Gianakaris and John H. Stroupe, eds (1986) *Drama in the Renaissance*, New York.

Davison, Peter, ed. (1972) *Critics and Apologists of the English Theatre: A Selection of Seventeenth-Century Pamphlets in Facsimile*.

Deak, Frantisek (1993) *Symbolist Theatre: The Formation of an Avant-Garde*, Baltimore.

Delgado, Maria M. and Paul Heritage, eds (1996) *In Contact with the Gods: Directors Talk Theatre*, Manchester.

Dessen, Alan C. (1985) *Elizabethan Stage Conventions and Modern Interpreters*, Cambridge.

—— (1987) 'Modern Productions and the Elizabethan Scholar', *Renaissance Drama*, new series XVIII, 205–203.

—— (1989) *Shakespeare in Performance: Titus Andronicus*, Manchester.

Diehl, Huston (1986) 'Iconography and Characterization in English Tragedy, 1585–1642', pp. 11–20 in Davidson *et al.* 1986.

Dobson, Michael (1992) *The Making of the National Poet: Shakespeare, Adaptation and Authorship 1660–1769*, Oxford.

Dollimore, Jonathan (1984) *Radical Tragedy*, Brighton.

Dollimore, Jonathan and Alan Sinfield, eds (1985) *Political Shakespeare*, Manchester.

Downes, John (1987) *Roscius Anglicanus*, eds Judith Milhouse and Robert D. Hume.

Dukore, Bernard F. (1981) *The Plays of Peter Barnes*.

Eccles, Christine (1990) *The Rose Theatre*.

Eco, Umberto (1981) *The Name of the Rose*.

Edwards, Warwick (1980) 'Consort Music', pp. 672–5 in Stanley Sadie, ed., *The New Grove Dictionary of Music*, vol. 4, 1980.

Eliot, T.S. (1963) *Elizabethan Dramatists*.

Ellis, John (1982) *Visible Fictions*.

Ellis-Fermor, Una (1936) *The Jacobean Drama* (reprinted 1958).

Emeljanow, Victor (1991) 'Grand guignol and the orchestration of violence', pp. 151–63 in Redmond 1991.

Erasmus, Desiderius (1978) *De Copia*, trans. Craig R. Thompson, *Collected Works*, vol. 2, Toronto.

Evans, Gareth Lloyd (1974) 'Judi Dench Talks to Gareth Lloyd Evans', *Shakespeare Survey*, 27: 137–42.

Evett, David (1990) *Literature and the Visual Arts in Tudor England*, Athens, GA.

Eyre, Richard (1993) *Utopia and other Places*.

Farnham, Willard (1971) *The Shakespearean Grotesque*, Oxford.

Fawcett, Mary L. (1983) 'Arms/Words/Tears: Language and the Body in *Titus Andronicus*', *English Literary History*, 50: 261–77.

Fish, Stanley (1980) *Is There a Text in This Class? The Authority of Interpretive Communities*, Cambridge, MA.

Flatter, Richard (1948) *Shakespeare's Producing Hand: A Study of his Marks of Expression to Be Found in the First Folio*, Melbourne.

Foakes, R.A. (1954) 'The Player's Passion: Some Notes on Elizabethan Psychology and Acting', *Essays and Studies*, VII: 62–77.

—— (1970) 'Tragedy at the Children's Theatres after 1600: A Challenge to the Adult Stage', pp. 37–59 in David Galloway, ed., *The Elizabethan Theatre II*.

—— (1985) *Illustrations of the English Stage 1580–1642*, Stanford, CA.

Foakes, R.A. and R.T. Rickert, eds (1961) *Henslowe's Diary*, Cambridge.

Fotheringham, Richard (1985) 'The Doubling of Roles on the Jacobean Stage', *Theatre Research International*, vol. 10, no. 1: 18–32.

Fraser, Antonia (1996) *The Gunpowder Plot*.

Freeman, Arthur, ed. (1974) *Commonwealth Tracts 1625–1650*, New York.

Freud, Sigmund (1960) *Jokes and their Relation to the Unconscious*, trans. and ed. James Strachey.

Fricker, Franz (1972) *Ben Jonson's Plays in Performance and the Jacobean Theatre*, The Cooper Monographs: Theatrical Physiognomy Series, 17, Bern.

Gair, W. Reavley (1982) *The Children of Paul's: The Story of a Theatre Company, 1553–1608*, Cambridge.

Galloway, David, ed. (1970) *The Elizabethan Theatre II*, Waterloo, Can.

Garber, Marjorie (1980) '"Wild Laughter in the Throat of Death": Darker Purposes in Shakespearean Comedy', *New York Literary Forum*, 5–6: 121–6.

—— (1992) *Vested Interests: Cross-Dressing and Cultural Anxiety*, Harmondsworth.

Garrett, Martin, ed. (1991) *Massinger: The Critical Heritage*.

Gellert, Bridget (1970) 'The Iconography of Melancholy in the Graveyard Scene in *Hamlet*', *Studies in Philology*, 67: 57–66.

Genest, John (1832) *Some Account of the English Stage, from the Restoration in 1660 to 1830*, 10 vols, Bath.

Gerritsen, Johan (1986) 'De Witt, Van Buchell, the Swan and the Globe, Some Notes', in *Essays in Honour of Kristian Smidt*, ed. Peter Bilton *et al.*, Oslo.

Gleason, John B. (1981) 'The Dutch Humanist Origins of the De Witt Drawing', *Shakespeare Quarterly*, 32: 324–38.

Goffman, Erving (1974) *Frame Analysis: An Essay on the Organization of Experience*, New York.

Gouws, John, ed. (1986) *The Prose Works of Fulke Greville*, Oxford.

Graves, R.B. (1982) 'Daylight in Elizabethan Theatres', *Shakespeare Quarterly*, 33: 80–92.

Greenwood, John (1988) *Shifting Perspectives and the Stylish Style: Mannerism in Shakespeare and his Jacobean contemporaries*, University of Toronto Press.

Gurr, Andrew (1963) 'Who Strutted and Bellowed?', *Shakespeare Survey*, 16: 95–102.

—— (1987) *Playgoing in Shakespeare's London*, Cambridge.

—— (1992) *The Shakespearean Stage 1574–1642*, 3rd edition, Cambridge.

—— (1994) 'The Bare Island', *Shakespeare Survey*, 47: 29–43.

—— (1996) *The Shakespearean Playing Companies*, Oxford.

Gurr, Andrew and John Orrell (1989) *Rebuilding Shakespeare's Globe*.

Guthrie, Tyrone (1961) *A Life in the Theatre*.

Halio, Jay L. (1985) 'Finding the Text', *Shakespeare Quarterly*, 36: 662–9.

Hamilton, Donna B. (1972) 'Language As Theme in *The Dutch Courtesan*', *Renaissance Drama*, n.s. 5: 75–87.

Hall, Peter (1993) *Making an Exhibition of Myself: An Autobiography*.

Hapgood, Robert (1988) *Shakespeare the Theatre-Poet*, Oxford.

Harbage, Alfred (1939) 'Elizabethan Actors', *Publications of the Modern Language Association*, 54: 685–703.

Harrison, William (1968) *The Description of England*, ed. Georges Edelen, Ithaca, NY.

Harrop, John (1992) *Acting*.

Hattaway, Michael (1982) *Elizabethan Popular Theatre: Plays in Performance*.

Hauser, Arnold (1965) *Mannerism: the Crisis of the Renaissance and the Origin of Modern Art*.

Hazlitt, William (1931) 'On Reason and Imagination', in *The Plain Speaker* (1826), vol. 12 of *The Complete Works*, 21 vols, 1930–34, ed. P.P. Howe.

Hearn, Karen, ed. (1995) *Dynasties: Painting in Tudor and Jacobean England 1530–1630*.

Heinemann, Margot (1985) 'How Brecht Read Shakespeare', pp. 202–30 in Dollimore and Sinfield 1985.

Herrick, Robert (1956) *Poetical Works*, ed. L.C. Martin.

Heywood, Thomas (1841) *An Apology for Actors*, 1612, reprinted for the Shakespeare Society.

Hibbard, G.R. (1972) 'The Forced Gait of a Shuffling Nag', pp. 76–88 in Leech and Margeson 1972.

—— ed. (1980) *The Elizabethan Theatre VII*, Waterloo, Can.

Hildy, Franklin J. (1994) 'Playing Spaces for Shakespeare: The Maddermarket Theatre, Norwich', *Shakespeare Survey*, 47: 81–90.

Holderness, Graham (1992) 'Shakespeare and Heritage', *Textual Practice*, 6.2, Summer: 247–63.

Holmes, Martin (1978) *Shakespeare and Burbage*.

Holland, Peter (1984) '*Hamlet* and the Art of Acting', pp. 39–61 in Redmond 1984.

—— (1994) 'Shakespeare Performances in England 1992–93', *Shakespeare Survey*, 47: 181–207.

—— (1995) 'Shakespeare Performances in England 1993–94', *Shakespeare Survey*, 48: 191–226.

—— (1997) *English Shakespeares: Shakespeare on the English Stage in the 1990s*, Cambridge.

Hopkins, Lisa (1994) *John Ford's Political Theatre*, Manchester.

Hosking, G.L. (1952) *The Life and Times of Edward Alleyn.*

Hosley, Richard, ed. (1962) *Essays on Shakespeare and Elizabethan Drama: In Honour of Hardin Craig*, Columbia.

—— (1975) 'The Playhouses', pp. 121–235 in Barroll *et al.* 1975.

Howard, Douglas, ed. (1985) *Philip Massinger: A Critical Reassessment*, Cambridge.

Howard, Jean E. (1984) *Shakespeare's Art of Orchestration: Stage Technique and Audience Response*, Chicago, IL.

—— (1991) 'Women as Spectators, Spectacles and Paying Customers', pp. 68–74 in Kastan and Stallybrass 1991.

—— (1994) *The Stage and Social Struggle in Early Modern England.*

Howard, Jean and Marion F. O'Connor, eds (1987) *Shakespeare Reproduced: The Text in History and Ideology.*

Hoy, Cyrus (1973) 'Jacobean Tragedy and the Mannerist Style', *Shakespeare Survey*, 26: 49–67.

Hughes, Charles, ed. (1967) *Shakespeare's Europe: A Survey of the Condition of Europe at the End of the 16th Century, Being Unpublished Chapters of Fynes Morryson's Itinerary (1617)*, 2nd edition, New York.

Hume, Robert D. (1976) *The Development of English Drama in the Late Seventeenth Century*, Oxford.

Hunter, G.K. (1994) 'Rhetoric and Renaissance Drama', pp. 103–18 in Mack 1994a.

Hunter, G.K. and S.K., eds (1969) *John Webster: A Critical Anthology*, Harmondsworth.

Hussey, S.S. (1992) *The Literary Language of Shakespeare*, 2nd edition.

Hutson, William (1987) 'Elizabethan Stagings of *Hamlet*: George Pierce Baker and William Poel', *Theatre Research International*, vol. 12, no. 3: 253–60.

Hyland, Peter (1987) '"A Kind of Woman": The Elizabethan Boy-Actor and the Kabuki *Onnagata*', *Theatre Research International*, vol. 12, no. 1: 1–8.

Ichikawa, Mariko (1992) 'Exits in Shakespeare's Plays: Time Allowed to Exiters', *Studies in English Literature*, 68: 189–206.

Ingram, William (1992) *The Business of Playing: The Beginnings of the Adult Professional Theater in Elizabethan London*, Ithaca, NY.

Jackson, MacDonald P. (1986) 'The Transmission of Shakespeare's Text', pp. 163–85 in Wells 1986.

James, Heather (1991) 'Cultural Disintegration in *Titus Andronicus*: Mutilating Titus, Vergil and Rome', pp. 123–40 in Redmond 1991.

Joseph, Bertram (1964) *Elizabethan Acting.*

Kastan, David Scott (1986) 'Proud Majesty Made a Subject: Shakespeare and the Spectacle of Rule', *Shakespeare Quarterly*, 37: 459–75.

Kastan, David Scott and Peter Stallybrass, eds (1991) *Staging the Renaissance: Reinterpretations of Elizabethan and Jacobean Drama*, New York.

Kayser, Wolfgang (1968) *The Grotesque in Art and Literature*, Gloucester, MA.

Keane, Dennis, ed. (1985) *Henry Howard, Earl of Surrey: Selected Poems*, Carcanet Press: Manchester.

Kendall, Gillian Murray (1989) '"Lend Me Thy hand": Metaphor and Mayhem in *Titus Andronicus*', *Shakespeare Quarterly*, 40: 299–316.

Kennedy, Dennis (1985) *Granville Barker and the Dream of Theatre*, Cambridge.

—— (1993) *Looking at Shakespeare: A Visual History of Twentieth-Century Performance*, Cambridge.

King, T.J. (1964–5) 'The Staging of Plays at the Phoenix in Drury Lane, 1617–42', *Theatre Notebook*, 19: 146–66.

—— (1992a) *Casting Shakespeare's Plays: London Actors and their Roles 1590–1642*, Cambridge.

—— (1992b) 'Thomas Nabbes's Covent Garden (1638) and Inigo Jones's Drawings for the Phoenix or Cockpit in Drury Lane', pp. 185–202 in Astington 1992.

Klein, David (1962) 'Did Shakespeare Produce his own plays?', *Modern Language Review*, LVII, 556–60.

Knutson, Roslyn Lander (1991) *The Repertory of Shakespeare's Company, 1594–1613*, Fayetville, AR.

Konjin, Elly (1995) 'Actors and Emotions: A Psychological Perspective', *Theatre Research International*, vol. 20, no. 2: 132–40.

Krause, Duane (1995) 'An Epic System', pp. 262–74 in Zarrilli 1995.

Lamb, Charles (1901) *Complete Works*.

Lawrence, W.J. (1913) *The Elizabethan Playhouse and Other Studies*, Stratford-upon-Avon.

Leech, Clifford and J.M.R. Margeson, eds (1972) *Shakespeare 1971: Proceedings of the World Shakespeare Congress*, Toronto.

Leggatt, Alexander (1975) 'The Companies and Actors', pp. 95–117 in Barroll *et al.* 1975.

—— (1992) *Jacobean Public Theatre*.

Lennep, William van, Emmet L. Avery and A.W. Stone, eds (1965) *The London Stage*, Carbondale, IL.

Levenson, Jill (1972) 'What the Silence Said: Still Points in *King Lear*', pp. 215–29 in Leech and Margeson 1972.

Levin, Richard (1989) 'Women in the Renaissance Theatre Audience', *Shakespeare Quarterly*, 40: 165–74.

Levine, Laura (1986) 'Men in Women's Clothing: Anti-theatricality and Effeminization from 1579–1642', *Criticism*, vol. 28, no. 2: 121–143.

—— (1994) *Men in Women's Clothing: Anti-Theatricality and Effeminization 1579–1642*, Cambridge.

Limon, Jerzy (1992) 'A Theatrical Emblem in *The Roman Actor*', *Notes and Queries*, September: 371–4.

Llewellyn, Nigel (1991) *The Art of Death*.

Loengard, Janet S. (1983) 'An Elizabethan Lawsuit: John Brayne, His Carpenter, and the Building of the Red Lion Theatre', *Shakespeare Quarterly*, 34: 298–310.

Luckyj, Christina (1993) '"A Moving Rhetoricke": Women's Silences and Renaissance Texts', *Renaissance Drama*, n.s. XXIV: 33–56.

McDonald, Marianne (1992) *Ancient Sun, Modern Light: Greek Drama on the Modern Stage*, New York.

McGuire, Philip C., and David A. Samuelson, eds (1979) *Shakespeare: The Theatrical Dimension*, New York.

Mack, Maynard (1962) 'Engagement and Detachment in Shakespeare's Plays', pp. 275–96 in Richard Hosley, ed., *Essays on Shakespeare and Elizabethan Drama: In Honour of Hardin Craig*, Columbia.

Mack, Peter, ed. (1994a) *Renaissance Rhetoric*.

—— (1994b) 'Rhetoric in Use: Three Romances by Greene and Lodge', pp. 119–39 in Mack 1994a.

Mackintosh, Iain (1993) *Architecture, Actor and Audience*.

Maclean, Sally-Beth (1993) 'Tour Routes: "Provincial Wanderings" or Traditional Circuits?', *Medieval and Renaissance Drama in England*, vol. 6: 1–14.

McLuskie, Kathleen (1989) *Renaissance Dramatists: Feminist Readings*, Hemel Hempstead.

McLuskie, Kathleen and Jennifer Uglow, eds (1989) *Plays in Performance: 'The Duchess of Malfi'*, Bristol.

McMillin, Scott (1987) *The Elizabethan Theatre and 'The Book of Sir Thomas More'*, Ithaca, NY.

—— (1992) 'The Rose and The Swan', pp. 159–83 in Astington 1992.

Magarshack, David (1967) *Stanislavsky on the Art of the Stage*.

Mangan, Michael (1991) *A Preface to Shakespeare's Tragedies*.

Mann, David (1991) *The Elizabethan Player*.

Marker, Lise-Lone (1970) 'Nature and Decorum in the Theory of Elizabethan Acting', pp. 87–107 in Galloway 1970.

Marowitz, Charles (1978) *The Marowitz Shakespeare*.

—— (1991) *Recycling Shakespeare*, Basingstoke.

Marsden, Jean I., ed. (1991) *The Appropriation of Shakespeare: Post-Renaissance Reconstructions of the Works and the Myth*, Hemel Hempstead.

—— (1992) 'The Rose and The Swan', pp. 159–83 in Astington 1992.

Mellers, Wilfred (1964) 'Words and Music in Elizabethan England', in Boris Ford, ed., *The Age of Shakespeare*, The Pelican Guide to English Literature 2, Harmondsworth, 1955 (revised edition 1964).

Mills, Howard (1993) *Working With Shakespeare*, Hemel Hempstead.

Mitter, Shomit (1992) *Systems of Rehearsal*.

Moore, Don D. (1981) *Webster: The Critical Heritage*.

Mowl, Timothy (1993) *Elizabethan and Jacobean Style*.

Mullaney, Steven (1988) *The Place of the Stage: License, Play, and Power in Renaissance England*, Chicago.

Mulryne, J.R. and Margaret Shewring, eds (1997) *Shakespeare's Globe Rebuilt*, Cambridge.

Murray, Linda (1967) *The High Renaissance and Mannerism*.

Nashe, Thomas (1972) *The Unfortunate Traveller and Other Works*, ed. J.B. Steane, Harmondsworth.

Neill, Michael (1992) '"Feasts Put Down Funerals": Death and Ritual in Renaissance Comedy', pp. 47–74 in Woodbridge and Berry 1992.

Newlin, Jeanne T. (1980) 'An Open Stage for Shakespeare', pp. 24–34 in *Shakespeare's First Globe Theater: the Harvard Theater Collection Model*, Harvard, MA.

Nichols, John Gough, ed. (1848) *The Diary of Henry Machyn, Citizen and Merchant Taylor of London*.

Nochlin, Linda (1994) *The Body in Pieces: The Fragment as a Metaphor of Modernity*.

Novy, Marianne, ed. (1990) *Women's Re-Visions of Shakespeare*, Illinois.

Nungezer, E. (1968) *A Dictionary of Actors and Other Persons Associated with the Public Representation of Plays in England before 1642*, New Haven. Reprint of 1929 edition.

O'Connor, Marion (1987) *William Poel and the Elizabethan Stage Society*, Cambridge.

Orgel, Stephen (1989) 'Nobody's Perfect: Or Why Did The English Stage Take Boys For Women?', *South Atlantic Quarterly*, 88, 1, Winter: 7–29.

Orrell, John (1977) 'Inigo Jones at the Cockpit', *Shakespeare Survey*, 30: 157–68.

—— (1983) *The Quest for Shakespeare's Globe*, Cambridge.

Orrell, John (1988) *The Human Stage: English Theatre Design 1567–1640*, Cambridge.

Orton, Joe (1978) 'Interview', *Plays and Players*, vol. 26, no. 2: 13.

Ovid (1986) *Metamorphoses*, trans. A.D. Melville with an Introduction and Notes by E.J. Kenney, Oxford.

Parfitt, George, ed. (1975) *Ben Jonson: Complete Poems*, Harmondsworth.

Pavis, Patrice (1992) *Theatre at the Crossroads*.

Pearson, Roberta E. (1992) *Eloquent Gestures: The Transformation of Performance Style in the Griffith Biograph Films*, Berkeley, CA.

Peat, Derek (1989) 'Looking Back to Front: the view from the Lords' Room', pp. 180–94 in Thompson and Thompson 1989.

Pentzell, Raymond J. (1986) '*The Changeling*: Notes on Mannerism in Dramatic Form', pp. 274–99 in Davidson *et al.* 1986.

Potter, Lois (1975) 'Realism Versus Nightmare: Problems of Staging *The Duchess of Malfi*', in Price 1975.

Powell, Jocelyn (1966) 'John Lyly and the Language of Play', pp. 147–67 in Brown and Harris 1966.

Price, Joseph G., ed. (1975) *The Triple Bond: Plays, Mainly Shakespearean, in Performance*.

Putt, S. Gorley (1970) 'The Relevance of Jacobean Drama', *Essays and Studies*, 23: 18–33.

Puttenham, George (1978) *The Arte of English Poesie*, ed. Gladys Doidge Willcock and Alice Walker, New York. Reprint of 1936 Cambridge edition.

Quince, Rohan (1991) 'Apartheid and Primitive Blood: Violence in Afrikaans Shakespeare Productions', pp. 215–24 in Redmond 1991.

Rackin, Phyllis (1987) 'Androgyny, Mimesis, and the Marriage of the Boy Heroine on the English Renaissance Stage', *Publications of the Modern Language Association*, 102, 1, January: 29–41.

—— (1991) *Stages of History: Shakespeare's English Chronicles*.

Rasmussen, Eric (1989) 'Shakespeare's Hand in *The Second Maiden's Tragedy*', *Shakespeare Quarterly*, 40: 1–26.

Rea, Kenneth (1989) *A Better Direction: A National Enquiry into the Training of Directors for Theatre, Film and Television*, Calouste Gulbenkian Foundation.

Redmond, James, ed. (1984) *Drama and the Actor, Themes in Drama 6*, Cambridge.

—— (1991) *Violence in Drama, Themes in Drama 13*, Cambridge.

Righter, Ann (1967) *Shakespeare and the Idea of the Play*, Harmondsworth.

Roach, Joseph R. (1985) *The Player's Passion: Studies in the Science of Acting*.

Rodenburg, Patsy (1993) *The Need for Words: Voice and the Text*.

Rowan, D.F. (1970) 'A Neglected Jones/Webb Theatre Project, Part II: A Theatrical Missing Link', pp. 60–73 in Galloway 1970.

—— (1980) 'Inigo Jones and the Teatro Olimpico', pp. 65–81 in Hibbard 1980.

Ruskin, John (1904) *The Stones of Venice*, vol. XI of *Works*, eds E.T. Cook and A. Wedderburn.

Rylance, Mark (1997) 'Playing the Globe', pp. 169–76 in Mulryne and Shewring 1997.

Salingar, Leo (1991) 'Jacobean Playwrights and "Judicious" Spectators', *Renaissance Drama*, n.s., XXII: 209–34.

Scott, Michael (1982) *Renaissance Drama and a Modern Audience* (reprinted 1985).

—— (1989) *Shakespeare and the Modern Dramatist*.

Shapiro, Michael (1977) *Children of the Revels: The Boy Companies of Shakespeare's Time and their Plays*, New York.

Shapiro, Michael (1989) 'Lady Mary Wroth Describes a "Boy Actress"', *Medieval and Renaissance Drama in England*, vol. 4: 187–194.

—— (1994) *Gender in Play on the Shakespearean Stage: Boy Heroines and Female Pages*, Ann Arbor.

Shaughnessy, Robert (1994) *Representing Shakespeare: England, History and the RSC*.

Shaw, Bernard (1931) *Our Theatres in the Nineties*, 3 vols.

Shearman, John (1967) *Mannerism*, Harmondsworth.

Shen Lin (1991) 'How Old were the Children of Paul's?', *Theatre Notebook*, 45: 121–31.

Shepherd, Geoffrey, ed. (1965) *Philip Sidney: An Apology for Poetry, or The Defense of Poesy*.

Sherbo, Arthur, ed. (1968) *Johnson on Shakespeare*, the Yale edition of the Works of Samuel Johnson, vols VII and VIII.

Skura, Meredith Anne (1993) *Shakespeare, The Actor and the Purposes of Playing*, Chicago.

Slater, Ann Pasternak (1982) *Shakespeare the Director*, Brighton.

Smith, Warren D. (1975) *Shakespeare's Playhouse Practice: A Handbook*, Hanover: NH.

Somerset, Alan (1994) '"How Chances It They Travel?": Provincial Touring, Playing Spaces, and the King's Men', *Shakespeare Survey*, 47: 45–60.

Sorelius, Gunnar (1966) *'The Giant Race Before The Flood': Pre-Restoration Drama on the Stage and in the Criticism of the Restoration*, Uppsala.

Speaight, Robert (1954) *William Poel and the Elizabethan Revival*.

Spencer, Christopher (1965) *Five Restoration Adaptations of Shakespeare*, Urbana.

Sprinchorn, Evert (1992) 'An Intermediate Stage Level in the Elizabethan Theatre', *Theatre Notebook*, XLVI: 73–94.

Stapleton, Michael, ed. (1983) *The Cambridge Companion to English Literature*, Cambridge.

States, Bert O. (1995) 'The Actor's Presence', pp. 22–42 in Zarrilli 1995.

Stanislavsky, Konstantin (1967) *An Actor Prepares*, trans. Elizabeth Hapgood.

—— (1980) *My Life in Art*, trans. J.J. Robbins.

—— (1983) *Creating A Role*, trans. Elizabeth Hapgood.

Steen, Sara Jayne (1993) *'Ambrosia in an Earthen Vessel': Three Centuries of Audience and Reader Response to the Works of Thomas Middleton*, New York.

Steig, Michael (1970) 'Defining the Grotesque: An Attempt at Synthesis', *Journal of Aesthetics and Art Criticism*, Summer: 253–60.

Stevens, John (1961) *Music and Poetry in the Early Tudor Court*.

Stewart, Susan (1984) *On Longing: Narratives of the Miniature, the Gigantic, the Souvenir, the Collection*, Baltimore.

Strong, Roy, (1969) *The English Icon: Elizabethan and Jacobean Portraiture*.

Sturgess, Keith (1987) *Jacobean Private Theatre*.

Taylor, Gary (1989) *Reinventing Shakespeare: A Cultural History from the Restoration to the Present*.

Tennenhouse, Leonard (1989) 'Violence Done to Women on the Renaissance Stage', pp. 77–97 in Armstrong and Tennenhouse 1989.

Tetlow, Elizabeth Meier, trans. (1987) *The Spiritual Exercises of St Ignatius Loyola*, Lanham.

Thomas, Keith (1971) *Religion and the Decline of Magic*.

Thompson, Ann (1991) 'Does It Matter Which Edition You Use?', pp. 74–87 in Lesley Ayres and Nigel Wheale, eds, *Shakespeare in the Changing Curriculum*, 1991.

Thompson, Marvin and Ruth, eds (1989) *Shakespeare and the Sense of Performance*, Newark, DE.

Thomson, Leslie (1986a) '"Enter above": The Staging of *Women Beware Women*', *Studies in English Literature*, 26: 331–43.

——— (1986b) '"On Ye Walls": The Staging of *Hengist, King of Kent*, V.ii', *Medieval and Renaissance Drama in England*, vol. 3: 165–176.

Thomson, Peter (1975) 'The Smallest Season: The Royal Shakespeare Company at Stratford in 1974', *Shakespeare Survey*, 28: 137–48.

——— (1983) *Shakespeare's Theatre*.

——— (1992) *Shakespeare's Professional Career*, Cambridge.

Thomson, Philip (1972) *The Grotesque*, Critical Idiom series, Manchester.

Trewin, J.C. (1971) *Peter Brook: A Biography*.

Tricomi, Albert H. (1974) 'The Aesthetics of Mutilation in Titus Andronicus', *Shakespeare Survey*, 27: 11–19.

Valency, Maurice (1963) *The Flower and the Castle*.

Vickers, Brian (1989) *Returning to Shakespeare*.

——— (1993) *Appropriating Shakespeare: Contemporary Critical Quarrels*, New Haven, CT.

——— (1994) 'Some Reflections on the Rhetoric Textbook', pp. 81–102 in Mack 1994a.

Wain, John, ed. (1973) *Johnson as Critic*.

Waith, Eugene (1957) 'The Metamorphosis of Violence in *Titus Andronicus*', *Shakespeare Survey*, 10: 39–49.

Waugh, Patricia (1984) *Metafiction: The Theory and Practice of Self-Conscious Fiction*.

Weimann, Robert (1978) *Shakespeare and the Popular Tradition in the Theatre*, Baltimore.

Wells, Stanley (1984) *Re-Editing Shakespeare for the Modern Reader*, Oxford.

——— ed. (1986) *The Cambridge Companion to Shakespeare Studies*, Cambridge.

——— (1988) 'Performances in London and Stratford-upon-Avon', *Shakespeare Survey*, 41: 159–81.

——— (1990) 'Shakespeare Productions in England', *Shakespeare Survey*, 43: 183–203.

White, Martin (1992) *Middleton and Tourneur*, Basingstoke.

Wickham, Glynne (1959–81) *Early English Stages, 1300–1660*, vol. I (1959), vol. II, pt 1 (1963), pt 2 (1972), vol. III (1981).

——— (1985) *A History of the Theatre*, Oxford.

Williams, Raymond (1968) *Drama from Ibsen to Brecht*.

Woodbridge, Linda and Edward Berry, eds (1992) *True Rites and Maimed Rites: Ritual and Anti-Ritual in Shakespeare and His Age*, Urbana and Chicago.

Woudhuysen, H.R., ed. (1989) *Samuel Johnson on Shakespeare*, Harmondsworth, 1989.

Wright, George T. (1992) 'An Almost Oral Art: Shakespeare's Language on Stage and Page', *Shakespeare Quarterly*, 43: 159–69.

Wright, Thomas (1971) *The Passions of the Mind in General* (originally published 1604; reprint based on the 1630 edition), Illinois.

Wright, Thomas (1865) *A History of Caricature and Grotesque in Literature and Art*, New York.

Wymer, Rowland (1995) *Webster and Ford*, Basingstoke.

Zarrilli, Phillip B., ed. (1995) *Acting (Re)Considered: Theories and Practices*.

Zimmerman, Susan, ed. (1992) *Erotic Politics: Desire on the Renaissance Stage*, New York.

INDEX